David Murdoch

The Dutch Dominie of the Catskills

The times of the Bloody Brandt

David Murdoch

The Dutch Dominie of the Catskills
The times of the Bloody Brandt

ISBN/EAN: 9783337300913

Printed in Europe, USA, Canada, Australia, Japan

Cover: Foto ©Andreas Hilbeck / pixelio.de

More available books at **www.hansebooks.com**

THE DUTCH DOMINIE OF THE CATSKILLS;

OR,

THE TIMES OF THE "BLOODY BRANDT."

BY

REV. DAVID MURDOCH, D.D.

NEW YORK:
DERBY & JACKSON, 498 BROADWAY.
1861.

W. H. Tinson, Stereotyper.

Geo. Russell & Co., Printers.

THE DISCOVERY.

LETTER of WESSEL SCHERMERHORN, *to the excellent and venerable* ABRAHAM HAASBROUGH, Esq., *New York.*

HIGH PEAK, *Aug.* 12, 1860.

MY MUCH RESPECTED UNCLE,

BY MY MOTHER'S SIDE.

I WRITE this from the highest point of land my feet ever have stood upon. I am now looking out upon the great valley of the Hudson, and can see the spires of Poughkeepsie, the cupola of the Capitol at Albany, the hills of Connecticut and Massachusetts. The White and Green Mountains rise before me in noble grandeur; all spreading out, so that it seems as if a great sheet were let down from heaven; while the North River, like a silver ribbon, is running through the resplendent garniture. We of Holland descent have cause of pride in Hendrick Hudson the discoverer; and as I look down, my heart beats with transport at the thought that MY ancestors have made all that land to become what I see, in fertility, richness and beauty. Chiefly my blood dances in my veins as I recall the history of those noble acts performed on the scene that lies before my view.

Knowing your great interest in all that refers to the past, I have, since leaving the Bowery, been collecting the antiquities of this region, especially such as may throw light upon the early history of the colony, as far back as the settlement of New Amsterdam—a matter in which I know you to be deeply interested, engaged as you now are in forming a museum, that may in time rival that of Plymouth Rock or Hartford.

I send you several cases per the "Vrow" sloop, Captain Post, in which are precious relics, valuable in your eyes: *Primus.* Dutch tiles that were brought over in the ship "Gilded Beaver," March, 1660; a china milk-pot that stood on Gen. Schuyler's table when the great Washington and his aid, Gen. Hamilton, sat at the same; a looking-glass that the light-heeled Dochter of Dom. Megapolenses saw herself in before she ran away with Michael Goosen, the tailor. *Secundus.* A piece of the Duffel cloth, the knife, and a button from the beaver that Aejie Hollenback got for interpreting between the Governor who then was, and Pewack, Chief of the Mohicanders, at the transfer of the land east of the Caulibergs, extending from the Heilderbergs, north, near to Albany, down to the south of Siepos Creek, which creek runs close to Kingston, which was ancient Esopus; also, in a small box laid in lint that grew on old Dom. Schuneman's farm, you will find a ring once worn by Annie Bogart, sister's dochter to Aneja Bogardus, that was second cousin to Anneka Janks, of blessed memory; next you have the staff or cane with which Dom. Schaet chastised the Lutheran dominie when he came off second best. *Tertius.* And what you will value most of all is the ancient manuscript, inclosed in double sheepskin. Its history is curious and might make the groundwork of a strange story itself. One of the dominies of the region being inquisitive in his disposition, and fond of tracing out all traditions of old Holland, found in an oaken, worm-eaten chest, books bearing the name of Dom. de Rainde, who had, with other good men, been driven away from New York when the British took the ancient edifice in William street, and made it a riding school. By looking into the records of the Collegiate Church, you will doubtless find the name and the history of that Revolutionary worthy, up to the time he took refuge in Caatsbaan, the ancient stone church of which lies just at my feet, and where I went last Sabbath, and heard the purest, and most eloquent

Dominie that now lives, of the old stock. Among those old volumes was this precious document found, and which I procured under the solemn pledge of conveying it to the hands of those for whom it was originally designed. Being proud to say that I have an uncle, by my mother's side, in the Grand Consistory of the Collegiate Church, the discoverer has intrusted the manuscript to my care, and which I send to you in perfect confidence that justice will be done to the venerable author by his no less venerable successors.

Here let me speak a word in behalf of the finder of this ancient document, who is worthy of all gratitude for rescuing such a relic from oblivion; and as you may be curious to know of him, I would merely say to you, and through you to the Grand Consistory, that he has not a drop of Holland blood in his body. When I ventured to ask him how he took such an interest in our "LITTLE ZION" here in North America, he rose to his feet, and with great fervor declared that the "true dominie's blood runs in the spirit, not in the veins; and that the sons of John Knox were, in dark days, nursed at the breasts of old Leyden, and that they still retain the same life in them, instinctively finding out those of the same family." Another reason he said might be given for his own attachment to the Hollanders on the west side of the Atlantic: his forefathers had been determined free traders from the coast of Scotland to that of Holland, sailing past the custom-house independently, which some foolishly styled smuggling; but whatever it was, "this son of Caledonia"—here he struck his breast with force—"is a free man, and has a strong love for all patriots in general, and a sincere admiration for his predecessor, DOMINIE SCHUNEMAN, in particular."

So far I tell, the secrets I keep till I see you.

Your loving nephew,

W. S.

CATSBAAN, *Dec.* 27, 1778.

To the Venerable Consistory of the Collegiate Church of New York.

TO MY BELOVED BRETHREN, GREETING:

Ever since the day I parted with you until now, I have longed to hear of your affairs; hoping that this will find your bodies in health, even as I know your souls prosper. Obliged, as I have been, to part from you, and to take up my abode here, even as the pelican in the wilderness, it grieves my heart sore, to think that my presence cannot be with you to comfort you in the midst of that cruel war which still environs you. Nevertheless, though you have in the abundance of your liberality declared my beloved associate and fellow laborer in the Gospel, the good and learned Dominie Rudolphus Ritzema, and myself, emeriti, *i.e.* amply providing for our wants; which I understand to mean that our presence is henceforth to be dispensed with, in lieu of younger and smoother tongued men who can use the modern speech of Sion to advantage, in the new state of things, I am content. My share of public delights has been given in times past; nor did I cease while going in and out before you to cultivate the Humanities daily; so that I might do honor and service to the learned-Kerke of Holland planted here in this desert land, not suffering any one to affirm that I was behind in anything which might commend the doctrines of the Reformed Churches, and that furthermore I might have within my own soul a spring of pure delight, from which I might drink in my solitude, and be satisfied, as the wise Solomon saith of the good man. Prov. xiv., 14.

Happily for me, this power of drawing from myself remaineth even unto old age. Could you but see me engaged in my regular studies, writing out my weekly discourse which I never expect to deliver orally; or reading out of the holy and learned Thos. Sherlocke, D.D., late Master of the Temple and Bishop of London, a volume of whose works my late and beloved colleague, Dom. Ritzema has sent me from his exile in Kinderhook (his own copy, Ex

Dono Reverendi Doctoris Samuelis Johnson, Connecticut), a wonderful book from which I have been drawing nourishment. Truly he is the Locke of Divinity, who anatomizes the whole system and illustrates its component parts.

Besides those weightier matters, I have not neglected my duty to my country: so I have been careful to record the passing events of the present time. I have written a history. It is after the manner of an old painter of the mother country (you know Holland has been famous for her artists); he sat down without plan, and putting down the objects which first struck his eye, threw the sketch aside, and found it next day to be a natural picture of the first order.

There will be historians in swarms who will give the outside of this great struggle. I have written of the quieter scenes of life in a disturbed state, and as it would not be safe to let the world know now what I have written, I send it to your care, so that it may be put into the strong box where we have hidden our records.

Some future antiquarian of sufficient enthusiasm may give my history to the world. One hundred years hence it will be read with admiration. To your care I commit it.

Never expecting to meet you again in the flesh, Voorts, broeders! zijt blijde, de God nu des vredes zal den Satan haast onder uwe voeten verpletteren. De genade van onzen Heere Jezus Christus zij met ulieden. Amen.

DOM. DE RAINDE.

POSTSCRIPT FROM MY LAST BED.—I have never found a safe hand whereby to convey my history, and so I trust it to Him who kept the Book of the Law till Ezra found it. Kind finder send it thither.

CONTENTS.

BOOK II.

THE BURNING OF SOPUS AND THE IMMEDIATE CONSEQUENCES THEREOF.

BOOK III.

BURGOYNE'S FAILURE; BEING THE REVELATION OF SECRET CAUSES UNNOTICED BY THE GREAT HISTORIANS OF THE TIME.

BOOK IV.

THE FAILURE OF BRANDT; SHOWING THE STRENGTH OF INDIAN AMBITION AND REVENGE, AND HOW THEY WERE FRUSTRATED.

BOOK I.

GIVING AN ACCOUNT OF THE

BLOODY BRANDT'S DESCENT UPON THE KAATSKILL VLAATS,

OCTOBER, 1778,

WITH OTHER MATTERS, KNOWN ONLY TO THE AUTHOR.

INTRODUCTION.

To read this book with profit to the reader, and with justice to the author, it would be to the advantage of both, were a survey to be taken of the region where the scene lies, on which such great events have transpired. The place for this will be that gorge in the mountain that lies half way between Elmira, Caatsban, and old Kaatskill. There is, when it is reached, a paved floor of stone. Through the crevices therein grows up innumerable small pines, where the bear and the deer find refuge, and the hunter lodges all night for his prey. Go forward to the brink of the precipice, and look out, where all New England stretches before you; then look northward and southward, where the Knickerbockers dwell.

On that spot where you stand the Indian and the Tory met to hold their bloody conclaves. The mountain range was the dividing line. The road from the settlements below, to Fort Niagara, runs over the hills beneath you up to this point, going through Unadilla and Scenedawa, by Queen Catharine's County, near Lake Ca-nun-da-saga.

From these crags the savage descended upon the peaceable Boermen of the vlatts like a hungry cormorant, or a wolf on the fold, sweeping the Whigs away to death or bondage. Should the time ever arrive when these mountains will be trod by civilized men, let them not forget that the privilege of looking out from them in peace has been bought with the blood of the patriot.

THE DUTCH DOMINIE.

CHAPTER I.

UNCERTAINTY.

"The great high an' low have but two prominent virtues—patience and courage."—SHERLOCK.

It was on an evening of October, 1778, that old Martin Schuyler, with his wife, the good Angelica, were sitting musing in silence, interrupted only by the ticking of the old clock in the corner, that had told the course of time to generations before Martin himself had looked up on the sun, moon or stars. So well had its present possessor become acquainted with the solemn regular tick, tack, that his pulse and his thoughts went in unison with the venerable timepiece. Slow or fast, he had come to regard the mysterious machinery of his soul and body as parts of the same creature within the mahogany case, so that whenever anything went wrong with the one, the other was sure to be out of order. The Dominie, who was the only doctor in his parish, knew this fact so well, that when he came on a spiritual or a bodily visitation he was sure first to administer to the soul, then leave some medicine for the stomach, and he as invariably set about putting all right within the old clock-case.

This essential regulator of the venerable mansion had given warning through the day of a hectic pulse, which brought on midnight before the natural time, making the old man give an unusual start as the hammer struck twelve. He had just finished his second pipe, and was pushing his finger and thumb into his bladder bag for a new supply when he found time to say:

"Anshela, vat's dat de Dominee said bout te spy in te camp, an sarch out te men in te city?"

"Awee," was the quiet answer of the vrow, for she perceived that her good man's mind was excited or disturbed, and she wished to allay his troubles rather than increase them; "te Dominee meant te king of the Jews finding te men dat ver 'gainst him."

"Ha! te Dominee, Schuneman, is a very cunning man, and meant to give Jake Overpagh a hit wid his gad; for I saw dat he looked straight in te rascal's face, dat made him bring down his impudent head like a shot duck."

Old Martin chuckled at his own jest, and waited to hear what his vrow would say to his conjecture.

But Angelica, with true woman's wit, knew that she was on dangerous ground when her companion's peace had been disturbed *before*, and she merely said: "Te Dominie drew his bow at a venture, and it might pierce Jake between te joints of te harness."

"I wish to te Lord," said the husband, with more haste than usual, "dat I could speak to te skitimylink through old Peg dere, and a hole would be made big enough to let te light in dat would make him spy from te toder world rayther than round Whig doors."

"Whish! whish!" said the anxious vrow, "stone walls have ears; better, Martin, to have a close mout' than an open skull."

All this time, while this unusually long conversation was going on, the one was preparing his pipe, and the other knitting quietly at the other side of the long chimney, in which smoldered the remains of what had been a proportionably large fire, now left to sink into red coals. All was quiet in the other parts of the capacious dwelling; cattle and negroes had alike been cared for, and the hour for that worthy pair to retire had nearly come. Conversation between the two was rather a luxury than a common indulgence. Like the two buckets of their own deep well, when the one was up, it was always left full on the curb ready for use, and the other was sunk into the profundity beneath, and though it took some time to bring it up, it was fresh for household service: it was always there when the traveller came, and welcome for his horse or himself. The bucket never came up empty.

The old Boerman gave a sudden start, as if something had struck him. Angelica saw that he was alarmed through some cause without doors. She was well acquainted with the habits of her husband, and knew all the circumstances of the country sufficiently well to enter immediately into the feeling of the occasion. *He* was not a man to be frightened at a shadow, nor was *she* unprepared for the exigencies of the period. When Martin, after cautiously looking up to the window, rose slowly on his feet, and stepped to the stair that went up to the chamber, lifting old Peg, as he passed, from her resting-place on the wooden hooks fixed in the joists over-head, the careful vrow ceased even to breathe, sitting as still on her stool as if she was stone; then, with an equally cautious step, followed her husband up the steps, both that she might aid him and obtain information, or give counsel. The house was one of those heavy stone structures, that seemed built more as towers of defence than as places for comfort; the walls three feet thick, with small windows, like ancient shot-holes, covered with heavy shutters, which, in the windy seasons, slammed like the gates of a sepulchre, and as dolefully loud.

Close by one of these in the dark, Martin stood peering out, when Angelica joined her sight to his; and thinking herself the first to perceive the cause of alarm, she whispered too loud, "Vat's dat dere, noo?"

Martin had seen it, but durst not breathe of it lest the ear of some one would catch the sound; and, turning around, he gave his good vrow a pinch on the arm, which was neither love nor hate. Pointing with his finger, he directed Angelica's eye to some living thing moving between them and a grey rock that stood but a short distance from the house; and nearer to them another of the same kind of shadows. Their blood ran quicker as that last object assured them both that it was a human form. Danger was abroad! All their negroes were asleep; no friendly person would be prowling around a house at such an hour. Massacres had been common; the Indians were on the hills, and the Tories had marked old Martin for their prey. His very name, SCHUYLER, was enough to render him obnoxious to the whole race. He loved his country, and had ventured to take the side he felt was right; but he was a man, a husband, and a father.

"The teeken vuur is blazing on the Kekute," whispered the trembling wife, as she came from looking towards the east.

Martin's courage rose as he saw the acknowledged signal. His friends were aware of danger being abroad; but here was something which came under his immediate inspection. Spies were around his house. Cool by nature, and rendered cautious through long experience in the woods and on the hills, neither animal nor Indian could double him, when once upon the alert. His own cunning was his greatest danger. He had fallen occasionally into his own trap; and trusted more to the judgment of his family than he was willing to confess.

"Where's Elsie?" he whispered to the wife. She was their only child, and had, in the lack of sons, become the chief stay of her parents in their declining years. Vigorous, prudent, and prompt in all her actions, she was equal to any young man in a case of emergency. It was therefore with some mortification and sinking of the heart, that he heard the mother say:

"Elsie, O the Lamashee has gone to the husking at the Bught. Take Cæsar wit thee; he is strong, and faithful; I'll go and waken him."

"Stay! stay! do not ruin us; dese blacks are sich cowardly critters, I would as soon take one of the ox steers wid me in the dark, I must go myself."

After he had said this, they came and sat down on the same place where we found him beside the fire, and composedly smoked the pipe he had began to fill when he was first disturbed. This was his manner when his brain was foggy; he saw his way best when the smoke whirled thickest around him; and as he feared it might be some time before he obtained more of this necessary of life, his first resolution was to puff a supply. By the time he was through, his mind was made up. Angelica had been anticipating the whole result; and while the smoke became slow and regular, she had gathered up some olecakes and rusk, thrusting them into his ample pockets; filling his horn with dry powder; counting out twenty bullets, and some buck-shot, which she deposited in the same place; brought a worsted cap of her own working, which she drew upon his head well over his ears; which he pushed up in an instant; and doing all this without a word, she sat down, bending her head forward on her hands, seeming to be in the act of silent prayer: which was evidently understood by the musing Dutchman; for he ceased to puff except in the most silent stream, that rose more as incense than as indulgence. Not a word had been uttered by them since they came from the chamber above, and the house had been made long since proof against all peering eyes; so that Martin only waited the proper time to go out; but that could not be till he was sure that the marauders had gone from the dwelling.

The house, as we have hinted, was large and solid as all the mansions are, except where the New England leaven has changed the taste of some rebellious youth, who was determined to ignore his Dutch origin. Martin Schuyler was not of that tribe. His father had built one side of the house, with the evident forethought, that his posterity to the fourth and fifth generation should continue to add to it; and our friend had done his share by raising wings larger than the original body, which was distinguished from the rest by being a few feet lower than the new sides. So that the house resembled some old men we have seen, whose head had sunk considerably beneath their shoulders, while their larger rear, required all the room that could be spared to them. It was literally so of Martin's dwelling built on a side hill, and so strong itself, it was hard to say whether the hill or the house was the most crowded. No matter, the high ground behind served a good purpose in these times of public tumult, when life and property were in such danger. A cave had been originally dug in the hill, to serve as a root-house: this suggested the idea of a hiding-place, which had been carried still further into the interior. Indeed so far, that a passage-way had been made sufficiently wide for a person to worm his way to an opening on the south side of the house. Into that receptacle, long since all the silver plate of Holland manufacture, all the milledoleors which Martin had saved, the China intended for Elsie, a castle of quilted work, indeed everything that could be dispensed with out of the house; so that surprise, was not to be so great if it did come at all, upon such cautious and cool heads. If there was aught neglected, it was more through too much care than too little. As in the case of the house being burned or surrounded, and they forced to flee, ready money was essential, so a round hole had been dug in the meadow below, out of which a piece of turf was carefully taken, the earth removed, and a pot of silver coin put in, all so well done, that Martin declared at the end of his life, he could "never find out the place himself to this day."

A few pantomime signs were only passed between the two. Angelica was preparing for retreat if necessary, and Martin for defence, when a slight noise was distinctly heard, as if some one had missed a footing, and had put out a hand to recover himself. Neither of the two moved a muscle, but their senses were now fully awakened to danger. "O, if Elsie were only here," was the internal wish of the anxious man. So rising slowly and quietly from his seat, he stepped into the back part of the house, through a panel which served as a door that opened at his touch. Angelica following to receive and give counsel.

"Where is Elsie said you, Anshela?"

"Down in the Bught at a husking bee," was the quiet and subdued reply; for the good wife and mother saw plainly that her husband was troubled. "Let me go out with you; four eyes are better than two; and you know that I have both caution and courage to meet any danger, when you are beside me."

"You speak like one of the foolish women, Anshela. I am only going to watch, not to fight—if I can help it. I shall go to the top of the hill, and return in an hour, but if not, send Elsie to meet me on the Sout Mountain."

"On the Sout Mountain!" the careful wife exclaimed; "why not rather light the teeken vuur and gather our friends?"

"Vrow! Vrow!" whispered Martin with great vehemence, before any friends could be here, our scalps would be reeking in that savage Kiskataam's fingers, our grey hairs twisted together. No, I must watch the redskin and see what deviltry he is up to, and trap him in his den. Elsie is the only one that can help me at this hour. You stay here quietly. There are only two of them. They are waiting till we sleep, and then they will go to the flat rock and light their warning fire. Ha! ha! cunning dogs. Martin is before you! Catch a squirrel sleeping. Thanks to Peet, for all that I know." The farmer and the hunter chuckled at the thought of outwitting Kiskataam, the Wild-cat, upon his own ground, the Kaatskills.

There was no more difficulty in bringing Angelica to agree to the plan. She was well aware that her careful husband possessed means of information which he kept to himself. So with a few more olecakes, and some quiet blessings, and prayers on his safety, she saw him crawl on his hands and knees through the narrow passage leaving her to close all up as quietly, and as closely as possible, without calling up any of the negro men, who were all asleep in the lower part of the house, in what is called the cellar kitchen.

Martin emerged from his underground journey like a rabbit that has found itself in the wide world, ready to return to its burrow quickly should danger be near. He lay still for at least five minutes, listening till he became familiarized with the silence and the darkness around him; when he gradually rose upright, standing so still that he seemed but one of the stumps of the field. Taking a wide circuit from his own house, he sought a patch of wood through which there was a cow path, guessing that the spies around him would take that on their way to their accustomed rendezvous. Nor was he mistaken, for, after waiting patiently a full hour, he heard footsteps distinctly, coming behind him. He would have been at a loss to tell whether it was man or animal, had he not also heard a human voice, which became more audible, but to him more mysterious, the nearer as it approached. Now it was the low guttural tones of an Indian; and again it seemed something else; but neither Indian nor Dutch. Here was something of which he had not dreamed. His secret informant of yesterday had not hinted of any one but Indian. Till now, he had been comparatively calm, for his experience had taught him that it was easier to circumvent ten Indians, than one true and determined white man of experience. But, judge of the still greater surprise of our watcher, when he heard distinctly, the tones of the English tongue; and that of a young woman. He started to his feet with an alertness the reverse of his previous sluggishness. Martin's acquaintance with the world of Albany, and of Manhattan Island had been frequent, among his own near relatives, who were of the first quality in the colony; enabling him to judge at once of these tones, and of the distinct words uttered; assuring him that this was a woman of polished life and language. Why brought hither to these wild regions? He lay down again, waiting for the persons to pass by; but so near that he might obtain a perfect view of their forms, and, if possible, guess into the mystery. As the Indian Kiskataam passed, carrying in his arms a young female, who was beseeching him to tell her why he was taking her through these woods. The heart of the honest Dutchman leaped to his throat, as he drew forward old Peg, with her muzzle almost touching the mean catiff that passed him; and but for the one he shielded himself behind, an ounce of lead would have decided his fate. But he was allowed to pass, while the name, "Mother! oh, my dear mother!" and another name, which Martin could not hear distinctly, rung in his ear, calling upon him for help.

"And help you shall have, my strange lamishee," said the tender father. "My own Elshie may be the next, and how could I come back to Ansbela, if I saw our own daughter dragged off in that way. The murderous savage that he is, I have long determined to give him the contents of Peg; and now is my time. No; now is his time; I will follow him and watch my chance. The dear lady, though she be of the English blood, must be set free, though the blood of 'Kiskataam flows for it."

The really excited Boerman was just about to rise, when there passed by on the same path, but in far quieter motion, another of the same race leading a dog by a bark string. At the sight of the man and beast, Martin ground his teeth with inward rage.

"Dunder and blitzen, were the Dominie here himself he would zweert, I will say—duivil. There is that duivil Shandaagan carrying off Rover, and here I must lie still and see all."

They who knew all would have pardoned the good Dutchman; even his swearing, when they reflected on the mean character of this second Indian, and the provocation he had given to Martin before and now. He was one of those offscourings of the race who proved false to all he pretended to serve. At this very time, he was pretending to be on the side of the Whigs. It was but the day before that he had been to the Hoogenhuisen, and seemed to be on the most friendly terms with all; yet, he had not said a word of this coming adventure, of which he was surely aware; and this decoying of the dog Rover away, was proof positive of treachery.

"Ah," said the mortified Martin to himself, "ever since that time Elsie caused contempt on his chieftainship, I have seen his secret revenge working; and now he thinks he has made himself sure, as the Dominie says, 'de Heeve wil en wij leven zullen zoo zullen wij dit of dat doen.'"

For these aggravating mortifications he had this to make amends, that Rover did not scent him out, when as he passed the place his master lay hidden; but went, seemingly as if aware, that both should bide their time. It was an augury to him for good; and as he was now sure of their destination, and had come upon their trail sufficiently, he was in no haste to pursue, but made up his mind to go slowly on and watch their motions; waiting for Elsie, who he was certain would meet him at the appointed place in time for the execution of any plan he could devise, which would set the feeble captive at liberty, and rid the world, if possible, of these two fiends, now bent on the destruction of the inhabitants of the region.

"They have gone to the pine orchard to prepare for that hellish congregation that's coming. Bloody wolves; they have tasted blood at Wyoming, and now we are to expect no better fate. That hell-hound, Shandaagan, has known all as well as myself, and his hunting around has been that he might lay his traps all the more secret and sure. The Hoegenhuisen will be among the first. They did not try it to-night. They have got other fish to fry. Maybe that is only bait they are carrying;" and the hunter grinned a grim smile at his own wit.

Taking a winding direction westward, Martin proceeded with perfect confidence of finding the skulking place of the party. Measuring his speed according to his knowledge of the length of road he had to travel, he was in no hurry, as any step he took was on ground as familiar to his foot, as the turnings of his own yard. His care was to keep sufficiently far out of the way not to be heard by the Indians on the one hand, and on the other to cautiously look around him, lest he might stumble on some stragglers of the party. The mystery of the English lady made him timorous. He had a certain intuitive perception that trouble was to arise out of that occurrence, to others, if not to himself. Crossing the Kaaterskill stream a mile above the opening of the clove, he left his own house to the south of him, and proceeded up the side of the hill which lies to the south; when, after an hour's ascending travel, he reached Puddingstone Hall, and sat down upon a slanting rock, that seems to have been placed there by some ancient Druid: for none but the beings who raised Stonehenge on their nice balance, could now put that stone on its sloping position. Martin had frequently, from his boyhood, sat on the same stone at all hours of the day, and of the night, and wondered how it came there; and how it hung there, and how long it had lain so; but now he had other thoughts to occupy his mind; for just as truly as he had conjectured, there were the very persons who had passed him by, now on the flat rock. The Indians were sitting before a bright burning fire; and near it was raised one of those wigwams, which all who live in the woods know how to raise in a twinkling of time. Still there was something about the whole scene here, which made the careful hunter feel insecure. That bower was more tastefully raised than the red man ever did such work; and the building of the fire was not after the fashion of that thoughtless race, but carefully made of dried wood, not found in the immediate neighborhood. The experienced eye of the unseen observer could discern other evidences of a superintendence which amazed and stultified his senses.

"God in de hemelin verlichte mijne oogen!" Martin prayed in his own tongue for light to his eyes; then almost out of breath in his anxiety, he said: "Oh, if Elshie were but here now, she could explain the meaning of these things."

In the meantime, he was too wise a man, and had been in too many different places, to let any chance pass, without informing himself concerning the actual state of things. Being on a height which overlooked all that was doing on the rock below, it was easy to see all that was moving; and lest there might be some prying eyes around, he lay flat upon the face of that leaning rock, with old Peg by his side, watching the chances which might come up. After he had satisfied himself that no being was in his own immediate neighborhood, he took a different position in hope that new background might discover some wandering shadow; but there were still the same Indian faces; and that of the young pale-face, which he could see plainly in the flickering glow of the fire as it rose and fell. Never was a man more puzzled to account for all these things. Here was a captive, and she could not be a Whig's daughter, judging from her English accent and foreign style of speech; and yet Kiskataam was in the pay of the king. Had he since thought of turning to the other side, making this the price of his double treachery?

"He shall not succeed," said the excited Martin, with a vehemence which nearly cost him his life; for standing as he did so near to the verge of the crag, he pushed with his feet so hard that a loose rock gave way, falling to the bottom of the precipice, over which, in the dark, he might have been hurled to his destruction. The noise reverberating through those wild hills in the night, roused up the beasts below from their lairs, and the party above were evidently much alarmed; for when Martin recovered himself, he saw that the two Indians were standing both upright like sentinels, ready for an attack. However, soon discovering the seeming cause of the interrupted silence, they sank back to their usual somnolence.

Our white sentinel on the hill had made up his mind to a plan, just as soon as he could obtain his expected help, which he thought must be near at hand; and with that in view, he took the most prominent point of Puddingstone Hall, where he stood like one of the black stumps of a tree, which even an Indian could not distinguish him from in the dark.

CHAPTER II.

DEEP DOUBT.

"Experience will show that as want of appetite supposes, and proceeds from some bodily disease, so the apathy the stoics talk of as much supposes, or is accompanied with somewhat amiss in the moral character, in that which is the health of the mind."—Bishop Butler.

Martin, though almost in agony for his daughter, never took his eyes off the wigwam. A fluttering leaf or the movement of an animal might arrest his mind unconsciously, still he never turned his thoughts on anything fixedly, so as to be moved aside from the object before him. He was certain now that the two Indians were only the instruments and outside actors in this drama, and his desire was increasing with every beating of his pulse to see the hand behind the scenes; so eager did he become, that he forgot that Elsie might arrive and not find him in the appointed place. He was drawing nearer and nearer all the time, fearful lest anything might escape his notice. He heard voices, but could not discern, at the distance he stood away, what was said. This induced him to step onward, till he found himself so near that he could distinctly perceive on one occasion the captive sitting up, while the ruddy glow of the fire showed him sufficient of her countenance to satisfy him that she was none of the maidens of the colony around, but one of those that he had seen riding out on the roads *round* Albany, who were birds of passage, gay in plumage and full of life, never intending to make this land their home. "Ruddy, and of a fair countenance," as the Dominie would say, though Martin inwardly thought "she has been stolen by this sinner, at the bidding of those wicked profligates that follow these fair doves as the hawks do their prey."

"She is no child neither, as I am a Schuyler, and as good blood as ever came from Holland; a lady of at least nineteen is she that walks out there before the fire, and she is talking just now to the Indian. I wish I could but hear her once. Yes, poor lamishie, you may well look out on that black sky, made darker by the very fire now in your eyes, for woe to thee, an unknown end is before thee."

With the true hunter spirit, the watcher was drawing closer and closer, so as to have a perfect view and reach his game in the best advantage. He could have brought down one of those dark shadows that stood before him on the flat rock with ease; the other he could meet singly without hesitation, but there were others here, and with white faces.

He was now so near that he could hear words indistinctly, and might have pressed closer, in his eagerness, but at this instant he was startled by something in his rear moving the shrubs close to the ground. He looked through the darkness, with the glare of the fire in his eyes, seeing nothing till he had time to recover from the effect of the light, and then saw distinctly two small balls of fire, so near to one another that he instantly felt that they must be the eyes of some animal about to spring upon him. His first motion was to lift Peg into her defensive position, but listening, with all his senses awake, he soon heard—what he had frequently heard before when he hunted on these mountains—the snuffing of a deer, attracted by the light, and thereby blinded to its own danger. Martin had been out on the little lakes near this very place in his canoe, burning pitch-pine knots on the prow for the very purpose of bringing the deer to him, and now one comes when he would have preferred to have it anywhere else. The pleasure and keenness of the hunter all but overcame his prudence, for his fingers tingled with the desire of bringing those noble six-tined antlers to the ground; but merely giving a side motion he alarmed the creature, so that it ran past the place where the Indians lay. They both sprang up with an alacrity little short of the deer himself, rushing after him with an agility not surprising to one who knew their habits and modes of life. Their natural love of sport, and their appetite, made keen by a whole day's travel, caused them to forget for the time the captive they had been watching over with so much assiduity all the night.

Martin felt that now was his time, and had already moved

a few steps forward to seize the trembling maiden, who was herself in motion to rush, she knew not whither, when there stepped out from the dark cover a new actor in the scene, who placed himself before her, saying, with some excitement in his voice and manner, bending at the same time on his right knee, as he seized her hand: "Dearest Margaret, I have fulfilled my promise made a year ago."

The lady drew her hand from the grasp of the intruder, as if she had been stung by a snake, and darted to the other side of the fire with the fleetness of the deer that had just passed that way. At the same time she gave a scream which echoed, and reëchoed, among the rocks and hills, till it seemed as if a hundred captive damsels were shrieking to their friends for deliverance. She would have rushed on, but now the man, who had been put aside so easily, rushed with an equal ardor, exclaiming: "For the love of God, Miss ——, do not go further or you will fall over the shelf and be dashed to pieces."

By this time he had hold of the exhausted girl, who gasped out: "O, why did I not know that I was so near to liberty, one leap and—and all would have been over. Let me go, touch me not with that foul hand; and if you will not, tell me why I am brought hither—for now I see who has been the cause of this wicked treachery. Let me die."

"Miss Margaret, you do me wrong, if you suppose that you are here through any desire to injure you. I mean the best that man can do for woman; and if you be patient and calm, you will hear it all."

"No, I will not listen to your false tongue;" and with that she shook herself free of the hold of him who stood before the angry girl, as Martin had seen a strong dog, who, having encountered a wild cat, is fain to stand off at a respectable distance, watching for a retreat. Abashed at the charge of treachery, yet mad at the epithet false; and afraid, lest by some sudden movement the excited woman should rush into destruction, the man stood more like a culprit, than as the director in some daring enterprise, which had doubtless required great tact and decision to bring it to its present crisis. Some new occurrence, it was evident, might disappoint him in his plans. He had succeeded in his end so far; but he was utterly at a loss to know what to do with the prize for which he had played so high a part, up to this time. Martin seeing this, was measuring the distance between himself and the traitor—for so he already regarded the man who was so named by the lady—that he might disable him and then fall upon him; but it was too late, for there were the two Indians returning; and three against two, and one of these only a feeble girl, was an unequal combat.

"Away from my sight, hateful wretch," was the exclamation of the enraged girl, once more uttered, as the man approached nearer to take hold of her hand; "Leave me to these savages; their presence is more agreeable to my eyes than the man who violates his honor as a gentleman, and his duty as a soldier."

It was now the turn of the man to show excited passion. The veins of his brow became swollen like cords, and his nostrils became wide as a war horse, when spurred to resistance; but with great effort suppressing his feelings, he said with trembling lips.

"My lady, urge me not to do what we both shall eternally regret; remember you are in my power at this moment."

"I am in no man's power. God will not suffer the innocent to be long without a deliverer. He is at my right hand this moment; I see him through the thick darkness." And she gazed so earnestly on the very spot where Martin stood, that he felt the blood rushing through his veins, faster than it had done for many years. So direct were her motions, that the eyes of her captor for a moment were turned in the same direction, as if in fear.

"Kiskataam, Kiskataam, I throw myself under your protection. I will pardon all you have done and said to me; I will obtain you pardon and a reward from my father, if you only save me now from the company of that traitorous man. Clifford, I hold you in scorn; and the daughter of an English soldier will bestow naught else on a coward who has betrayed his friend, and would now spoil the peace of the family where he has been nursed, and confided in from boyhood. Oh, Bertram, why do you not come to me!"

With this effort, which was too much for her, the excited lady sank down helpless on the ground; presently she was lifted by her tormentor, as he would have lifted a child, and placed on the bed of laurel which had been prepared for her. As he laid her down, Martin saw that the man put out his lips as if he could have imprinted a kiss on the pale brow, but the weakened woman gained new strength at this insult offered to her modesty, and struck up her hand with such force that the insulter staggered back a step or two, while the poor captive hid her face and sobbed like an infant, calling out, "Oh, mother! mother! come to me."

The eyes of the inactive spectator melted at what met his senses, and groaning in his spirit, he longed again for Elsie. Then he set about imagining what would have been his own feelings had it been his own daughter who was going through such an ordeal as he now was witness to. "Ha!" said he to himself, "I only wish that the hand which smote that rascallious cheek had been as heavy as Elshie's. He would feel it warm now, and remember Pine Orchard to the end of his life. But, there now, these savages are skinning that deer, which fairly belonged to me; and which, if my heart tells me true, they shall not live to eat. Three shots in Peg would settle the question; but, unlike the Pegs of the Yankees, mine, like Anshela, can speak but once at a time, and I am slow at loading."

Apart from the place where the bower and the fire were built, the red men were busy skinning the deer which they had succeeded in killing; while the man who had appeared so suddenly, stood as sentinel near the lady. There was great nervousness displayed in his movements at times, and an uncertainty in his step, which could not be hidden from any observer. All at once he came forward to the side of the prostrate captive, calling out a full name which Martin did not catch. "I have a plan, Margaret, that I will lay before you, and choose."

"Kiskataam! Kiskataam!" was again shrieked out by the feeble prisoner, with a vehemence which brought to her that sedate chieftain, who, like all of his race, was not easily thrown from his self possession; "Indian, take me under your care. Have pity on a poor helpless girl, take me back to the river, I will find my way to the ship. Good Kiskataam, you have had young squaws of your own forced away by the Senecas, and they were returned to you. You told me of them when you sat beside me in the big canoe. Take me back. The red soldier will make you king of the Six Nations if you release his daughter."

The Indian rose to his full height, showing more emotion than common in his countenance and voice as he slowly said,

"Does the Panther have pity when he has the Fawn in his mouth?"

There was evident bitterness in his words. Why should the Fawn seek pity from the Panther when the Lion has come to her protection?

"The Fawn, as you have been pleased to call me, would rather trust the Panther than the Wolf. The Lion I would trust. Alas! that I should see any bearing the emblem of the lion, becoming more cruel than the cowardly dog."

This last was said in an undertone which evidently was intended for the one who took it up in anger, which shot from his eyes in flashes of revenge.

"The Lion," continued the Indian, "would raise the Fawn in his hall of greatness."

"And then give me over to be devoured by the wolves. No, Indian, protect me or not, as you please; but hear me, I would rather have my poor body destroyed by the meanest reptile that lives in these wilds, than be possessed for an hour by the Lucifer who has betrayed his friend."

The man, whom we shall henceforth call Clifford, had stood with his arms folded during the conversation, wishing to be regarded as calm, but this last stroke made him turn himself aside as if he felt afraid of showing his feelings of growing passion.

"Indian has a beautiful wigwam," said Kiskataam, when he saw that the white man had moved out of earshot—"Indian built it for his squaw, that would come from the rising to the setting sun. Wigwam beside the clear lake where the trees grow thick, and the leaves shine in the glittering light. The Fawn would hide in the darkest spot. Kiskataam would bring the flowers of the cloves to deck her hair, and the softest skins for her bed."

The astonished lady could scarcely believe but that the whole was a dream, and her amazement was so great, that she could not make any reply otherwise than by her looks, which the quick perception of this other tormentor easily interpreted; whether he was sincere or not in his daring proposition will never be fully proven, but in the present instance turning his fawning tones into keen sarcasm he continued:

"Has not the Fawn said she wished to run upon the mountains, and along the streams that flow down their feet? Did she not sigh to see the brooks, that blue eyes never looked into until her own gazed therein, as she said the first squaw did in the white man's paradise."

"Oh! distress me not with my romantic folly. All was beautiful in fancy, but it is terrible in reality. Sad is my fate! The victim of both the red and the white man."

"But the Fawn has not yet seen the place where the milk-white deer run tame, led by the young squaws to the wigwam door. She has not fed the young eaglets fluttering in their nest. There are bird-songs too in the forest that the Fawn would love to hear. Soft skins of the bear and the beaver, of the fox and the catamount, which Kiskataam has tanned with his own hand. On these would the Fawn sleep, and dream; she would forget her troubles, and not be afraid of the Wild Wolf any more."

The Indian began this long description in the uncertain tones of half reproach, but ended in the soft mellow sounds with which his race speak in their times of sadness or of entreaty. Nature is imitated by them, and is successful at times in evil.

"Kiskataam," said the enraged lady, "do you mean what your words imply? Have you stolen me away for yourself or for another? Come forward Clifford, and tell me whether you mean me to be the wife of an English soldier or the squaw of an Indian chief? for it seems I must choose between being in Howard Castle, or plant corn beside the Susquehanna. Clifford! Clifford!" and the rocks rang with the sound of his name. He was at her side in an instant.

"I was," said the lady, "a moment since ready to have trusted the Indian rather than you. I confide in none of you. Your minion there seeks to preserve a separate suit of his own. He is as mean as some white men are, and betrays his friend by seeking to carry off the victim."

"By this time the two associates in guilt were confronting each other, with those looks of hate which traitors put on when found out. So long as each of these caitiffs could make an instrument of his companion, in accomplishing a selfish end, blandness and generousness were the features of their intercourse; but now the disguise had fallen, at least from the Indian, and the man Clifford felt mortified at being made the dupe of one he called a barbarian. With his ears still ringing of treachery, charged upon him by one that seemed fully to know him, and who so defied him, he was in no mood to take an insult from any third person. He was only too glad to find one object on whom to wreak his vengeance.

"You Indian dog!" was the first word he could utter in quivering passion through his teeth. "How dare you come between me and mine. Have I not pledged my word of honor to pay you?"

Here Clifford stopped short suddenly, seeing that the lady

was watching the coming word. She felt that she had gained a point in setting her two enemies against each other. Whoever lost, she could be in no worse hands; so rousing herself up, she stood prepared for the smallest chance of escape; and also, for knowing all that concerned herself. But the suppressed sentence which would have revealed something was lost; and the burst of passion ended as it began, with "Indian dog!" Clifford was choked with rage.

"English fox hold his nose to the ground;" was the bitter retort of Kiskataam. At the same moment he was handling his tomahawk, which hung at his girdle, in rather a sinister manner. The Englishman showed nothing of the coward, but the sight seemed rather to swell him out to larger dimensions; and, without even yet discovering that he had any weapons of defence about him, he stepped up nearer to the red man, demanding the object of this show of fight.

"Does the Indian chief seek war? Blood is sweet to the Panther just now. Would he fondle the Fawn? would he carry her to the beautiful lake away by the Susquehanna?"

All of this was uttered in that mingled bitterness of sarcasm and anger which the English people know so well how to give to any enemy when they wish to provoke him to do a desperate act.

"The Panther loves to worry the Wolf," was the no less determined reply of the Indian, who stood his ground with equal courage to the other; and Martin, watching the result with an almost breathless interest, bent over the whole scene, without thinking for a moment that were his presence known, it would turn the anger of both these men upon himself. The lady, with an equal interest, forgot her captivity, waiting for the crisis of the present affair.

"The Panther would worry the Wolf—ha! and lick the Fawn's blood at his leisure: a dainty meal! He must fight first with long teeth. The Wolf, as you would have me to be, has got snapping jaws:" and with that the click of a large pistol was heard in the hand of Clifford; nor was his crest in the least degree, at this moment, like the wolf, but terrible as a real soldier appears in the time of danger.

Kiskataam seemed undecided, but it was not the indecision of fear, for his eyes glanced fire, though not a muscle of his face seemed to move, except in that nervous rapidity which is more like the stream of electric fire that runs over a cloud before the storm breaks, making the beholder wait timorously for the glancing lightning and the report, than anything in human action. The true savage stood with hand on the tomahawk, watching the eye of his opponent, and wheeling in a twinkling, he hurled the weapon in the direction of the lady, grazing her head, so that the knot which held her hair, was cut asunder; but passing her, it lodged in the tree against which Martin was leaning; and by which he was watching the transaction so near to him.

The occurrence was the doing of a moment. All, with the exception of the actors, were confounded; and by the time they had recovered from their surprise, an event was taking place which diverted the attention from the design of the Indian.

CHAPTER III.

A HARVEST FEAST.

"If Roger is my Joe, he kens himsel'
For sic a tale I never heard him tell,
He glowers and sighs, and I can guess the cause,
But wha's obliged to guess his hums and haws,
When'er he likes to tell his mind mair plain,
I'll tell him frankly, ne'er to do't again."

RAMSAY'S PATIE AND ROGER.

ELSIE SCHUYLER was an only child, a rare thing among the Holland Dutch, which rendered her more the companion of her father than she would otherwise have been, had he had sons to bring up and lean upon in his old age. Of strong will, clear mind, and a pious spirit, her actions were prompt and fearless, as her father's were slow and uncertain. With his daughter beside him, Martin seemed as if her soul stirred and moved his body. He thought immediately as she did, and with all his strength he set to the fulfilling her desire. Yet he never would have understood the man who would have ventured to tell him he had no mind of his own, nor could Elsie have known any thing of controlling the action of her parent.

In truth, even with her strong will, she had been all her life under great moral restraint. Her education would have been regarded as deficient in New York; but such as it was, the grand end of all education was gained by her in prudent self-control, rapidity of thought in times of emergency, and fearlessness of action when danger required it to be met. All of these essential elements were the result of training, which had no plan in it, but grew out of the nature and habit of the worthy parents, who taught her the usual course of reading in the Bible and the learning of the real orthodox Heidelburgh Catechism. Though she spoke the vernacular low Dutch of the region where she lived, yet it was the ambition of the parents that their daughter should also speak the English tongue, and she was accordingly sent to a school where the English Bible and other books were read. This, as she grew up, was of immense advantage to her on account of the intercourse she could have with other parts of the colony, where more could be learned than on the sides of the mountains. Elsie had every year since she was sixteen paid an annual visit to her friends in Albany, and even New York; for the Schuylers and the Van Cortlandts were not too proud to have their country cousins visit them in the cities, when they had such fine opportunities of returning these courtesies among the hills and the vales of the Kaatskills.

It was in this school that the daughter of Martin Schuyler was fitted for life in any home where Providence might place her, though it suited the plan of both father and mother better, that some of the young farmers of the region should come in, and be a son to them in their old age. There were many qualities in Elsie which other circumstances would have developed, and she had already acquired habits of thought, of feeling, and of manners, which no new training could have possibly repressed. Her mind, and modes of thinking and acting, could have been polished to a superior power. She would have been more fascinating in her smile, softer in her voice, have had a smoother rhythm in language, have trod the soil with a daintier tread, and moved around her father's house with less noise. But then the rocks and the hills were rough on which she stepped, and the doors, the painted floors, and the big jambs of those rooms, were not after city patterns. It was rather the house of the Boerman than the palace of the Stadtholder of Amsterdam, that Martin had lived so long in, and where Elsie had been brought up. She was a true-hearted young woman, who had neither been allowed to waste her existence in the seclusion of a country life, where much ignorance and rudeness have so covered the genuine precious stone that its polish and beauty have never come out; nor had she been sent to the city and so ground down upon the wheel of fashion that not a streak of truth remained either on face or person. The man of the world, possessed of tact and having an insight of human character, would have chosen her, like a learned lapidary, as a precious stone capable of the highest lustre; and had Martin seen his Elsie in the big halls of the Van Rensselaers, he would have wondered, after asking where that young vrow came from, to hear that she was the gem of his own mountain farm.

On the night of our history Elsie was down in the Bught—a peculiar piece of land which lies in a bend, or "bight" of the river—where there was a husking-bee, which brought all the young people of the country together, from the West Camp to the Van Bergen patent. Fun and frolic were in full force. In the large, sloped-roof barn sat groups of lads and lassies, among bundles of corn-stalks, out of which they were stripping the yellow treasure, and throwing it into bushel baskets, which some old men were removing as fast as they were filled. This active business did not hinder the tongues of all from going, only as Dutch tongues can. But it would have defied the most learned philologist that ever studied at Babel, to have followed that modern confusion. It was not the numbers, though there must have been a hundred, nor was it the harsh guttural *ughs*, that sounded underneath, like the soughing of the wind in a storm; nor was it the sharp shots which flew so that the blood rose to the faces of some of both sexes, as red gleams pass between travelling clouds; but it was all three, and in addition there was what no community in the broad continent can produce except on the North River, and only on the west side running for fifty miles, viz., a mixture of French, Low Dutch and German, so combined that it would have put either Frenchman, Dutchman or German to utter confusion. It seemed literally as if jaw bones were thrown across the barn, till they struck against each other in the whirlwind which lifted them into the air.

Still all was not uproar, and even that seeming confusion had nothing of the keen wiriness which other nations exhibit in their frolics when a man knocks his neighbor down through pure love of fun, when his over-good sweetness turns so suddenly into vinegar. Here and there among that busy throng were small, quiet parties, who enjoyed themselves. Hearts were drawn nearer, and lips followed, as a matter of course. Experience can sit anywhere, feeling composed and self-possessed, while the vulgar mind is sure to be attracted by the least sound or sight which may occur outside of themselves.

"Ha! ha! Jerry, are you there? Show your wrists to the folks here. What makes you look so red in the face, you spalpeen?"

"What should make me show my wrists any more than you an empty pocket. Mexican pillars can save a Sabbath-breaker's conscience. Ha! who is red in the face now?"

These rude allusions were made by two rough-looking youths to some recent piccadilloes in which they had been both engaged, but the one having money could pay the fine imposed, while the other, being poor, had to stand three hours in the stocks in front of the church door—a species of punishment which had been imported from the mother country, and which was regarded as a great disgrace. Sabbath-breaking is one of the crimes; no one is suffered to ride except to church, only "It shall be lawful for the *Post*, or any other person in his Majesty's service; or to bring a Physitian or Mydwife." Such is the law of the colony.

"Jerry had quite a crowd around him outside the kerke door; more than the Dominie had inside." This was put in by a great laughing lout of a fellow, who made the rafters ring with his own approval.

"You had better look to yourself, Dirck Dietrick. There are worse things than the jugges in these times," said the goaded Jerry, who was in no mood to be tormented while his wrists were glowing with the iron rings. "There are stone jugges, where some folks would be if they got their own."

"Don't be angry," was the mellowing response of Dirck; "for the Dominie said, after you went away, that he believed good came out of it. He preached all the better for your example."

"Aye," said Jerry, "just as some folks would be better whigges if a cowboy were tied at the koort-house door every morning."

"Come, come, no more of dat," said old Tobias, the good Boerman, in whose barn they all sat; "we have no more of dat; come and eat de sheeps, and de bearen, and de chicken, and drink de rum and de cider."

In a corner, away from the most roystering of the company, sat Elsie, along with a few of the best class of young persons. Both sexes regarded Elsie as a superior person, and were never too familiar in their approaches. Such as, like herself, had relatives in the large towns, or who had improved themselves by the best company whom they could find, were usually found near Martin Schuyler's daughter, and were fond of quoting her as an authority. Among the young men was Teunis Roe, who had, either by accident or affinity of disposition, found himself side by side with Elsie upon several occasions of public gatherings; and he had not been an entire stranger at the Hoogenhuisen in former days. Indeed there was a time when old Egbert Roe and Martin Schuyler were sworn friends and brothers. But, oh! that weary war! it had proved what they had often heard the Dominie say: "De vader zal tegen den zoon verdeeld zijn en de zoon tagen den vader."

This was literally the case, for Teunis in his heart was Whig, and his father was in his heart a Tory. It was the son against the father, and the father against the son, and both in the same house, sworn foes, but as yet in part secret. For so long as Teunis had to remain at home he must keep his principles to himself. His peculiar and hard case was fully understood by Elsie, though not by Martin, and consequently the intimacy of the two families was broken up, so far that there was no longer any interchange of visits, once so pleasant in the long winter nights, between the old people; nor was there the same liberty felt by the young folks themselves when they met. The actual position of Teunis was fathomed easily by Elsie, but with tact and delicacy she avoided all allusions to the public affairs of the country. She never inquired after the reason of his absences, yet seemed to expect him to embrace such occasions as the present for meeting her, and talking over local matters, of which there was always a sufficient stock on hand.

"You were not at the wedding of Peggy Wolfin on Friday last," said Teunis, as he took up a large stalk of corn, balancing it on his right thumb-nail, as if he cared but little whether he husked any more that night or not. "You were expected to stand as bride's-maid, and there was some disappointment you may be sure."

These last words were uttered in a low tone, which the heart, if inclined, is sure to feel; and the damsel had not a heart of stone.

"These are not times, you know, Teunis, for young girls to go much alone, and my father had heard something which made him more than usually afraid of my going out. Indeed,

I am here just now more on my mother's leave than on his. Do you not think these are hard times to marry?"

"That depends, Elsie, upon whether both be of one mind; in some things union is strength: and two sticks tied together are stronger than the same two sticks taken separately." Teunis here threw the ear of corn into the basket, just as Elsie cast one in at the same place; and then laughing at the conjunction, asked the maiden whether she would like to see how the two lay in the basket, heads or thraws.

"O, you may look if you please," said Elsie, half blushing; "Nelly Schutt there, would take that to be as certain as the good book, but"——

"See, there they are lying side by side, as cozy as two kittens," said Teunis, as he held down the basket to the candle; and to tell the truth, woman's curiosity, or something else, inclined Elsie this time, as before, to look and laugh at the folly of the sign.

"There now," said Teunis, "is a quarrel getting up between these onwijzen."

"Teunis, mind what the Dominie says: he that calleth his brother fool—you know the rest."

"I know, Elsie; but what can you call that Dick Deidricht but a fool; hear how he is provoking Jerry to bring up matters which should be kept out of our homes, and from these friendly gatherings. I must go and keep them quiet."

And off he moved; but before he had time to put in a word, Tobias was giving out the bill of fare, in his own peculiar manner, which had the same happy influence upon Dutch blood, that the smell of good dinners has upon hungry dogs, and hungry princes or princesses; for animal nature during a time of hunger is much the same in the quadruped and the biped.

It would require more words than can be spared, to describe a supper among the honest Dutch on the Hudson River. They must have inherited their liking from their ancestors on the Scheldt, and in the Low Countries; where the sturdy Boerman, after working in the deep bogs, came home to his vrow and fed heartily and slept it off. And, imitating the burgomaster of the place, on his great occasions, he too called in his "Vrenden en de geburen en bringt het gemeste kalf en stagt het; en laat ons eten en vrolijk zijn."

The old Hollander was very orthodox, and in killing the fatted calf, and being in a vrolicke—(Anglicè, merry). He was never hurt by a good supper. He lay all the easier, like an old Roman on his couch, that the citadel was well provisioned. It would be an interesting history to tell all that lay on the vast table, made of doors taken from their hinges, and covered with linen sheets, on which lay piles of meat in huge wooden dishes; not carefully selected, the one animal from the other, but the bear and the cow were together, and the chicken and the rabbit were on the same plate. Equal hillocks of bread stood ready to be distributed by the bustling fat hostess, who moved around as we have seen a Dutch scow among other craft, coming square up against one and another, till she succeeds in laying a portion equally as large as Benjamin's share, before each guest. She repeated these acts of kindness to the end of the feast; every now and again urging them to partake; saying to one, "You don't like our victuals, Jake." "Take up the leg of that turkey and send it with the rest, Tim.' "Now, Elsie, eat till you burst; I wish you may." "No ting like good victuals."

She did not mean all she said, but she intended to do her best at being hospitable; and being among her own kind of people, it was a satisfaction just to see her good natured look as she surveyed the ample table, with her guests devouring far more than all the worth of the labor they had performed; but it would be so rich to tell afterward, that she had cooked two more sheep, killed five more turkeys, and twenty more chickens than dame Languendyck ever did. Besides, every one had at least a yard of sausage put on his plate, a pound of rolichie; cabbage and onion, apples and cider, all came on just as if they had not eaten anything for a month. Never were a company more unfit, according to city notions, of taking themselves to the ball-room; but the spirit of these folks was just rising. The plentiful draughts of cider and brandy which were drank, without injury to the perpendicular position of the guests, helped to carry them through the contra-dances, without being hindered by their abdominal gravity. The barn floor, during the supper, had been cleared by the negroes, who always worked with right good will when there was to be—gezang en het geric—*music and dancing;* and even the good Dominic would stand at the door and see his children vrolicke. All was full of glee and merriment, and fairly on the way to a happy termination, when old Fred, the head man of Tobias, came rushing into the middle of the floor, his jaws chattering, and his face the color of his grey head, screaming and acting as a lunatic may be supposed to act, under a black skin and African features.

Not a word could be got from him except the sound "Vuur en sulfur—Gog en de Magog. Ingen barbareen." These words came out in the form of squeals and grunts, more than like human speech.

Of course all amusement came to a close at this sudden apparition, for while some declared that Fred had seen a geest, others a spook, some had, with more presence of mind, run to the door, and coming back announced the tidings, more alarming than anything of the witching-kind, that the vuur teeken on the Keekute was in a blaze. This was the acknowledged beacon of warning, and was like the fiery cross of the Scottish clans, the gathered signal in approaching danger. The combustible material had been brought together early in the summer, and was in fine fitness for the torch. An onset was expected from the west, as already referred to, and now that the glare was reflected from the sky, the yells of the Indians almost sung already in the ears of the helpless and the cowardly. What added to the anxiety and uneasiness of the occasion, many were known to be secretly friendly to the savages, now near at hand, and were mingling with the very persons whose lives would be sought out with as much horror and fiendish delight as was usual on such occasions. All the company prepared to go; some to their homes, and others to the general rendezvous.

Elsie, with the rest, had risen in the moment of surprise, and after looking to the Keekute on the river-bank, she turned her eyes to the west in search of the hill above Hoogenhuisen; and there, too, rose up the great flame, like a fiery tongue speaking to heaven for relief. Her heart smote her for being in the midst of pleasure at such a time; while without uttering a single word, except a low whisper to Teunis, who stood waiting her will, though he had spoken not a word.

"*De tijd is nabij; laat ons van hier gaan*, Teunis?"

"I am beside thee, Elsie, and am ready. Meet me at the outside of the big poorte. I shall be there with the horses;" and without a word more, he was off on his errand.

Elsie was soon out and mounted on her sheepskin saddle, and was carefully adjusting her foot into the iron, preparing for a sharp gallop, when, without looking up, she said in low, but somewhat agitated tone of voice, "Teunis, there is no need of your protection just now. The road is good, the night clear, and filly is sure-footed."

Had the young man been struck by some unseen hand, the effect could not have stupefied him more than these words, which he interpreted into something like a suspicion of his honor. He had not recovered himself yet when Elsie continued:

"And now there is the less need of your proteccion, for upon my word there is Rover come out to meet me. Oh, something bad must have happened. He has either been sent hither by my mother, or his own instinct has brought him to warn me beforehand; and without another word, in the agitation of her spirit, she struck her pony a sharp stroke with her whip. Teunis, true to his Dutch nature, while trying to open his mouth for an explanation, was left on the road beside his impatient horse, who would hardly allow the master time to mount on his back. But once there, he galloped after Elsie with the fury of passion aroused, and came up easily to the leader before the end of the first mile. Once alongside of the eager damsel, he called out in nervous earnestness:

"Elsie! Elsie! why in such haste? I want you to tell me if you"——

"Be quick, Teunis," said the hurried girl, as she held in the panting animal, "for you see that doggie there running before me is saying, as plainly as he can speak, 'the Tories have your old father by the throat, and the Indians swinging your mother's scalp by the grey hair.' Oh, Teunis, do not stop me just now."

And with that, she struck her horse once more, giving him rein, so that it was with difficulty that her follower could keep up with her, though well mounted himself, and holding a capital bridle hand for a colonist and a dull Dutchman; as all the Englishmen were accustomed to speak of every one but fox-hunters who pretended to ride.

"The Tories are not so cruel as you take them to be, Elsie; but tell me if you have any suspicion of my putting a straw in the way of hurting"—he was going to say Elsie, but he changed it to "any of the volke of Hoogenhuisen?"

"No Teunis, no, you would not with your own hand, I know; I could pledge myself for you, but there are"——

"There are more Tories than Teunis Roe, you would say, Elsie. I thank you for the confidence you place at least in me, though you almost called me by a name I am not deserving of: But Tory or not, the hand that is raised against Elsie Schulyer is aimed against a heart not far from her."

"Thank you, thank you. That is all I can say just now; I was going to say something about our not being seen together at such meetings as we have come from, but there is no time for anything but action. See how the sky is glowing all around us; and, O mine Goden, why am I away from the side of my fader and my moder?"

By this time they had rode at least three miles, and in fifteen minutes more they would see, from a small hill, what was the state of things at Hoogenhuisen; for the fear all the time in Elsie's mind was, that the mansion had been fired, and that the blaze they saw reflected overhead was not the signal, but the dwelling. This made her spare neither horse nor herself, till finding that the faithful creature required a few minutes to breathe, she slackened her pace, and began by saying:

"You see, Teunis, that I am now near home, and it will bring trouble on you, on us both, if we be seen together on such a night as this. Let us part now. Part here till this weary war be over; and then"——

"And what then?" said the eager youth. "Shall I come back then to be rejected for my cowardice at this hour, in leaving you in danger of being scalped, that I might save myself from disgrace at home? No, Elsie; I am a man, though I have not stood out for my country yet, as others have done; and I have a man's heart that would not suffer a hair of any woman's head to be hurt by those savages, could I hinder it with my hand. Least of all would I stand back and see a foul finger put on your fair skin; so help me God!"

The tears started into Elsie's eyes at this burst of passion, so gratifying to her kindly nature; and, struggling with herself, she endeavored to give such a reply as might not betray her real sentiments; though the more she repressed them, the more they overcame her; so dashing forward at a rapid pace, they stood looking from the hill toward Hoogenhuisen, when both at once exclaimed—"It is the teeken vuur! the teeken vuur!"

"God be thanked," said Elsie; "my poor parents are safe yet, and my father on his waakt toren: Now, Teunis, you have come as far as it is safe for you to be: When these times are over, I will think of this night."

She held out her hand as the parting signal. The hand trembled, and all the more that Teunis held it longer than a mere good night would require. When he found words, he said:

"Do not forbid me to come, before these dark days are

over. You know where my feelings are, where my desire is at this moment."

Elsie interrupted him by saying, "This is no time for feeling, but for convictions; and where duty calls, the Dominie says we should be: mine is now to be on the waakt toren alongside of my father. Go you where your conscience points."

"Mine is also on the watch-tower; and to-morrow, if I have heard aright, shall decide the fate of more than one."

"Teunis, do not tell me of anything you have heard below, for I cannot tell you in confidence any of our concerns: so God guide us both, and save the righteous cause."

And with these words she gave her impatient horse the reins, and off she started, as if mounted on a deer, and was out of sight in a moment, before her agitated companion had time to recover himself.

However, Teunis, instead of obeying the mandate to go back, slipped from his horse, tying him beneath a tree, a little way distant from the road, and taking a near path to Hoogenhuisen, was at the door watching the movements of the inmates with great earnestness. He had his fears that all was not right. He was well aware how much both Martin and his fearless daughter were dreaded and hated by the Tories; so he resolved to become their secret protector. How far this was the result of feeling or conviction, he did not stop to inquire. It was enough that he had heard dark hints, secret cabalings; and that he knew the Indians were on the hills, waiting the proper moment, when their friends would give the signal. The teeken vuur, or signal fire, showed that the Whigs were somewhat aware of their danger; still it was with a beating heart as Elsie felt, that he saw the dog Rover by the side of his mistress: all the superstition of his nature aided in making him afraid. Nor were his suspicions set at rest, as the sagacious animal passed him again without recognition, going straight to the side of a rock, and giving a slight but earnest whine, as if seeking for something which he had lost in the dark. At that moment an object glided like a ghost, through the barn-yard toward a corner, where it remained in the stillest quiet, more as a shadow seemed than a body moving. Had the moon been up at the time, the watcher would have expected a man to have followed, but neither sound was heard, nor form seen, though the eyes of Teunis were fixed with painful interest upon the place.

"Some one must be watching here as well as myself; I must see the end of this; for it cannot be for good that any one is here at this hour." But then he thought within himself of how Martin Schuyler would scowl were he to meet him in his yard, at this hour of the night. "I must see the end of this. Something is out of its place here, and my help may be of use to my friends; and if I prove myself to be a friend indeed, I may get farther into a corner of the old man's heart."

CHAPTER IV.

THE RESCUE.

The Challenge: "How say ye to my soul, flee as a bird to your mountain?"
The Answer: "The Lord is in heaven."—PSALMS.

In the meantime Elsie had been seeking for her parents all through the house, calling to them in a low voice as she went from room to room with a beating heart. Finding all in silence, and the very bed of her mother empty and cold, she was now certain that some enemy was abroad. Carefully gliding, lest some spy might perceive her, she reached the rear of the dwelling, where was the hiding-place, or, as it was known in Dutch, the verborgenheid, which she entered and found the anxious Angelica waiting for her.

"I am afraid," said the anxious wife and mother, "dat somewhat ill has taken place. De teeken vuur has been blazing below at Overpaugh's all the nicht. De niggers heve all crept into bed, and den Rover snuffles round de barn-yard as if he kent mair dan he spok."

Elsie did not give utterance to her own superstitious fears about the dog, but turning aside her mother's thoughts from her present fanciful notions, she inquired into the reality. Where was her father, and who could have kindled the teeken vuur on their own hill?

Angelica only answered with groans, for of that she was herself ignorant, and saw in the lighting of the signal certain destruction.

"Mammy, lie you here and I will go to daddy. Some friend is at hand to aid, and more will be here soon. No enemy would kindle the *teeken vuur*. Lie still and trust."

The brave girl was giving encouragement when she needed strength herself, for the dark night and the wild road were sufficient to alarm an old soldier or an old hunter; but it is questionable if either of them would have gone forth at mid-day with more cheerfulness than she went out under the stars, since duty to her father demanded her presence. Now she thought of how she had dismissed Tennis, whose company would have been a pleasure and a protection. It was too late to regret, so she set about the necessary apparel for such a journey as she must take. While engaged in this, her ear caught sounds of retreating footsteps in the rear of the house, and on moving to that part she felt something fall at her feet. Groping in the dark, her hand touched a paper, which she knew must have been put there by some one out of the family, so carrying it to the most secluded corner of the house she lighted a candle and read:

Fear whispers:

"O night and shade,
How are ye joined with hell in triple knot,
Against the unarmed weakness of one virgin
Alone and helpless."

Courage calls:

"Virtue may be assailed,
But not enthralled:
Surprised, but never hurt."

"Strange man! Are you around, restless spirit? How I wish that I either knew more or less about you than I do. I tremble for myself when near you, and yet you fascinate me with that eye at times; but, oh! it burns my cheek to meet it. Surely those eyes must be the furnaces of some smoldering fire on the brain. They have glowed so for a month past that they seemed more like the air-holes in a coal-pit, when the wind blows fierce at night, than the eyes of a human being. What terrible passion has made him now like a wild beast, roaming all night and watching all day. He could tell me something of what is going on, but I dare not seek him, but guess. There is danger, but I may go on my errand. Why not speak it out?"

Crawling through a secret passage she reached the open ground, where, cautiously looking round, she gave out a sound like *chick-a-dee, chick-a-dee*, when Rover came to her side in a fondling manner, which she returned gently. He said, as plainly as he could: "I am at your service;" while she, putting down her hands to his head, seized his jaws between her fingers, pressing them so that, if possible, they came more closely together. The dumb animal seemed to understand that he must be silent as well as speechless, for all through that night not a sound escaped from him.

Elsic, swift as a deer, and now as fearless, urged her way under the star-light. Rover ahead, trotting with his tail up proudly, coming back now and then to receive the encouragement which his mistress never failed to bestow upon him, passing her kind hand along his back; nor was it long before she reached the place of appointment on the South Mountain. On the same large, slanting rock, where her father had sat an hour before waiting for her, she leaned to rest herself. Rover had left her at this point, and though she called the secret chick-a-dee, she heard only the echo of her own voice, but not the reply of her father. She expected that Rover would in this way bring them together. Growing impatient, she rose and took another position, where she saw for the first time the fires which blazed red and clear. In her present high excitement all her motions, mental as well as of body, were rapid, so that it did not occupy her long in comprehending the whole, the moment she noticed the peculiar wigwams, and the different figures moving in the light. The bower in the centre was as yet a mystery which her keen spirit was not long in penetrating. She had come up close to the very place where her father was watching so intently, when that quarrel we have already recorded was commencing between the chief Indian and the Englishman; and seeing a figure standing between her and the light, she was not a moment in deciding it to be the one she was seeking. Taking hold of his arm, she whispered in his ear:

"Ben't vreest niet"—Be not afraid;—for Martin trembled more than he had done at any previous part of the night; but soon recovering himself, he felt doubly strong, and was able, with his daughter by his side, to withstand any danger.

"Elshie, see you that poor crying lamishie," were his first words, "in the hands, in the teeth of these wolven. A Tory's dochter, maybe, but we must save her, with God's help."

"Patience, daddy, we must wait the right time." Here the heroic girl sighed and wished now for the strong hand of Teunis.

The quarrel between Clifford and Kiskataam was becoming every moment fiercer and fiercer; exciting not only the captive in the wigwam, but also Martin and his daughter, who, in their eagerness, were unconsciously drawing nearer to the scene of action, till they stood behind the tree that grew at the very rear of the frail wigwam. They could have touched the captive; but their attention was absorbed in the conflict. Suddenly the Indian threw his tomahawk, aimed at the head of the lady, but which struck into the pine trunk behind her. Clifford, seizing him by the throat, gave Elsie time to say in Martin's ear:

"I will take the lady to the North Mountain. Stay here about till her enemies be turned the other way by you and Rover;" and with that counsel, she darted into the bower of bushes, and whispering, "Be not afraid, let us escape," and putting her arm through that of the prisoner, they were out in the darkness before the two combatants had risen to their feet. Indeed, so intent were they on revenge, that every other passion was swallowed up; and even the object which had cost them both such sleepless vigilance, was for the time forgotten. Rolling on the ground like fierce buffalo and panther, their eyes sent out flashes of deadly hate. Now it was the lithe muscle and the quick movements of the red man, that was gaining the ascendency; then it was the firm grip and main strength of his enemy. The natural cunning of the savage enabled him to wriggle out of the hold which kept him down; but he was no sooner up than Clifford's knowledge of the wrestler's art, placed him on his back.

"Yield! you false villain," were the first words of the enraged Englishman. He would have said traitor—but the word, as it had been uttered that night, burned on his brain. "Yield! and leave this region, or, by Heaven, I will toss you over the precipice to the wolves;" and he shook his victim with a force that showed his power. And it might have ended as he threatened, had not the artful Shandaagan yelled the whoop of his tribe; which, taking Clifford by surprise, caused him to raise his head, when he discovered that his bird was either fallen or flown. The war-whoop rang again from both Indians, in the ears of the flying girls, causing the blood of the late captive to curdle in her veins.

Clifford, when he saw that the lady was not standing where he had seen her a few moments before, feared that the tomahawk of the savage had done its work, and he ran in to lift her up; but not finding her, he rushed about like a madman, foaming out all kinds of avowals. His oaths of fidelity froze upon his tongue, and in a measure brought him to his senses, when he found that the wily Indian was also out of sight, and might come upon the lost treasure by himself. In the present state of affairs between them, no chance was left for him to have a share of the booty, and this maddened him all the more; but the sly Kiskataam, now sure of his revenge, and cooler in blood, had already made up his mind and was moving in a track of his own, which would have baffled the intellect of a whole regiment of Englishmen, were they on the hills pursuing him. Noiselessly he crawled among the tangled brushwood, intending to take a wide circuit, when this innocent Fawn must be entrapped. Her fear in the dark, her ignorance of these regions, and her inexperience of all savage life, rendered her escape, as he thought, impossible. He was transported in spirit—first, in being revenged on Clifford; and next, in having the lady to himself.

"She shall grind the Indian's corn. I will build her a wigwam by the Big Horn, on the island of the crooked Chemung. The squaws of the Great King will wonder after the Fawn;" and he smiled in bitter hate. "Big soldier shall whimper like a woman."

Here quietly the cunning savage lay down with his ear to the ground, as he had often done on the war path. As for Clifford, who had by this time lost all track of his company whatever, he was running through the woods alone, like one possessed of a devil. Shouting loudly, he called the name of the lady or of the Indians, as they came to his lips.

"A thousand pounds for the capture! I will swear to you, Miss Margaret. I pledge my word as a man of honor; by my sword as a soldier: only come back and you will be taken to New York or"—— Here again he would shout in terror of himself. The meanest human being he ever saw would have been hailed by the proud spirited man with a welcome, in preference to wild nature, in all her magnificence. But he was there alone, and had neither God nor mankind to commune with him.

As yet the two fugitives were out of the net of the fowler. Elsie knew the mountain paths as well as her pursuers, and had a place in her mind to which she was guiding her helpless charge. At the beginning, Margaret—the late captive—ran with a speed that surprised Elsie; but it soon was seen to be impossible for her to proceed far without help; and that of more aid than one of her sex could afford her. They both sat down on a fallen tree, unable to articulate through their exertion, when the sound of their pursuer's voice rose again on their ear and seemed to be coming toward them; here Elsie took hold of the lady's arm, and found, to her terror, that she had fainted and was falling on the ground. Now was the time for the fearless heart to rise above all enemies. Taking the light creature in her arms, she lifted her up, and was carrying her onward, when she heard the rustling of the branches behind her. Standing still as the stump she leaned on, hoping that the enemy might miss her and pass on, what was her astonishment when the words of the Dominie's last Sunday's text were pronounced quietly and softly, "Ik zal hesen gaen in de micht of de Lord"—I will go in the strength of the Lord.

"Oh, Teunis Roe!" were the words of the startled Elsie as she fell against his manly breast. "You never were more welcome," she whispered, drawing herself back abruptly.

Tennis had found his way into the house of Martin, and by calling out and knocking around, succeeded in bringing Angelica to him. In him she always had confidence, so that it was not difficult to find out the destination of Elsie. He ran with an eagerness which proved him to be in earnest. Yet he failed to reach the rendezvous in time to aid in the escape, though from a short distance he saw father and daughter counselling behind the tree. Afraid to meet the old Whig, he stood back viewing the struggle on the rock, and the rescue of the lady, by Elsie. He then lost all track of them, and but for the fainting of the lady could not have found them at all.

Between these two guardians the late captive was carried to a cave, known to the hunters of the mountains, where a soft bed was spread for her, of the leaves which lay around thick and dry, yielding a not unpleasant fragrance to the wearied sleeper, who lay as yet unconcious of the safety of her retreat. From her starting and muttering, it was evident that her dreams were of being pursued and of falling into the hands of her persecutors.

CHAPTER V.

DOUBTING CASTLE—GIANT DESPAIR.

"'Then,' said Mr. Great Heart to Mr. Valiant for Truth, 'thou hast worthily behaved thyself; let me see thy sword:

"'Ha! it is a right good Jerusalem blade. It is; let me have one of these blades, with a hand to wield it, and skill to use it, and I could venture upon an angel of the high places with it.'"

OLD BUNYAN.

SHANDAAGAN had heard Elsie giving the sound of the chick-a-dee, and immediately guessed the cause. The stern old Boerman of Hoogenhuisen was more dreaded than any one else on the mountain-side; and this Indian had been all the previous day skulking around the place as a spy; but knowing the vigilant character of the daughter of the settler, he readily concluded she was on the hills. When the *chick-a-dee* was heard he gave an involuntary ugh! for the mystery of Rover's leaving him in the early part of the night, was solved to his dull mind. The Boerman was on the hills himself, and that accounted for the restlessness of the animal, and his haste to get away. As we have hinted, he was no stranger about the farm-house. From his boyhood he had been accustomed to stop there on his way to and from the east, passing through Stony Clove, on the road to his native lodge. Elsie had not only become an acquaintance, but also an object of interest. She was of a nature to deal kindly with all, but was sure to show her superior nature toward intruders; so that when the deceit of the Indians discovered itself in anything, it met a rebuff, unpleasant to a malicious nature like Shandaagan's. It was, therefore, as much to gratify himself as to serve Kiskataam, that he entered so heartily into this enterprise. Revenge for some supposed insult put upon him by Martin, years ago, and a secret human liking that he had for the company of Martin's daughter—of whom he was afraid, but never could pass by—fascinated him whenever she choose to keep him on his way. It was not love, it was not hate: it was infatuation, or fascination, that brought him wherever she was; though latterly she would have seen one of the devil's imps sooner, of her own choice, than his black shadow.

And if we can suppose one of these same imps as full of

malice as they are said to be, with three objects near him, and he uncertain as to which he should venture upon first, we can have some idea of this low Indian, with fear of his chief, malice toward Martin, and his undefinable liking for Elsie. The first of the three, at any time presented to his senses, would have had the victory. In this state he was wandering through the brush, sometimes creeping like the snake; and then, as he thought upon his chances of success, he lifted his head high enough to look around. He was well pleased to see the quarrel begin between the two leaders. It was to him a matter of delight; so much so, that he inwardly hoped both would be killed, and then he would make his own bargain with the captive. Watching the progress of the combat so intently, he forgot all other things, nor was he aroused from his intentness till he heard the fearful alarm of the two combatants, now separated so strangely. He soon understood the cause. The same sound had raised up Martin to his full height, within a few rods before him, and now revenge gained the mastery; for, coming softly behind the Dutchman, who was intently watching the movements of the two captains, lest they should get upon the track of Elsie and her charge, he had lifted Peg to her proper position, when he was seized by the strong arms of Shandaagan, and bound in an instant above the elbows, and thrown upon his back, with the muzzle of his piece pointing to his ear.

The astonished and grieved man gave a slight groan. A thousand daggers passed into his body would have been less felt than were the agonies of his spirit. His country, Elsie, Angelica, and the poor captive Fawn, all came up before him ere his own sad captivity was thought of. But he was not devoid of that power of endurance which is found in noble natures, allied to true courage, and in his own way he expressed it, "Uw wille geschiede"—thy will be done.

"The Hedgehog is smooth and tied," was the significant sneer of the Indian, as he gave a quiet chuckle in his throat, which indicated more pleasure than the loudest shout of triumph from a white man; "the Hedgehog must creep fast."

This hint was accompanied by a touch of the muzzle of old Peg, which Martin knew well was irresistible, no matter in whose hands she was held. Her word was law.

"Where do you mean me to go, you cowardly redskin? Have I not fed you? has not Anshela clothed you? and has not Elsie picked the thorns out of your feet, when you could not move? and now you bid me walk after you have tied my arms with these deer-skin strings. Let me go about my own business, and be off with you to your miserable hut among the ice-beds."

The red man never gave a sign to all this outburst, which intimated the least feeling, except at the recollection of Elsie's taking the thorns from his feet. He moved from leaning on the one foot to the other, as if pain or pleasure was seeking the topmost scale; all his reply was, "The Hedgehog must wait till Brandt comes."

This was the same as if the sentence of death had been pronounced upon him; for the name of that great Mohawk had spread terror through the whole western country, from the Hudson to Fort Niagara. The Dutchman groaned in his spirit, and was troubled; but after a moment's prayer he recovered himself, and whispered, "Ik ben bereid niet allen gebonden te worden maar ook te sterven"—I am ready not only to be bound but also to die. His chief sorrow was that he should be absent from his post, at this time when he knew that so many were depending upon his vigilance in lighting the teeken vuur—the watch-fire above his own dwelling; but to his great relief, as he chanced to pass along to his appointed prison, he cast his eye down toward his home, and saw that all was blazing; he would have clapped his hands in rapture at the sight, but was quickly reminded of his helpless condition by his not being able to bring them together. He satisfied himself by quietly repeating in Dutch, "Ik word nu tot een plengoffered geofferred"—I am now ready to be offered.

Martin was a pious man, and knew his Bible better than any other book; quoting its sayings, always with much point, when either sunk in distress or rapt in enthusiasm. He felt stronger through seeing the watch-fire blazing, and when he reached the stream, he bent down for a drink, for which he seemed so grateful, that the Indian thought he must have read some sign in the flame, which white men can only understand. Martin was repeating to himself what gave him courage even now, "Zyn neet Abana, en Pherphar, de revieren van Damascus, betters dan alle waterin Israels."

It was evident to Martin that by the time they had gone a short mile to the westward, that Shandaagan was wavering in his purpose, and that some other object was beginning to arrest his attention. Hoping, therefore, to turn this vacillation to his own account, he tried to lead the wily savage into conversation, so that if possible he might obtain a cue to his intentions.

"The Wildcat has been a long journey with the Panther since the sun rose. Wildcat must be tired and weary afoot, going through briers and thorns. The Wildcat will soon rest and wait for the great Mohawk."

These different objects were presented purposely to confuse the mind of the Indian, for Martin understood his uncertain character, and hoped to have his mind diverted from himself. But revenge, for the present, was the ruling passion, and he had his victim in his own hands. At the same time he felt that he had made a great sacrifice in losing sight of Elsie and the captive, and resolved to secure the father, trusting to his hunter's skill to find out the daughter before morning, through the help of Rover, who was now trotting on before them, to the great mortification of the prisoner, who seemed to read the thoughts of his captor.

"The Hedgehog must lie down there till the second moon rises;" said the dogged Indian, as he pointed down to the foot of the ravine, where Martin knew full well were the highest falls on the mountain, over which he inwardly suspected it was the Indian's intention to cast him, where he would be dashed in pieces. Roused by fear and indignation, he determined to resist, and make at least one effort for his life. He was hesitating, as he felt the muzzle of his own gun pressed against his back, when turning suddenly, he seized Peg, and would have wrenched her out of his captor's hands, but for the bindings on his arms. The struggle was unequal, and he had to yield. His last chance was past. The wily and cruel savage could not be caught again off his guard. The prisoner still hoping, descended into the gorge, stepping on to the rock over which the stream was pouring, and there he felt it was but a step between him and death. Shandaagan made his captive sit down on the rock, under a young sapling that he had been surveying with his eye. He pointed the gun to the breast of the Dutchman, in a threatening manner not to be misunderstood. Then bending the birch back from the edge of the fall, he placed a stone upon it, just sufficient to keep it down. On the trunk of the tree he tied tough thongs, cut from a green skin, which he, without warning, attached to the body of Martin. A few moments completed his work.

"Shoot me, you false geveinsde"—hypocrite—was Martin's

fierce expression when the manner in which he was bound was plain to him.

The Indian had no such intention; but putting parched corn within the reach of his victim to preserve him alive till some future time, he proceeded to smoke the fragrant weed of Virginia, sitting near enough to his prisoner that he might inhale its influence, and thus tormenting him as much as possible.

"Shandaagan," said Martin, in a tone of petition, and yet of superiority, "unbind these strings, and tell me what you want. Is it Milldoleors? You can have them. Come to Hoogenhuisen when the sun rises."

The revengeful savage shook his head; he had made other calculations. He loved a sweeter morsel. Lighting his pipe again, he put it to the mouth of Martin, who instinctively began to puff away as if the old clock stood ticking at his elbow in the corner.

"The Wildcat will return;" was the brief reply of the Indian, as he walked away, not deigning to look once behind him. His thoughts had gone back to Martin's daughter, and with Rover's help, he was sure of finding her; and with her, the English lady. By these means he would secure both the favor of Kiskataam and the reward of Clifford. He could make a bargain with all for himself; more especially as the onslaught of Brandt would furnish him with the means of escape, should he become entangled.

We must leave Martin to his solitary reflection, as the Indian pursued his way. He had put in one humbling petition as his captor moved off: "Shandaagan will not hurt the squaws at Hoogenhuisen?" He looked up for an answer, but the bronze face of the redskin was imperturbably fixed.

"Let the Hedgehog sleep," was all he heard. The bitterest of the parting moment was to have Rover, when the Indian drew him away, whine round him, and even lick his lips. But a kick from the red man made him follow, leaving the disconsolate master without a single earthly friend within call. Death by falling over the precipice was certain, the instant that the thongs were cut away; and they must be cut asunder to let him go free. He had nothing before him now but to wait for day, and hope for relief.

The Indian in the meantime pursued his return to the pine orchard, where the capturing party would be waiting for his report. They knew that he had gone on the pursuit, and he must say something. He determined to affect ignorance of what he really knew concerning Elsie. He found Clifford alone; so walking right to the camp, he cast a curious glance into the bower as he passed, and just as he thought himself discovered by Clifford, his eyes dilated sufficiently to express surprise at the place being vacant. The Englishman was standing out on the verge of the rock, as near to the edge as it was possible for him to stand, as if he watched the approach of something that was at hand. He gave a quick start as Shandaagan came up to him, saying:

"They call you Wildcat; your steps are as soft and sly as that animal's. Where have you been hunting all night? Have you seen aught of our Fawn?"—he was going to say, but he checked himself, and said: "Our friends from above? Anything of Brandt?"

"The Dutchmen have kindled their fire on the hills;" and pointing with his finger to the river, he said, "their fiery tongues are crying back to the mountains."

"Oh, you mean to say that the whole country is alarmed; well, I suppose that must be the case, from all the signs of the times. Have you met any of our scouts? or have you seen the"—

And with that, he pointed with his finger to the empty bower.

Shandaagan shook his head, and said softly—for he wished to keep in favor with Clifford, and yet elude his questions—"Wildcat cannot catch Fawn."

"No, but Wildcat could hunt for Fawn, and then," holding out a purse through which the coin glittered, he said coaxingly, "that shall be the reward for bringing her in today or to-morrow."

This was just what the Indian was seeking—the commission of search; and if Kiskataam would join the Englishman in the wish, he would begin immediately. He was listening with eager ear for that wily chief, whom he knew could not be far off; when, all at once, he appeared, as if he had risen out of the ground. He had heard the sinister tones of Clifford, and soon saw Wildcat, and came to prevent a conspiracy which he suspected already. He was sure that the Englishman could never find out his captives without help; and now the only help he could find was on hand; his best way of preventing a combination against himself, was to enter into the fellowship, and be one of the leaders. He could act for himself none the less. He hoped to control the movements and skill of his brother Indian, and thus leave the Englishman at fault. So, assuming a bland look, he came forward as if nothing had happened to disturb the equanimity of the night; sat down at the fire and prepared his pipe, pointing at the same time to the slain deer. Shandaagan understood the movement, and proceeded to cut off choice collops for their breakfast, which he put with care upon the red coals, now in a fine condition for broiling that tender meat. In half an hour all the three were in the best possible temper of mind. Clifford had a flask of brandy, which had the usual effect of exhilarating the spirits, and drowning all care.

CHAPTER VI.

THE EYELIDS OF THE MORNING.

"Within a savage cave beneath the mount,
Closed in the shades, the warriors passed the night
But when the sun from Heaven's eternal fount,
Thro' the brown forest shed his golden light,
'Up, up!' at once they cried; and either knight
With rival zeal along the track of frost,
Began the ascent; when on their startled sight,
Whence they knew not, in various colors glowed
Their onward path, a fierce and frightful serpent crossed."
TASSO.

DAY had dawned upon the east, before the fugitive lady and her deliverer had risen from their couch. Teunis had undertaken to watch while they slept, and faithfully did he fulfill his trust; and though urged by Elsie, in softer tones than she would have given forth at another time, he remained alert and vigilant still, by their side. They all three stood behind a jutting crag on a higher shoulder of the Kaatsbergs, than that flat rock on which the lady Margaret had been rescued on the previous night. She had already learned that they were her friends. Indeed, her confidence in them was entire on the instant they had found a resting-place, free from alarm. They had done all that any human beings could have done to quiet her agitation and induce her to fall asleep. She called them her guardian angels, sent in answer to her mother's prayers; and, though she started in her dreams several times, still, as Teunis reported, she seemed to sleep soundly for two hours, when she opened her eyes in surprise, but not in alarm.

"Delightful vision I have had!" were her first words. "I was on board the ship once more, and my mother rocked me in my little hammock, singing the old lullaby. 'Hush, my dear, lie still and slumber.' What do you think, Elsie, for so you say I must call you, is that such a dream as forebodes good?"

"Yes, my lady, all dreams in which a good Providence is seen are of the right kind. Our Dominie tells us in his preaching, that the angels are 'allen gedienstige geesten, die tot dienst uitgezonden worden om dergenen wil, die de zaligheid beërnen zullen.' But I forget myself; you do not understand our tongue—it means that the angels are servants to the pure hearted, and no doubt but our Heavenly Father has sent these holy spirits to your pillow, my dear lady, this night."

"Call me Margaret if you will," said the pleased and bright blue-eyed damsel, already recovering from the effects of her horrid captivity. "Tell me, if you please, what your parish priest says about those good things, for he must be a good man, since you are so kind."

"Not our priest, Miss Margaret, but our Dominie—our minister; it is true he is one of the good men, whom we love to hear speak, and you would love him too, were he here just now, looking out on that rising light. See where the dawn is just peering out above those hills far out yonder. It is but a narrow border, yet watch, and see how it will spread.

"Yes, I cannot help looking, and it reminds me of that beautiful Psalm that says, 'I will watch for thee, as they who watch for the eyelids of the morning;' for see how like that is to the opening lids of a child, when it looks up for its mother. But I wish I had not thought of the word *mother* just now; as I look upon that scene, it seems as if it is selfishness not to forget everything else."

"This is no place for despair, fair lady," said Teunis, who hesitatingly took part in the conversation. "There are hundreds of good friends below who will risk their lives for you. Rest must be taken here to-day, and I will go down to prepare the means of deliverance."

"Thanks, oh, a thousand thanks to you, and a rich reward awaits you. My father will give up all he is worth for his daughter. We are a happy family, when together. But oh, how miserable that cabin is at this moment."

"Look up, my lady," said Teunis, for he was becoming bolder, as he saw the sad state in which the poor exile was.

"Look up; see, there is hope for you. The dawn gets brighter; now wait and watch till the sun springs out of his bed."

"Glorious! glorious king of day rejoicing in the east! never did I see thee before. No marvel, though the heathen fell prone at sight of thee. I shall not think of myself here amidst such majesty. Not a cloud up there except these two in the very zenith. Sparkling golden studs growing pale; and that azure! was ever aught so pure over this world before!"

Teunis, who felt a personal pride in the scene, and who considered himself bound in honor to uphold its reputation over all the world beside, stood ready to show off all the great points of sublimity; and Elsie, equally interested, well knew the features of beauty, so that between the two, the English maiden was likely to be well instructed in mountain panoramics.

"See the sun, how he rises like a great captain, surmounted by a helmet of gold," said the young man. "Don't wink lest you lose a single ray."

"O God!" said the enraptured girl, "what must Thou be thyself, since thy servant is so bright and beautiful?"

Elsie was muttering to herself a Psalm in the Holland tongue—Gy kept voor maels de ae'rade gegrondet, ende dé "keenelen zen tiwerk uwer handen."

"What is that you sing?" said the lady, "tell it to me in English; it must be good for it makes your face shine."

"I am saying what you know to be true, perhaps, at this hour more than you ever thought before. 'Of old thou hast laid the foundation of the earth, and the heavens are the work of thy hands.' But, Miss Margaret, you must look below, as well as upward, if you would see all the sublimity of this scene."

And with that the stranger looked down, exclaiming in amazement, "The ocean, the sea, the sea!" An infinite mass of vapor lay so thick upon the valley that it seemed more like the rolling waves than a cloud of mist. "And is it possible that we are not on the seashore. Hark! I think I hear the surge as it breaks against the rocks? But no, we are on the mountain, as I know full well from the journey of yesterday. Tell me if it be possible that people do live and breathe down there in that awful gulf."

"Yes," was Elsie's reply; "thousands are at this hour asleep. No marvel they should have heavy dreams, compared with those we have had up here in this blue ether. See how high the sun has bounded already on his journey; not a star to be seen now. Yes, there is one, the *blinkende morgenster.*"

"You mean the morning star. May I take that as the sign of deliverance? I would not pray to that orb, but to Him who said, 'I am the bright and morning star.' Be thou that so to me, O Saviour of men;" and the poor, feeble girl was again turning to thoughts of herself, when Teunis called out to see how the whole earth was in motion below.

Grand and terrible was the scene; even these two natives, who had frequently looked on the like before, held their breath when the huge masses divided and turned, as icebergs are seen to sink and rise when some change takes place in their weight. Then, as if relieved from their anchorage, they made a sudden plunge, which sent the waves far out to the verge of the expanse. It would have been some relief had there been the least noise, but the silence to the ear when there was such agitation to the sight, reminded one of what we have read of the gulf which divides time from eternity—neither life nor death.

"I have read somewhere of the North Seas," said the most intelligent of the spectators, "of the hummocks of snow and ice which move through these death-like seas, and where the sky is like living crystal. See that mountain there, rising up as if giants were beneath it lifting it. Have you not read, young man, of the gods piling mountains?"

"I know nothing of such books," said Teunis. "There is one passage that exactly expresses my mind, where it describes the clouds as the dust of the Almighty's feet."

"You are right," said Margaret; "no book can furnish us with words fit to express our ideas of nature equal to the one you quote from, and yet I have read in other pages descriptions which at this moment come up to the pictures passing before us. See there, that moving tower, pursuing the one still vaster that swells upward and onward. I can imagine the great warriors of antiquity on it, roused up in their ancient armor, bent upon a great expedition, obeying the voice of the leader. But the trumpets are silent."

"The sun is their only leader at this moment," said Teunis. "He is drawing them after him. Till he appeared all was quiet, but you have observed that from the instant he showed his face there has been a great and general commotion.

"He is like a strong man," said Elsie, "going forth to run

his race;" for she was anxious to give as much moral influence to the conversation as might strengthen her new friend for her day's work; and so pointing with her hand to one of the figures which appeared on the clouds below, she asked of her companions if that did not "seem like what they had conceived of the angel who would put his foot upon the sea and upon the land, lifting his hand to heaven?"

"Yes, and we standing up high, as we do now, seeing the rising dead. These misty shapes make me feel awful, even at this moment. Shall we be able," said Margaret, "to see the dwellings in the valley when the mist is gone? I almost think these must be their shadows, grown huge, that are lifted up?"

These observations were disjointed and interjectional, followed by pauses which showed that the spectators were full of thoughts that partook more of the spiritual than of the earthly. It was reverie uttered at intervals; musings which elevated the soul into that fellowship with spiritual existences, afterward to be remembered with calm delight. The sight recalled to the more highly educated of the three some of those images which till then had lain sleeping in her memory, and half whispering, she repeated to herself those fine lines of the greatest of uninspired sacred poets:

"There is a cave within the mount of God,
Fast by the throne, where light and darkness
In perpetual rounds lodge and dislodge
By turns, which make through heaven
Grateful vicissitude like day and night;
Light issues forth, and at the other door
Obsequious darkness enters; but now goes
Forth the morn' arrayed in gold empyreal."

"There! there! is the earth at last!" shouted out the enraptured Teunis. "I have never seen it as we see it now, but I think on the sailor crying from the mast-head, land! land!"

"I never see it," said Elsie, "but I think on the morning stars, shouting for joy when the dry land appeared at creation. Is it not beautiful, Miss Margaret?"

"It is; but what is that we see, like a white line, passing through the whole, as far as we can look, north and south?"

"Let the lady find out herself without our help," said Teunis; "watch and you will see;" and the young Dutchman, full of honest feeling, looked from the face of the eager spectator to the object she gazed upon, and back again.

"The river! the river!" said the enraptured gazer. "The famous Hudson, where the Indian canoes once swam as lightly as the swan, till the enterprising Hendrick Hudson came and sailed up as far as Albany. He says he 'saw very high mountains on the west of him, and very old men on the banks.' How high we must be, for it seems but a narrow stream. Alas! I ought to know it well, after what I have endured near it since I left the ship. The ship! yes, oh, the ship must be seen from this height. I think I see it lying close by the shore, there waiting for me. Look, dear Elsie, and tell me if that be not the broad pennon of St. George that we see yonder."

"I am afraid not," said the mountain girl. "There are too many clouds floating there yet to allow us to see any vessel from this distance. See these shadows how they pass and repass all along the river, so silently, and, I was going to say, so solemnly. They always picture to my mind the valley of death, where they say spirits are moving before the eyes of the dying."

"It is, indeed," said Margaret, "a scene that might well impress awe upon the superstitious. A Greek could imagine that river to be the dark Styx, and these the ghosts of heroes crossing in Charon's boat. See how large everything seems, and how far they move from us whenever a larger cloud comes over. I wish that veil would clear away. I long to look down into the eyes of the sleepers."

"Lady Margaret," interrupted Teunis, "it is time for me to leave. There is soon to be bloody work below; and I must be there to act my part. You will be as well taken care of as if I were present."

This was said as a word of encouragement; for the speaker perceived that fear was overcoming the unhappy girl, and that his presence was becoming necessary to her comfort, as she had not yet learned to confide in one of her own sex. "The troubles below," continued he, "will divert the attention of your pursuer from you. After a few days, we will find means of taking you to your friends. In the meantime, Elsie, keep away from the *kekutes;* for these wily redskins can tell a woman from an owl in the dark; and give them but a glimpse of your bright hair, dangling in the sunshine, and a bullet shall be sent to you that will bring you down. Then, what shall I say to Martin Schuyler?"

"Oh, you can say that the Tories have run away with Elsie," was the sly answer of the Boerman's daughter. "Go, as we planned it alr[illegible]y, and be sure and bring some olecakes and cheese, and a bottle of milk; and—a word more," after he had gone a few steps, she running down the hill till she came close up to him, "Go in and comfort mammy, as you pass. Tell her good news; the best you can frame. And" ——

"And what, dearest Elsie? One word more, and let that be HOPE. You know how some words put life into the feet of the runner: and the Dominie says, 'want wij zijn in hope zalig geworden.'"

"Yes, Teunis, 'we are saved by hope,' but that means for another life. We have something else to think of than the present world, in these sad times; but if"— And the damsel paused, and sighed, and then looking up, said, "Go, Teunis, and my prayers shall go with you."

"And your word, Elsie, is hope?"

"Hope, then," said the modest maiden, as she returned to her charge; feeling all the burden of her responsibility, now that she was left alone with the feeble thing that she had dared to rescue, as a bird out of the hand of the fowler.

Both of the young women felt lonely; and something like terror crept over them as they were watching the movements of their departing companion, which they could not long discern, as it was not for the safety of either party that he should let himself be seen from above. So, Elsie, who was the strongest in mind and in body, as well as larger in experience, turned the attention of her ward, as soon as possible, to other objects than herself. She had already got the key to her natural character—a wrapt enthusiasm for nature—and she wisely used that for her own benefit.

"Here we are, then, upon the high hills, and how small we look to ourselves when we turn our thoughts upon our frail forms. Do they have as high mountains in your country, Miss Margaret?"

"No, Elsie, we have not any lofty mountains," said her sorrowful companion, who was making an effort to overcome her feelings, as she guessed the kind design of her comforter. "The mountains of England are not so high as these, but I have seen the Alps, which are much higher than these Kaatsbergs; and I am reminded by the scene of this morning, of similar grandeur; and my thoughts run to friends who were there with me, and I am afraid that I shall make but a poor follower of yours to-day. I have seen the day when I could have wished myself an eagle, that I might perch on that highest point; but now, I could cra[illegible] on the lowest part of the ground. Trouble humbles the proud heart, dearest Elsie."

"Oh yes, lady. So I have heard our good Dominie say, and he has been on those high mountains you speak of in his youth. And sometimes in these days of trouble, he will break out in great raptures, and sing in the words of the good book, so that we all feel quite strong, and ready for any trial. I wish you could but understand Dutch."

"Say it to me, if you please; though I do not understand it, your voice will direct my mind away from myself to the Good Being, who only can deliver me now."

"That is true, and the words are comforting, and always cheer me, as you may be sustained if you could but understand them; but I will try and give you their meaning: O myne duve synde in de kloven der steenrotsen, in't verborgen, eener steiler plaetse toond my uwe stemme hooren want uwe stemme is zoet en uwe gadaente is lieffelyk. Now, I wish I could give you the English of that; but it is about a dove in the cloves of the mountains, in the secret places of the stairs; and then it says" ——

"Oh, I can tell you the other part: 'Let me see thy face, let me hear thy voice; for sweet is thy voice, and thy countenance is comely.'"

"There now; I have often heard these beautiful words," said the stranger, "but never till now have I seen their beauty, and their promise of deliverance to myself. Here I am, a weak dove on these high hills, but I cannot fly. Those who love me are far from me. O! God, let me see thy face in these secret places. Let these mountains whereon thy feet shall come, be as the stairs of thy palace, that I may be delivered. Surely, dear Elsie, these words were sent to your lips by the Good Spirit, for me. Let me hear more of them."

"We have spoken enough of these fine words, young lady, it is time for us to do something to provide against coming danger." And with that, the two young women, like sisters, moved on, where the strongest led the weakest by the hand, as a mother leads a child. So helpless was the late captive, and so easily would she have been again ensnared, but for the prudence and love of her guardian.

CHAPTER VII.

REVENGE IS SWEET.

A monster, huge and hideous, void of sight."—COWLEY.

THIS was a busy day for the young Dutchman. Like all his race, he was slow to move, but once under way, he was like one of those arks to be seen on the Scheldt, which nothing can stop in the current. Now being wakened up, his duty was becoming more evident. The country stood out in its size and importance more than ever; and, like an arch into which they were just pressing the keystone, he heard a cheerful call of Elsie, saying, the more you put on me, the more can be borne. He grew stronger, and more decided at every step; for his mind and conscience were alike in action.

"I owe a debt of gratitude to my father;" there are other persons in the world he would have said, but he remembered the uncertainty of his condition at the moment, and he hesitated to say the words "Elsie and country."

"Country," thought he, "what have I done to merit a country; standing like a great goose, as I have been, first on one foot, then on another, as I felt it hot or cold, or was tired. I must stand on my two feet if I deserve the name of a man; and the love of Elsie. She is not the girl to favor a goose:" and the slow intellect of the meditator smiled at his own wit. Like all honest men, he was trying to satisfy his conscience first, and then he hoped to pursue his own interest the more successfully. That was after all paramount. His conscience was on the side of the country, and it was all the easier for him to work in his new harness, since his heart was there, because Elsie was also there; and it only required a small force in addition, to place himself wholly there. At the present moment he must work prudently; but he would do his duty, and not flinch to-day.

"I ought first to go to Hoogenhuisen and see how Anshela gets on, for I am afraid all is not right there in the absence of both Martin and Elsie; but then I have been so long from home, they will suspect me in these suspicious days unless I show my face; and daddy will miss Grey more than myself, for it is past the time of his feeding him: and now, when I think of it, the poor animal has stood all night tied to that tree. There he is whinnying just now that he hears my step."

By this time he had reached the foot of the hill, and was astride of his good nag, that was not unwilling to receive his burden. Perhaps had the animal shown the least inclination to go up to Hoogenhuisen, where he had been so often, and where he had been fed with many a good mess of oats, the man would not have checked the rein; but he trotted freely down the way to his own stable, the master saying to himself, "well, go; I shall find out the state of things below, and be all the better prepared to elude these redskins, whether led by Brandt or Kiskataam; for Brandt, after all, is at the bottom of this game, though the mountain chief seems to be playing the main part up here just now. The lady, in some mysterious way, has been taken by the Tories, for some Tory purpose. Why she should be of their own blood is more than my dull head can see through. Elsie says she can understand the reason, but I cannot; and no matter. It is onr duty to deliver her; be she of the Whig or of the Tory race, I will fight on her side."

With such reflections in his mind, new to himself, and therefore all the more oppressive to his breast, he came within sight of his home, that lay, like most of the houses of the early settlers from Holland, in a hollow between two of the low hills that lie at the foot of the Kaatsbergs. The mountain stream ran through the meadow before the wealthy Boerman's door, surrounded as that was with trees of the forest, which had never been cleared away; or had come up a second growth since his grandfather took up his abode there. It was a rich farm, and had been one of those spots on which the aborigines had raised their "maize, their beans, and their pompkins." Some of the ancient apple and plum trees, which came from no one can tell where, were now yielding their fruit to the hands of another race.

Teunis was met at the foot of the hill, as he was passing through a bunch of pines, by an old negro wench, whom they all called mammy, who stood up in the road and stopped him, by holding up her finger in a warning attitude; which he, in his present state of mind, was unable to despise; though he did his best, by trying to pass her with a "Good morning, mammy; what brings you here so far from the pigs and the chickens, so early in the day."

"Mammy's chic'ns fly like de patriches, and me must follow dem."

"Well, have you found them, Dora?" said Teunis, affecting to understand her literally. "They must be ducks you are seeking, or they could not cross the creek."

"Nae, nae, duck neber flee to de mountains, chick'ns keep 'bout de doors. Patriches run avay, and hide der eyes, den tink nobody seed dem."

"Explain yourself, Dora," for the young man saw that she was in earnest about something, and he was anxious for information which might unfold what he wanted to know. Besides he knew that old Dora was faithful, and he needed a confident friend in some one: so he at once said, "tell me mammy, has any one been seeking after Teunis last night?"

"Mammy had dark tream," and here the poor creature's tears began to run. "Teunis baby boy again; but Teuny fall over the vlat rock and got wings, den flew away to Hoogentuisen vere Martin feed him wid whiggee corn."

"Come Dora, none of that nonsense," said Teunis, impatiently, "tell me what you are here for. Have you anything to tell me about the Indians?"

At that word the old creature became as bright as an old African can be, and opened her bag of secrets to Teunis, so perfectly that he became fully aware of his danger, and before he left her, had made out, in his own mind, the plan he should pursue immediately. The conversation was carried on in a low, quiet whisper, for at least ten minutes. At parting she looked in his face, as if examining the lines of feeling that might be traced there, and at the close of the investigation, she drew her own palm over her brow, saying,

"Look to de high peak ven de storm is past, de vind sweeps de vet dust off, and the face is clear as de morning."

Teunis rode on, taking the hint by bringing his thoughts and looks into proper subjection, before he met his father, who Dora told him had been asking after him twice since six o'clock. In ten minutes more he was in the barn attending to some duties, which he knew belonged to his share of the usual work, with as much earnestness as if nothing else was in his mind. There his father found him. Whether he was aware of his absence through the night or not, did not appear; but the moment he came within sight of his son, the working of his lips showed that an unusual agitation had been moving him all that morning, and was now to be expressed. The son feared that his own thoughts had become known in some mysterious way, as they had been already partially revealed to old Dora, as he found from more than her dreams. There was some medium between her and the mist on the mountain, which he could not trace, and from her former character, he was still more inclined than ever to believe that she held communications with the geests * she had so often frightened them with when they were children. For the fact was, that sometimes being overborne by the noise and the rudeness of the youngsters, when they intruded upon the kitchen, her own proper domain, she had to have recourse to the very means which white nurses have of stilling their noisy brood, bringing the *fetish* on them, which was equally effectual with geest or witch, only that her goblin was of African color, where she declared there was one so large, that he could swallow an ox and three pigs for his supper, with as many little white babies as could be found. All of these stories had their influence on Teunis—not yet abated entirely. This morning had renewed his wonder; where the old wench could have obtained her knowledge of him and of his very thoughts when she had not seen him since the morning before! When Jacobus Roe then stepped into the barn as he did, his son Teunis was in some measure moved in feeling through sympathy, and might by a more skillful or more suspicious parent have been thrown off his guard. Luckily for him, the old man could only entertain one idea at a time, and the idea now was the King and his cause. To sustain Toryism he was ready to sacrifice all he had in the world, family and farm; nor did he dream for a moment that he could come to a loss, since Brandt had arrived to carry off the Whiggies. After they were moved the whole country would be as quiet as his pigs after the bieren—bears—were driven away, and they lying down in their straw, well fed. The Whigs and the bears were the same thing in a measure, to the old Boerman.

"Teunis, sonnee, I vant tee to run for me to te top of"—Here Teunis looked into his father's face ready to frame an excuse, or in some way to get rid of being hindered in what he must do, whatever should be the consequence, to save Elsie and her captive friend; but to his great relief, he found that he might both run his father's errand, and serve his own cause; for the father, going on slowly, said, with some hesitation and under his usual tone, "Tee must run to te top of te clove and look sout' and-nort', and stand allee day till tee see smoke rising from Sopus, den come back vere tou vill be vanted. Tak de sorrel mare wid tee, and do not spare de spur nor de vipp, nor yourselv."

* Ghosts.

This was an extraordinary license on the part of old Yaacob, who loved his horses with an affection that approached the human feeling, as near as it could come. By this token, the son saw that the crisis was drawing to a point; and lest he should be laid under some definite obligation, he hastened to fill the letter of the injunction, with an alacrity that pleased the old man, so that the smile of satisfaction came up over his grim face, breaking after five minutes into words. "Ha! deze jougeling * vill make de Whiggees run, I guess." That lad was the pride of his heart, and he hoped to see him made a captain before long.

At the door of the kitchen, where Teunis had stopped on a visit to old Dora's larder, he met his mother, who was under as much emotion as her large frame would allow her to bear; as she came forward she merely looked at him, whispering in his ear, "*geen huisknecht kan twee heeren dienen*;" † and with her heart full, she turned and left him in amazement. She was no sooner out of sight than Dora waddled up, putting her fingers to her lips, intending to impose silence on Teunis; a state she could not remain in herself; for, with as much solemnity as she could put into her dark face, she said, as she touched him, "Miene kinder ‡ dere be geesten vatching de, tak dat;" and she thrust a smooth black stone into his bosom, throwing a thong, made of a snake skin, which ran through it, over his neck; mumbling something, seemingly a prayer, as she went back to her work. This stone Teunis had seen a few times before, on occasions when Dora was excited, as she was just now; and he remembered once when he was a boy, that going on a hunting excursion, when Dora thought he must be in danger, that she did the same thing as now. His leaving his paternal dwelling under all these circumstances, was calculated to waken up any dormant sensations that might be sleeping in his breast. The double errand on which he was bound, the responsibility laid upon him, his own interests in the events of the day; and the parting he had just made with those who loved him, together with the hope of securing the approval and the love of one now dearer to him than life, made him solemn. But the words of his mother were to him the heaviest sounds: "No man can serve two masters." "Mother," said the honest youth to himself, "you are right. This shall be my last service to King George; and if I guess right, it will not displease you, that it should be so. I have long thought I knew where her

* This young man. † No servant can serve two masters. ‡ Child.

heart was, and maybe she has heard me speak in my sleep; for I have dreamed before this of shaking my head clear of the English colors, when my father, honest man, was putting the flag over me." With these reflections, he put spurs to his horse, that felt the spirit of his rider and was off like an arrow, up the hill. He was noticed by Dora, whom he did not see; for there seemed to hang over the whole scene a stillness, which, to the oppressed and superstitious mind of the rider, was in the highest degree ominous. Not a living thing could be seen; cattle were driven far into the woods; horses were tied in some cave, and even the poultry were caged in the bush. The houses seemed to be all deserted, except where some old negro slave, and his ancient wench of a wife, were left to keep a sort of watch over things of no value. It was a lonely and melancholy ride; and to add to Teunis's sense of the fearful, as he went on at full speed, he saw, crossing his road at a little distance, one of those bears which were numerous in these regions. He moved slowly till the horseman came near, when he sprung up a tree that overhung the path, looking down through the branches at the intruder upon his domains, with a calm superiority which was provoking to a hunter's spirit. But there was no time to waste in parleying with Bruin; so, on the rider went, marking the tree with his eye; for he saw that the sweet tooth of the animal would incline him to return there some other time, when they might be on more equal terms.

Truth to tell, Teunis was less afraid of a bear than he was of things that had neither shape nor sound. The tales of old Dora had more influence upon him than the substantial objects he had chased over the mountains; and as he rode at full speed in the darkness of the forest, where, on his right hand, he heard the dull sighing of the trees; and on the left, the monotonous murmur and brattling noise of the stream, he remembered he was coming near to the "*spooks den*," which, from his infancy, he had regarded as the abode of the unknown sprites of the hills. It was not without a feeling of tremor that he slackened his horse's pace, that he might survey the scene, before he fairly entered into the mouth of the demon, if there was such a being. He was a young man, above the average in intelligence; but that did not save him from the usual fears of mortals, when engaged in earnest work, as he was at that moment. All that he had heard of the place from Dora, and the other old blacks; together with the tales which adventurous hunters had lately told, some in fear and others in sport, came up to view at this instant. By this time he found himself walking his horse slowly toward the dreaded place, which lay at the foot of the hill, just where the road he must take turned off to the left. He knew that there was a hut there, and a well, which was supplied from some spring on the side of the hill. He was about to descend from Sorrel, that he might allow her to quench her thirst, and then slake his own lips, which he suddenly discovered were drying; when to his great surprise and fear, he perceived smoke issuing from an aperture in the roof of the rude cabin; and, as he listened, he heard plainly the sound of a human voice. His first impulse was to remount Sorrel and ride back over the road he came. But his horse was too thirsty to allow herself to be deprived of the beverage so near at hand, and before the rider had time to recover his bridle, the animal was at the brink of the rude log trough, out of which was running the purest crystal water. Teunis knew the place, for it was past it he had gone when Dora first put the charm round his neck, to protect him from the spooks; and whether through instinct, or because he had faith in the old African's incantation, he suddenly thrust his hand into the place where the black pebble lay, and held it as a weapon of defence. He had just time to dip his own lips into the water and take one long draught, when he lifted his head and saw, to his horror, an object which, had he seen before he drank of the spring, would have made him fall to the ground. But his nervousness departed with his thirst; and what was of itself sufficient to encourage him, he saw that Sorrel was not in the least afraid. Quick as thought, he remembered what the Dominie had said, "that the dumb creatures are terrified for geesten, not for men, in whatever garments they come. But when you ride in the dark, or on a doubtful business, see that you be not wiser than the beast you stride. God may put light before his eyes. Mind how Balaam was rebuked for his iniquity, "*want het jukdra* gende stomme dier sprekende met menschenstem heeft des profeten dwaashied verhinderd,"—or, as the English Bibles have it, "the dumb ass, speaking with man's voice, forbade the madness of the prophet."

"This is no angel then," said Teunis, "sent to hinder me, for Sorrel is not afraid. I have heard that there was such a creature here before, and now I know that he must be but mortal."

The young farmer, though he had lived in simple seclusion, was not unacquainted with those trials which show the true character; and once put into a close corner, he soon regained his natural courage of heart; and though it may tend to lower him in the estimation of some, we must tell the truth, old Dora's charm in his hand was not without its influence.

By the time these reflections had flown through the brain of the youth, the figure we have alluded to came out into the road where Teunis was to pass, if he went up the hill at all. There was no other path. A deep ravine was at the left, where a waterfall dashed on the rocks; and on the right there stood frowning a steep hill, overshadowed with woods and bushes. Teunis mounted his horse, and was gathering up the reins, that he might pass at a sudden, when chance might offer itself; but he soon perceived that he had to do with one who was more than a match with him at manœuvering. The strife was now which would longest remain silent. The two stood facing each other. He on the road was a tall, bony man of great strength, which appeared from the steady stand he took, without wincing or moving a muscle. He had on a cloak of bear-skins, and a cap made of the skin of the common wildcat. Under the cloak, which was worn close to the body, gathered in by a belt which had once belonged to a soldier of his majesty, was hung a straight sword, of about a cubit's length. Other weapons he had, as the turning aside of his outer garment showed, though he did not bring them forth for use; as he could readily have done had occasion called.

Teunis, at length gathering courage from his sense of duty, said in a respectful manner: "Would it please you to let me pass; I am on important business, and have been detained too long already."

"Have you been detained by me, Teunis Roe, from doing the business of the cold-blooded Brandt? One might think that the smell of scalps was sweet to your nostrils, since you want to be on the hill to tell him that it is now time for him to descend like a hawk among Dora's chickens, when he pounces on the best."

Teunis started at the allusions all through this sarcastic speech, for it was delivered in that strain which has so grating an effect upon the sensitive nature of an honest man, who spurns at even an insinuation.

"I am none of Brandt's tools," said the man addressed, with some spirit, "nor do I mean to serve his master; I have other work upon my hands."

"Pray, who is Brandt's master?" said the singular being,

who evidently spoke more for the purpose of drawing out his new acquaintance than because he wanted information. "We have been taught that the Great Mohawk is a king himself, and bows down to no man."

"The one that Brandt serves is his master, be it Satan or St. George," was the tart reply of Teunis, for he was becoming bold and impatient. "Let me pass." This time he did not add "if it be your pleasure."

The other, not noticing the demand, proceeded to speak in reply to the sound sentiment expressed of service; "You are, then, neither a servant of Brandt, nor of St. George, nor of his grim majesty of the black regions. Whom may you serve, then, young man?"

"Who is it that demands the information?" was the quick response of Teunis. "I have not come up here to be put through my catechism."

"Well spoken, friend, and I like you all the better for your chariness and spirit." Here the speaker with the hairy robe stood looking Teunis in the eye, for at least ten seconds, till he succeeded in riveting him to his place, when he broke the silence by saying, "The black stone in your hand, and the serpent skin that binds it round your neck, seem fitter for a man who is bound to the devil than to God."

Teunis looked into his hand, and saw that it was the charm of Dora he was grasping with such firmness; ashamed at his being found out, and actually fearing that it was from the devil, he took it from his neck, and flung it with all his force into the gulf, where it hung suspended from the branch of a sapling, far down.

"So you deem yourself free, young man, now; but know this, that no one is his own master; and some are more arrant slaves than Dora's children."

"So you seem to think that I am in bondage with the rest. It shall not be my fault if freedom be a stranger to any who tread these mountains."

"No doubt you are very much in earnest when your particular interest is at stake. A man's own feeling renders his judgment very decided. Would you have been so far from home had the liberty of the country only been in danger? We do not always perceive our own bent."

At that instant Teunis felt not unlike Sorrel, with the bit in her mouth, restless, and ready to spring at the first opening. He had been surveying the height of the hill, while the stranger was feeling the pockets of his inner garments; and to do so found it necessary to unbuckle the girdle of his cloak. Now was the time, and quick as thought the spur gave Sorrel the hint, who took it willingly, and at one bound was on the other side of the opposer, who was shoved to the right with some violence, which both disturbed his intention and his temper for an instant. Wheeling around, Teunis said, "I beg your pardon, but I must not be hindered by any one." The discomfited man gave a scowl that brought the blood quickly to the heart of the rider.

"Young man, it is well for you that I have a deeper interest in you than you are aware of, else your stolen passage would not serve you. If I meant you harm, it matters but little whether I look at you from the south side or the north. There are reasons of more moment than merely holding this palaver with you, why I should know you." By the time he was done with these words, he affected to look in the face of Teunis, who was standing up in his stirrups, with his eyes staring on the man who was addressing him: who said with a cool, sarcastic voice: "You seem to be in no hurry now, that you have made such an effort to pass me; are you shot, that you are speechless? What do you see?"

"I see," said Teunis, "what makes me believe that you are either better or worse than other mortals; and now I have to beg of you to let me go on my proposed journey."

The strange man had put on his breast a small miniature picture, and around it was a blue silken chain, which Teunis recognized as one that he had himself bought in Albany, and put over the neck of Elsie at their parting, a year ago. He could see, too, that the likeness was that of Elsie. The sight blinded him and struck him dumb, and the only thing he could say was to beg permission to leave.

"I see," said the strange mortal, "that we in part underderstand each other. Go! I have been watching your movements. I saw you hail the beams of the rising sun. Remember that he is a great discoverer of secrets. He sends his rays into bright eyes through tears; and more than three can stand on a high cliff. Nothing hides but the valley, or the grave under its clods. But blood will ooze out of even the deepest pit; and the eyes of conscience, and of revenge, can see the stains, without sunlight."

These words, at the close, were said with a bitterness which froze the spirit of the listener; and as if to relieve himself, he turned to the speaker and said: "Can I serve you in any way? Do you want anything? I cannot help but pity you."

'Want! Have not I water there? sun enough when I look up? and shall not I have earth enough when I lie down to sleep my last sleep? Yes, but the earth would not be still should I die before "——The rest of this sentence was in pantomime which no one could see and not comprehend that a deadly purpose was in his soul.

Here, turning to Teunis, he said: "Swear;" and he held out a large pistol, with the muzzle to himself—"swear," he said firmly.

"And what am I to give oath concerning? for that is not a matter of common import."

"Well, swear," said the wild man, for he was more in the character now of a savage roused to the highest excitement, than a being of this reasonable world: "swear that you will not tell a word of what you have heard, nor describe a token of what you have seen, till the sun has risen and set six times."

As Teunis looked at the portrait that hung at the breast of the one that was invoking him by an oath, he hesitated; for there were questions of deep interest to him, which he would wish to have solved; and if he gave his oath, all inquiry was shut up. He looked on the features again, that he might be sure, and then to the face of him who wore the gem, who understood his wish, and said:

"I know what you would ask; you cannot know. *She has sworn;* swear! I say," and he gave a shriek that was reverberated through the valley, as if a thousand demons were responding to their leader. Teunis said no more, but following the words dictated to him, he swore to be silent till the appointed time came.

"Now, go your way; you will have a friend while you are faithful to the trust you have undertaken. Hear this, and be quick. Brandt will descend before two suns set; but your first business is above, for the Indian hounds are scenting out the footsteps of the feeble. Go; but here, wait!" and he seemed to take the same black stone that Teunis threw away in his fury, from his pocket—how he took it from the tree where it hung, Teunis never could guess—and put it over the head of the rider as it was before. Then taking it in his own hand, he touched a part of it, when out sprung the nib of a whistle, which he put to his mouth, and made the air resound. Bidding Teunis do the same, he said curtly:

"When danger is too strong for you, let that be heard." With that he turned, and the horseman sprang up the hill, as if relieved from some force that pressed him to the ground, so that he rode up the hill free. He felt that the spell which bound him was removed, and now his circulation was become so rapid, that wings seemed to be given to the animal he rode. It was really so, that he found himself on the shoulder of the mountain in half the time he was wont to take; but it was at the expense of his horse's energy, for by the time his mind had come to its balance, the creature was blowing like a grampus, as Judge Abiel, who had sailed to the West Indies, was accustomed to say of his oxen, his horses, or his negroes, when driven above their strength.

"I have been in the hand of the Philistines," said Teunis to himself. "Did ever any one see such a creature in the shape of man! It is like the picture of the sailor left on the deserted island, with his nigger Friday. Such a beard; not much grey in it. He is not as old as he pretends. His eyes are quite round, and his teeth all firm, and then he could move when he chose. I declare! he had all but the hold of my bridle, when I leaped past him. He would have thrown us over the precipice, Sorrel but for your quickness;" and he vainly stroked the neck of his friend in need.

With more caution, and at a slower pace, the young man moved on, full of thought concerning the person he had left. His seclusion, his knowledge of his own business, his acquaintance with Dora, and with the black stone he was wearing; and above all, the mystery of the picture, were puzzles which must remain unsolved for at least a week. His oath must seal his lips, and Elsie's silence could be accounted for, since he had never heard a lisp of the spook in the glen from her. Why be on such terms of intimacy with him? She was unlike all the girls in the country around. He had heard Dora say that *fetish* had wakened up the sleeping man of the mountain. Some trick in all this, connected with the descent on Brandt. His underdress would point him out as being on the side of the King; but then would Elsie allow any of that side to possess an article of hers? Was this after all the old Rip Van Winkle that his grandmother used to tell about? or the old Hendrick Hudson that the Indian Sachem keep a tradition of? Thinking on in this desultory way, the young Dutchman fell almost into a sound sleep from the want of his usual rest on the previous night.

CHAPTER VIII.

WARS AND RUMORS OF WARS.

"There was whilom by days of old,
A worthy knight as mene told;
Wifeless he was, Florent he hight:
He was a man that mòchel might,
Of arms he was desirous,
Chivalrous and amorous,
And for the love of virgin thought
He rode the marches all about."—CHAUCER.

TEUNIS in eager haste was soon on the crown of the hill; the sun being now about four hours high, and for the first time since he had loved Elsie, did he entertain the least hope of success; but knowing well that he had no common heart to reach, he was rousing himself to do his best for her and for himself. He determined to deserve success.

At full speed, and wending his way through among the trees, over a very rough road, in a manner which a woodman only can do, he reached the verge of two small lakes, more in size like the artificial ponds in an earl's pleasure-ground than the head spring of a mill stream. Clear as crystal, and cool as in winter was the water, surrounded by trees that were reflected from its glassy surface. Now that the sun was high, his rays showed the soft alluvial bottom, on which lay the trunks of a former time, preserved from decay; nor did the smallest wave ripple these tiny seas at the time our traveller was gazing down where undisturbed fishes were sporting in large schools. These two little lakes, that seemed like the eyes of the mountain, if we allow ourselves to believe, as Kiskataam told the Fawn, that the Mountain was once a monster, who devoured all the children of the red race, and that the Great Spirit touched him, when he was going down to the salt lake to bathe, and here he remains. His eyes are open all the summer, but in winter they are covered with a thick crust, and a heavy film. But whether he sleeps or wakes he sheds tears always, and they trickle down his cheeks as may be seen. The cunning chief laughed under his red skin at his own wit of invention and at the simplicity of the English maiden for receiving such a tale.

Turning to the right from these lakes, Teunis sought out the bear's den; but what was his horror, when he did not find the objects of his search. At the moment he supposed that they might be still lingering in the neighborhood, so he set himself to find out their new hiding-place. He crawled through the brush, carefully marking every point, to see if a footprint had been left behind. He imagined he saw evidences of their presence, and he did at last in one spot, where the ground was soft, see distinctly where they must have been. Here he was careful that all should be obliterated, as he was not sure that he would discover the signs of their whereabouts. He knew that other eyes as well as his own were prying into the ground, for he could plainly see here and there a larger footprint, that was pointing after the other. He wandered for at least an hour, but to no purpose, and would have remained longer had not his horse, which was tied outside of the bush, grown impatient, and was neighing for his master. Teunis having a tint of superstition in his nature, regarded the call of the animal as the voice of instinct, if not more directly the intimation of Providence to return.

Great was the surprise, if not fear, of the anxious youth when he emerged from the thicket, to see a man coming toward him from the side of the lake, tall and of a commanding presence. He was of about thirty-five years of age, dressed in a half military garb, boots and buckskins, with coat of blue cloth, made in the English fashion, having large skirts which came to the knee, and was made so that it might be buttoned to the chin. At present, however, it was open, and showed a vest that was trimmed with gold lace, over which hung a cravat of the purest muslin, that evidently had been but recently put on, and that with care. His beaver was soft felt, but shaped into a smart negligence which betokened the man of fashion, seeking to look at his ease as he wished to feel. Teunis looked at the new comer as if he desired him to be the first speaker. By his voice he had made up his mind to judge, and he waited to hear; and so he was standing at the side of the saddle when the other approached.

"Is not your horse the first creature of the kind that ever drank of these waters?" said the stranger, as if he wanted to draw out the young Dutchman by an indifferent topic. "He seems to be impatient to go. How far may you be desirous of travelling this warm day?"

There were more questions here than one, which allowed Teunis a choice, of which he felt glad, for he had no wish to reveal his business to a stranger, so he answered: "I have seen greater creatures than horses here before, and where one animal of four feet has been, others of the same number may come without hurt."

"You would not say, because a cat could climb these rocks, that a heavy-footed horse could follow up to the same place?"

"I have seen some creatures as heavy as Sorrel who could outrun cats, and climb the rocks as easily."

"You jest, young man; such animals as you describe could not run up trees as cats can climb. You would have me believe that a Dutchman can beat an Indian at a race as easily as an Englishman can fight a Yankee rebel." This last was said more by way of feeling the pulse of the native American, and thereby finding out the sympathies he had with the king or country, than because he wished to provoke ill-nature. But Teunis had been schooled too long in self-restraint to give way to his temper. He merely replied:

"Bears can climb as high as cats, and deer can run faster than either. It is not weight, but muscle and sinew which make the difference."

"And blood, young man," said the stranger, evidently well pleased to escape out of the place he had put himself in, without reflecting on where his ignorance of the mountains would carry him. "You are a native of these regions, sir?"

This was said in the gentlemanly, yet commanding tone of one accustomed to receive a direct answer "Have you heard news from the river side this morning?"

"I am a native of these hills," said Teunis, "and have been sent to gather news, not to spread it. One of the first duties a messenger performs is silence."

"That is a non-performance, as I judge. All the more faithful you must be to your master, and on that very account I should wish to engage you on a business of my own, if you would take a reward of value."

"You mean, I suppose," said Teunis, evading the object of his interrogator, "that you would employ me to stir up the game we have been speaking of; but let me assure you that a good dog, or an Indian scout, would perform that duty better than I could possibly do it. But I must be gone;" and with that he leaped into the saddle and was ready to hasten away, where he had determined upon in his own mind during the few moments he stood parleying with the stranger.

"No," said that gentleman, putting hand to the reins of Sorrel, and gently holding them. "The game I am after is too tender to be caught in hunter fashion, but requires the most careful handling when caught."

There was a lurking leer in the eye of Teunis's new acquaintance which at once wakened suspicion in the mind of the innocent listener, and all at once the light broke upon his understanding concerning who this was. He almost betrayed himself, when he found that he was in the presence of the much dreaded Clifford, but he soon became at rest when he found that even he was as ignorant of the hiding-place of the young women as he was himself. He inwardly resolved to divert attention away from all that side of the mountain, where the chief danger lay of their being found out.

"What say you to my proposal, young man," continued Clifford, "of being my aid for a day?"

"You mean to hunt deer?" said Teunis, affecting to take him literally; "or rather the fawn, if I may judge from the tender way in which you speak of them. No. I must go; the king's business requires haste. There are Indians on the hills now, who would serve you better, as I said before. There is one coming this way now; and who can outrun any fawn that was ever stolen from her dam." By this time, Kiskataam was there close by; and Teunis, raising his voice, called out, "Can the Sachem find a fawn for the king's pale face, here?"

This hit at random, struck both of these wily betrayers; but was said in such a manner as neither the one nor the other could resent it without discovering his own secret. Nor durst they combine and demand an explanation of the doubtful expression. It might be chance, or it might be directed to both. They wisely remained silent, and Teunis was rewarded for the risk, by seeing that as yet the girls were safe.

Here Sorrel was restive under the hand of Clifford, and would have sprung away at a bound, had not the Indian laid his hand also upon the reins on the other side with a menacing look; pausing before he spoke, and with a meaning which said, "refuse, and you are a dead man." But by this time, the rider had become excited, with his horse, and demanded why he "was hindered upon his journey, and that too, by professed servants of the king."

"It is because we are the king's servants, that we stop you in these troublesome times," said the white man.

"Indian chief rules up here on his own hills," said Kiskataam, "Young Tory Whig must go to the pine grove and wait for Braudt; and not hunt up here now against law."

"Kiskataam," said Teunis, sharply, and with some haste, "does not mind the great Father's word always: but Indian does not know law so well as pale face. Doe, buck or fawn, or any sort of deer, can be hunted from August till January. But, in the king's name, I demand a passage," he said to the two men; who were still uncertain as to the figurative or the literal meaning of his reference to the deer, doe, buck or fawn; terms which they knew were in the law.

"Since you claim to be on the king's business, young man," said Clifford, somewhat sternly, "you can, at least, show us some missive from his majesty."

"What if I cannot?" said Teunis, with promptitude. "Shall any one dare to hinder me? You are a stranger here, and this sachem is not in commission."

"Since you are so bold and brave, young man; let me tell you, that both Kiskataam and myself believe, that under that clownish face, more knowledge concerning a business of ours is lurking than we are willing to let go along with yourself; and, to come to the point at once, we demand your meaning of the word Fawn!"

Even the Indian was surprised at the question, and fixed his great mysterious eyes on the rider's face, which remained as stolid as it was possible to be. To release himself and gain time, he merely grazed the side of Sorrel with his rowel, who reared and sprung; so that he freed himself from the Indian's grasp, but not from the more experienced Clifford, who suspected the manœuvre, and reiterated the question in fury, "What did you mean by using the word Fawn?"

"Sir," said Teunis, "I see by the dress you wear, that I am in the presence of one of the king's officers. I am now, myself, on the king's business, and my own, and I refuse to tell you aught but what I am forced to tell."

"You shall not get clear by that pretext, young man. I see plainly, that by some means you are acquainted with my secret, and you must either tell all you know of it or die." And with that, he drew out a sword that was hidden under his outside coat. "It would be dangerous to allow a living man to go away from us at this moment, with that in his breast which must ruin our plan. What does Indian say?"

Kiskataam nodded assent, and swung his tomahawk around his head, ready to strike. At this moment, the round black stone of Dora came to Teunis' mind; and, without thinking of aught else than his self-preservation, he took it into his hand, then pressing upon the hidden spring, the words of the fur-clad stranger came to his mind,—"Call when you are in danger." He blew with a force which startled the two men at his saddle, for they evidently expected some new development, and lifted their arms as if in defence, when the report of a musket came, and then another, which struck the weapons from the hands of the interlopers; so that before they had time to recover themselves, or their weapons, Sorrel was rushing on between the two lakes, at a speed which defied all pursuit.

Flying was more like the movement of the rider and his horse, than running. There was a path wide enough; and which had been well travelled, as the ground showed, over which Teunis rode, bending his head beneath the low branches, and wheeling to the right or left, as he required. The way was becoming clearer; till suddenly he turned into a narrow and rugged defile, that brought him down into the wide glen, or clove through which the Kaaterskill was heard falling from step to step, on its descent. On coming to the top of one of those more prominent than the others, he was alarmed by seeing Shandaagan, the grim shadow of Kiskataam, of whom we have spoken before, suddenly fall to the ground, as if he had been struck by a club. Teunis knew that it could be for no good that he was there; and while it would scarcely serve his purpose to notice him, still he must not be left in his rear at this time, for he might do him injury; so, boldly riding up to the spot where he saw him sink, he stopped; and first spying out the place where the red man lurked, like a serpent in his way, to bite his horse's heels, he called out as if he were speaking to the chief himself, and not to his aid:

"Kiskataam has come far since the new moon rose. The chief has got many king's heads in his belt."

The effect of this side speech was evident upon the sly Indian, who was at a loss to persuade himself of what it might mean, and with great caution he opened his eyes, when Teunis, seeing that his trick took, gave one of those hearty laughs which are sure to disconcert an Indian when he is found out, by a cunning like his own. Shandaagan rose and looked cautiously around, when seeing no one but the rider and his horse, he gave a significant ugh! which might mean either pleasure or displeasure.

"Shandaagan sleeps early," said Teunis. "Hunting deer

when the laurel is red requires clear eyes in moonlight." This was said to throw the savage off his guard, and put him at ease with himself, for it was too evident he was on the same errand which engaged others, and now Teunis felt at rest. None of them had found the trail of Elsie and her charge, though all were on the search. He was in no hurry to ride on, nor willing to say more than would serve his own ends. So he waited the answer he might receive.

"The deer hides in the bush all day," was at length the reply of the red man, "and scents the hunter in the wind. Pale face has a call of his own that brings them to his pond."

Here he cast the pupils of his eyes quietly around, marking the effect which his hint might have, as if he expected that it would be understood.

Teunis answered in the same enigmatical style. "Indian has more traps than the pale face, and has bright eyes for a night trail. When he has no moon he kindles his fire, and gets scalps;" and with these words, pointing to the top of one of the little hills, he was silent, but watching the face of his companion for the moment, his heart beat with anger and with some fear. "There now comes the great dog himself with all his hounds of cruelty."

"Brandt" was the name that the Indian muttered between his teeth.

"Yes, Brandt, the mighty hunter before the Lord, come to burn and murder. His dogs' tusks are sharpened at hell-fire, and he and Kiskataam, and Clifford"—here he paused before he spoke—"and Shandaagan will crunch the skulls of all the fawns they can catch, but, by all the great spirits in the universe, let them keep out of my way."

And with that furious speech Teunis rushed down the hill, as if he were a fiery flying angel, sent to defend the weak against the strong. He was now on the road to Hoogenhuisen, where he hoped to find Elsie; though how she could have got there was out of his calculation. Still, she possessed so much self-reliance, courage and strength herself, he had full confidence in her, but not in the power of her companion.

"She is a feeble-looking thing, that Margaret, compared with Elsie," said the young admirer of the Dutch built maiden; "but there is wonderful spirit in some of those trim tight limbs. Those blood horses that the red-coat officers have would do but little at the plough, driven by old Cæse and held in by Dad, with his dander up, among pine stumps; but then put old Brown and Bet in one of these curricles, with their heavy hips, I am guessing they would be left behind. But then Elsie is not so heavy as she looks along side of that English miss. Put her beside Nelly Van Zant, or Peggy Troumpour, and see them waddling through the barn-yard after the cows : their weight and a three year old would about balance the scales. I would match Elsie in triggness and spirit with Sorrel here at a race, and for a step equal to Miss Margaret, with all her fine gracefulness and quick movements. Well, I am glad she is so nimble and strong; there is the more chance of her escaping these red skins and that haughty sinner of an Englishman. It is for no good he is there. I wonder what he means by kidnapping his own flesh and blood. One thing I am sure of, that I am in for some great venture, and here I stake my life, fortune and honor on the side of humanity, be that king or country.

With thoughts full of earnestness, he pursued his journey till he arrived at the door of Martin Schuyler, with some trepidation lest he should meet the old farmer himself, of whom he had of late a wholesome dread. He was studying in his mind how he best should convince the stern Whig that he was a true man and no spy, when he met Angelica herself, who was about the yard superintending the household affairs, as he thought, when in reality she was giving orders in the place of Martin himself. That worthy and careful farmer had not returned, for a reason that we know of; but as yet his good vrow was in the dark, nothing having been heard from either him or from the daughter. Through the day she had driven off the young and the old blacks to see if they could find any trace of them, who always went a little way from home, skulking among the woods and the rocks, thinking of spooks and of Indians, and then lying down in a safe place, where they were sure to go to sleep long enough to allow them time to search all the places to which they were sent, and return with no tidings but bad reports of everything horrid. None were faithful and brave except old Noll, who had been abroad before he came to Martin, and knew something, priding himself on his "trabels among the vild men of Batikoo, ven he was kidnapped by de Spanish." Noll had been bought by Martin when in New York, and he gave him the name the Yankee had given him on his passage, from the resemblance he saw in the nose of the negro to that feature in the face of a famous Puritan whom the people of New England delight to honor. Nor was the name unworthily nor unwittingly bestowed. Noll was a courageous old soul, and faithful to boot. So much confidence had Martin in him, that he once hired him out on a voyage to the West Indies, which was undertaken by Garret Abiel, who went from the Bught with a load of cattle, and staves, and other produce, bringing back rum and molasses. The Elder declared that Noll was the best hand he had on board, and could mount the shrouds faster than Jake Van Orden, his chief mate.

Of old Noll many tales are told, but on the occasion of Martin's absence, he was all astray, and had just returned before Teunis's arrival, with no news of his master, and sad news of the vuur teeken burning from every kekute from Albany to Sopus.

"Did tou see de Meester on the Berg* any vere? Did tou go to de Sout Mountain, and to de Nort Mountain? Did tou see any blood upon de vay? Did tou see Elsie or de dog?—vat did tou see? Spak dis moment, Noll. O wee! O wee!"

All this time the careful wife was collecting together silver spoons, chinaware, and other nice things known only in the best houses of the colonists, who had came from Holland, or who still held intercourse with the mother land. The chief of those things, in which, as a good wife, she prided herself, had already been put aside before that day, in anticipation of such an onslaught, as it had been threatened many a time; but the remainder was now gathered up with care. When all the young brood—children of Noll and Minerva—were sent out of the way, these faithful servants of the household, who could alone be trusted, were bidden to gather up the bundles, and carefully stow them into the hidden corner, which was not opened to any eyes, except to those who would give up life sooner than reveal the secret.

"O wee! O wee!" came ever from the lips and the heart of the anxious Angelica. "Dere is de sucker kuppe † dat mammy gave me on my bruiloft ‡ day, ven I was a young vroflicken lass, like Elsie. O wee! O wee! Vere is Elsie noo."

Noll, as if her name suggested another of a different age and place, here chimed in with what she had seen on the road, where he had been.

"Yah, vele, may the goede vrowe seek for Elsie. Dat ole Torry's kinder § was on de hill, running like de wile cat seeking Elsie."

Angelica looked up, as if she had been struck a blow on the temple, and almost gasped with earnestness, "And vay

* Mountain. † Sugar bowl. ‡ Bridal. § Son.

do you call de Torry's sonne, Noll? Answer, negur, for your life."

"Noll cannot spak when goede vrowe scolds; Noll must wait ande tink—Teunis Roe rode down de hill on de sorrel, ande stop near de spring haf vay, ande speak to de sly Indian, Shandaagan—Noll looke from de doder side of de clove."

A thousand hopes and fears rushed through the anxious mother's mind at this information. She had always encouraged Teunis in the face of all Martin's prejudices; but here was something like holding communication with the enemy. It was just in the midst of her cogitation that the young man himself entered, and said, almost as soon as he put his foot within door:

"Has Elsie come home, Anshela? Tell me, if you would save my life?"

"Ande whar's Elsie? and whar's de Meester? dat I vant to kenne," said the anxious wife and mother; "dis de lange * dai en me leven,† Teunis; all is goen to destruction; no a wench vill do aught but cry, de Indians! and every negur of dem hiden himself."

"You have not seen Noll run, vrowe goode; yet Noll did not run when the Spanish tooke him by de leg an tied dim; and dis scalp vill be but poor glody;" and like all his race, when he was not crying during excitement, he was sure to laugh.

Angelica and Teunis had retired to another corner, where they were in earnest consultation concerning what was to be done; for now a crisis in the affairs of all had come, and it must be met. There was no other way than to abandon all the houses and the barns to the cruelty of the savages, who were almost sure to wreak their vengeance on Martin's head and property. Teunis gave Noll such advice as the old negro would take from him; which was but little till the mistress of the house backed it by her word. The cattle were driven off to seek refuge on the hills. All had been buried that could be put in the ground; furniture was sent off to caves, and under water-falls, and clothing distributed among neighboring friends, who were not likely to be exposed to the ravages of the enemy. The most difficult matter was to dispose of the negroes in such a way that they could be taken care of. Like all animals, they clung to their first nest; and as some of them were now nearly as old as Angelica herself, and some she found when she came to Hoogenhuisen to be mistress,

* Long. † Life.

it was the most trying part of her duty to put them in a way of securing themselves against injury. There was an old house still standing down in a glen, in which they stowed away lumber and useless tools, and things which Martin hated to burn: into that building Noll was to move all the black family, and as the greatest part of them were his own offspring, of two generations, he succeeded in collecting them in a drove, and putting them under the direction of old Bet, who managed amidst screams and cries of no uncommon kind, to bring them safely to their house of refuge.

All this had to be done before Angelica could move; but when all was accomplished she sat down beside the large fire-place, where the greater part of her life had been spent, and though the worde O wee! O wee!—alas! alas!—were frequently on her tongue, she did not give herself up to despair and to inefficiency.

In the meantime Teunis was out surveying the whole ground, so that as much property might be secured as possible. Returning toward the house after helping to d●●e off the cattle and the hogs into the woods, he stood on a knoll, from whence he surveyed the warning-fires, that rose all along the river, and on the King's Ridge, like a string of lamps lit for a festival, where was to be feasting and frolicking.

"Yes," said Teunis, speaking to himself, "there will be noise and commotion soon. The ball is just opening, and unless God interferes, many a hearth will be desolate. What should I do? Humanity is the first duty. What does the Dominie say? '*Die vader of moeder liefheeft boven mij is mijns niet waardig.*' 'He that loveth father or mother more than me is not worthy of me.' Well, I love one more than father or mother, and she is exposed to the wrath of a cruel enemy. But would I venture my life and honor for another girl in the Kaatsberg, or on the airth? and yet I feel that I am but following out my conviction; only I have been as undecided as my pistol is when it hangs fire. This trouble has made me pick my flint. One thing I am sure is right now—help Angelica in her trouble. The Dominie again must help me here for encouragement. '*Kleenen te drinken geeft alleenlijk eenen beker koud water,*' A cup of cold water to one of these little ones, will ease my conscience, more in my last moments than a sea of blood in the cause of King George.' "

In the midst of these musings his eye was fixed on a small fire that twinkled among the heavy trees that grew on the opposite side of the gulf from were he stood. The secrecy of the place, and the silence, convinced him that the time was at hand for the threatened attack; and without further delay he hastened back to warn Angelica of the danger. As he turned to enter the door-yard, he saw between him and the barn wall a figure moving hastily from him, and disappearing in the shade. This was no pleasant reflection, for he was convinced that it must be some spy sent from the enemy, who was posted near; so he ran toward the place as lightly as he could, and just succeeded in obtaining a glimpse of Shandaagan, but that was all. It was in vain to pursue him further, so he hastened back to where he had left Angelica, but it was with equal fear and surprise that he found all empty. The fire burned on the hearth, and other things were in the same condition as he had seen them an hour ago, but all was silent.

He turned to go, after a vain search, satisfied that the vrowe had retired to some hiding-place of which she knew herself. He was mounting the impatient Sorrel, when Angelica came to him, and with great tenderness and emotion took his hand.

"Teunis, tee vele be kind to Elsie. Martin vill yield. O, wee! O, wee! dis may be our last meeting. My dochter! my dochter!"

Here the feelings of the mother overpowered her.

"I cannot leave you," mother, he was going to say. "Come up behind me here on Sorrel, and you will be put safe down in any place where you wish to go;" for he knew that he could not offer her a place of refuge even with his mother, lest his father should find her there.

"Nay, nay, Teunie, I must wait here. *De wolf zal met het lam verkeeren ende luypart by den guiten bok nedderlegen zal all doyven ;* and with that, she suddenly turned from him and disappeared, where Teunis could not find out, and, as he rightly judged, she had sought the hiding-place, and did not wish that even he should know the spot, he rode off at full speed for the Baackouter, where his father was expecting him with great impatience.

"The goode vrowe," said Teunis to himself, "spoke a prophecy, and more than she intended, when she said the wolf shall dwell with the lamb ; for my fear is now, that that greedy wolf, Kiskataam, will have my lamb beside him before the morning, and the English kid will be at the mercy of that cruel leopard, who evidently would lick her blood. But let me not despair; Elsie will go through where any other would stick fast."

Going on at as rapid a rate as the ground would allow him; for he had turned into one of those byways which he knew well, he came to a low marshy place, where the ground was like a thick carpet; so soft that the shoes of his horse made no noise. One reason why he chose it was, that he might avoid any scouts sent to spy the public road. All at once his horse pricked up his ears; a certain warning, which a cautious man never despises. Nor was it needless in this instance, for both rider and horse were in a moment all alive. All eye and ear, Teunis looked round, and paused that he might hear; and well it was that he did use all these precautions, for just as he was about to put the spur into the flanks of Sorrel, and escape out of the narrow defile, he heard a low bark on his left, which assured him that some one was close by. He wheeled his horse round a rock, which stood near, and there behind it was the Indian Shandaagan, holding the dog, Rover, by a bark string, from which he was evidently trying to escape. He was holding the dog's jaws between his fingers to prevent his giving alarm. Teunis was the first to speak, as a white man, however slow he be, is always sure to do.

"Shandaagan is kind to Martin's dog. The folks of Hoogenhuisen want the dog. They need all their friends. The Indian always got milk and succotash at Martin's house."

These words were cold thrusts to the wily Indian; and he was at a loss whether to interpret them as the expression of simple earnest, or intended sarcasm. Had he been sure concerning the young Dutchman's knowledge of recent facts, he would have had some cue; or were he sure to which side of the public contest he leaned, the difficulty would have been less; but in doubt he yielded to the suggestion of giving up the dog to the rightful owner, by putting him at the disposal of Teunis.

"Indian knows Martin's dog, and dog loves Shandaagan." This was said as an excuse for his having the property of Martin in his possession.

"Dog loves Shandaagan with a string," said Teunis, laughing, so that the other felt the rebuke, and let go his hold, which Rover no sooner found out, than he leapt up in recognition of the new comer. This so mortified the Indian, that he betrayed some feeling, and was ready to execute any contrary manœuvre, which might divert the Dutchman from the game he himself was endeavoring to entrap; for, as all may guess, it was after Elsie and her companion that he was tracking; and the dog he had been using to this end all the morning, since the time he had succeeded in capturing the unfortunate Martin. Knowing, as he did, the political bias of old Jacob Roe, he presumed that any information of the movements of the king's party must interest the young man. So stepping up close to the saddle, as if he were confiding a secret to the rider, he almost whispered, as he pointed his finger in the direction where Teunis had seen the fire, and said:

"Brandt's braves slide down the mountain. The pine trees shake with their feet."

Teunis started at this announcement, and checking up his rein, he sat erect, ready to spring. "Where is Brandt and his men?" He was nearly saying verwerpelyk—reprobates—when he bit his lip, which the sly Indian did not see, or he would not have replied as he did.

"See! there they are now, and the young Dutchman is wanted by King George's men."

"Where then are the rest of the king's servants? Where is Kiskataam? Why is Shandaagan not there instead of lying here behind a stone, nursing a dog in a string?"

This cut to the quick, but the red man was on his guard, and quietly walked off, saying something about "watching the fire on the rock." He gave a careless whistle, intended for the dog, but the latter preferred liberty to a chain, and ran barking and leaping up before Sorrel, who sympathized with the spirit, by making up for the loss of time by his increased speed.

Down the mountain the three went, each one apparently more eager than the others; but Rover was always in the van, with curled tail; and as he turned occasionally around, he seemed to say, "I know more of them you seek, than you can ever know without my help." The thought of using the animal in finding out his mistress grew before his mind, till it became a settled thing with him, by the time he stood on the hill that overlooked Baackouter, where his father's house was; when all at once the question rose to his tongue: What should be done with Rover? They will ask me where I have been, and then as quick as one question is put, the next will be—"Have you been at Martin's?" They all know Rover, and my liking for his mistress; and she is a Whig, and as they will be sure to abuse all Whigs, her father must take the chief share. They will torment me till I break out in a passion and declare myself. I will send the dog back. He will find out his friends, and help to protect them. He tried to drive Rover back, but he ran all the faster; then hiding himself, he would come up at full speed, and pass the horse with a bound, as if proud of his feat.

"You must take your risk then, poor dog, though I fear if Dad sees you, there will be but little mercy shown to you, Whig as you are."

CHAPTER IX.

THE DEPTHS OF SATAN.

"Do thou but threat, loud storms shall make reply,
And thunder echo to the trembling sky;
The drudging sun, from his old beaten way,
Shall at thy voice start, and misguide the day.
Heaven's gilded troops shall flutter here and there,
Mocking thy eldritch tones around the sphere."
COWLEY.

MUSING was new to this young man. He had sat for hours gazing into the fire, seeing droves of red deer and swarms of wildcats running over the hills, but his mind went no farther than the fire. His ideas were all gathered from the narrow bounds of his nativity. But here, on his horse, he sat in silence, while his thoughts, new fledged, were floating in an atmosphere of love. Suddenly waking up, he rode down hill at full speed, and in the twilight was, after the exciting events of the day, in a proper state of mind to become superstitious. Still, being now in great haste, he left the main road for a bridle path he knew well, and which led him through the bed of a spring stream that ran down to the flats below. The land lay high on both sides, and the little light at this hour was almost entirely shut out. On the side of one of these little hills was a deep pit, which tradition said had been dug by a crazy German, who had conceived the notion that some precious metal lay imbedded there. From the time of the discovery of the Hudson River, gold seekers had been all over these mountains, and wonderful tales were rife of silver mines being found when sinking wells and while hunting wolves. Some one had shown Heindrick

Van Guilder a shining stone that he pronounced gold, and this set him crazy that he might find out the bed where it came from. He bought the secret at a high price, and for months, alone, day and night, was he found dig, dig, digging still, in hopes of reaching the treasure. He had one answer to all that found him out. "What are you doing there, Heindrick?"

"Het köningrijk der hemelen or dis het my graf." He would either have the kingdom of heaven or a grave.

A grave he did find, for one day some hunters, following their dogs, came into this hollow, when, horrible to behold! there stood, in his pit, Heindrick, with his spade in hand, looking down into the ground. They called to him, but he gave no reply. After a while, one more daring than the rest ventured down, and found that the body was stiff and frozen. They laid him out as he was, covering him up with the earth he had thrown out himself. Ever after, superstition and natural fear combined to render this a haunted place. A slight shiver came over the young Boerman as he passed the place where the disappointed gold digger lay. It was said that groans and sighs had been heard coming out of the pit, as if some weary man were expressing his sorrow over something lost; and these would continue till they would be interrupted by shouts of contempt, as if the poor wretch were taunted by those who had themselves known what disappointed ambition was, and were now too eager to have a companion in their misery. When these reports were brought to the Dominie he generally smiled, whether in doubt or belief no one could guess, but when Bromie Van Guisen told him that he saw a terrible thing in the moonlight, that was the very shape of an ass, the good man could not restrain telling him he was frightened at his own shadow.

Teunis this evening passed the pit almost expecting to see something, at the close of a day in which he had seen so much already. Sure enough, voices fell upon his ears. At first he was determined to believe that they were in his imagination only, but his horse, pricking up his ears, proved to him that the animal, through her instinct, felt herself to be on devilish ground. What startled the young horseman still more, was the flight of Rover, who had retreated homeward with a speed which the man was just about imitating. As it was, he now was brought to a stand-still condition, and listening, he heard sounds not unfamiliar to his ears. It was the *tam-tam*—the African drum—which the negroes used in all their jollifications. Its being beaten at that time, though evidently under restraint and at intervals, intimated to the listener that something was going on in the nether regions.

"These are not spooks," said Teunis to himself, "that I need be afraid of. If they be entertaining old Heindrick Van Guilder, he has better company than the country believes. Let me find out these geestes."

With these reflections, he tied Sorrel to a tree and followed the sounds, which became more distinct at every step. Climbing up one of those steep ascents, found at the base of the mountain, about one hundred feet, and proceeding hastily in a southerly course, he saw lights shining from below on his left hand. On looking narrowly, he perceived that those lights and sounds came alike from a deep defile that was hidden by the trees and bushes, which grew thick on the sides, and spread their branches so as to meet across, making a dark, damp, though spacious apartment, far down from the place where Teunis stood. He remembered the place, having entered from below through a small, covered, natural entrance, where the fox and the bear found a refuge during the gloomy months of winter. It had in former times been a retreat for the Indians. Ashes, cinders, pipes and arrow heads were found here, together with their utensils for cooking fish. The mill, in which some ancient squaw had ground her corn to meal, had been dug out from one of the recesses in that rock, and stood as an ornament upon Garret Abiel's mantelshelf, left there, no doubt, as in a place of safety, till her return; but alas! the place that once knew her, now knows neither her nor her race any more.

Their cave was occupied at the time Teunis gazed down, by another race, whom the great Mohicans, in the days of Etau:o-quam, king of the rivers, would have despised. About sixty negroes of the jettest black, male and female, were assembled around a rough stone furnace, about three feet high, which looked like one of those ancient altars at Baal, seen in the pictures of old Dutch Bibles. On the top burned a bright fire, fed by pine cones, gathered near the place. The heat and smoke were diffused around; finding their way up to where Teunis lay, looking down upon the whole crew with curious amazement. They sat on their haunches in a circle round the fire; a man and a woman alternately, all naked to the waist. Their elbows rested on their knees, while they held out the palms of their hands, between their faces and the fire, as if to catch the heat and turn aside the blaze. In this posture they chanted some outlandish words, which were varied by a chorus, which came nearer to the squeaking of pigs than any sound the listener ever heard. When his eyes were set so as to distinguish objects and persons sufficiently plain, he perceived that the company were all known to him, belonging as they did to the families around. Most of them were direct from Africa—some brought hither when young, but there were ruling spirits among them who knew the difference between the country of their birth, with its customs, and the one in which they now lived. First and seemingly highest in the seat of honor was Cuffee, Abiel's chief man of all work. The Elder, on his way back from Jamaica, where he had been with horses and cattle, landed at New York, where he exchanged molasses and rum for a lively black fellow, who being able bodied, and sometimes too able minded for the Dutch boys of his own age, became quite an important personage in the Bught, far and near. He always maintained that he was the oldest son of an African king; and one of the favorite entertainments of the fireside on winter nights, was to get Cuffee to tell how he was kidnapped when he was on his bridal tour with Coomba. He would say:

"She was'm gran' sodger. Had great body guard ob young febels, like herselb; all very hebby and very lubby; hebby as massa's young steer, ebery one."

He made out a long story about breaking through a fence, for a sacrifice that Fetish must have, for getting him such a good wife; and how just when he had secured the finest young maiden of the village, the men of the place came behind them, seizing him and others, putting a bamboo girdle round him, to which they tied his hands down to his side, till he was put on board ship, and landed in King George's dominions at New York.

"Served you right," the young lads would say, to provoke him. "Good for you, Cuffy," the old vrows would cry, "to be brought here where the good Dominie would make a Christian of you, if you had not zeven duivels in tee; yaw, zeventig maal—zeven maal duivels."

"Juggue man for me," he would answer with haste; and sometimes with a stroke of paganism that startled his honest hearers. All the authority of his master could not make him enter the church door, nor bring him to sit patiently while the good pastor catechized the other members of the household.

The other actors in this hidden drama—or whatever else it was—did not yet appear, were Dora, and her son, a miserable hunchback of over twenty-five years of age, though only about four feet in height. His breast protruded far out, while his head sank down between his shoulders so that when he walked it seemed to rise regularly up and down, as if his spine struck, every step he took, upon a spring at the root, that sent it back with a force which kept the upper knob bob, bobbing, making his height vary about four inches at each step. Nor was this all, for his eyes and ears obeyed the downward and upward motion; almost meeting when he stretched, and rolling off when he crouched. The effect on the spectator was to keep him half way between terror and laughter, every time the strange figure moved. Along with these curious contortions, he had the unnatural power of ventriloquism, which his mother had found out early, and encouraged for her own purposes. He had a shrewdness that was remarkable; and most seen at the time he was left to himself, for then the use of all language seemed free. In his mother's presence he seemed but a part of herself, and understood every sign she gave, watching how he might carry out her designs. This arose from her constantly telling him that the Fetish god was in him; and so rare and singular was the power of double speech, that the whites around them hardly knew of it: and as to the blacks, they all regarded Unga Golah as the mouth of the Fetish, and Dora as the regular and true Priestess.

Teunis, however, was not altogether ignorant of these things. From daily intercourse with the blacks, and especially with the hunchback, who was nearly of his own age, he had discovered this hidden power of speaking double. Recently, however, he had observed that Dora had checked him, and that some strange notions had taken possession of her brain. He had found her at home, and also in the bush, training her oracle, by putting him through a kind of drilling in the African language; as he or she would respond to it in Dutch or English, or a gibberish of all three.

The influence which the black crone had over her ignorant associates was sufficient to turn her head, and her son's with her; and no one, knowing the barbarism from which they had emerged so recently, need wonder at the rites of superstition practised by them in secret, since the fear of a Great Supreme was not lessened by their translation hither, even when it was directed aright by instruction in the true faith.

What astonished Teunis was the actual earnestness of the whole band. Accustomed as he had always been to the loud and frivolous mirth of the blacks, he waited after their first song and their dance hand in hand round something that stood in the middle of the rough floor, with Dora and Unga Golah by it, to hear them break out in a confused Babylon of tongues, laughter, and shrieks; but no such noises followed. He was then convinced that something serious was going on. Surprise gave way to curiosity. He now remembered what had been talked of some time since concerning the witchcraft of Dora and Juggy—for by that name the hunchback was known all over the region—and how Cuffee was seen to plunge into the woods at certain times, said to be at the full moon, till at last suspicion was aroused, that conspiracy was going on among the slaves, when they were followed, and watched by David Abiel, who reported something like the very scene Teunis was now witnessing.

"Let me tell you," said the Elder to the Dominie, "that strange doings are going on below Face outer."

But the common sense pastor hooted at it, and smoked away at the other pipe.

The Elder, somewhat piqued, said: "Dominie, you don't mean that our David is a *luegnaar?*"

"Nay, nay, Elder, he is no liar, but he may tell very large truths. This cuppee of good Hollands would be good stuff were you to throw it into your water cask out there; but I vow, I would rather have the water by itself, and another cuppee—pure, though less of it."

"Well, Dominie, you are a wise man, but I believe that Cuffee is a red hieden en de tollenaar; and that Dora, for all you praise her and her kinderen, is niet else than a Tooverd."*

The Dominie laughed, saying: "Strange to find Cuffee a heathen and a publican, in an elder's family; and believe me that some other folks are more of the witch kind than Dora."

The truth was that Dora attended the kerke regularly, and was on the outside all Christian. Naturally apt and cunning, she had picked up many of the practices she saw, and used them, the better to blind the white folks and carry on her designs: though it would have been difficult to say what these were, beyond the self-gratification of having others afraid of her.

After chanting the song that Teunis first heard, the circle

* Witch.

widened for the dance. Half naked as they were, their bodies glittering with oil and vinegar, so that the gloss might remain, they stood out waiting for the sign which was given, when Juggy threw some mixture into the fire, that sent up a greenish blaze, like what salt and brimstone, when burned with alcohol, will produce. Teunis stood aghast when he beheld them all with their green eyes glancing, their white jaws chattering, and their limbs going like the legs of large toads in a putrid pond, when the sun is hot and the trees shady.

To heighten the effect of her power, Dora poured upon her hands some liquid, and proceeded to take up some coals of fire, tossing them unharmed from one hand to the other, and even putting out her tongue as if she could eat fire. Teunis knew of her tricks in this, but her followers shouted "gree, gree man," giving her sacred honors. This was the word by which the old witch had often frightened Teunis when he was a child, but this was the first time he had seen its meaning to be heathenish, and as connected with herself. He had once heard her, when in a rage, utter a mixture of words, which he supposed to be a pagan curse, when gree, gree, was the burden of the rhyme; and Tom, the Dominie's man, had often been heard to say, that Dora was a *gree gree* priestess in Guinea. These things were current, but witch was the highest title bestowed upon her among the whites.

The dance over, there was a long, rough box produced from a recess in the rocks, and laid down with great care. It was ornamented with different colored cloths, not unlike the quilts, or chair cushions, found in old houses of wealth, where the ladies have time to be ornamental as well as useful. On laying the chest down on the ground, there ran through the whole circle the sound, Fetish! fetish! Teunis knew this word well from hearing Dora repeat it in her prayer, in the same breath with Heeren, Goden, Fetish; which he supposed was but the African word for God. He now found the true meaning. This must be some kind of an idol; and she was the acting priestess. Uncovering the box, she moved round it in a beckoning gait, snapping her fingers, which was the signal for the whole company to follow with the same movement, and the same sound.

After this, all stood still, when the voice of Dora was heard calling out Unga Golah; and the deformed imp came forward, crawling on his hands and knees, close up to the box, asking in a loud whisper, at the opening in the end of the box, in the African tongue:

"Who shall be king of the colored regiment?"

When an answer came as if out of the inside, loud enough to be heard through the cave:

"Who should be captain but de King of Dahomey and de Prince of Bungalore?"

Cuffee gave a start, so well feigned that it was considered real, and as no one but the initiated understood the trick, and these did not exceed three persons present, it was no wonder that all ran back in fear, when Dora opened the box, and out sprung a rattlesnake, with its fiery tongue protruded from its mouth. More horror still seized them, when the hunchback, without the least hesitation, lifted the reptile in his hands, twisting him round his short neck, with the open jaws of the snake before his face, so that the mouth of the human monster was ready to speak in question or reply. Walking back into the furthest recess of the cave, he stepped upon a shelf in the rock, when he put his lips out, and his head at the highest, and calling in a loud voice:

"Who be captain of de black regiment for de great King George?"

"Mongee Cuffee, prince of Dahomey." This answer was in an entirely different voice; and to those who saw the ugly snake, how it writhed and turned, putting out its tongue fiercely, and many times, the reply evidently came from it; for Juggy had covered his own mouth so that his lips never moved. Besides, the voice was neither that of man nor woman, but a sound which any superstitious mind would interpret as a fiend's answer.

Teunis began to see through this trick and its object, and was curious to ascertain, from actual observation, how far Cuffee's mind accorded with the hint given. It was evident that all eyes were fixed on him, expecting some demonstration, when he rose, bowing himself all the way up to the place where the snake and his master stood, and asked:

"Vat vill de Fetish hab de King of Dahomey do first?"

"Gib de big Elder 'Biel into de han's ob de great Ingen dis night."

What deceived even Teunis so far was the number of times this was repeated. It seemed as if it came out of the rocks, behind and from above, again and again, ten times over, assuring him that, well as he knew the cunning dwarf, there was something more in the power he possessed than a mere double voice. Nor did he fully understand it till afterward, going into the same recess, he spoke a few words, which were echoed and reëchoed so often, that he became startled lest he had wakened up the African *gree gree* of his childish days. By repeating, the secret was revealed, and certainly it was well fitted for the cell of a necromancer; more especially for such a one as Juggy, with his double voice.

As the play went on, between the hunchback and the snake, Cuffee assumed more boldness, becoming desirous of having his future fortune told.

"Fetish say dat Cuffee vill be big capden en king's black army, dat is to be. Wat coat sall Cuffee wear?"

"Red like de coal, and de color of de blood, when de pigs squeal. De coat sall glitter all de over wid silver, like de plum-tree in de spring, when de birds sing small abobe de windows."

The great stout fellow stood out at full length, well satisfied that his time was come to act; and so turning to the rest, who were looking with perfect admiration, he addressed them in what he intended should be a moving speech.

"Colord bruders of de good Guinea blood, dat has run like de Cauterskill Creek, through three generations. Bruders, you'd 'members de day when de sun rose before you, and set when you'd put out de finger at him, till he would get blood in de face. No whip den make Cuffee jumb; no ox waitin' for him chewing his cud; no milk den, but to drink it all. All de earth beautiful as missis' gownde when she go out to drink tea; and de trees sparkling like de butt'ns on massa's Sunday coat. De dolphins sport in de water like de calves when de cow-bell tinkles in de woods, and Cuffee lying on de ground, make believe in de sleep and dream.

"All dat seek dese fine tings, meet Cuffee at Phœbe Hotel, where de bounty will be paid down in bright dollars, out of de big chest dat lies in de back room, under de ole man's bed, when de key is put into dis place by de big Indian, at twelve in de middle of de night."

The secret was out—Teunis saw through the whole. The Tories were at the bottom of a devilish plot, stirring up these blacks to massacre their masters, and the reward was to be the spoils. This cunning dog, remembering former times, and having his vanity fed, was ready to do whatever came to his hand. He had influence with others, and what he lacked Dora made up. Laws had been passed against negroes meeting by themselves, and many alarms had been raised in Teunis' time. He had heard of a great conspiracy during the French war, when hundreds ran off to Canada; and doubtless here was something of the same kind. These ignorant creatures were as likely to kill on the one side as on the other. The mind of Teunis was made up to frustrate this bloody attempt, and by the way of beginning the counter plot, he resolved to disturb the horrid assemblage at this present time.

As he was casting this about in his mind, Dora was preparing some new cantrap, and had cast fresh fuel with some sickening stuff into the fire, which rose up to the place where Teunis lay, making him sneeze so loud that it must have been heard, only that they were all sneezing themselves in chorus. When they became quiet, Cuffee was questioning the dwarf more minutely concerning his future prospects; and was dancing in perfect rapture at the thought of having gold lace at his shoulders, and a cocked hat on his head, with a red and white feather. The answer to all his demands came from the alcove at the far end of the cave, where the box with the mysterious snake had been carefully deposited. So perfect were the sounds, that a stranger could not help being imposed upon. The attention of the whole company was thus purposely diverted away from the doings of Dora, who was engaged looking down to the ground, at a place where Teunis remembered there was a clear spring. When ready, she called upon Cuffee, and bade him look, and ask whatever he pleased. He obeyed, when a voice came up out of the water, that made him start back with amazement. She called up another of the company, but prompted him to the question, which obtained the answer that the hunchback always gave as out of the spring. Two of these will give the general drift.

Up stepped a merry-looking fellow called Jerry; and as he bent over the pure water hole that glittered in the torch light, he called out:

"What sall Juggy make Jerry in de great army?"

"Jerry shall have de care of all de rum in de cellar of de King George; and of de pie and olecakes for gibing to oders."

Nothing could please this worthy better than this, as he showed by the width of his mouth when he rose.

Here an old grey-headed, merry-looking, man knelt down, asking in a laughing tone:

"Shall Cæse hab a place in de gran' army? Moder Dora, bid Fetish speak."

The answer came up: "Memby Cæsar play 'pon de sackbut and harp, de psaltery and de organ of King Solomon."

Cæsar came away grumbling to himself, "Noting said 'bout de good fiddle and de bow."

True to their Ethiopian nature, their blood began to circulate freely, and their bodies became restless for motion; Dora, to indulge them, brought them together in a ring, which ran around her and the dwarf in rapid motion. His head rose and fell as that of a turtle, when excited by some mischievous boy. Voices were heard all around encouraging the mirth, as if coming from the invisible world. A stroke of humor came across the mind of Teunis at this instant, and in that vein, following out his resolution of breaking up the assemblage, he took his powder-horn, which had been filled fresh that morning, and making an opening with his knife into the gin-flask, that he intended to have left with Elsie, but which was still nearly full, and putting the horn into the gin, he prepared to set fire to the liquor; but how was that to effect anything at the height he stood above them? A lucky thought entered his head; his stocking was worked with worsted of the strong, firm kind, more like hempen string than soft lamb's wool; the unravelling of one of these from the top was but the work of a few minutes, and with the yarn he lowered his vessel, now on fire, over the brink of the precipice. It soon attracted the eyes of the revellers below by its bright blue flame. With the exception of Dora, all regarded the new luminary as a part of the ceremony, and waited with open mouth, nose, and eyes for the next act. Not so the prime mover, who became alarmed lest her own tricks had called down the wrath of a greater than Fetish; and giving a scream, too natural not to be felt as genuine fear, all were ready to join in the chorus, when the fire reached the powder just when the flask touched the rock, on which the mysterious box stood, and the explosion came, calling forth echo and reëcho from the inner chambers of the den, till it seemed as if they would never cease. The shricking and yelling of sixty frightened wretches were not so easily set at rest. Taking their cue from their priestess, they ran, she following, or rather leading them toward the narrow entrance, where they leaped over each other like cattle crowding a gateway.

Teunis, in telling the Dominie afterward of the occurrence,

said that the most amazing thing of the whole to him was the terror of Dora, after what he heard her say, and when he saw the boldness of her actions.

"You needed not that case to explain to you what you have often heard me say, that the wicked run when no man pursueth; and then see how the witch of Endor was more afraid than any of the company, when she saw the doings of the Lord. But tell us," the Dominie asked, "how that imp of Sathanas behaved? I mean Juggy the Hunchback."

"He seemed the only self-possessed mortal of them all. He danced and leaped frantically, till he spied, after the smoke passed away, that the sacred chest was shattered into a thousand pieces, when he immediately, and in haste, crawled on his hands and knees around the spot, calling out "Groote draak—great dragon—aude slang, old serpent, Duivel en Satanas, Fetish-gree-gree;" all in Dutch, English, and African mixed up, till at last, finding what he wanted, the snake, he held it in his hands, uttering some gibberish which he intended for a lamentation. Finding that life was gone, and that there was nothing in the dead worm either for his fear or his love, he threw it on the ground, stamping on it with a revengeful look and loud curses, ending the tragedy with a fiendish laugh, which I, out of mischief, returned in the same tone. It was now that the imp showed signs of fear; for knowing within himself that this was not his own double, he fled as fast as his shuffling feet would allow him, throwing, as he passed the fire, a handful of the stuff into it which had caused the green flame and the pungent smell which had made us all sneeze. I left the mouth of the pit saying, I believe this is the devil's snuff, and a proper place it is to expect to get it, for that is nothing else than the bottomless pit."

CHAPTER X.

THE PERILS OF A PILGRIMAGE.

"Let not a torrent of impetuous zeal
Transport thee thus beyond the bounds of reason;
True fortitude is seen in great exploits
That justice warrants, and that wisdom guides;
All else is towering frenzy and distraction."

ADDISON'S *Cato.*

THE young Dutchman reached home that evening tired, and full of a thousand reflections all new to him, and he had already laid down a scheme for the next day, which, like many such plans, was to be upset before he fell asleep.

He found the main room of the house filled with men, and all sitting in dense darkness. It was a secret conclave, such as Teunis had witnessed before, when some event of moment was expected. The men spoke in whispers, and had by this time nearly finished their discussion, and were about to take action. It appeared, from gathered conversation afterward, that the subject was of an offensive and also of a defensive character. The Dominie, who was of a determined and hot temper in political things, took strong side against the Tories, no matter whether they were of the active or of the passive kind. He had of late forced some of his people to show their hands, and had threatened to bring them all out. To obtain ecclesiastical authority, and to bring the recusants and the lukewarm to their senses, was the object of a journey he had taken that very day to Sopus, where he was to meet his brother Dominies in their classis. To get the start of the reverend man, and prevent his severe discipline on his return, which they of the king's party were sure to receive in its utmost severity, was the intention of the present gathering. They had, after many a whiff and jabber, fixed upon their plan, and were waiting for volunteers who would carry it into execution. As none but the old men were admitted into the counsel, it was difficult to see how their meeting could result in anything practically beneficial. The seizing of the Dominie himself, along with the whole consistory, was a bold stroke for a few dull-headed men. But nothing short of this was their aim, and for this very purpose Brandt was called east after his raid upon Wyoming. His scouts had given warning of his approach, so that "now or never" was the word. The chance was opportune, and yet there was a hesitation with some on conscientious grounds, and with others on superstition. There was a fear that the scheme would fall through for want of young men. The leader in their counsel saw the deficiency, and regretting it, had, with adroitness, brought in a fresh supply of the genuine Virginia tobacco, lighting his own pipe first, so that the nostrils of the company were soon regaled and demanded another pipe. It was while they smoked this, slowly, that several young men came in who had been sent for intentionally. Teunis entered along with them, as of right.

"Tee zal never get me nor myne sonne at trappin de Dominie, like as we do de great bieren in de pig-pen. He is de servant of de Lord for gooden."

"There now," said Tim Samp, "Dick is giving us the Scripture about magistrates. Let us have it all through, and then we shall have the very authority we want. Let every soul be subject to the higher"——

"No more of dat, Tim; hev no I been in de consistory two yearen, ende vas no de Dominie above us alle? ende vas no I higher dan de justice?"

"But, Dick, we are all King George's men, and we are sworn to serve him before saving the Dominie, though his neck should stretch for it. He will not save ours. My mind is, send him and his consistory off to Niagara by Brandt, where they will learn him manners to the king, and cool his hot blood in that big water."

"Our Dominie serven de Heere ov heeven, ende nae man may putten his hand upon his skin buldt en dey touchen mynne, sure as my name is Dick Burget."

This unexpected explosion, in one supposed to be completely on the true side, was received in silence, and was likely to break up the whole scheme unless some way could be made for getting old Dick removed aside till the whole was acted out, which would be in a few days. Amidst the thick smoke little knots were consulting, with their heads turned in to one another like sheep in a hot day under a tree, concerning the best method of disposing of this new difficulty, when the matter was resumed by Dick Burget again, who was willing to sacrifice every one of the consistory but the Dominie. In this he found an ally in a neighbor whose terrors were more from the influence of priestly power than enlightened piety.

"I am wid Dick," said Conrad Post; "for de man wid dat tree-nooked hat can bring de tunder ande fire down on us."

"Yaw, yaw, Conrad," put in Dick; "here again de Scripture zays, 'op wien hij valt, dien zal hij vermorzelen.'" *

"Away with your nonsense," said the man at the head of this movement, who was losing all patience; "do you think that if the Dominie were a stone, he could fall on you and grind you to powder? He would prefer blowing you up. I have a plan that will settle all trouble. Let us send Teunis Roe here off to Sopus, and hear how the Dominie speaks in the Classis about the discipline; and if his tone be peace and moderation, I am for saving his black coat, and will stand by Dick here to the last. What say you?"

To this all agreed at once, and before Teunis had time to object, he was inducted into the office of messenger or spy, as friends or enemies might judge of him and of his actions. With true Dutch caution, the young man went to bed confused in mind, yet feeling that the sun-light would enable him to determine his proper course, for as yet he still ranked with the men who were signalling to Brandt.

In the morning, before sunrise, his father was at his door, rousing him and warning him of his ride. The young man himself felt the responsibility of the office imposed upon him, and in the wavering state of his mind, felt anything but at ease in the prospect of acting a double part. He lay a few moments reflecting on how he should act, when he remembered that Elsie whispered in his ear at parting: "Be sure and tell the Dominie of the first signs of danger." Her warm breath seemed yet to blow on his cheek, as he leaped from his couch, saying, "and now Providence has put that in my power."

When he descended from the chamber, he found that Dora had his breakfast laid out for him, to which she had added her choicest dishes. Evidently well pleased with something, her elfish son was receiving tit-bits aside at the jambs where he sat, swelling up and down as his chest fell or expanded. Teunis, remembering the scene of last evening, eyed them askance, wondering in himself whether they were witches enough to know the cause of their late dispersion. They gave no sign, so he concluded to watch the current of events.

* "Upon whomsoever it shall fall it shall grind him to powder."

His horse was ready for him at the leaping-on-log, held by his father, who stood beside a stranger, whose voice Teunis recognized to be the same as led the discussion of the previous evening.

"You are sent, young man, on this duty because you can be trusted. All the instructions you require are to keep yourself as much hidden from Dominie Schuneman as you can, and bring a true report of his sayings back with you. Your reward is a captaincy in his majesty's service: a prosperous journey."

The sun had but streaked the hills of Connecticut, and the horseman, gathering up his bridle, was fixing himself firmly in the saddle, when his mother's voice called him to a corner, where she stood weeping. From her yesterday's warning, he comprehended the nature of her fears; and anticipating her, bent down his head, while she kissed him and blessed him, and he rode away through the dim woods. Near to him he heard a voice that spoke in the English tongue, in answer to one on the opposite side of the road, in Dutch. He slackened his pace to listen. Smiling, he soon discovered that Unga was attempting a trick upon him, which did not succeed. Fairly on his way, his good steed soon carried him into old Sopus, where after stabling him, Teunis went straight to the court-house door, where a crowd of people was assembled.

Determined to take no active part in anything, Teunis went among the men with eyes and ears open. They were of the class to which he himself belonged, and notwithstanding that Sopus was so near to Kaaterskill Vlatts, there were but few whom he knew intimately, and these were the kind who possessed the pass-words and signs with which he was well acquainted. From even these, however, he was resolved to keep away at present.

A debate was in progress to which the new comer gave heed—the peculiar merits of several Dominies. It was Myer and Doll of Ulster against New York and Jersey, and the world to boot—old Jacobus Elting, of Vlattbush, on the one side, and on the other a large broad Albanian, full wigged, dressed in smooth brown coat, who was boasting over Doctor Dominie Westerloo, the chief of their Sanhedrim.

"No doubt of it," was the slow retort of the other, "after the new fangled notions of the day; but the man that tells his own consistory that their hearts are no whiter than their own niggers, would not be heard here in Sopus. You must be mean dwaazan * to stand that; and then his advice to throw off all allegiance to the old mother of Amsterdam."

"There now, you have set your tongue a-going, and we will have the question of the day discussed before we go in doors. Leave politics to the Provincial Congress, and let the doctrines of the Kerke be attended to, so that all be according to the canons." This was spoken by a square-built man, of sedate appearance, whose presence was impressive, and well placed. He continued to say that "the rational and calm declaration of the altar, whence come the high obligations of practical righteousness, are more acceptable to the Maker than all the zeal and talk we have sometimes about things which human nature cannot stand."

"A wee! A wee!" said another, "to hear such things said by men in the consistory—human nature never can stand to hear the truth against itself."

"Never mind," said Elder Van Vleck, "after these troubles are past, all these things are to be settled by the Dominies themselves. Let us help them through with their quarrel this day, and we will let the next day take care of itself. There comes Colonel Haasbrouk and an eastern stranger with him, if I may judge from his dress."

"Yes, judging from his dress; but when did a Connecticut man step like that, and keep his head so firm on his shoulders? As I live," said Jan Freer, he is as like the man that I took up to Van Lueguens as any man I have seen since, and I have had my eyes open all the time."

"Nonsense, Jan, the man coming is dressed in the colors of the Connecticut Rangers, and has a commission, as you may see from his buttons. There he is now handing his credentials to the colonel."

"If I hear him speak I can tell; and it would be a good test to put him to, just to ask him to count over fifteen and saxpence; the dearest money ever I earned, since it cost me four weeks in the common jail of Sopus, for helping a spy. The more I look at him the surer I am. There he comes, and good Santa Claus, I shall watch him this day."

By this time, the two new comers had arrived within earshot, and were engaged in earnest conversation, which was held loud enough for all to hear.

"I will tell you this, Captain Whittesley, that our minister, or Dominie, as we entitle him, is one of the best of men, and the bravest of soldiers."

* Fool.

"Colonel, in these days the qualities you give him are possessed also by our parsons in New England, but it seems to me that the learning needed in their holy calling cannot be ripe." This was evidently said more for the purpose of keeping up the discourse, than out of any wish for an opinion; for all the time he either listened or spoke himself, he was glancing his sharp blue eye in all directions.

"I can only speak for our Dominie Doll, that he has been a most faithful student in ancient universities, and that he never fails to speak like a Boanerges. Lively in his spirits, he is ever on the stretch for new fields of action; and now that the wave of war has reached its height, he rides on it as if it were his native element."

"And I suppose," said the captain, "like priest, like people."

Here Colonel Haasbrouk introduced his acquaintance by name, and as one of the aids of his Excellency, here on public business.

The discourse took a new turn. The stranger, who was one of those easy moving men, who can turn the most trifling matter into food for discourse, soon led off by referring to the gatherings he had seen of the militia on his way, and of the excellent appearance they made.

"Yes," said our Albany friend, "they are good enough for such a place as Sopus, or for such a county as Ulster, but they cannot compare with our men, nor with your men in the east."

This brought, as it it was intended, a rejoinder from one of the Soposonians, who declared himself ready with "a company of Ulster men to do what the Bunker Hill men did not do—keep the hill from the redcoats."

"Oh, yes," said the bantering Albanian, "they have hard heads, but soft places in them, that a ramrod would pass through without touching a letter of the alphabet."

The Ulster member, somewhat piqued, pulled out a roll on which were inscribed the names of a whole company, signed by themselves, and handing it to the man called Captain Whittesley, asked him to say if "that was the sign of ignorance."

"I declare," said the stranger, "this is all in good writing of hand and few proxies. You must draw back your insinuation, friend, and it is well. Their courage will be tried if I am not mistaken. These granaries placed here, in case Schuyler should be forced to fall back to Watervliet, must be greatly needed."

While the stranger said this, he looked full in the face of Jan Freer, so piercingly that that worthy's tongue failed him as he was about to ask him if he was not the man who sailed up to Saugerties with him in the middle of the night, three months since. But by the time the courage of Jan had returned, the conversation had taken an interesting turn.

"Do you apprehend," said Colonel Haasbrouk, "that the enemy may pay us a visit on his way up; I find on my dispatches, *haste*."

"There are many rumors abroad," was the reply, given too loosely for an orderly, "that the enemy has several points of attack in his mind. The chief object is to form a junction with the north; but General Vaughan is one of those soldiers who love to take responsibility, and may be tempted out of his way form the mere love of adventure. A little sport with him is a great thing; and as the Provincial Congress now sitting here would afford him such an opportunity, it seems unlikely that he could resist the jest. Do you suppose that your Congress would sit on were he to land his men and a couple of guns?"

"What if he does see them running off? My men will be found here at their post," said the colonel; "and we hope to do our duty as good citizens and soldiers. The country will be here, though Van Cortlandt and his congress do run, which I am sure they never will."

"Nor will the Classis run," said an old man in a clay-colored coat, which had seen some wear and tear, but was still becoming to the wearer. "The Dominies will be put to their trumps, and I will venture my word for at least one-half of them. Dominie Doll at the head of the good and true, and there is Dominies Dirck and Schuneman, of the Kaatskills."

"How does it happen, my good sir, that you have two congresses sitting in this old town of yours—an ecclesiastical and a political? Surely you have not thought on uniting church and state, as in the old time?" The New Englander sneered a little as he said these words, as if he meant to say: "You are behind the age."

"We Hollanders," said Haasbrouk, "have skulls that are not so easily penetrated as a pumpkin"—here the colonel cast a side glance at his guest—"and consequently we neither give up our cherished notions so readily, nor receive new ones so easily, as you eastern folks can."

"Ha! ha! excellent, my dear sir; the inference you draw

then is, that our Yankee heads are soft. Ha! ha! That is good. We are even. But tell me what is all this commotion among your clergy? In every tavern and farmer's kitchen I could hear of nothing but the coetus and conferentia. Greek to me, indeed. Are these the passwords of a secret society?"

"The words have a meaning to the men who use them, but, so far as I know, they who make the most use of them are neither better men nor better soldiers. A meaningless jargon. I pray the Lord to send us a real enemy, so that our pastors may become united about something. If Vaughan does nothing else, he may do that, and to some purpose. I see that my words are giving offence to my friend here."

Things were taking too warm a turn, when the stranger adroitly proposed judging for himself by the assemblies called together. He did this with so much grace and dignity that he won the favorable opinion of all except the cautious and the experienced in men and things. It was evident that Jan Freer had not laid aside his suspicions; and notwithstanding that Colonel Haasbrouk had carefully perused his commission, a lurking doubt still lingered in his mind every time he looked at the stranger's face and heard his voice.

Strange as it may sound, our young friend, Teunis Roe, was one of the few who suspected the pretensions of the man called Whittesley; standing back in the crowd, he had time to observe all his motions and listen to his voice, and though the Kaatsberg youth had not exchanged a word with any one there, he felt sure that he had seen this man before in a different character than he now assumed. His acquaintance with the underworkings of society gave him opportunities of seeing much that durst not be spoken on the housetops. The man became a new object of interest to him, and for the moment he almost forgot the errand which had brought him hither.

To that he was soon recalled by one of the venerable men who was there offering his services to the stranger as his guide into the church where the reverend pastors were to meet, having adjourned since the last evening for the purpose of discussing the very point that Teunis was sent to hear and report upon.

The feeling of suspicion, which was awakened in the minds of a few at the first, fell upon a larger number by degrees, until it spread among the more intelligent, so that by the time the Classis met for business there were no lack of watchers upon the stranger's steps. His movements were not the least impeded by those nods and winks which were interchanged by the company, but they rather seemed to give him dignity of look and a defiance of danger which held every one in check. As his eye ran over the faces of the crowd, it fixed a moment longer on Teunis than he was able to bear comfortably. It was evident that, whoever he was, he recognized in the Kaatskillian's countenance something of an interesting nature to him, which he would have inquired after in another and quieter place.

At this time the signal for meeting was given, and, wending toward the temple of God, were seen the venerable men, whose life was one of self-denial and of honor. Their steadfast look and stately steppings impressed the spectators with awe, making even the frivolous Jan Freer to speak under his breath as they went past.

"Now, Captain Whittesley," said Elder Swart, under whose care the stranger had been put, "let us go, since you wish to compare our Dominies with yours in the east. They say that you are greatly indebted to them for that spirit which the Yankees show in the good cause."

"It is true, sir, that I have heard many a rousing discourse from them upon the rights of man, and the obligations of kings being nursing fathers to the church instead of dashing her children against the stones; but a coward may be in a black coat as well as a blue."

"And a hero in bands as well as wearing a sash at his side," was Swart's quick retort, which brought the blood slightly to the cheek of the New Englander, who parried the thrust gracefully by saying: "It requires all the manly qualities of our common nature to gain the crown of honor or the crown of glory."

The assemblage soon dispersed, and as the form of the last Dominie in the procession disappeared within the church, Teunis determined to hear and see all he could; but his first object was to obtain a private interview with Dominie Schuneman, and fulfill his promise of warning.

Colonel Haasbrouk called an officer to him, when he saw no one watching near, and said in a low voice: "See that you follow that new comer everywhere through the whole day, and into every place. See that he leaves not till he has my pass."

"Colonel," said the astonished officer, "he holds a permit

from head-quarters, and how could that have been obtained unless he be true and on the right side?"

"It matters not," said the colonel; "if he has not worn a red coat in the regulars, I never saw a man step so like one in my life. Had he said, I am a deserter and on your side, I could have believed him sooner than his mimicking the Yankee."

CHAPTER XI.

SAMSON CARRYING OFF THE GATES OF GAZA.

"When gospel trumpeter, surrounded
With long eared rout, to battle sounded,
And pulpit, drum ecclesiastic,
Was beat with fist instead of *a* stick,
Then sir knight abandoned dwelling,
And out he rode a colonelling."

HUDIBRAS.

THE Elder Swart was a grave man, of homely presence, but of more common sense than first appearances indicated. He would remain so silent and dull, when hearing an important subject, at times, that it was doubted whether he understood any of the questions. An hour afterward his acquaintances, from his remarks, were surprised at the queries he put. He was a profound admirer of the Reformed Church of Holland. His body expanded largely as he entered the porch of the holy building with his new friend, looking first with reverence on the men, who had already begun their business by an act of devotion, and then on Whittesley, endeavoring to guess the effect which such a sight might have on one of the wise men of the east. That singular man looked on all without any apparent surprise; indeed, it seemed to Swart that the Dominies, on looking toward the pew where he sat, were under some kind of fascination, as they looked more astonished than their new visitor. Teunis, who had taken a seat in the next square pew to the Elder, sat with his back against the captain's, so that he could both see and hear to great advantage when he chose to look in that direction, or listen to their words.

The Classis, constituted as it was of clergymen and their elders, who were laymen of note, sat by a huge oak table, which served as altar, on which now lay a pile of papers, under the care of a secretary. Above him, on a raised seat, was the president, robed in full clerical dress, with cloak and bands. Beside him stood a large gold-headed cane and a three-cornered hat, somewhat the worse for wear. He was a man of about sixty-five years, with a keen black eye, that moved in his head—which scarcely ever turned—as if a set of spring nerves were secretly kept in use, now that they seemed needed for watchfulness over the company under him. The others were less prominent till they spoke, when they stood as high up in their boots, and some of them seemed to take pride in looking as keen as their leader. One of them, on his feet, took occasion simply to remind his reverence in the chair, that "we are all brethren." "Go on and speak to the question," was the grave rejoinder.

The Elder and the New Englander sat down in a high, square pew, which was sufficiently capacious to have held a Dutch vrow and ten daughters, all Dutch built. It was covered over with maroon cloth, and studded round with brass-headed nails, which gave it quite a golden appearance. The Plattekill man whispered, This is Captain Conrad Elvendorp's pew—one of the new fangled race rising up in Sopus.

Whittesley's attention was directly turned to the business in hand, which was evidently of an exciting character. The speaker who was holding forth, was a tall, thin, pale man, of a soft voice, which went far into the ear, with a nervous power which made it tell upon the feelings more than on the conviction. He spoke in deep tones, which proved his earnestness, and was more for moderation than for extreme measures. "That's the good Dominie Direk Romeyn, now on his feet," whispered the Elder Swart. "He is always for peace, and so far does he carry his wish, that he would sacrifice the state for the church any day; but his heart is always as clear as his tongue is smooth, and every one loves him. I wish that Dominie Schuneman and he were carded through one another, then we would have a perfect Dominie, and a complete Whig. When the captain had got his ear clear of the Elder's mouth, he heard the voice of the speaker, though so soft that it filled the house, rising into warmth, and sparkling with energy, so that even his opponents were listening to the easy flow with a restrained delight.

"In these days of trial," said the reverend speaker, "it becometh the servants of the Lord to throw oil upon the troubled water, instead of raising the tempest to hellish fury. This poor Reformed Church is at this hour like the Ark of Noah, high on the waters of the deluge; and but for the strong arm of the great pilot, who seems to be asleep in the stern, we might despair; but we have a duty to perform as the ministers of Christ, and not as captains of companies, going forth with spear and buckler to fight in the open field. We have Joshuas in great number; let us give ourselves to prayer and the word, standing like Moses with our hands lifted to heaven, and these Aarons and Hurs will help us, if we only keep our own passions in due control, being baptized by the anointing which abideth. Oh! my soul is melted into grief when I think of how some of my fellow-ambassadors have fallen off, who were ordained to this good work by the laying on of hands by the venerable fathers of that ancient mother in Holland, whom we all love and revere. Alas! alas! that the day should have arrived, foretold by the prophet: 'I am like a pelican in the wilderness.' She who has fed her young ones here with her own blood, drawn from her own breast, is now to be disregarded and thrust forever aside. Do we not see but too plainly, that these unhappy troubles are fast rending asunder the ties which bind us to the mother church. Under the thin veil of patriotism there lieth too manifestly the canker of licentiousness; and to the pleasant cry of independence in the state, there is added the demand to bind and loose, after our own skill, and by our own power. My voice is—'let the potsherds of the earth strive with the potsherds thereof; but woe be to the man that striveth with his Maker.'"

The speaker sat down in great emotion, hiding his face in his hands and literally sobbing aloud. The effect was visible upon all the tender-hearted; and in other times than those, when tears were of small account, the eloquence of that man would have carried the day. But like the few drops which fall just before the wind changes from south to north, these pathetic symptoms were the turning of public sentiment on that day.

"They have been talking all of yesterday," said Elder Sickles, who came into the same pew, "but they are now beginning to warm up, and we shall soon see the lightning, and hear the loud thunder, after that shower of rain, with a few hailstones. For Dominie Frelinghuisen can hit hard though his words melt as soon as they come down to the ground."

"Yaw! he reminds me of Stephen Zabriskie, that would

cut his nigger, Cruse, till he would bring the blood, and then he would cry at the effects of his own whip-cord. But there rises Dominie Dirck Romeyn of Mombachus. Hear him, but first look at him. How like he is to our dog Tiger, when he smells a fox, ready to spring before he has quite measured his distance."

The eyes of the whole company were directed to this person, who stood up tall, but so eager to begin, that he stooped forward like a racer that has already started. His face was neither pale nor bilious, but seemed like one that had just risen from his bed on an errand, which he deemed of vital importance to the cause he had at heart. His hair was cut short to his head, and his dress, though snug, was put on after a fashion of his own. He seemed nervous, but determined; and but for a nose of great length, through which he blew off passion, as an eager horse blows when restrained for a few moments, he must have fainted before he commenced.

"Let me," were his first words, "throw a bomb-shell into the enemy's camp. We have covered up the truth too long, and I am for tearing off the cover at once. Speak of peace and quiet at this moment, when King George and his bull-dogs are at our gates. Do you not hear them bark now, and their teeth of iron which have crunched the skulls of men, women and children, gaping wide that our flesh may be torn? And what do we see but strong men of God covered with the panoply of heaven, crying like children for their dear absent mother over the sea, under the name of Peace. No! my voice is now for war, and the resolution before us, which we are asked to pass in favor of hot defence, and if need be, of hot pursuit, even unto death, is one that I shall require my consistory to pass as one man, else we part next day. It is the only way to wean us from our mother's breast, that we be required as a Church, to do what our country has done; live without all help, advice, authority or counsel from Europe. Let those who have been born on that famous continent, or those who have drank of the milk of Leyden, still snifter after the pap of a Holland cow; for my part I believe that the meadows of this new world yield as good fodder as the bogs of those low countries. I despise all whining when we should be fighting, with the sword bathed in heaven, where it can only obtain the temper fit for slaying the foes of liberty and of religion. Let me warn my brethren who vacillate on this good cause, under the professed appearance of keeping the peace, that the people are before them;

and let them neglect the opportunity now given of putting their names to this patriotic resolution, and another chance will not be afforded. Like the ancient Sibyl bringing her books, the chances of obtaining them decrease, and thus enhance their value."

The speaker went on in this strain for a full hour, pouring forth a torrent of eloquence, which made the coldest-hearted rise to a pitch of enthusiasm which it would have been dangerous to have impeded, or even turned aside, without using the greatest wisdom and power. When he sat down, every one thought the question settled; but the president, whose strange black eyes had been wandering at the beginning of the last speech, became so fixed toward its close, that it seemed to all as if two coals of fire were glowing to a red heat, and that some secret bellows blew the fire into an intense ardor, so that it became impossible to gaze upon them. Quietly he gave a secret sign to some one to come up to him, when he moved out of the chair, which was occupied by a substitute of less dimensions, but of equally solemn gravity.

"Now we shall have the other side. A sound man is Dominie Rysdick, but behind the times. He would have this big continent bound by his cable to a Dutch scow."

"None of your sly hits, Hanchie Sickles. You would send the world round like a teetotum, and banish every good and wholesome doctrine for the newest thing, if you only heard it in the English tongue; but I should like to know if you ever heard a good Dutch prayer answered in another speech than Dutch."

"Oh, yes!" said the young Elder Sickles, "and I have seen a Dutch water-finder get a spring with English hazel; and I have seen a cut made with an English knife healed by keeping it warm behind a Dutchman's fire-place; and a lame horse cured by whispering 'Indian' in his ear; and old Anikja on the hill can speak a burn away."

All of this was said with a cunning look, and so sedately that the Plaattekill Elder Swart did not at first take the drift of it; and before he had gathered up the sense, Dominie Rysdick had begun, in a slow, swinging way, with his eyes half shut, and his back half turned to the audience, as if entirely unconscious of any one being present. He was like a man speaking in his sleep; or perhaps more like one that talks into the next world, and feels quite sure that he will be heard by those who can understand and appreciate what he says. When our friends in the square pew had time to listen, they heard the slow, hesitating voice of the speaker, like the rough rumbling of a stream when it is diverted from its course into a mill race, as if nature angrily resisted the hand of man.

"I am forced to rise out of my seat, where I supposed I might take my rest till this question of years had been disposed of; but it seems that we are on the verge of destruction: there are men who will play with the whirlwind. A few winters since, a reverend divine, now present, went up the mountain there on a journey of curiosity. He was not satisfied with taking the plain road, but he must strike out a path of his own; and though he went as fast as any sober man should travel, he put himself in the eye of the wind, so that he might have the pride of saying that he rode upon a whirlwind—that he took it by the forelock. Alas for human vanity! he was swept from his feet, and obliged to lie prone on the cold ground, or take the chance of tumbling over the precipices headlong, as some would now fall."

With this quiet hint, and telling hit, at the rashness of those who are not satisfied with taking the natural road to their end, he was seemingly about to take his seat again, but the current of his thoughts, like the stream, had now got into the mill flume, and onward it began to run. He had made a sensible hit at some of the rash men who were clear for riding on a fiery steed of war; and while his secret design might be to prevent giving aid to the friends of the country, his course showed a wish of keeping a passage behind through which he might retreat in case of the strongest being the conqueror. Though born in the province, his honors had all come from abroad, with which he kept up a close intercourse, and was connected by marriage with some of the noble families of England. Withal, he was a true lover of his native land, and conscientiously believed that she had prospered under the fostering care of the mother country, and would prosper. But since there was no chance of resisting the tide of public sentiment now set in, his aim was to turn the torrent aside. The little anecdote he told of the reverend brother was adroitly put in, to show the danger of disturbing existing relations between the mother church and the colonial daughter. The Dominie to whom he referred was one of the fiercest Whigs of the Classis, and had been an open and determined advocate of independence from Holland.

All of this was told to the stranger in an undertone, so that he understood the nature of the question, and the character of the individuals who were debating it with so much unction.

"You will hear for yourself how Dominie Schuneman will get out of that when he rises. He is a cunning man that is now speaking, and maybe he thinks, now he has got the laugh upon the Whig, that he will spoil the edge of his sword; but wait and hear."

"I have seen," said the Reverend Doctor Rysdick, continuing his harangue, and raising his voice, "that there are some men whose judgments are like the eyes which are full in youth, and others whose judgments are like the flattened eye of riper years. As age advances, these change; youth takes a narrower view—age sees at a distance. Those men who look only at the present, and the nearest objects, see no danger beyond them. I am old, and know something of the former times which I have seen; but lest it be said that I am therefore all the less able to see the future, let me declare that faith in the man of age is the second-sight by which he penetrates the clouds; while the young man of fleshly vision is satisfied with the figures which play upon the surface, and please his fancy. We cannot question, but appearances favor the young and the ardent; but you know what the master sayeth: 'Oordeelt niet naar het aanzien.' Yes, judge righteous judgment. Take in the whole history of the church, and of the people from whom we have sprung, and say if it be wise in us to sever every bond, and let ourselves float away into the current of a noisy world, that would cry one day Hosanna! and the next crucify him. We are set for the defence of Zion, not to aid in the clamor of the passionate multitude. Are there not a sufficiency of voices in the public streets to shout sufficiently loud to wake the dead, but we must, in the midst of our quiet and repose, cause our voice to be heard in the street? Remember that the servant of the Lord must not strive: Niemand die in den krigj dient wordt ingewikkeld in de handelingen des leeftogts.* We are soldiers, but the war we are to wage is with the world, the flesh, and the devil. These few sheep in this wide wilderness must not be left by me. I will retire to my hillside and wrap my cloak around me, waiting for the storm; with these old eyes looking through the tempest, and this trembling voice calling to the weary and to the wandering while life remains; joyful that the Chief Shepherd who called me to his fold still is the

* No man that warreth entangleth himself with the affairs of this life.

same as he was when first I entered thy sacred walls, O Leyden! the Alma Mater of those who have long watched with me here. Go away, my fellow-shepherds; leave me alone in this bleak and dark world. Go, seek after the novelties and the carnalities of time and sense. Find the new existence you dream of, but let me still have my early loves, and, if you will, my early hates. 'Chose you this day whom you will serve,' but if I forget thee, O Vaderland, let my right hand forget her cunning, and my tongue cleave to the roof of my mouth, if I count not thee above my chief joy."

The aged and venerable man sat down, far from being overcome, but agitated as the old tree that moves in the wind that rises with increasing force, making its strongest branches wave aloft, while the trunk stands as firm as the rock on High Peak. He walked slowly and with dignity to his seat, which was yielded up to him by his adsessor, who was blowing his nose to hide his tears of admiration rather than of grief.

There was a brief pause here which no one seemed inclined to break in upon immediately. The question was upon the duty which devolved upon the ministry in the present crisis of the country, and it came up in the way of resolution, recommending all the Consistories to move in the patriotic work of defending the Declaration of Independence with their property and lives. Some, when first urged to this open act, hesitated, as we have heard, but the popular feeling had already gone far before them, and there were ministers who took the van, willing to ride the whirlwind, as the last speaker had said, in rather a sneering manner, considering his dignity.

The effects of the last speech beginning to subside, there were several who rose to their feet at once, but the President's eye rested on a tall man of subdued look and demeanor, whose age seemed to be a few years over thirty, though his manner so grave and his words so deliberate, were at variance with his voice and figure, which showed him to be rather below than above those years. He was dressed like the others around, in clerical garb; but had he been met in a log cabin, dressed in homespun, cut and made up by a wandering tailor, he would have shown his breeding as a gentleman and his training to be a scholar. Perhaps a keen eye would have discerned the theologian spread over all.

A slight buzz ran through the house at the sight of his person, and at the prospect of hearing him the Elder said to Captain Whittesley: "Here is a man of some importance!"

And accordingly he put his mouth to the ear of his cicerone, and whispered: "Who is that?"

"Dominic Livingstone," was the short reply. "He is now living at the Manor with Baron Livingstone. He has been forced to leave New York. His church has been turned into a riding-school for the red-coats, and he has come up to help us in this strait. Good man, he loves the church and the country, but he is one of the peaceful men who are not willing to fight unless we cannot help it. I hope he will not follow in the same rut with old Dominie Rysdick. But he belongs to the true Whig race. These Livingstones are all good blood. But he has commenced."

"I desire the peace of Jerusalem, and I love them that love her peace," was his opening sentence; and he paused as if engaged secretly in mental prayer for wisdom to speak the right words. "You know that I am here an exile from my dear people. Driven away from my home, with many who love liberty more than life, the place of their birth is deserted, so that with the weeping prophet, I may say of New York: 'How doth the city sit solitary, that was full of people? how is she become as a widow, she that was great among the nations and princess among the provinces? How is she become tributary!' Nor is this the whole, Mr. President, but the house of the Lord, where so many songs of praise have risen from joyful hearts, and prayers been uttered by the lips of the goodly servants of the Lord, is now a dunghill; a place for the swearer and the infidel to tread upon; a scene of revelry and riot. The enemy has made it a place for his horses and his soldiers to exercise in, and we are shut out of our holy house. 'Alas! for the day! for the day of the Lord is at hand, and as a destruction from the Almighty shall it come. Is not the meat cut off before our eyes? Yea, joy and gladness from the house of our God?'"

The effect of this exordium was evident upon all the hearers, not even excepting the members of the court, who, from their pride and staid dignity, seemed unwilling to yield to the pathetic in a day which required sternness; but they were here overcome for a few moments, while the speaker paused to recover himself, which he soon did.

"Mr. President," continued he, "there are two extremes in the men of this day—those who look entirely to the past, and would build on those foundations fabrics exactly as the original buildings were; and there are younger minds who cry: 'Raze it! raze it!' and must have new foundations and a new dwelling-place. I say let us build the new on the old foundation, for the best reason in the world, that the old is founded upon a rock, and is to be preferred to the sand"—and he paused, looking round—"to that of Holland itself. The time has come when preferences are to be made, and if the wisdom of the present generation is perfect, then let them burn all the books in Vandalic rage; and if the wisdom of the former ages was complete, how comes it that we are reduced to the state we are in this hour?

"Our church, like our country, is an orphan, left of its natural mother, Holland, and of its natural father, England, so that nothing remains for her now but to say: 'though father and mother forsake me the Lord will take me up.' Nor has she been thrown off quite helpless and bare of all means; on the contrary, with a good charter from heaven—a good catechism from Holland—and a wide country all before us where to choose, there is nothing to fear in looking forward, nor anything to long for in looking back. Like the famed Eneas, of whom we read in our dear old Leyden, we are sailing this day between Scylla and Charybdis. On the one side I see my venerable fathers sailing, or wishing to take refuge in the haven of ancient system, and on the other, my fellow-brethren are determined to launch away in their individual ships, independent of the admiral. The one will rot in port, and the other will be swamped in breakers. Hear my counsel and sail between, and God will bear you to a fairer land than the Great Trojan. Fathers, take heed that you restrain not the spirit of this young church, feeling the impulses of a generous pride, in being able to live in hope till better days arrive; give them the liberty of putting up more sail, instead of bidding, or demanding, as you from your age have a right to do, that they should haul in and cast anchor, waiting for day, instead of putting out boldly to sea, which is always safest in a storm. And you, my young and brave fellow-sailors, remember that old heads on board, who have weathered storms before, are not burdensome but safeguards, which we do well not to despise."

With this speech of moderation, the young doctor sat down, leaving the reverend body to make the application—not difficult to do, after what had occupied the Classis all the morning. The question really was, whether the consistories of the several churches should be called upon, to take an active part in the defensive and offensive war, now waging, in their capacity as a church court. These bodies in the old

Holland Church, as in all the Reformed churches, still took active measures against criminal offenders, and had a power of trial and of punishment, subject to appeal in the higher court. But the final court to which the American branch was subject had been Amsterdam, where was now the court of appeal. One had been formed here, but from the natural prejudices of the old Dominies, and the present state of the country, it had not yet got into working order. The machinery had indeed been imported and put up, but it had not been tried; nor were the legitimate engineers experienced men. The danger, therefore, of giving power to single churches—the same power of acting in cases which might be construed into offences demanding discipline—might become dangerous precedents, and yet to forbid them at the present time might be construed as treasonable acts by the Provincial Congress. Here was a dilemma, to a cautious man, of the most puzzling nature. The men of Tory predilections chose one horn, and the fiery Whigs fearlessly took the bull by the horns, and laughed at his stamping fury. They saw with pleasure that the revolution in the State was the sure deliverance of the church from its ancient vassalage, and so they pushed the necessity of every consistory having an ecclesiastical power over political offences, and thus cleansing the camp of every Achan within it.

The last speech, coming as it did from Doctor Livingstone, who had already obtained great influence over the Colonial church, both from his own personal character for piety, learning, great executive talent, and his connections with the Whig family of that name, as well as for his own banishment from New York, to which he had referred, made an impression which was ominous of temporizing measures, such as would have crippled the hands of the ardent friends of the country. For it was well known that many influential families were in constant communication with the Tories. Those could be reached through the church, when they might not be touched by the magistrates. At any rate, the warm partisans were determined to try this lever upon the old Dutch bodies of rich Boermen, such as Paulus Troumpier, of Catsbaan, and Johannes Lasher, of Kinderhook; and others that could be named. The disaffection had gone down to the very core of society, and it was necessary that it should be traced throughout, though that should be to the splitting of the churches.

"Give the Consistories power to bring up their neighbors

who differ from them in matters of a political kind, and what shall we see but one setting himself to watch another, so that no one is safe in his shoes? Have we not trouble enough in the towns and in the country without taking the same into our churches—setting father against the son, and the son against the father? No; let us have at least one peaceful place, to which we can turn in these days of turmoil and war. Let the Sabbath bring all our people to one seat on earth, as they must all appear before one Judgment. To their own Master must each man stand or fall."

This speech was uttered in great fury by a high Conservative minister of this conclave, who had stood out long for conferring with old Holland in all religious matters, and who, from his very stiffness of spirit, thought it impossible for a country to exist as a Christian land unless it had a king. "The Israelites had a king," said he, "and the church was now a kingdom, modelled after the plan of the upper Kingdom: Take the title of king away, and you would spoil the Book where the word occurs so frequently." Besides all these reasons, there were in his own parish some who secretly acted with the king's men, and he naturally trembled both for them and for himself.

During the time of this debate, the Elder Swart got so much in earnest in listening, that he entirely forgot the presence of the man whom he had taken under his care, and would have let him slip through his fingers had he been Arnold himself. Others, however, were not inattentive to the motions of the strange man; but his whole conduct was to them a puzzle which they could not unravel. It was evident that he was not the man he pretended to be; and yet the persons he was holding communication with were all of the true side. Salutations were exchanging between him and some of the best Whigs, clerical and laical; and yet a sort of restraint was on these, which was felt more than accounted for. One side of his character was decidedly suspicious—the interest which the blacks had in him, and the whisperings held among themselves concerning him. In the nervous state of some men possessed of slaves, the cause of this might have been found, and there rested, had it not been for the fact that one of the most active and turbulent fellows of his race was seen to steal round to the back of the stranger, and put something in his hand, leaving the house with the same caution with which he entered.

Whittesley, without appearing to notice these things,

inquired about a man who rose at that point in the debate, which seemed to be turning against the liberal side. The person referred to was a square-built man, of middle age or over, weighed at least two hundred pounds, and was more remarkable for force than polish.. He was what the Dutch call a magtigen * man—strong—strong in lungs, strong in arm, and strong in character; and withal full of wit; one of the warmest-hearted souls in the world, with the most ungracious mode of showing his goodness. When he rose there was a general expectation of a scene.

He began with a text from the Dutch Bible, and indeed throughout he made more use of that translation than he did of the English.

"How happens it that this prejudiced Dutchman is on this side of the question? What's his general character?" asked the mysterious stranger.

"This is Dominie Schuneman, of the Kaatskills," was the reply of the Elder. "A great admirer of the Low Countries, and believes that the model of our new republic should be found there. In fact, he declares that Jefferson has copied the Declaration of Independence from those United States of the Nederlands. He prides himself on looking backward and forward. Some one said as much in the presence of his nigger, Tom, who went to the kitchen, where he was heard laughing with the rest, and saying: 'D' real trut', massa hab eene in de hole ob him's neck back; hem see bot ways ende de all round.' But hark, the storm is up. Dominie Schuneman for ever."

"Evenwel het vaste fondament Gods staat, hebbende dit zegel: De Heere kent degened, die de zijnen zijn," were the first words distinctly heard: [" The foundation of God standeth sure, for the Lord knoweth them who are his," was the translation whispered by the Elder.] "We cannot know everything, though we be Dominies; but we have, from our position in society, more opportunities of feeling the public pulse in the right place, than any justice on the bench. We must let our lights shine so that all may see the men who are on the side of their country and of their God," said the earnest man, as he looked round on the lukewarm and the temporizing. "This is no time to hesitate; as that worthy Scotchman, Wotherspoon, said truly, 'the pear is ripe and rotten,' and it is too late to speak of going back, and I want the authority of this court to call before me the men who, like

* Mighty.

'the children of Ephraim, being armed, and carrying bows, turned back in the day of battle.' We have too many of these deceitful friends, who come like wildcats round our dwellings through the week, at night; and on the Sabbath day are found purring softly in their pews. I want the power to say to Monus Diedricht or Bromie Layman, seize them there, and we will try them on the spot. If you do not give us this authority, by the Lord we will take it. You laughed incontinently at the man who was ready to ride the whirlwind. The Reverend Doctor, heavier in his jesting than Goliah with his greaves of brass, could have told it more to his purpose, had he been with this humble servant of the Lord on that day, when the wind came like lightning through the gorge of the mountain, carrying him forward as a feather is tossed in the gale. Did the man laughed at hesitate? No; but borne to the verge of the precipice, he seized the top of a tall pine that God had planted for him a hundred years before, where he swung upon its topmost branches till he recovered his balance, and found time to descend, and be sheltered under the shadow of the great rock. The same man stands before you ready to engage in a more perilous strife; to mount the wildest horse that war can produce, and be in the van of the flying cavalry. Who among you are willing to lead or follow? Who shall go up to Ramoth Gilead to battle? Cowards are next to traitors, and when the Lord's will is not followed out, Israel shall be smitten before the men of Ai."

During the time of this fierce call, the back of the orator had been toward the place where Elder Swart and his companion sat; but in the course of his gesticulations he turned, when his eye rested a moment on Whittesley's face, which seemed to operate as a new impulse to his already highly excited spirit and manner. The strange captain gave a sign which was understood by the enraptured man, for lifting his voice higher than ever, he called:

"Hearken, O men of God, to the sounds which the demons are already making on the sides of the mountains. I hear even now the war-whoop of the savages, within sight of my people. My own Mary is calling upon our little ones to come and hide themselves away. She sees the traitors around, skulking, and rubbing their hands, saying, 'Our day has come;' and here I am, begging the privilege of defending our hearths against the men in league with Brandt and Butler. The messenger who has brought me the report is now in our midst. To your tents, O Israel!"

The effect of this speech on the whole congregation was electrical, and moved the most phlegmatic Dutchman present, so that it would have been dangerous for any one to attempt resisting the influence. Persons had been seen during the sederunt, coming in and putting missives into the hand of the speaker, which now were understood to be reports from the upper country; and as usual when a company of men rise into an excited state, the call made to their patriotism, as well as to their personal fears, roused them to enthusiasm. All rose to their feet; the president was the last up, but as if the truth had at length penetrated his skull, he lifted his hands, pronouncing the apostolic benediction in a slow, solemn voice, every syllable of which was heard throughout the house, when all left the place.

"Let us go and visit the other house," whispered the strange captain.

"You mean the Provincial Congress?" said the Elder.

An inclination of the head was all the answer, and the two went out together to the Court House, where that body were then met.

Our Kaatsberg messenger had become so absorbed in mind, while seeing and hearing, that he forgot his intention of obtaining a private word with his own Dominie Schuneman, so that by the time he recovered from his surprise that worthy was gone, and already far on his way homeward.

CHAPTER XII.

THE BRAVE BUT BLOODY BRANDT.

"Hercules had tried his strength on Antæos often without success, till at last he saw that frequently, as his enemy was thrown upon his mother earth, she threw him back again; the hero at last lifted him up in his mighty arms, and squeezed him till he breathed his last breath."—GRECIAN MYTHOLOGY.

DOMINIE SCHUNEMAN found his horse ready for him at the church door. The means of return had been provided during the last hour by Dominie Doll, whose horse was furnished to Tom, the Kaatskill pastor's man, so that he might go back with his master at full speed, while at the same time the favorite nag of Sopus might be out of harm's way in case any attack should be made upon the village, as rumor went, and as the importance of the place invited.

Off minister and man flew at full speed, only pausing at every second mile, that the animals might take breath, when Tom was plied with more questions than it would have taken a day to answer in a calm time.

"Tom, was the teeken vuur blazing last night on Round Top? Did you take in the Van Bergen apples, and put the others into the cider press? We must have our cider-brandy made when we go back. Has Captain Van Vechten called out the sodgers?"

The last question was the one that touched Tom's fancy with most vividness, for he answered at once: "Yaw, yaw, massa; dere vere tree vistles an a trum, ende dey made sound like de saltery of de King Jew's harp."

"King David, you mean, you blockhead. How often have I told the people about the kind of music they had in old times, and tried to show you the way they held their instruments; but it is all one, blunder after blunder."

"Lorra! Massa don't mean that Tom know no more den te men who never crossed the big water like massa self."

It was one of the Dominie's favorite boasts that he had been to Holland as well as the best of them, and knew something. Tom used to say the same thing, only he put the name of Guinea always in. He considered himself a travelled gentleman of color, and as holding a place among his own class equal to that which the Dominie held among his brethren.

The spur was again at play, and away the two went at full speed, Tom keeping his horse, as in duty bound, one length behind his master; for the animal he rode was not equal to the other, but he was the lighter in weight and the best rider of the two. The usual visits which were paid at other times to the dwellers in Vlatt Bush and Catsbaan were dispensed with on that day, though the memory of the good horse every now and again prompted him to turn into the different barnyards where he had tasted the good fodder of the landlord. A dig with the Dominie's heel was all the answer given, and if the creature had any mental feeling at all, it must have been surprised at the unusual self-denial of his rider, who loved his friends so well that he never passed their door, nor suffered one of them to pass his, without tasting the cup of kindness in cider or good Santa Crux, while the faithful steed ate his corn.

But this was no time for palavering, and on the two riders rattled, bringing to their doors the inhabitants, black and white, wondering at the haste of the Kaatskill Dominie, who was always a welcome visitor to the master, while Tom was even more welcome to the servants. It was sorely against the grain for the latter personage to pass by the house of old Bennie Languendyck, where a lively wench lived for whom Tom had a sneaking liking, and within a mile of the house he made up his mind to stop at all hazards. How this was to be accomplished was the problem he set himself about to solve. He trusted to his luck, which meant in his case the effect of a certain charm which he tried at such times. He had learned a Dutch rhyme, which sounded like a psalm to his ear, and in some way he supposed there was virtue in it. If it failed, he had bad luck; sometimes he succeeded, and then he had good luck. Tom said his say, and then, like wiser folks, he set about accomplishing his wish. He loosened his saddle-girth as the first thing to be done, and giving his master's horse a sly prick in the rump, the two started away at double speed, when just as they were close by the garden fence of his desired place he slipped down, saddle and all, as if he had fallen, while his horse bounded forward, taking for the barn-yard as a matter of course, into which the Dominic, horse and all, followed as straight as an arrow.

All that Tom wanted was gained. He wanted his supper, and he did not care for any other wench preparing it but Flora; and this was sure to be done. So, coming in limping, and holding his hand on his hip, at the same time making so many wry faces that it was difficult to restrain laughter, though all thought he was seriously hurt; and, indeed, he had not escaped without a few bruises more than he had calculated upon. Of course all was laid to the loosening of the girths, and he chuckled within himself at the trick. Once off the horse, the Dominic was easily persuaded to let his friend lead the animal to the stable and himself into the ample parlor, where the best in the house always waited for him. This was not his own parish, but he was as well known here as at home, and loved the people nearly as well. Bennie Languendyck was one of the regular descendants of the Huguenots, full of piety and good will, which were written on his face by the finger of God, and could not be misunderstood. His feelings were all, next to his God, for his country, and just as soon as there could be a quiet moment he began to make inquiries after the matters of the church, which were so intertwined with the affairs of the state that in speaking of the one they fell into the other. Bennie had a great deal to learn, and some things he could tell. The Dominic was the very man he wanted most of all to see at that hour. He had a reverence for his learning, his office and his piety, which made him humble and glad at the same time, which the good man was the last in the world to take advantage of, though, to tell the truth, a stranger would not have believed so of him, judging from his gruffness and decision. These traits were the results of his intercourse with slaves and inferior men, whom he thought were more impressed in that way than by a milder manner. But all knew him to be one of the warmest-hearted men in the world, and they loved him as much as they feared him.

"Te Dominie het been to tend Classis, and can tell vot vas done to de Tories," said Bennie, in a half inquiring strain.

"Yaw, and a set of Tories some of them are, who were there, afraid of their own shadow or else of their own ease. They stand in fear of man. We have Ahitophels in the camp, and in the court of the Lord. But, Bennie, mark Dominie Schuneman's words, he will root out the Tories from the Hilderburgs to the Kaatskills, if there be power in his Consistory."

"Glad am I dat dere is one Dominie villing to do his duty, ende much need is there of power and skill to do all dis. Has de Dominie heard"—and the old Dutchman, lowering his voice to a whisper, looked round the room as if afraid of an enemy in his own house—"has de Dominie heard of de rising to be among de placks?"

"Rising among the blacks!" repeated the confounded minister, as he rose up from his seat, looking around the room in his turn. "Who said the blacks were going to rise at this time? That would be the Gibeonites turning traitors, after we have nursed them in the very bosom of our families, giving us over into the hands of the Amorites. Speak, Bennie, and tell me all about it, for am not I a father, a Dominie, and a master myself. I will pursue, I will overtake, I will divide the spoil; speak, I tell you."

"Dere is no need of haste, before de avondmaal * pe ready. You kenne vat ve say, 'empty stalls make biting horses,' ende dere comes Flora to bid us set too."

She was a young jet black damsel, of about twenty years of age, and was also one of the original Africans, imported in large numbers before the Revolution; some of them direct from their native country, and others brought from the islands

* Supper.

of the West Indies, in return for trade. Flora was a superior wench, had been apt to learn the manners and the language of her master, and had become a favorite with all; so much so, that she had an influence beyond her place.

"Ha! Flora, are you there, with your white teeth and grey eene?" said the Dominie. "I wonder who is to carry you off from old Bennie. Are Tom and you not going to make it up? I guess now the reason why his saddle-girths gave way. Come, see if you cannot make it up; and then we shall see what we can bargain for; I cannot part with Tom, so you most come to the parsonage."

Flora, who was waiting-her chance, pretending to place the dishes till this speech was over, gave a sly look up, saying as she went toward the door, "Dese be no dimes for marrying and gibing in marriage."

"She is a smart wench, Bennie, and if Tom and her can draw up, I would be willing to hand you over two hundred pounds for her."

"We will speak of dat again, Dominie; say away," and the grace was asked with reverend deportment. The meal was excellent. The earnest minister had been so engaged since the morning, that he actually was not hungry till he sat down and smelt the dish of new chickens, and saw the white bread made of new wheat flower, with vegetables in abundance. The victuals now began to disappear and there was a lull. The good vrow slily poured out from a beautiful china tea-pot, into cups of the same kind, the rare beverage, tea, while the old man, from a black, square bottle, which he had hidden till now, filled a crystal goblet, placing it on the opposite side from where the wife's tea was put. The Dominie looking from one side to the other, gave one of his hearty laughs, and tasting first the one and then the other, he said:

"Ha! we have found out the thief that broke into the storehouse at Sopus. Well, you are more deserving of grace than King George, and I will not tell. But, Bennie, was not that a sly thing of these mauraders to get in, and the sentinel walking before the door with fixed bayonet?"

"Nay, nay, Dominie; dem dat hides kenne vere to seek. Ticklish times raises up ticklish men. Have you said yet vot the Consistories are to do wid de Tories?"

"I am going home," said the Dominie, "to summon every Tory in the parish before us, and forbid every one of them from taking sacrament, and then hand them over to the committee for punishment; I shall spare not one of them. I will," and with that he lifted his great hand in the same way as he would take his oath, "I will not spare my own brother if he stands in the way of the country and her cause."

Just at this moment a young man entered, the son of Bennie Languendyck, with evident alarm upon his face, and said he wished to tell what he had just heard. After some length of preface, it came to this—that a report had been spread about of the negroes rising, and as he knew that Flora and Tom were in the secret, if there was anything in it, he had stowed himself away, so that he could hear their conversation.

"Well, what did Tom say?" was the Dominie's quick demand.

"What did Flora say?" was the demand of the master of the house.

"Give me time," said the youth. "Tom was making love to Flora, and she was making it a condition that he should join the black regiment they are going to raise on King George's side. She says she will get him made a captain. Tom says he will think of it till the day after to-morrow, when he will come down and tell her. But Flora, who seems to know a good deal more than she lets out, says the Indians are coming down to take the Dominie off to Niagara to-night, and she is warning Tom against being in the way, lest he be shot and his scalp taken."

"The duivel!" was the first words of the Dominie; and then, correcting himself, he said: "God knows what will be the end of all this, but I must face the evil and prepare against it. It is according to the information which Tom himself brought: Brandt is on the mountain, and I shall be his first mark. But we shall see when it comes. I must go and meet the Consistory at the Baackouter, on my way home. There we can plan. Take you care of that wench, Flora, and I will watch Tom. A man's foes are those of his own household. Peace be with you."

The minister and his man were soon at full speed again. Tom had not a single pain, nor a wish except to get to the stable and tell what he had seen to his near associates. He was not ignorant of the purposed uprising, but, possessed of more wit and cunning than the majority, he had heard all, but committed himself to nothing. He even pretended to Flora that she was the first to tell him. He was full of his own thoughts, and rode further behind his master than usual, as if to avoid being questioned on the state of things. The master's mind was as full of thought as the servant's, so that scarcely a word passed till they came near to the ford that allowed them to cross the Kauterskill Creek, which at that time was swollen, it being after a heavy rain. As they both mounted up the bank, the hind feet of the Dominie's horse slid back, which nearly unseated the rider, just as Tom came up in time to give his master a helping hand, keeping him on the saddle.

"That was well done, Tom: you might have pulled the other way, and got me out of the road, sending me down stream."

"Lor' forbid, massa!" was the first impulsive cry of the slave. "Tom knows better who feeds him than touch a hair of massa's head at any time."

"Oh, I did not mean you to take it so much in earnest as that. One might suppose, from your speaking so, that you had been told to do it;" and here he looked in the negro's face.

But Tom had recovered himself, and smiling said: "Lor', massa, you look so, and talk so like red rooster when afraid of de black cock."

This was touching the Dominie in his weakest place, for fear was that which he never knew, and to speak of it when there was actual danger was likely to make him angry.

"Afraid, you scoundrel! who is afraid? Afraid of what? of Brandt, or of a whole black regiment with a Tom captain at their head. All that I need to do is to lift my whip, and they will run."

By this time he was holding his raw-hide over the nose of Tom, who stood aghast, not so much at the threatening, as at the words "black regiment," which had incautiously in his passion passed the lips of the master. He had intended to keep that secret to himself till the time of revealing was properly come; and, feeling the prompting of his anger powerfully within him, he wheeled round and rode off, nor did he stop till he was before the door of Monus Diedricht on the Baackouter, where he had appointed a meeting for catechizing the children, and with the members of his Consistory. He found that all were met, so that with his accustomed diligence, and as if he had been in his study all day, he proceeded with his religious duties, the same as in a time of peace.

An hour being occupied with devotional duties, he called his counsellors together, who were grave men and well tried. All were present but one, Martin Schuyler, and it was agreed that something of great importance must have kept him at home.

"You see, Dominie, that the teeken vuur above his house was to be the signal-fire for all the rest on the Cauliberg, and sure enough it did blaze out from the Hoogenhuisen in a full glow, and that was enough to keep him."

"True; but he would have been here or sent word, unless something else kept him. I am afraid that the Indians have taken hold of him on the way down. Rumors have been rife all day from our scouts, but nothing definite yet, though we are expecting the news every moment."

This was said by one of the men of mark in the neighborhood, who was requested to remain and tell what he knew of the state of affairs. His account was gloomy enough. All day the Tories had been observed passing in and out of the woods at well known places, where it was too likely some secret plans were perfecting. No one could be found bold enough to venture near the centre of the woods, which lay between the mountain and the king's road; and the most they could judge by was the smoke which lay there in the morning, showing that fire had been kept burning through the night. Through some secret source, which no one could trace, a report had come down toward evening of the Tories' intention being to join that night and attack the Dominie's house. To meet this, a company of men had gone over there about an hour ago.

"Thank you, friends, for that; but what will the 'Yfvrow do without my help? I must go as soon as we get through here."

All gave a sly smile at the Dominie's fear about the 'Yfvrow, who was well known as the ruler of that domicile, and needed less of his help than he required of hers; still, he always believed himself to have the mastery, which he had in all other parts of his parish, except in the parsonage.

"Let us proceed to business;" and the usual formalities were gone through, of a devotional cast. Afterward the President stated the order he was determined to pursue in all treasonable cases. Debar them he would from the sacramental table, and if they did not repent, hand them over to the civil law. To all of this not a word of opposition was offered, except by Elder Abiel, who was a man not to be put down, even by the Dominie. He hated Tories as he hated the devil, and if he were sitting on the bench of justice, he would go the length of roasting some of them around here; but as an elder, it was another thing.

"I have known Dominies to change sides, and who knows but our Dominie here may be killed in this war. And supposing we get one of the double-sided men, who are all king with king's men, and all country with me, and he chooses to sit in judgment on me as a Whig, what shall I deserve?"

"Garret Abiel," said the Dominie, with earnestness, "your faith is failing. Do you for a moment believe that we are to lose the ground we have gained, if we be true to ourselves, and stop these traitors, who are prowling about our door all night, waiting for our carcasses? Tender mercy at this hour is severity, and I call upon you to make out a case of public scandal against Petrus Sax, Jacobus Roe and Johannes Troumpier, and others to be named."

At this point in the proceedings, some one called over the half door where they were assembled, "Garret Abiel, tous vanted at home," and at the call the elder rose, putting the pipe, that he had just filled for the fourth time, into the cinders, giving a few whiffs to be sure of its kindling, and he left, bidding the Dominie call on his way home, and he would send David with him on the road home, as a convoy. Abiel's house lay in the Vlatt, about half a mile from Monus Diedricht's, which was perched on the side-hill close by the military road, which went through Unadilla and the lake country, to Fort Niagara. The road to the Elder Abiel's, from the place he was in, was uneven, and fenced on both sides by alder bushes and small trees, which were left in the meadows, and by the rail fences. Besides, it was necessary for him to cross the creek before he could reach his own door.

It so happened, in the course of events, that Teunis Roe was on his way toward the house of Garret Abiel. He had returned during the evening from Sopus, whither he had been sent; and having missed his own aim—telling the Dominie of his danger—he was in no haste to return and report anything to his prejudice. All he could do was to be as near as possible to him, and avert from him the injury intended.

His father met him with as much excited pleasure as it was possible for him to display outwardly in his stiff, clumsy manner, and to all questions put concerning the Classis, he gave evasive answers, which satisfied the old man, and made him rub his hands in prospect of the captain's cap that waited for his son Teunis; other means of information were not wanting concerning the sayings and the doings of that day; nor had the movers in the plot, of taking off the Consistory bodily, waited for the result of those resolutions discussed at Sopus. The temper of the stern Whig Dominie had been felt too often before this, not to be dreaded now, whether he had the authority of the church or was left to act without it. Either *he* must be removed out of the way, or *they* must escape for the present. Brandt's presence was now their only chance, and already the train was all laid, waiting for the spark.

"Noo Sonne," said the burly Boerman, "hev de glass of de gin schnaaps, ande here is de plack for tee face. Tee must be tee young Ingin," and he looked as if he were laughing, when not a sound came from his throat. Gin had been plentifully drank all round, of which the old Tory had swallowed a good share.

Teunis was shocked at the disguise he saw the company in, and his feelings revolted from the garments brought to him, so that on the first impulse he said warmly, "Dad, I cannot hide my face like the owl."

"Ende vat vor no like de oders? Tee vill vecht alle de betters," said the really astonished Jacob.

"Nae, nae," said the son, becoming more decided, "if I look like the devil I must feel like him, and maybe I may turn and blow brimstone on those who set me on fire. Daddie, I will remain and be a man, and respect myself. In that way will I do my duty, all the better to my God and to my country, and to"——

The cautious mother saw where all this was tending, so stepping in between father and son, she whispered something in the ear of the old man, which tickled him greatly, for breaking out well pleased, he said:

"Goodt, goodt, sonne; den go down to de creek ende, votch for de big Whiggee Abiel, and see dat he off wid Brandt once, Dominie or no Dominie."

Teunis, on reflection, saw that he might aid in the rescue of the Dominie, should he be taken, all the better if he put on the disguise provided for him; and in the event of his being taken, there would be at least one friend near, who might aid him in his attempt to escape. Without any more parleying, he endeavored to ascertain the exact state of affairs, and started to the edge of the stream over which Elder Abiel must cross before he could reach his own door. Then and there he hoped to obtain a quiet interview, and reveal to him all he knew.

All at once he heard the very man he was waiting for,

shouting at the top of his voice, and swearing a little in Dutch, at some one who was waylaying him.

"Take dat, Dunder-bush! more comin' before morning. He! he! he!"

Tennis knew all the parties well. It was the Elder and his slave Cuffee, that arch negro with whom Dora was in compact, now carrying out the scheme which had either been put into their hands by Satan or his imps. The whole of that dark scene in the cave came up before the vision of the hidden sentinel, and in present circumstances the plot seemed likely to be successfully carried out. The private and the public enemies of Abiel had found in this black knave a fit instrument, as they saw, of effecting their purpose. He possessed great shrewdness, with more fire than usually falls to the share of his race. Certainly there was a deeper malice in that bosom than was known, till the times showed him up in his true colors. All the chastisements he had ever received were treasured by him, lying at interest, which he now determined to pay at a compound rate.

This now being the set night, and nine o'clock being the hour when a clean sweep was to be made of the whole country, the Dominie with the rest, Cuffee was set to watch the door, and keep all away but friends. But the malicious slave, remembering his stripes and rejoicing in his revenge, resolved to have a little fun, and do a little of the punishment with his own hand; so he had the Elder Abiel called out from the rest, that he might waylay him in the dark.

"Tak dat vonce more 'gain. Love cat-ende-nine-tails; he! he! he! Domily fire all his cannons at him. No dead yet; one heavy gad kill no ox so big."

"You black sinner, what do you mean? I'll beat you white," and here the worthy master was groping round in the dark for some stick or stone that he might defend himself with, while Cuffee was dodging him in all directions, and dealing out such strokes as he thought fit; sometimes from behind, and then on the side, all the while laughing his "he! he! he!" so provoking, that the sound went further into the old man's spirit than the gad went into his body. It was just as the master was fairly worn out that Tennis stepped in and gave the black a stroke on the temple, that laid him flat on the ground, but he was no more hurt than if he had been a bull calf. Rising quickly up, he ran with all his power from the place, and disappeared in a thicket.

Tennis, finding himself alongside of the very man he

wanted to see, thought of the two messages sent by him to the Elder. One was to watch him lest he should escape from the designs upon him; and the other to warn him so that he might escape. He resolved to follow his heart, and warn him, but how to begin, in the present confused state of the old Dutchman's brains, was a question of doubt. He had been so completely thrown off his balance by the suddenness of the call in the midst of his argument with the Dominie from fear lest something serious had happened in his absence, and was so hastily passing through the dark, that the stroke from behind, and the beating which followed from his own slave, was, when all had passed over, a maze through which he could not see. When, therefore, the first man he met was no other than the son of his mortal enemy, he was inclined to consider it but a part of the plot of which he had heard that night for the first time.

"The devil take that son of his own! When I get hold of him, I will make his flesh as raw as he made old Grey's back in his last night's ride." The negro had been out with the Tories all the previous night, and rode one of his master's horses almost to death.

"Maybe," said Teunis, "I can explain to Uncle Garret the cause of Cuffee's rebellion."

Before another word could be got in, the old man was up in a rage and with his staff high in the air, was threatening the speaker with the punishment he meant for the black.

"The rebel! Who speaks of rebellion here? Who will hint at rebellion to me, you mean Tory, and the son of a far meaner Tory?"

But for the promise he had made to Elsie, this sudden onslaught might have upset the good intentions of her lover, but his real desire of warning the honest Boerman of danger kept him calm and to his purpose; so, loosening himself from the grasp made upon his throat, he quietly said:

"I did not mean you were a rebel, Elder, but that Cuffee was in league against you, and rebels were in your own house."

"You lie!" was the hot answer of the old man. "I do as the Dominie advises, and as he tells of Abraham, who commanded his children and his servants after him. My house is a well-ordered house, as my good whip this night will testify."

By degrees, however, Teunis found the way to the angry man's understanding; so that by the time he had reached his own door, he had a tolerable notion of the state of things and of what he must guard against. Had he but another hour to collect his thoughts, clear his brain, smoke his two accustomed pipes, and give Cuffee his promised chastisement, it would have taken more strength than the Tories had mustered at that time to have overcome him, except by taking him by surprise. As it was, Cuffee had anticipated the threatened attack, through his love of mischief, so that instead of getting the whole Consistory—the Dominic with the rest—they must be satisfied with the next important personage, Garret Abiel. The rage of the Tories was uncontrollable when they found themselves balked in part; and in all likelihood the country would be roused before they could accomplish anything. The negro had run to his employers, whom he now regarded as his equals, telling them, with great glee, how he had "trashed de ole man so that he roared like de black bull;" but instead of getting praise for his pranks, he was near receiving thirty lashes, and would have been tied up, only it was thought best to use him in carrying out their plot.

Cuffee was ordered into the ring and told how he must act.

"You must go into the kitchen," said one of the disguised figures in the group, "and sit within the big jambs, and be there when the Elder comes in, and deny everything. You will be scourged, and you deserve it; but if you do not submit to your master's whip, you must take one here from us."

Cuffee looked as a big, cowardly mastiff would when he fain would bite some one. He expected different treatment.

"Massa yet. Me thinks free man do as he pleases; king's man free; and den ole Phœbe will tell all, let me lie as I like. She'll tell de trut to shame de devil. Her mind and conshness truble her if her tongue go crooked. Her Christshan words straight as hoe-handle."

"Cuffee," said Helmers Ousterhout, who knew that the nigger was more afraid of the fat wench than he was of even his master, "hide the ladle and she cannot strike you."

"I'll not go in once again. I'm de son of King Quackledom myself, and de free as'll the best of them."

Here a tall, straight figure, who had stood silent in the shadow of the rest, stepped forward and seized the African by the wool with his left hand, holding in his right a bright, glittering knife, with which he made three flourishes round Cuffee's head, at the same time giving him a shake which gave the black ague fits. At the close of this little pantomime, he was ready to do as he was bidden, and in he marched, just in time to take his seat close by the fire on the floor, and feign to be fast asleep.

Once embarked in the plan, Cuffee was the very one to go through with it, and he put on a face which almost deceived the spectators, who had taken their places at the kitchen window to watch the progress of things. The fire just blazed, while the other negroes were preparing for their several beds. A few little elves, who had had an early sleep, were playing, naked as little pigs, on the floor. Luckily for Cuffee, Queen Phœbe was down in the cellar, preparing for the morning's repast. It was not long before she came up, when Cuffee gave a start and a snort, as if he were wakened out of a dream, then falling back again into the land of drowsiness. Just then the door opened, and in stepped the master, whip in hand; and an angry man was he, as he stood over Cuffee, and roared:

"Strip, you black dog! You sinner of Satan!—en de groote draak oude slang—duivel en Satanas! Strip!"

The Elder, for want of words in English, had recourse to the Bible, and heaped dragon, serpent, devil, satan, all in one, on the head of the devoted Cuffee: but strip was the word which went furthest into the ear of that worthy.

"What'll strip for now? Had von flogging already, to-day. No'll worked for so much, and no more."

"Strip," said the angry master, his rage rising with his efforts to restrain himself. "Your rebellion must be checked. Ha! you are going to set up for yourself, King Quackledom, and your subjects are to gather in the morning. But it will take all the black regiment together to save you just now, for that stroke you gave me in the meadow. I knew your he! he! he! You son of the devil! You heathen! This is what you learn of that Fetish cantrap that you have at full moon, instead of learning your catechism."

"Lor' blessy, massa, me been back all de way to Guinea coast, 'long side of King Quackledom, chewing monkey snout, an' trinking spittle schnaps wid Prince Maskity till I fell down on de floor. Phœbe knows, dere, herself; an' she tell de trut always, Domilie, and 'hole Consisry say amen."

All of this was said in the utmost gravity by Cuffee, with his back to the wall and his face fronting the back door, which he kept watching with the intensest interest, for through that he expected his rescue. On his right hand stood Phœbe, and on his left her daughter Peggy, who had for the cunning, frolicsome fellow a hankering kindness; the master stood in front. The small fry had all run like rats into their holes, for well they knew that when the blood of old Dunder Geest was up, he dealt his blows with great impartiality all round within his reach.

Peggy stood ready to declare anything, but Phœbe, who was really what Cuffee had said, truthful, felt herself in a tight place when her master demanded if she had seen the black scoundrel fall on the floor.

"Mammy," said she, "black as Cuffee; massa vite as Godde made him. If massa saw Cuff loll on de grass, me seed him loll on de floor. Tat's all Phœbe say."

The Elder was beginning to get confused, and by way of clearing his mind and regaining his quiet, he resolved on giving a few lashes, for he knew that if Cuffee was not guilty, he would be guilty before long, so it was as well to make things sure, and give him payment beforehand; but ere he had time to lay on, the door opened as quietly as a Dutch door will, when in stepped two of the disguised Indians; then Cuffee also stepped out and seized the whip, which the master was flourishing round his head, by way of giving it force and effect before laying it on.

The Elder, again taken all aback, looked as if coming out of a dream, first at the new comers, and then at the impudent slave. When he found his tongue, he threw himself back to the wall, and ordered them out of his presence.

"You red sinners, as you only seem to be, get out of my own huisen," and he flung them aside as if they had been children, for he was still a man of great strength, and had once been the most powerful man in the whole region. Six feet three in his stockings, and shoulders a yard broad, he stood straight as an Indian, with arms ending in fists that weighed like a blacksmith's force-hammer. "Get out of my huisen, you scallowags; adderen gebroedsels, ye dressed up geveinsden. Get out, before I lay you low with my hands!" and springing forward, he felled Cuffee to the floor at a stroke. Phœbe rushed in between the master and slave, or he would have trod him down under his feet in a moment. The brood of blacks, seeing their queen in the midst, screamed and squealed like young bears when their den is rifled, while the old leader roared at the full pitch of his voice for his sons. "David! Egbert! Charlie! All of you come."

But it was useless crying. The house was surrounded by mock and real Indians, headed by Brandt himself. When Garret found out the actual state of things, he submitted without another grumble, only that he made one more effort at giving Cuffee his due, and it was the most effectual of any attempted by him. As he was passing out of the door between two guards, that ungrateful slave marched ahead in mock dignity, shouldering the old man's whip, which had done such good service on his own shoulders so frequently, when the master seized the big, thick, heavy clasped Bible in his large fist, and threw it with such force that it lighted on Cuffee's skull, making him turn a sommerset before the whole company, causing laughter that was heard up to Monus Diedricht's, so that they were deceived by it, and believed it to be a frolic rather than a fight.

When they gained the outside of the door, old Garret was doubly mortified when he saw that his son was put alongside of him, a prisoner. Brandt, who led the party, saw the necessity of dispatch, for already the alarm was spreading far and wide. The Dominie flew like a madman from house to house, rousing the true Whigs from their beds, and sending the young and eager after others, and appointing a rendezvous for all to meet, so as to make a stand and deliver the men now kidnapped. But the leader of the marauders was too good a general to linger till his enemies should muster their forces, so he ordered a march.

The old and respected farmer who had sat all his life in the midst of plenty, ruling his own house at a word, heard the word march, with a strange kind of incredulity, and it was truly pitiful to see his patient spirit yielding to the necessity of the case. He was not without experience in travelling, for he had seen more of the world than the majority of his class; having been several voyages to the West Indies, with cattle and horses which he took on his own venture. He built and loaded a vessel in a bught of the river, the first ever built on the stream, and returned with rich profits, of rum, sugar, and negroes, all of which he was now forced to leave. Still it was better with his experience than it was with most of those around him, who never went to Sopus or Albany but they first made their wills.

Garret was an older man than he had been, and his habits were more fixed, so that ease was become agreeable; and no wonder though his spirits for a time sank, as he went up the side of the hill that overlooked his own rich domain, with his son David by his side, nor that he gave vent shortly to his grief:

"And are we come to this? I have thought for a long

time that my head would lie in the valley there beside my fathers, and my friends, but awee, awee! this is to be the end of all my patriotism. Like King David, I am leaving my house. Well, David was a good man, and suffered worse than I am suffering after all. His son did that, my slave does this. He was forced to leave bareheaded and bare-footed; I am not quite so badly off as that yet. Shimei went up cursing him; well, I have my share of curses from these Tories. Curse on; the Lord hath let them. I say as that better man said, 'I will bear it all for God and my country!'"

So, down-hearted, he went on; but a little incident occurred which roused him out of his melancholy, and actually put new life into him. He was going on cane in hand, with the knapsack on his back, which the old vrow, though in tears, had filled with her olecakes and rusks, and leaning in part on the shoulder of David, his son, when that malicious Cuffee came up before him, bowing with mock gravity, and took his hat off his head, putting his own skull-cap on in its place, and marching off as before, with the authority of King George's men. The Boerman waked up as out of a dream, watching his time, and when Cuffee once more came around demanding obedience to "de king of Quackledom," the hickory stick of the aged prisoner laid the impudent fellow once more low, and this time so effectually that the nose sprang blood. He rose with the full intention of resenting the stroke, when Brandt came forward, and laying his hand on Abiel, simply said, "Mohawk's prisoner," and ordered the negro to restore the hat and take his own chapeau. The Elder had no more trouble from any quarter, since he found himself under the special protection of Brandt, who took such a partial liking to his prisoner that he ever after showed him favor above the rest. "The Indian," he would say, "loves to see a man, though he be an enemy." *

Wearily and sadly did the prisoners mount up the hill, mocked all the while by the false Indians, and pitied seemingly by some of the real red men, who were acting as a diversion in behalf of the two branches of the British army above and below, so as to keep the men at home in self-defence. The majority of the militia had gone, which will account for the difficulty of raising a company that night, till it was too late.

The Dominie and his friends followed the party of marauders up the hill, and came upon them so near at one time in

* See Colonel Stone's Life of Brandt.

the dark, that Garret Abiel insisted upon firing in among them, when the Dominie put his hand upon the young man's shoulder, and said, "What if you should shoot your father?"

There was too much sense in it to risk a volley; and so well aware were their enemies of this, that they placed their prisoners where they were sure to receive the bullets if they came. "Let us go and gather a strong force of men, and intercept them before they reach Unadilla. They will wait for more prey on the mountain, and we shall watch their motions. It will be safest for us to leave sentinels behind, and have signals appointed, and by the day after to-morrow, we will be well ready; for I know the Indian is not yet satisfied with the booty he takes away, and will return to have the rest. We shall see. God will teach our hands to war and our fingers to fight." All being accustomed to regard the Dominie's word as law, agreed; and having left their watchers, and appointed signals, the main body returned.

Brandt and his prisoners having gained the Kauterskill Clove, ascended the side of the hill due west, where, on a table that runs some way north and south, they made a halt. The old man having the rank of captain in the militia, was put upon his parole, and allowed to range freely; and passing his word for his son, the same privilege was extended to him. So confident were the Indians that he would keep his word, that they lay down and slept with their feet to the fire, and their arms stacked. Toward morning, one of the prisoners came close to the ear of the Elder, and whispered: "Now is our time; we can kill them and run." The old man lifted his head from the knapsack, and saw it was possible, but he sank back, saying, "I will rather die than break my word."

Toward morning, just as the sun was up, all were ordered to march. Upon the eastern hills the light was shining clear and beautiful, and the whole sky was purpled over with the red glory of the coming day. The spectators interpreted the sight in accordance with their feelings. The prisoners saw in it the promise of deliverance to themselves and to their country; the Indians said the Great Spirit was angry with the rebel; and the Tories, in their mean disguise, were ashamed of their hypocrisy, as they looked in the face of the man whom they knew was their superior, and who had done nothing worthy of death or of bond.

When they gained the height of the South Mountain, the whole company gazed down the river, when a redness was seen upon the sky in that direction, dark and lurid, which betokened something unnatural, being of an entirely different hue from all around.

"Sopus is on fire!" was the burst which came from every tongue. "The rebels are roasting!" was the fiendish shout of the Tories, who, in their transport, threw aside all their disguise in speech, leaping and huzzaing like men really possessed of the devil. They danced round the old Elder, making all manner of faces at him whose nod had up to that moment kept them in check. "Vat does de Elder tink now?" was the triumphant cry of an old neighbor's son, whom the insulted man had befriended only the week before. "Vat will the good cause do now? The great Provincial Congress could not keep the goot king's troops out."

"Sopus will rise out of its ashes more beautiful and richer than ever," was the quiet reply of the old man, though the tear was in his eye, as he sighed in spirit; but rousing up, he uttered himself freely in the language of the book he loved. "Behold, all ye that kindle a fire, that compass yourselves about with sparks; walk in the light of your fire, and in the sparks that ye have kindled. This shall you have of His hand; ye shall lie down in sorrow."

"Hear the old Whiggee prophesying," said one. "De old nest is down at last," said another. "Te king's powder too strong for Washington's guns," was a third cry. "Why don't the Dominies turn the Heidelburg cannon at the sodgers." This was a climax, and brought the whole company down with laughter.

In this way the prisoners were insulted; but the chief of these was content with muttering to himself, and in the ear of his fellows, such consolation as his religion gave him. "Als hy ze doode zo Naegden z na hem ende keerden wider ende zogren Godt vroeg ende gedachten dat Godt rotssten was ende Godt de Alderhwojste haer verlosen."

"What does the old oak say to the wind," inquired Brandt of one of the attendants, to whom the Mohawk paid more respect than the rest. "Does the heart of old oak break at the sight of fire?"

"No, no, not at all," said the other; "he is taking comfort at the sight, and would not yield, though you were to turn him into the flame."

"Repeat his words in English, since he is talking to the Great Spirit; the Mohawk can know his feelings. Christian and Indian Spirit all one."

"Here is the translation of the big man's words: 'When he slew them, then they sought him, and they returned and inquired early after God, and they remembered God was their rock, and the High God their Redeemer.'"

"Ugh!" said the brave Indian. "King George should bring his priests to fight these goot men. Mohawk find no scalps here," and he walked off to a place by himself, followed by his own braves, who, instead of hooting and yelling, as the false troop did, stood looking down the great and glorious valley upon the gloomy smoke, in the most stolid composure, as if no tide of feeling flowed through their veins; more like a part of the inanimate objects around them than human beings. A Tory of the name of Sharpe came up to Brandt, holding out a bottle to him, and loudly asking "if he did not wish he were down there to get some scalps from those snivelling Whigs."

"Indian does not love white man's blood;" and the Mohawk turned away from the despicable wretch in disgust; and when the latter laid his hand familiarly on his shoulder, he threw him off with a vengeance that made the man grow pale enough in the face. Especially when the knife of the red man glittered in his hand, and he said significantly, "Scalps can be had nearer than down at Sopus."

Sharpe, who a moment before had been so well satisfied with his own dear self and his transports, and who supposed that all on the king's side must be made of the same coarse materials, fell back with confounded surprise, till he saw that Brandt was in earnest, when he left him, muttering to himself, "These Ingins such a proud race, they should be taught to respect good king's men in these times."

The sky, in the meantime, grew redder and redder, and looked as if the bolts of vengeance had shot up from hell upon the devoted place. From where the spectators stood, so high above the plain, it seemed as if the mouth of that bottomless pit was belching forth flames, as every now and again the different stores of powder and of rum blew up, and blazed blue among the red and the black, with which the conflagration was mingled.

"Dat is but von place," said one of the disguised Tories; "dere vill be red fires, stringing like the gooldt beads on Mammy Dorland's neck, all up de Nort River. Vat say you to dat, Elder 'Biel?"

"When they persecute you in one place, flee to another, the good book says. Burn us out on the Vlatts, we will run to the mountains, like the first Christians." This was said in perfect calmness; for by this time the bitterness was past in the old man's mind.

"Dutchmen from Holland cannot live on hills," said some one by his side, who seemed to stand by himself, but who was watching all, far and near, with a keen eye. "They are water-fowls, frogs rather, and live best in the marshes."

This was none else than Clifford, whom Teunis, who had now joined the troop, at once recognized, though in his own present disguise, he was not so easily distinguished as the man so lately seen on horseback by the side of the little lakes.

The pine orchard being the place of rendezvous, new parties were coming in all the time, bringing more prisoners. Teunis watched every fresh arrival with eager eye, till he saw Kiskataam and Shandaagan come from the northward without any attendants; and he began to feel satisfied that Elsie had eluded their search. The interview he witnessed between these Indians and Clifford, convinced him still further that the trail of the two fugitives had not been discovered. The heart of the young Dutchman beat against his side with gratitude to God, who had saved them. He resolved to find his way during the day to Hoogenhuisen, and hunt for himself.

CHAPTER XIII.

BLESSED ARE THE PURE IN HEART.

"These thoughts may startle well, but not astound
The virtuous mind, that ever walks attended
By a strong sided champion—conscience."
MILTON'S COMUS.

ELSIE and the young lady Margaret have been too long out of sight. We left them when Teunis did, on the side of the North Mountain. He went below for the purpose of obtaining information concerning Brandt, and that he might be of service to the friends of Elsie. The fact of this lady having been forcibly carried away from those whose duty and pleasure were to love and cherish her, was a mystery which must be unravelled before her freedom could be obtained, and it lay heavily on his mind; but the occurrence may have been forgotten by us, while following after that gang of land pirates, whose object was revenge, under the color of patriotism.

But our narrative, like the marchings and counter-marchings of an army of observation, must go back as well as forward. It was so that Teunis Roe had to ride on his unexpected expedition. First to Hoogenhuisen, then down the mountain to the Vlatts below; up again on the outlook for Brandt, when he turned again, at the impulse of his feelings, in search of the two females he had left behind him that morning. Since they were missing he came at once to the conclusion, that Elsie, in whose prudence he had the utmost confidence, had deemed it best to leave their retreat for some place of greater safety. He was well aware of the different ways by which one acquainted with these highlands might succeed in getting safely down; and he felt quite sure that this must be the case now.

But in all these conjectures he was mistaken. The events of that morning were deeply interesting to both the captives; for the two had become identified, and the absence of Teunis was felt, even by Elsie, to be the cause of more anxiety than she would have allowed to any one. They sat down on a smooth place to break their fast upon the fragments which Elsie had carried with her from the husking bee. Dame Myers, according to her custom, had not only heaped up the plate of her favorite with Benjamin's share, but had watched so as to be sure that she ate enough, since they had plenty, and more to cook. After feeding the maid of Hoogenhuisen with what would have satisfied a hungry soldier at the close of a day's march, or at its commencement, with nothing to expect for week, one of these piles was thrown into Elsie's apron, which, in her haste, was carried all night long in her arm, so that when she unrolled the bundle, it showed krowlers, olecake, sausages and roleshees, lying all snugly together. To a nice and delicate stomach such a mess might not be delicious; but with appetites sharpened by fasting and the morning air of the mountains, there were no objections offered, even by Margaret, who was heard often to declare that the sweetest meal that she ever partook of was on a rock, three thousand feet above the sea, in the dark grey of the morning, with the Indians on her trail.

"If ever I return again to my native England," said Margaret, after she had broke her fast that morning, "I shall have a breakfast, as near as it can be dressed, like this once a year, on the top of Snowdon. But we have no such heights in old England as this. Oh, what a glorious panorama, now that the mist has all rolled away. But tell me, Elsie, is that plain we look upon level down to the river brink? I thought, on coming up, we rose up over little hills before we ascended this main giant. There do not seem to be any inequalities whatever; but tell me, can that be the great river that I have read of, and sailed upon so lately? Now, from here it seems but like a silver ribbon, drawn through a fawn velvet robe—so narrow. The Thames and the Rhine are not to be compared to it. Not a vessel on its bosom."

"You are mistaken, Miss Clinton"—for by this time Margaret had informed Elsie who she was—"that stream is broad and deep, but the woods, the plains and the mountains are all great, and you are judging the river in comparison with these. They correspond with the continent we live upon. My uncle says, that while he was in England he was all the time trying to contract his views. You are obliged to expand your powers of comparison. That was the way he explained the difference of feeling to an English officer whom he met up here once. 'See those hills,' said he, pointing to the Green Mountains. 'They lie on the borders of Canada. Opposite to you are the mountains of Connecticut; and these on the right lie near the coast of New York.'"

"And who was that officer of England that came up here with your uncle?" said Margaret, "for I thought none of them ever had been so high up in this land."

"His name was Calderwood," said Elsie, "and he spends his time in examining all the curious points of the region, and explaining the causes of things to us."

"Spends his time up here; and his name. It cannot possibly be the Calderwood that I know."

"Did I say spends his time? I meant," said Elsie, "he *did* spend his time. There was an evident hesitancy in the communication of the maid of the mountain, which her companion was too quick not to observe, and too well bred to pursue it; still the name lingered on her ear, and the passing hint excited an interest more than other passing remarks had done. Here Elsie gave a sudden start, as if she had seen something that awakened her horror. She stood on the highest point at hand, scrutinizing a dark mote on the river, which was plainly becoming more visible every moment.

The mountain nymph changed colors more rapidly than an April sky, but was still silent.

"What attracts your eye so intently?" said Margaret, at the same time gazing down in the direction she saw her friend looking; when, with equal rapidity, her countenance grew pale and red in an instant, as she exclaimed: "A ship! A ship! I have seen a ship before, at sea, but one from such a height as this never before."

"Yes," said Elsie with some bitterness, "a king's ship, where she has no business to be. Oh, if our people had but a match for her, I could stand here and see her driven back to the sea, and clap my hands at her."

"It would be a grand and awful sight to you; but to me, my dear Elsie, how terrible, when I tell you that my father and mother are on board. Oh, my dear parents, how I long to be in your arms."

Here she stretched forth her arms, as a child does to grasp the moon; and as vainly. It was indeed the Vulture, that had, after the abduction of Margaret, remained near the place where they first missed the Indian Kiskataam. On this account the attack upon Sopus had been delayed twenty-four hours; while in the meantime the cruel kidnapper was making his way where no ship could swim. This moment of seeing the ship was, on that account, one of intense interest. There she was, like a large bird of prey, hovering over her victim.

"She is well named the Vulture," said Elsie, "which is a kind of eagle, the Dominie tells us, that scents carrion far off. There she spreads her wings, and before night her cruel beak will be in the heart of some innocent Whigs, whose only fault is, that they love their country and their liberty better than they love King George."

"Have pity on me, dear Elsie, I am in your hands, and you are kind to me, and I cannot be angry with you, though you are severe; but no wonder though you both love your people and love liberty, standing up here, feeling all the rapture of this scene. My parents are in that ship, and my brother is there, and one very dear to me is there who would shed his blood willingly for me—all are suffering. Oh, if they could but see me, as I do them at this moment."

"Well, I shall repress my feelings, Miss Clinton, for your sake, and please to forgive me in my ardor, but remember that this is the day Brandt is expected to come from this very mountain height, to join hands with the Tories below;

and that ship is hovering there to help them. No wonder my heart is glowing with anger, when I know that my father is in danger, and all my friends exposed."

"Elsie! Elsie! forgive me, and cast me aside, for I'm not deserving the trouble and the risk you run on my account. Oh, God! what have I done that I should be sent here to these wilds, and within sight of the happy heaven that I love so well down there. There is a hawk sailing down; if I had but his wings for a few minutes!—and yet I think myself far above him in wisdom and in sentiment: yet ten minutes in possession of his power would put me beyond all harm."

"Lady Margaret, you were on board of that ship, and all the power of great England was pledged to defend you, so long as that flag waved, and yet you fell into the snare of the fowler; you trusted a human arm and it failed you. Here am I who have lived all my days in these wilds, and yet I am free. The hand that holds up that hawk, teaching him to stretch out his wings toward the south, will carry you carefully home if it be his will, and if not, all the armies and navies of King George combined cannot insure your safety."

As is common in these high regions, clouds began to gather round the tops of the peaks, enveloping everything in mist, so that the river and the plain soon became invisible. Margaret was almost in despair at the thought of being cut off from her home, which seemed so near, and could scarcely refrain from crying aloud to her mother, whom she knew would be vainly gazing upward in search of her. Elsie, more prudent and in sober earnest, was trying to persuade her weeping friend to come under some shelter before the rain should commence. The eager daughter would look down where she knew her mother was; and long after all was thick darkness, her eyes were vainly penetrating the cloud, that hung over the river. A sudden breeze springing up, dispersed some of the misty layers, when the vessel was seen rising up out of the water, huge, and seemingly removed far off.

"She is leaving me, and I must be cut loose from all that I love; O, Father! O, God! send me help in this hour of my trouble."

Again all was cloudy. Elsie here took hold of the young lady's arm, drawing her gently to the ground, beside herself, while she pointed to the ledge of flat rock near them, where the hated Indian stood, gazing in the same direction with themselves; and evidently absorbed in the movements of the ship, which his keener eye still saw through the thick mist.

This was enough, the frantic voice of Margaret was calmed in an instant. Fear rushed through her bosom like the gust of wind that swept noisily through the gorges of the mountain. Tame as an infant, she laid her head upon the lap of her friend, where she rested and recovered her strength. A cave that Elsie knew of, where she and her cousin had once taken shelter during a storm, was the place to which she determined to remove, immediately after the sun had passed his height. In the meantime they lay close to each other, near the spot where Tennis had left them, still overlooking the grand valley of the Hudson. It was a small place to lie easy in, but the fear of being seen, by eyes which they knew were near and watching every movement, made them lie close.

Margaret, gradually recovering from the agitation caused by the sight of the ship, was anxiously watching the face of her friend, to read from that, if possible, what her own fate might be.

"Elsie," said the partially excited girl, "say something good to me in your own language. Something that your kind minister says—that Dominie you speak of. It must be good, for it makes you so kind."

"We might sleep one hour till the shower be past. When the sun comes out after rain, it always makes me feel strong," said the Dutch girl; "and gratitude to the Creator makes me still stronger."

"And I am stronger now that you are speaking. Tell me what you have learned that is good for me to hear."

Elsie repeated in Dutch:

"'Ik zal in brede t' samen nederliggen ende slapen; want gy o' Heese allen zult my doen zeker womeen.' The English of that you no doubt know. I will both lay me down in peace and sleep."

"Oh, yes," said Margaret; "'For thou Lord only maketh me dwell in safety.' I have read that in the Psalter."

"Lie still, Miss Clinton," said Elsie, in a whisper, "for an Indian has ears quicker than a white man, and a thick cloud, I have heard, gives out strange sounds. Hark! there are voices not far off from us. Let us trust in God like Jacob when he lay with a stone for his pillow, while troops of angels were looking down on his face, keeping his eyelids quiet and his heart from beating too hard. Hush! There they are again. Hush!"

In this way they lay till all was quiet, when both fell asleep; Margaret dreaming of home. A ship sailed beautifully before her dreaming fancy, and the whole world was gay for a moment, suddenly to be overcast the next. As for Elsie, she was too well aware of the danger to allow herself to be overcome by sleep so as to dream. She merely slumbered; for all the time of this calm she was planning in her mind what would be the best way of escaping out of the toils which she was certain must be spread already around them. Prudence said, wait till night throws over you his thick cloud, unless the present mist continues, when the chances may be quite as good. Besides, she felt as if Teunis would return again during the day, and perhaps bring aid with him, when it would be best to remain where she would be in the way.

When Margaret awoke, the rain had blown past, and the mountain-tops were clear, while all below was in terrible commotion. The storm had descended, and was then raging in its fury. The two refugees felt refreshed, and exulted in feeling at the sight; and, placing themselves in a narrow cavity, which hid them on all sides and left the view to the east still open, they sat down to contemplate the scene at their feet, like the goddesses of the storm.

"Do the storms," said Margaret, "continue so much longer below than they do up here? I have always supposed that there was more rain, winds and vapors on the hills than on the plains."

"There are sometimes great hurricanes up here when they are safe below; but it seldom happens that any one has the chance of seeing such a storm as that from this height. See there, how the thunder is bursting out of that darkness. Look—oh, look! how these lightnings break out on all sides. Do you see that flash there, Miss Clinton?"

"Really, dear Elsie, that is majestic. They seem like serpents rolling themselves in the dust raised by an earthquake."

"Or rather, my lady, like what we read of Sinai, that sent forth thunderings and lightnings and a thick cloud."

"Yes, Elsie, there it comes sailing along from the north, like a great admiral ship. How calm and powerful his advance! Now he comes more swiftly. The sight of the conflict impels him forward. Now he will speak. He is charged with fire and wrath. Why, the whole Armada run at his approach."

"No," said Elsie, taking up the enthusiastic language of the proud girl of the Queen of the Seas, "they are but playing round your admiral till they get a better place. See how they send their fires into his sides! Ah! how the Dominie would shout at that, and clap his hands, singing: 'What aileth thee, ye mountains, that ye skipped like rams and ye little hills like lambs.'"

"Ah, I see my great admiral has scattered; he is in fragments. I have heard my uncle say that great ships were not always great victors."

"That may be true: I know that great Goliath fell before little David, and a great king that shall be nameless may learn that the battle is not to the strong. Great clouds are but the dust of the Almighty's feet."

"Let me repeat to you, Elsie, words that I learned in school, that I never have seen pictured before my eyes till this moment. They describe a great battle in the heavens between the good and the bad spirits:

"'In his right hand,
Grasping ten thousand thunders, which he sent
Before him, such as in their souls infixed
Plagues. O'er shields and helmed heads he rode;
Of thrones and mighty seraphim prostrate.
As if a herd
Of goats, or timorous flock together thronged,
Drove them before him, thunder-struck, pursued
With terrors and furies, to the bounds
And crystal wall of heaven.'"

"My lady, that sounds grand, though I do not understand it fully. My mind, you see, always runs to the words of our Dominie when I see such a sight. When he describes the last day, when seven thunders utter their voices, and when I see the clouds chasing each other as they do now, it puts me in mind of what the good book says about 'giving their flocks to the thunderbolts.'"

"Well, Elsie, I confess that your old Dominie and his book beats my Milton. But here comes a new turn in this divine panorama. There, the scattered troops are wheeling into squares, just as I have seen in Hyde Park on a review day, when the several regiments moved to the rendezvous; while the numberless spectators, like those broken masses that remain in the distance, remind me how the crowd fringed the outside, impatiently watching the centre till it would spread out again. Do you suppose that the army is about to disperse to their quarters, and leave the heaven as clear as it was this morning?"

Elsie replied to this question, that she thought rain would descend in torrents upon the whole Hudson valley and this she foretold truly. The different layers of vapor became one great sheet, fastened to the sides of the mountains eastward, where it lay as in silent rest for a short time, till it seemed to move, internally giving out its abundant drops. Not a shred of the river, nor a point of high ground were seen; and yet the sun was shining above High Peak, and to the west of where the two spectators stood, for it was now an hour past meridian. Elsie was the first to speak, for she was familiar with the scene, and could in a degree foretell what might arise; while her companion was too much rapt in viewing the awful mystery beneath, to anticipate the coming change.

"Look, Lady Margaret! see in the south, how the rainbow is forming. Now see again in the north."

"Glorious!" was the exclamation of the enraptured girl, "if it forms all through as perfectly it will be worthy of the Almighty hand that paints it. I have been on the side of the Alps, but never beheld anything like this. Hush, dear Elsie, do not speak, lest you mar its perfection by a breath." All the sorrow she had felt an hour ago was forgotten, and lifting herself up, she whispered, "Oh, mother—Oh"—Bertram, she would have said—"could you but see that bow of promise, you would hope as I do. You cannot see it, for the rain is above you."

"That bow," said the proud Elsie, "is over the land of the rebel."

"No matter; if all the people of the country be like Teunis and my own Elsie, I could kiss them in purest love;" and she embraced her friend in tears and smiles together. "Alas! I was thinking only of myself when you spoke just now, Elsie. Poor worm that I am, when all around me ought to lift me above, and give me a sense of the greatness of Him who has set his bow in the cloud, as the sign of His beauty. Can you read signs, Elsie?"

"Let me try and read this," said the good girl, willing to chase the gloom and despair away from the mind of her companion at a moment when so much depended on energetic exertion. "There were thick clouds this morning; you began to climb these mountain heights in despair. The sun came out and dispersed the gloom: Teunis and I, like the stars, have led you here to this place of refuge; your enemies are still around you, muttering like the thunder beneath. Now the bow of promise appears and you will be delivered from all your fears."

"Thank you, thank you, dearest friend; I should trust, since you have been sent to me in this wild region, like an angel from heaven, where I had no right to expect any one but an enemy at this time. But see, the bow has fallen flat on the ground."

"It is only the sackcloth cloud that is spreading out farther to the east. We girls of the hills say that these bright colors we see, are the eyes of good people below, shining through to their friends in heaven; and that black parts cover very wicked folks. The rays of the sun never get through to them."

The ears of the English girl were not shut to this fancy of her companion, but her eyes were the most awake lest she might lose the smallest change in the wondrous bridge.

"There, it rises again," she exclaimed, "as it was before, as if Michael and Ithuriel had stood at its opposite points, raising it as an archway to the celestial city. I have read in the Psalter something about lifting up the everlasting gates that the King of Glory might enter in."

"Yes, Miss Margaret, and no grating sound on these hinges. How rich the gilding, and the form how perfect. Have you ever seen anything like that, near kings' palaces?"

"Oh, Elsie! but see: like all earthly grandeur it departs. Already it gives way at the centre of the curve. Dimness is now passing over the whole; what remains even now is more in memory of what was, than in assurance of what is."

"True, Lady Margaret, every one walketh in a vain show. That jewel is gone; so we must wait for that sight which is seen in heaven."

"And are there rainbows in heaven, Elsie? Any gems as resplendent as the one we have seen pass? Heaven shall seem more glorious than ever it did, after what I have just looked upon."

"Oh, yes, Miss Clinton, there is a rainbow there round about the throne, in sight like unto emerald. Our Dominie would tell us that these are figures of realities. The everlasting beauty of heaven, and the unfading splendor of its riches; I have heard him preach about the rainbow, when he told us that Noah stood on a mountain, five times higher up than High Peak, and saw a bow stretching over a plain through which the river Euphrates runs."

"And what good did that do to his simple people. Our parsons tell us what will be of practical good to us. What the better were you, Elsie, on that account?"

"We were told by the good man that the bow was the signature of God, put to the covenant he had made with Noah; and that the bow in heaven was the sign of our salvation being fully secured."

"Ah, I see," said Margaret, "and the good you obtain, is in believing that God is faithful to his covenant. That is good; I will believe in the sign; I feel stronger when you speak of that."

"There is other business for us, dear Miss Clinton—look down there," said the watchful Elsie; and in the direction where her finger pointed the eager eye of her companion was turned, when she saw, to her horror, Clifford in close conversation with Shandaagan; and the chief Kiskataam was coming up toward them. They were engaged scrutinizing closely the ground, as if they had discovered some footprints. The rupture between the Englishman and the Indian had been apparently made up; and one thought filled them both, though it was plain that as yet they were all at fault. No question but they were on the trail of the two fugitives; and had they followed on in the direct line, it would have brought them to the spot where they would have found the cave—empty; for a few feet further, and the girls were prepared to swing themselves over the face of the precipice, as foxes do, when pursued by hunters. But the pursuers lost track of their game at the point where they were seen. Elsie had made, extempore, out of her under-dress, two pairs of moccasins, which had no special form after a human foot, and they completely stultified the red man, who could not decide the kind of animal to which it belonged.

What more particularly diverted their attention at this critical moment, was the sound of Teunis' horse's hoofs along the rocky path. The two Indians glided out of sight, so as to elude suspicion, leaving Clifford to have an interview with the young Boerman alone, which ended so as completely to change the whole front of the affair, and save the two fugitives from making a desperate venture in another direction.

CHAPTER XIV.

A TRIAL OF FAITH AND FORTITUDE.

"Fifty thousand pannier loads of devils, with their tails chopped off by the rumps, could not have made so diabolical a scream of it."—TRISTRAM SHANDY.

NIGHT came gratefully to the fugitives, and Elsie had, in her own mind, determined to get down into the valley, and reach early some place of refuge. How to get through, when enemies were around, so quick in eye and ear, was the question that came up to her lips. Her knowledge of the Indian character, and her present acquaintance with the cause of Miss Margaret's trouble, made her fully aware of the vigilance of their enemies. Add to all, the threatened raid of the great Mohawk was near at hand; so that should they escape Clifford and his satellites, they were in great danger of falling into the line of Brandt's party. In that case Margaret resolved upon giving up at once, well persuaded that the daughter of an English officer must be safer in Brandt's hands than in Clifford's. But then, what must she, the daughter of a Schuyler, expect, but bondage. No matter; her first care was to get through the lines of Kiskataam, whom she knew must be watching with the eye and the ear of a catamount.

"Let me take one full view of the stars from this high observatory, before we go back into the darkness. I may never see the like again. What does your Dominie say of them that does you good? It will do me good to hear it."

"He says," said the honest Dutch girl, "that were the sun always to shine, we would lose one half of the glory of the heavens; and that were we always prosperous, there would be no star dust scattered over our path."

"I suppose he adds one thing more—that if there were no death, there could be no heaven. Let us go: had I not been stolen away, I would never have seen Elsie, nor these resplendent scenes that have risen upon me this day from early dawn till dewy eve."

At this instant Elsie almost shouted, and would have clapped her hands, had not her friend, who now had learned caution, prevented her, when, pointing to the southward, she said, "the *teken vuur* is lighted on the keekute.* I knew that Teunis was true to his word. It blazes, see, from the back of that hill. My mother! we must find our way to her. The sky is all red above the hill. I gathered these pitch knots myself, and helped my father to build the pile. My heart and my hand shall go together."

"Then Teunis had not the promise of both this morning when he left?" inquired Margaret, willing to lead the mind of Elsie away from sad thoughts, which, in her turn, she now suffered to intrude upon her usually vivacious spirit.

"There are reasons, Lady Margaret, which you cannot fully understand. I would not divide myself from my country's cause. My heart must not be put on neutral ground, nor yet on the king's."

"King's men are more esteemed in London than other men, and Teunis would be promoted there."

"May be," said Elsie, "but the blood tingles in our veins here at the sight of freedom and of truth."

"I have wondered all this day, when I have heard you express your patriotism so strongly, where you could have learned such sentiments. Have you mingled with others than your own people?"

"My dear Lady Margaret, were you to sit one day under the pulpit of Dominie Schuneman, you would not wonder any more. Oh, I wish you could hear him, when he is rousing up the minute men. How the fire flies out of his eyes when he bids them bring back their shield, or be brought back on it."

"What makes you look down there so earnestly, Elsie?" as she saw the anxious girl gaze into the dark. "Tell me if you see anything alarming?"

"Nothing, only I see the red skins are kindling a fire on the flat rock, as a signal for their fellow-murderers below. There will be hot work all around us before the morning. Let us go, and trust to Him who takes care of the young fawns up here over these mountains. Kiskataam has named you the Fawn. Let us look above all man's power."

They set out upon their perilous journey, and as Elsie knew that the narrow road which runs between the two ponds was most likely to be watched, she at first determined to go around; yet considering within herself, "If the Indian suspects my presence, he will guess that I am more likely to avoid such a trap, and fall into the other. It will be better

* "Look out" is the English; "keek oot" is the Scotch.

for me to go forward and examine for myself." So communicating her plan to her companion, she left her, with instructions how she should proceed in the event of her being kept from returning.

"Go back," said the intrepid girl, "to where we have been all day. Stand on the place motionless, and wait. If I am alive, help will find you before noon. Wait here till you see the Ellwand *—those three stars up through that tree. If I am not back then, do as I have bid you; and remember you are a soldier's daughter, and God's arm is with you in all places."

"But, dear Elsie, what if those cruel men keep you from helping me? They are cruel enough to kill you."

"They dare not. I have power over them by myself, which I could not have with you by my side. But if no one comes to you, there is one who will help you at the foot of the hill. Try and find your way down the road you saw Teunis take. But do not fear."

With that, Elsie went on into the dark alone. While Margaret, with a palpitating heart, saw her depart, it seemed as if the last link was broken which bound her to the world. Elsie moved through the tangled underbrush with the utmost caution and quiet. Accustomed to such journeys, she knew no fear of aught except the danger of falling into the ambush that might be laid for her. The farther she went, the slower was her progress, creeping rather than walking. Her present aim was, if possible, to get a glimpse of the persons who might be around the fire, and when she did get within sight, Clifford was the only figure she could discern. This assured her that the other two were out as scouts. Creeping along to the westward, where the path is narrow, she judged it to be the most likely spot for a sentinel to be placed; but how to find it out, she stood utterly at a loss: when, turning to the left, close by the path on which she came down upon her father's trail on the preceding evening, she went up high enough to let a heavy stone fall in the direction where Clifford stood, who, startled at the sound, fired off his gun, which in ten minutes brought in the other two. The Englishman was evidently in the greatest consternation, which rendered him nervous and made him act ridiculously, which, to an Indian, is always an unpardonable offence. They evidently treated the whole as the result of his own

* Yard-stick.

imagination, and, with characteristic coolness, stretched themselves out before the fire preparatory to rest. This was enough for the brave girl, so hastening back to her terrified companion, she communicated the joyful intelligence of a speedy deliverance.

Margaret was standing like a young roe that had heard the shout of the hunters, and expected every moment to hear their baying hounds in her thicket. So near was she to danger, that Kiskataam passed the other side of the rock where she was, and might have stumbled over her had he taken the other side; but she had escaped, and Elsie, kissing her, said:

"There shall not a hair of your head fall to the ground without His permission. Brace up now, my lady, for we have a long walk before us ere the day dawns. We must be quickly into the clove."

"My dear Elsie, I am firmer than you take me to be, and can stand more fatigue than you suppose me capable of. I have been out with the chase before now, and you must know that we English girls are great walkers."

"You will require all your strength, Miss Clinton, when you come to make the comparison between those smooth lawns you told me of, and these humpy roads. Lean upon me, and be sure to notice when the rags get loose from your shoes, for we must not leave a trace behind us for these Indian dogs to scent us out."

They were now fairly on the way, and as Elsie determined that the safest plan was the boldest, she led her companion straight between the small lakes, passing close to the fire, along the edge of the pines that grew in the crevices of the rocks. Half carrying her charge, they crawled up the South Mountain, slowly and carefully, lest they should loosen any of the stones that lay anchored there, and so disturb the quick ears that lay watching so near them. Once up, they sat down to rest upon the big rock. The two maidens, like two birds that have just made their escape, stood up on this height and looked down, with a half contemptuous smile at the superior skill with which they managed to outwit men of such reputed cunning.

Thus taking short journeys, and resting during the intervals, they reached the gate of Hoogenhuisen, where the first welcome that met Elsie was the leaping of Rover coming out to meet them, who, though he had been carefully taught not to bark aloud, could not restrain making a noise equally significant and audible.

Angelica, the mother of the lost girl, was up, and seated at a fire, which then was needed in the cold of that October morning. Her pipe, which was always the first mouthful of comfort she took on all occasions, was between her teeth; while her eyes settled upon the growing blaze as if she could read in that the fortunes of the new day. On the entrance of the daughter, she did not fly into an ecstasy of feeling, as one of a more excitable race certainly would have done; for besides being a true daughter of Holland, proverbial for their phlegm and slowness of action, women in these days have learned through hardship and danger, to possess their souls in patience and quiet. The Reformed Protestant Dutch Church is equally Calvinistic with the New England Puritan, and its doctrines are equally felt among the people, operating upon them in producing that hardy endurance, as essential in times of trouble, as gallantry and courage in an onset of battle. Angelica was a sincere believer in her religion, and acted out her faith to the last.

In reply to the few questions put to her by Elsie, she quietly, but evidently in deep concern, stated that Martin had been away two nights. Teunis Roe had been up yesterday, inquiring after things; he had left only in the darkening. Some Indians had been seen prowling about. Tories had passed the house on the back road. These were the days that old Martinus, her grandfather, had often foretold would come.

Margaret had been left at the door by Elsie, till she prepared the way, and held a brief conversation with her mother before telling her that she had a stranger with her that had fallen into trouble. That was at any time enough to awaken the sympathy of the kind-hearted vrow. "Let her come in, we will share what we have left with any poor wanderer."

"My mother," said Elsie to her friend, "has just been repeating one of her favorite texts, which gives her strength in her old days: 'The world passeth away, and the lusts thereof; but he that doeth the will of God, shall abide for ever.'"

"Mammy, here is a stranger needing rest and refuge. I have brought her to you, and you will be a mother to her." With that Elsie conducted her new friend up close to the fire, that the two might see each other.

"Tee's welcome, sae lang's I'm here myself; nay one can tell vat te morrow vill bring varth."

"Where do you think is daddie? that you are sitting at the fireside at this late hour, alone?" Elsie had her doubts all along that her father was entrapped in some way; but she hoped still that his absence might be voluntary.

"Nefer sene hemme since tee was here dat nicht," said the sad mother, as she blew out a double mouthful of the smoke that she had been keeping in till the question was wholly asked.

The answer was a thunder-stroke to the affectionate daughter, but she was too good, and too wise a comforter, to suggest more fears than were already preying upon the mind of the anxious wife; so inwardly revolving the different views of affairs, as they came up rapidly in her mind, she felt that the best plan for the present was to rest till daylight, and then act. So taking Margaret by the hand, she led her up a back stair to the chamber above.

"You must feel for the bed, my dear lady; misery has no choice. Lie down, but be ready to rise at a moment's call. Never fear, for though you be surrounded, you will escape, so long as I am by your side.

"Oh, Elsie, dear Elsie, I wish that I could lie down as contented in spirit as that good woman, your mother, feels at this moment. I now know why you can be so forgiving and so kind to me, though my people are doing you such injury. Hush! I want to hear your mother's voice praying, though I cannot understand her words. You will interpret them for me."

Angelica, immediately below, was saying in her own language, "Looft den Heere myne ziele en all wat binnen in my is zynen Heiligen name."

"What does your good mother say, Elsie? I love to hear her voice."

The kind-hearted daughter, who was weeping to herself, and wishing to hide her feelings from her companion, could scarcely articulate an answer. "She is full of gratitude, Miss Clinton, to think that I am spared to her, and the words you heard her utter were, 'Bless the Lord, oh, my soul, and all that is within me, bless his holy name.' Sleep, my Lady Margaret, for we must be up betimes, and work for liberty and life; judging from all that I see on the earth and in the sky."

Morning rose upon the world, in many parts as it had done before; but these quiet regions, which knew no memorable change before, had a new page added to their history.

All over the mountains to the westward were seen pillars of smoke, which plainly indicated the approach of the dreaded Brandt, from the fields of blood on which he had been committing havoc. Elsie had risen from the side of the weary fugitive, and was surveying the scene around, so as to determine the course of that day. She had some hope that Teunis might come to her aid, for she saw herself completely surrounded. Her heart for a moment misgave her. Had she done right in risking all for this stranger? Might she not be sent, so that she would become a hostage, and so insure the safety of her own people against Brandt. Would it not be well to retain this lady? "No, God forbid," was her impassioned cry. "Providence has placed her under my care. Neither parents nor enemies would approve of treachery; no, nor the Dominie, nor my own heart. And now, that every hour in the company of this young lady has made me more in love with her, I will act out my feelings and my convictions and hope for the best."

As these reflections gave place to resolutions of good intention, she felt stronger, and was ready to perform whatever duty came first to hand; nor was she long in finding out work to do. She stood up to her full height on a jutting point of the rock, in the grey mist, and to a stranger in these parts, who had never seen an object through a cloud, she would have appeared of gigantic size. Her hair as yet was untied, and hung over her shoulders; the loose dress which she had on flew forward in the wind, while her excited feelings gave her an earnestness of manner which could not be hid, even by the misty veil around her. Lifting up her arms to the Almighty, whom she recognized alone, she invoked His blessing on her and on her parents in that day of trial. "Send us a deliverer, O God; give me wisdom and courage, power and patience to guide and be guided through our perplexity and danger."

Turning her eyes downward, she plainly saw a strange figure approaching the place where she stood. In the mist it seemed also of gigantic size, but that did not deceive her, accustomed as she was to judge by things around her; still the man who drew near could not be an Indian, from his walk; nor was he a native of these regions, as indicated by his gait and dress. He did not bend forward, as all those do who have climbed up hills from their infancy; and his garments were worn with an air which showed that he knew what was dignified and becoming, though he affected to despise both, from the loose way in which the long grey cloak he had on was thrown around him. Elsie was not afraid when she came to see who it was; for she knew the Hermit of the Hollow, who, at that moment, was most welcome. She of all the young women of the hills was his especial favorite, and indeed the only one who met him heartily, and not with pity. She had sat with him for hours, hearing his tales of other countries; asking him questions which did not intrude upon his own affairs; and anticipating his wants in such a way as to impress him with a high regard for her natural ability, which he took great pains to elicit and foster. He was a many-sided man, and had to be studied carefully, which all could not do, and were accordingly repulsed by him, so as to make some believe him mad, others a fool; and not a few that he was a spy upon the country, and in league with the Indians. Elsie believed him to be sound in head and in heart, except on one point, a burning revenge against some object of his hatred, that haunted him night and day. All her sagacity could never find out the direction to which that passion pointed; so that she had come to suppose that it was in his own imagination.

"I have been searching for you, Elspeth, and have found you where other eyes, less kind than mine, might have seen you. Do you know that these hills are crowded just now with your enemies, and a ball could have brought down the Maid of Hoogenhuisen without any one being able to tell whence it came? How often have I told you to keep below the rocks, instead of standing on them."

"There are times when fear should not interfere with duty," said Elsie, "and this hour is one of them."

"I have waited for you two days. Have you lost confidence in me? Where is the token of my friendship and of my power, that you neither brought it nor sent it to me?"

Elsie blushed at these words, which were intended as a reproof, for something understood between them; but turning to her visitor, she told him that it was impossible for her to have come. He must take her word without any explanation just now; but here was the token still safe, and now, if he could help her, the time had come.

"Yesterday is past and gone; to-day there will be blood and fire. For that you must be ready. I have come to warn. The enemies of your country and of your house are near. You have just time to hide before they be on you. Hear them now on their way to the Dog Pool, where Martin is bound a prisoner. They will bring him round here, that they may gloat their vengeance in seeing him lament over his burning home. But, Elspeth, the day of vengeance is at hand; I saw my enemy in my sleep, writhing in agony; I could have brought him down with my gun this morning; but no, I shall wait a while yet, that the sweet morsel may become sweeter. I am enjoying it in the prospect so much that I am sorry that the time is so near when I shall swallow it. Like the wildcat that I saw yesterday, playing with the rattlesnake, I will sport around him, mortify him, goad him to death, and then *smite* him." Here the infuriated man turned to the place where the gathering was, around the flat rock; shook his closed hand, gave a wild shriek, and left the place, for Elsie to reflect alone upon what she had seen and heard from him.

Whatever opinion Elsie had of the rapture of vengeance which this mysterious being indulged in at the close of this interview, she understood the warning in a literal sense, and made haste to take advantage of the time allotted to her. Angelica was immediately informed of the necessity of the case. The most valuable part of the property had already been hidden away; china ornaments, and a full tea-set that Skipper Van Vrankin brought home from the Indies as her mother's marriage present. A silver teapot was rolled up in a flannel undershirt of Martin's, that he might have something clean and warm to put on if he lived. A satin gown that had been but twice worn, and was carefully aired, spring and fall, and kept for Elsie, when she married, was put into an earthen pot, and sunk into the deep soil of the garden. A huge pile of bedding that had long stood in a corner, from the floor to the ceiling, with other articles of warm clothing, which hung on hooks and nails along the walls and on the joists, so that scarcely a vacant spot could be seen; and these were the special idols of Angelica's fancy. She kept looking into that room, saying, "awee! awee!" wringing her hands at the loss of thirty years' labor. No wonder though the careful housewife should have for a moment given way to sorrow, when she thought on all her plans being thus blasted in a morning. Elsie reminded her mother of the Dominie's text the last time they had been at the kerke of Kaatskill, "wentelt uiven wegh op den Heere en ver trourot op him: hy zal 't maken."

"Tell it to me in English," said Margaret; "I need it as much as your mother."

"I am telling her," said Elsie, "to commit her way unto the Lord, and he shall bring it to pass."

All was business and haste below-stairs, while every now and then Elsie went up to the highest part of the house, taking a survey of things around. The place from which she anticipated the danger was above them. Down the Clove road she was led to expect the band of ruffians, who were to come with her father a prisoner, and her main object now was to be ready to receive them into an empty house, and her mother with herself and Miss Clinton to be out of sight. Dismissing all the negroes, not excepting old Noll, by telling them that the Indians were coming, she took her mother by the hand, and led her half forcibly up the hill at the back of the house, where the secret retreat had been prepared for more than two years; she opened the door, that was but a fissure in the rocks, against which a stone lay, as if it had dropped down by chance; she pointed to it silently, that her mother and Margaret might go in first, which they effected by crawling on their hands and knees. Then following them, she let fall before the entrance a heavy block of stone, that had been prepared and balanced for this purpose so effectually, that it was both a natural and an artificial defence. Loop-holes were prepared both for seeing and shooting through; and from the position of the fortress the garrison could overlook whatever was going on around the dwelling below—on the back road which ran past it—between them and the back door, which at this time was left wide open, so as not to provoke assault.

The inside of the hiding-place was a natural cave, formed by the percolating of the waters and the action of the frost together; the latter loosening the rocks, and the former carrying off the debris; so that, in the course of time, there was, as is common in these lower shelves, a wide subterranean passage-way, which was kept a secret from all except the family. Like all such caves, there were roomy landing-places, where a troop of men might lodge; as the Dominie said once, after pressing himself through the narrow entrance: "The gate is strait, but David and his men might hide themselves from Saul and his forces; and let me tell you, Martin, it may become to thee and Anshela, like the cave of Engeddi."

Safely landed, and at comparative ease, the three hunted women placed themselves so that they might see the outside of the prison through the stone grating. Nor was Elsie without the means of defence in case of requiring to defend herself and friends. There lay beside her the long duck-gun, well loaded with heavy slugs, and a pair of large horse-pistols, which her father had used in the cavalry when a young man, in the old French war. Provisions enough to victual a garrison for a month, and bedding sufficient for two generations.

The attack did not come that day, notwithstanding they were so warned. However, it was kindly given, doubtless in full knowledge of the enemies abroad. From their secret refuge they saw the two Indians prowling around all that day, and they had good reason to know that a watch was set upon them through the night, yet they all three slept and were rested, when the light streaked the crevices of their rocky prison.

Soon were heard noises that increased every moment, till ten men disguised in mock Indian garb appeared. Flannel shirts to their middle, notched round; short breeches, joined to leggins of buff deer-skin. Round the waist they wore a belt of raw-hide, in which were stuck such side-arms as they carried. In the centre of this vanguard walked our friend Martin Schuyler, looking as calm and as dignified as ever he did when sitting in the Consistory of Kaatskill church. His hands were cruelly and unnecessarily tied behind his back, and his large soft hat, which had been first contemptuously knocked down on his head, was, on his coming near to his door, drawn as far back to his neck, that he might the better witness his own disgrace and the destruction of his property. They halted opposite the gate, and wheeling into the yard, the captain ordered a full stop, drawing his sword, which he laid flat over the back of his prisoner.

"Now, you old Whig sinner," said the ruffian, "you see that Konig George has got long enough arms to reach you at last. The Dominie has made you believe dat you leeven in de kloven der steen rotzen ende verborgen; but the nest is not too high for Brandt's claws."

The man who said all this was one of the leaders, and one of a better class. His speech showed that he felt malice as much as loyalty, and that he only wanted the power to execute a wicked will.

"Tell us," cried out one coarser grained still, "where the old vrowe has hidden away her milledoleors. We must hear them clink, or by George and Saint-ne Claus, we will hang her up for smoked meat."

"She is smoked already, Nick, and that long ago; ha! ha! ha!" said a great ugly, toothless fellow, with a foot like an elephant, who came stamping round Martin, giving his nose a pull that brought tears into his eyes, not from the pain so much as the mortification of being the jest of such heathen. To the sudden surprise of all parties, the last insulter received a back-handed stroke that made him reel around, just as he was about seizing the two ears of the patient Boerman. This arrested the attention of the whole company, who had by this time come up, and were taken aback in some degree at seeing quarrelling in their own ranks.

"Treason! treason!" shouted several voices at once. "What is that for, Teunis Roe, that you strike your friend?"

"I am a man," was the reply, "as I have always been, and will not stand by and see a prisoner insulted by meaner men whom he would not have set with the dogs of his flocks in the days of his prosperity."

"Blessings on the Indian," said Angelica, who had witnessed this acting from her retreat, and almost cried out in horror at the manner in which her venerable partner was struck.

As for Elsie, another of the same acts would have brought upon him the contents of the long gun, that lay with the muzzle in rest; and the shot would have been sure. But the gratification was even greater when she saw under the disguise one that was willing to expose himself to death on behalf of her father; and the duck gun fell from her hand, as if she had become helpless in an instant. Her eyes followed that youthful, active form wherever it went; for it seemed to her it was in every place where most needed, though all his efforts could not save the impending doom that hung over Hoogenhuisen. While he was watching over Martin, keeping his head from further insult, the spark had been put to the barn, and already the smoke was rising from the roof, shooting up like the breath of fiery serpents, fed by the fuel beneath, that was reducing the whole of the precious produce that had been gathered in with such industry and care by the man who had to stand and look on the destruction of his labors.

The disguised defender turned away from the place he could not save, planting himself in the door of the house, as if he said, "He that enters here goes over my body. All this destruction is useless and revengeful, and is not desired by the king, nor yet by the commander of the forces, and must bring disgrace on those who are engaged in this day's riot. Stand back, I say, as you value life and limb."

This resistance excited the suspicion of the villain Kiskataam, who had come on in the hope that he might fall in with his victims; and seeing the position that Teunis took, he suspected that Elsie and her companion were hidden in some part of the dwelling; so, stepping up, he confronted the guardian of the threshold, saying, "The double-faced seeks to hide the young she-cub."

"I do not know whom you call the young cub," was the tart answer of the guardsman; "but if it be Martin Schuyler's daughter, I have some interest in her welfare, and in the welfare of all who go along with her; and we will go together, unless the chief can hinder me."

With that, the man in disguise led the way through the house that was so well known to him.

This was taking the red man where he did not want to go; but since he saw that Teunis was bent upon a search, and fearing that he might lose his prey, he followed, from room to room, until he came to one that was fastened within. The Indian was evidently sure of his object, and gave a sign which brought Shandaagan to his side, when he began to show marks of restiveness, and blood was in his eye. Teunis stood at the door with pistol in hand, for he feared himself that the young women might be inside of the room; with his back to the door, he gave a shout, calling for the "Mohawk chief to come up and receive two prisoners."

The cunning Kiskataam turned pale with mortification at the defeat of his plan, for this was one of the main points of his dread, being found out by Brandt as one engaged in kidnapping from the camp of their friends. So, turning on his heel, he left the house quicker than he had entered it. Teunis, well pleased with his victory, and with his fortunate discovery of the vulnerable part of the redskin, succeeded in getting a peep within the room, and was satisfied in finding it empty. Coming down, he found out that a fire had been kindled on the roof, and that it was all in vain to expect to save the house where so many men, worse than barbarians, were bent upon its destruction. He found Kiskataam waiting for him, who came up and said, in his low, guttural tones:

"The deer belongs to him that has first trapped it."

"Well," said Teunis, "it is mine, for I have been here first."

Becoming again provoked at the defeat, he said bitterly:

"Young Boerman's tongue cuts like the north wind;" and, leaping forward, he seemed determined to examine some part of the house himself, while, quick as thought, Teunis shut the heavy half-door, so that the Indian fell against it, rendering him ridiculous in the eyes of the others, who by this time had become interested in the contest between the white and the red man. All this time, Martin cast glances of gratitude upon his young friend, whom he now discovered to be Teunis, and was at no loss to guess his motive. Thanks from the old Whig were grateful in the highest degree to the Tory's son; but it would have added a thousand-fold to his heartfelt joy had he known that his whole conduct was marked by eyes that swam in tears of love and pleasure, almost inviting him to come and receive his reward while it was in the fullest bloom.

The work of devastation proceeded. The flames rushed upward and onward; inviting materials, they were throwing on to feed them; and the winds, like evil spirits, flew through the notches of the hills, as if to concentrate their forces where they could do the greatest injury, alongside of the incarnate fiends who aided them, howling and yelling as if they gave voice to the invisible troops of hell. The animals which were not beaten down escaped, running, lowing, to the woods, while the old team of horses, which Martin actually loved next to his wife and daughter, screamed and shrieked as the fire came round their stalls, adding fearfully to the din. What made much amusement, and not a little trouble even to the destroyers themselves, was an army of well fattened rats, who came through the yard around the feet of the men, who stamped and slashed on all sides, killing many and hurting more. The Indians especially were alarmed, and ran out of their way when they could, in a manner that caused great fun to their allies, the mock red men. One of these huge savages, to show contempt for both rats and Indian courage, paid for his temerity, when, seizing two of these grey-bearded captains, they caught his fingers in their teeth and made him "roar like Garret Abiel's black bull, Smut."

This little episode, which was causing such sport below, had like to have seriously affected the females confined above, through these frightened creatures seeking a refuge among the rocks. Led on by two ancient patriarchs, they were making their way to the crevices in the face of the hill, and had they found the first hole, no power could have hindered; but Rover, who from one of the loopholes saw the state of things, had his nature roused, so that seeking a passage in the opposite side he came round to the front just in time to seize the leaders by the neck, choking them, as the main army dispersed in other directions. After doing this, the faithful creature went up and licked the hands of his master, who had still a kind word for his friend.

The word "forward" was given, and when Teunis was congratulating himself that Elsie and the rest were escaped, he saw a close council held between the two Indians and Clifford, who now made his appearance on the stage for the first time. He was ashamed to be seen, yet he could not trust his instruments of cruelty even with the great promise of hire; and he durst not tell the Mohawk chief the real facts of the case; so that with a guilty purpose in his mind, a mortified pride to contend against, and the fear of exposure, he now became the most miserable and restless of all the creatures around him. Teunis saw with some uneasiness, that while Clifford and Kiskataam marched in the rear, the other Indian, Shandaagan, was left behind. No doubt as a spy upon the burning homestead, in expectation that the members of Martin's family would return, and discover their retreat. The young man had great confidence in the sagacity of Elsie, but how could she baffle the cunning of three such knaves?

CHAPTER XV.

THE SPECTRAL LOOKING-GLASS.

"That the dead are seen no more," said Imlac, "I will not undertake to maintain against the concurrent and unvaried testimony of all ages. That it is doubted by single cavillers can very little weaken the general evidence; and some who deny it with their tongues, confess it with their fears."—JOHNSON'S RASSELAS.

MARTIN SCHUYLER was marched to the same camp where his friend Abiel had been carried the previous night. Two of the Consistory, the friends met each other with calm faces, and a single sigh. They were pious men, and true patriots; so they bore up, as became their character, and all the more bravely in the presence of their sworn enemies, who looked at them with that grim smile which tries to hide the real feeling at the root of the soul, when success renders the position taken insecure, upon which victory has placed them. What was to be done with these men; and how were they themselves to come out from behind the false faces which they were wearing? "What if these two good men ever returned; and was not the prospect after all, that the Whigs would triumph in the end?"

In the meantime it was evident, from the preparations making, that it was the intention of the leaders to remain some time in this encampment; probably because all the captives expected, had not been brought in; or that some word from the general had not arrived. It was noon by this time and the Indians were busy with their meal, which chiefly consisted of venison brought with them, and parched corn gathered from the fields, through which they had passed, where it stood in stacks, ready for drawing in when the men had leisure. Apples they had in abundance, wild plums and other natural fruit. These they shared freely with their white companions, bond and free. Liquor there was none, except the pure water brought in gourds and skins from the little lakes close by.

It was one of these dull drizzling days so common in those high regions, when the fog becomes so thick that it might be cut. Nothing could be seen outside of the rock, and to such as knew the depth of the gulf beneath, it was a frightful consideration, that the thick darkness hid thousands of living souls, happy beneath such a heavy cloud. Moral reflections, however, were not the kind that were now passing through the minds of the men surrounding the different fires, kindled for cooking and for warmth. They who were around the crackling branches were more like a hunting party than persons engaged in the serious business of war. Smoking, eating, singing, jesting and telling stories were all going on together; and a full report of their conversation, with a picture of the different groups, would furnish amusement and instruction for a week. Ever and anon, as another prisoner was brought in, it produced a buzz of excitement, which rose into madness on the part of the one side, or sank the other into bitterness and cursing. But, on the whole, there was, at the end of an hour, quietness and resignation. Brandt kept the wild Tories in restraint; and the calm example of the two old men prevented any outbreak of anger from the Whigs. Martin Schuyler felt that he was one of the class who might expect the hardest treatment. Placed as he had been on the outskirts of a wide camp, his position required the utmost vigilance; and in absence of others, he had frequently to take arbitrary measures, which brought on him the whole responsibility. That he now must bear; nor were his judges the most impartial of his fellow-men. He saw around him in disguise many who had suffered in their families, and otherwise, through the course he had himself pursued; but the current of events had thrown the chances now into their hands. He must submit. Mercy he did not expect. The way in which his property had been destroyed that morning before his eyes was only the glaring light which showed him the way to his own personal ruin. He thought but little of himself; and gladly would he have suffered all they could have inflicted upon him, were he sure now that Anshela and his daughter were in a safe place. But how could that be, when so many were hunting after them; and those hunters so wily, and practised in the craft? "I have seen," he said to himself, "the deer hide away in the thicket for a short time, while the dogs were in pursuit; but the moment the man arrived, he saw at a glance what all the instinct of the combined pack could not discover."

As for Teunis, he wandered, like a spirit ill at ease, from fire to fire, listening eagerly to all that was said, so that he might use the information he received as a guide for future movements. His intention was to get a quiet interview with Martin, so that he might unfold his plan to him, and obtain his counsel; but there were eyes constantly following him. Clifford and Kiskataam were seated at different points keeping watch; still Teunis was a privileged person, and they durst not interfere with his liberty without revealing their own secrets. By and by the young man became bolder, and felt more independence, and finding himself, after some manœuvering, by the side of his old friend, his first desire was to possess the confidence of Martin.

"I hope," said Teunis, "that you do not think me capable of doing you any injury, or that I had any hand in what happened at Hoogenhuisen this morning."

"They say that a man is known by the company he keeps, Teunie, my lad. But you have your own reasons for being there and here."

This was said in a softer tone than the young man expected, and gave him courage to proceed.

"That is true, my friend, and the time will come when you will justify my conduct. Be quite sure that nothing in the world can bring me to hurt a hair of your head, or"——

His heart failed him to say the rest.

"Or that of Elsie, you were going to say. I believe you. She is worthy of all the blood you can shed on her behalf, Teunis; and there is old Anshela, her mother, who never shut the door upon a dog, and always left it open for you."

The old man's eyes swam with tears at this, and he turned round, as if he wished to see how High Peak was appearing at that moment.

"I swear to protect them," said the young man, in a whisper.

"We are noticed," said the senior, and pointed with his finger to an opening in the clouds, saying, loud enough to be heard, "The wind is changing—there is a change of fortune, too, coming in good time."

But for the cool and more constrained manner of the old man, Teunis, in the inward delirium of his real joy, would have given vent to some expression which might have caused him trouble. There was nothing he would not have dared to do at that moment in defence of Martin and of his family. His course was fixed, and the only consideration with him now was, "How shall I best reach the end I am seeking—show my true colors, and deliver Martin's family?" Honor and love had overwhelmed the ideas of life and fortune, and he could have faced a whole tribe of mock or real Indians to battle, were Elsie the object contended for.

"We are watched," said Martin. "Let us part for the present, and come to me when a chance presents itself."

At this point in their conference, a movement was observed among the different groups, as if some object of interest had arisen. Agreeably to Martin's prediction, the wind rose from the north, lifting up the black cloud that had hung like a heavy sheet behind them, and was rolling it up as a scroll is wound around, so that the sun was visibly coming out in a clear sky west of the mountain. On the flat rock were all the persons already known to us, evidently arrested by some object of great interest. Brandt, Clifford, and the Elder Abiel, stood together on the verge of the cliff. Martin and Teunis came up close to them, so that they formed part of the same half circle. When their attention became properly fixed, Teunis saw, for the first time, what he had frequently heard the old hunters tell of, the *geest wolk waren*—the spirit of the mist—seen only at rare times in these regions. So far as he could judge, there were huge masses of vapor passing in different strata, some of which were denser than others. That which was nearest to them at that moment was thin and transparent, reflecting all the objects which stood between it and the light thrown upon it by the clearer sky behind. In reality, it was a moving mirror, that slowly passed as a panorama is unreeled before a company of spectators. There was this difference between nature and art: the faces and forms of the persons looking on were the figures in the picture before them, taken instantly and held up to them. Every one saw himself distinctly, and his nearest neighbor only less vividly drawn. The whole was more like an artist's dream than a reality. It seemed as if they could have walked out and touched the picture, till a moment's reflection made them sensible that the whole was but a shadow. Teunis gazed first on his own outline, then on the tall, straight form of the Indian, who stood immovable. Behind the group of which he was one himself, he saw those who had lain down on the laurel bed, and beside them, several starting up in evident alarm; others were rushing forward, with curious and hasty looks of wonder at the strange sight; and round the place, where hemlock branches had been woven into tents, some of the Indians could be seen stooping like Arabs when an alarm has been given, caused by the mirage when it has lifted the forms of an enemy above the level of their plains. Be assured there was not an uninterested spectator on the rock, for so rare was the sight, that scarcely one of the whole had seen the wonder before, and those who had heard of it were more inclined to regard it as the vision of a frightened imagination than a fact.

Even the educated Englishman, Clifford, though affecting through philosophy a superiority, could not help showing an intense eagerness to see all to the close. He had read of the like phenomena among the Alpine heights, and had a way of explaining these to his own mind; but all his soul, for the present, was absorbed in the one sense—*sight.* Indeed, all were more eager to see than to speak, except one man, a Scotch highlander among the loyalists, who, knowing of these sights in his own country, was anxious to tell of the famous spaeman of Ben Cruachan, who was the seventh son of a seventh daughter in Lochabar, who saw in the mists of the hills the warning to Lochiel. Donald was almost out of the body as the cloud went on, carrying his own shadow with it. He swore a highland oath that he would give the best bit of tombacht in his spleuchan, for one word of Luath McGregor, just to tell what was going to take place.

"How the man wi the second sight would stan' up there afore hersel' the big chief Brandt, and show him whare he should be kilt. Grat satishfaction it would be to himsel'."

The Mohawk was deeply absorbed. The sight was new even to him; born and living mainly on the flats to the north. He looked on with a solemnity which amounted to dread, as if he had really reached the spirit land, of which the traditions of his fathers spoke. His whole tribe present rose to their full length, expecting to behold the figures come out into actual substance. Not accustomed to see themselves reflected from artificial mirrors, they were ignorant of their own forms. Gradually, as they began to comprehend the true nature of the appearance, their fear gave way to a silent admiration.

The faculties of the whole assemblage were awakened to the intensest eagerness; their apprehensions of things rapid, and their decisions unhesitating. Every one had come to some conclusion, and had felt sentiments in harmony with his opinions. One thing was evident—all were under an undefined feeling of superstition, as if that before them was a writing on the wall, like what the profane king saw, ominous of his own doom. The sheet cloud went slowly by, figure after figure melted into thin air; and it was affecting to hear each one tell, after, of how he felt an internal shiver, as he saw his own body dissolving, before his eyes, into nothing. There was not one present who would not willingly have avoided the conclusion, but his fate was irrevocable. Into the dark gulf he must plunge and be lost—forever.

In a short time the whole east was covered with the same black cloud as before, while the white, thin vapor, which had served as the reflector, was wheeled round to the south, and settled against the sides of the hill, which rises bluffly a few hundred feet higher than Flat Rock. There again, it became a new speculum, and of a far different nature from what it was when in its former place. Instead of each individual spectator seeing himself, he saw his nearest neighbor, to the right of him. The fact had an influence upon the events of that day in a striking manner. Fear and superstition had given place to curiosity; and, as a natural consequence in men of their order, chiefly gathered together through a spirit of adventure, frolic and fun began to show in their faces. One trifler, who had been the most cowardly of the crew, gave a caper in the air, which threw others into the same absurd attitudes, till a hundred more were seen dancing round, and hallooing like madmen. Solemnly and silently the figures in the cloud mocked the fools outside.*

Those men, however, with whom Teunis had stood all through, were not inclined to act in that pantomime. They were either engaged studying the reasons of those things before them, or quietly observing the movements, and waiting for the lesson which nature was teaching. Clifford was inclined to rally the two old Dutchmen upon their sober visages; and was asking of them how his own face appeared under that veil, when, as if struck by an invisible hand on the heart, his countenance assumed an appearance of such strange fear, that it was plain, even in the mist, that some awful change had come over him; and as he grasped the arm of the Elder Abiel, it seemed more like that of a drowning man than the grip of a brave soldier. Teunis, who saw that his face had become purple, and his eyes fixed in their sockets, came up hurriedly to his side to support him from falling, as he was evidently staggered; when, being on the same line of vision with Clifford, he chanced to look forward, and obtained a glance of a figure he was sure he had seen before, and which was evidently that on which the eye of Clifford was fixed. It came from a higher point than that on which they stood, and as if from a tree near by, where a face gazed through upon them. The figure was as if a man stood up, clothed in shaggy vapor, with a beard of enormous length; and though the expression of the countenance could not be defined, the gestures were of a threatening aspect. Teunis, more self-possessed, looked and saw the figure of the hermit whom he had seen lately, gliding away to the side of the cliff, below which he disappeared by some way known to himself. The Englishman, recovering from his surprise, shook off the friendly hand of Teunis, asking roughly, why he held him so firmly.

"Kindness," was the reply, "makes no choice of its subjects when they are falling through fear."

"Who is afraid, young man?" and the hand of Clifford instinctively was at his side. "You need support yourself, and you dream that all must be like you."

"I have no cause," said Teunis, "of being afraid of *him*. He never had any harm from me in his life. I have heard that those who injured him have reason to tremble."

By this time the countenance of Clifford was literally livid

* The Fata Morgana, seen so remarkably on the Straits of Messina, has been observed on the Catskills to perfection. The vision, as described in the text, was seen from the balcony of the Mountain House in 1845.

with anger or terror, or a mingling of these passions; and he would doubtless have done something dreadful at that moment, had not his companions interfered, apologizing for the young man's ignorance of manners. The Mohawk put his arm through that of the Englishman, while Martin said, in a whisper: "Hot blood. Let us away till it cool."

None seemed to know the cause of this strange movement; and in the rapid current of things of a marvellous nature, none inquired minutely into them. Teunis felt some desire to know, and passing over the cliff at the same place he had seen the hermit go, he pursued after him, in hope of getting an explanation.

In the meantime, nothing was talked of but the remarkable vision. The company were calmed down to soberness, for a short time at least. Clifford, who had really, from some cause known to himself, been the most startled, now affected the utmost lightness of spirit, and seemed anxious to turn the conversation away from himself. He avoided all his companions for a time as carefully as he had been ready to meet them before; ashamed of a passion he had indulged in without cause, he became talkative, and even sprightly, with all around, jesting the Indian upon his solemn looks, and the old Elder about his religion. That worthy man, more direct and simple than men of the world, traced all he saw to the GREAT CAUSE least understood. One of the younger men was explaining the wonder by his grandmother's looking-glass, that she brought with her from Holland.

"Maybe," said Paulus Wynkoop. "But how can twae put together make dem shine?"

"You saw yon black cloud," said Jack Adams, who had taught school in the town, and knew some things; "it was not all dark. Behind, it was light; that was the quicksilver. The other cloud was the glass, and our faces were reflected from that surface."

"Well, what do you say, Jack, to the other, where we could not see ourselves, but our neighbors?"

"That," said Adams, "beats me; for I declare I saw one face that I have not seen here this day; and I never saw such a shape before, so that I am guessing there was more in that cloud than the Dominie could tell about. I wonder what he would have said to all these things!"

"Oh," said Martin, who was near, "he would have told us about the openbaring * and the shifting scenery Johannes

* Apocalypse.

saw, when looking-glasses, brighter and greater than all these, revolved round the heavens."

"And he would have told us," said the Elder Abiel, "about the angel that sat upon the cloud with the sickle in his hand; and the other angel that cried, 'zend uwe sikkel en —for the time is come.' That was a warning of things expected."

"Surely," said Clifford, "old man, you do not call those things miracles, since they can be all excellently well explained, without calling in the help of the Creator?"

"Surely," said the Elder, "you would not take the Almighty's works out of his own hand; and may he not be showing us what is going to happen?"

"Oh, I suppose our red friend, the great Mohawk, saw the sires of his people in that cloud too, at their council fires. Was my brother studying the work of the Great Spirit? Were you not afraid lest you should see the ghost of your father, chief?"

The chief was displeased, and merely grunted out, "Pale face grow paler at the ghost of his father."

Clifford understood this to be a direct thrust at a tender place he was doing his utmost to guard. He attempted to laugh it off, by saying, "If our fathers be reduced to such substances, it would be folly to entertain fear of them here, or hereafter."

"And you should honor your father's name, my good sir, if you would be honored yourself; you obeyed him in the flesh."

"And you would add, 'Why not in the spirit?'"

"Yes; why not in the spirit?" were the Elder's words. "I am more afraid of spirit than I am of flesh, though I scorn to tremble, as I have seen some at their own shadow."

This last was said unwittingly, but it convinced Clifford that it was dangerous for him to continue the subject; and seeing Kiskataam standing aside by himself, he went on, walking slowly toward him, as if at ease in mind, while he was really eager to know from him what had become of Teunis, who was now missed from the rock; for agreeably to a plan laid down, that young man was to be tracked in every place.

That prudent youth had proceeded on the trail of the mysterious being, man, or shadow, whose spectre had produced the effect of terror on the hardened Clifford, and was soon out of sight.

The main body, waiting upon the will of their leaders,

were disposed, after the excitement of the appearance in the cloud, to find employment according to their fancy, and were watching the rolling up of the misty curtain that hung over the land below. The outline of the hills beyond, became every moment more visible, till at length the view, long and sweeping, attracted every eye, as if in expectation of some object new and interesting, when a cry, "The ship! the ship!" rose with a shout.

It was the Vulture in search of more prey, and like a creature possessed of instinct, she was sailing up the river. She was hailed by the spectators as if sent for their special amusement. There was one great drawback to their sympathy: the ship was too far off to allow the movements of the sailors to be seen, or the voices of the spectators to be heard. There was real pantomime in the ship. She represented the crew. The movements she made was the speech, that was interpreted freely. Nor was there any difficulty in understanding her language, when first a flash came out from her side, then blue smoke, that curled upward, followed by a report that echoed among the hills.

"King George is speaking," cried out an excited Tory, "and the Baron Livingstone must answer. Ha! ha! Brave Whig, you are put to your trumps at last."

"I wonder," said Hank Van Schaik, "if he has not some of Captain Kidd's doubloons in his coffer yet. The Vulture would take a mess and be gone."

"Shame upon you, Van, for thinking the king's officers would be bribed by that old pirate's gold."

"Ho, ho! is that all you know of these things? Why, that old pirate, as you call him, had a good deal of the witch about him, and might throw dust in the eyes of a captain of the royal navy. He never hid money but he killed a big nigger beside it; and as they say he hid a good sum in the baron's house, who knows but an army of blacks may come out to meet the marines, should they venture to go on shore?"

"Venture! I guess they'll venture; and the king's folk will search that old house for his own. I suppose you know that Queen Bess had an interest in Captain Kidd's venture; but old Livingstone took her part and his own. 'The king will have his own again.' That's the old song. See, there, they have cast anchor, and a boat is lowering, as I am a living man. Now we shall see fun. I wish to goodness I had wings; if I would not put my foot on that roof before five minutes were gone."

Clifford, who carried a small spyglass, lifted it to his eye, and surveyed the vessel's outline and movements. He then offered it to the Mohawk chief, whose vision was of that nature which sees far off, so that he did not require aid; but handing it to the Elder, he looked, and saw that something fearful was about to take place. All waited anxiously; nor had they long to wait. A little cloud was observed to rise above the ancient mansion, that grew in size every moment, till there rose a shout of fiendish joy from the enemies of the Whigs, that made the welkin ring above them. Tears and curses, not loud but deep, came from the other side at the destruction which was now going on.

The blaze soon ascended through the black smoke, till there was nothing seen but one vast sheet of red flame, that shot up into the sky like a great tongue, invoking the vengeance of heaven upon the perpetrators of this deed. The spectators had been so lately the actors and the sufferers in a similar transaction, it seemed but the continuance of the day's work; more especially, when it was recollected that the Schuylers and the Livingstones were not only fellow Whigs, but related in the same family ties to each other. The king's ship on water was only carrying out the acts of the king's servants on land. Accordingly, the Tories danced and screamed, at the sight, holding out their hands like children when they seek to be warmed at the fire they have kindled themselves.

The sad prisoners were reminded anew of their sorrows, and of the losses which their friends were undergoing, and were fain to be silent under the jibes and the reproaches continually thrown out, while the fire blazed before their eyes.

"Let us be patient, Martin," said the good Elder; "all this will be explained by and by. You remember that the silver must be put through the fire before it can be known as the good and pure."

"If I only was sure that Anshela and Elsie were in a good, sure place, my mind would be at ease," said the really tried man.

"See," said the Elder Abiel, "there is Teunis Roe, and he seems as if he had some message for you, as he is now signing to you, not to me."

It was so, and fortunate it was for them both that they could hold a consultation unobserved. So eager were their guards upon the sight before them, that they had nearly forgotten the prisoners; and Teunis was so sensible of this, that he hinted to Martin the possibility of escaping. But that could not be after the word of honor he had passed on that day to Brandt.

The eager young man urged this till Martin grew angry, and told him that if he had no better comfort to give him than that, he might go; all he asked was help for his family; if he could in his conscience give it when an opportunity occurred.

"I think it is possible," was the reply of the humbled youth, "if you confide in my honor, and tell me where is your Binenkamerin."

Had Teunis struck the old man on the face, it would have caused far less surprise than asking him where his *secret chambers* were; first that he should suspect their existence, and next that he, the son of his enemy, should inquire after them. But checking himself, he merely replied:

"You demand what even my best friend, the Elder there, would not venture to know about; and you will have to give me very good reasons indeed, young man, before I answer your question now, though I be a prisoner of Brandt and of your king."

Teunis hung his head, knowing that he had so far forfeited the confidence of Martin, by asking him to violate his word of honor; but the case was too urgent to stop short at this point. He had, as we saw, followed the Hermit down the face of the cliff, unobserved by any one, during the time all were attracted to the vision on the cloud; and being swift of foot, he soon came up with the mysterious man, who seemed aware of being followed, and suddenly turning, he demanded why Teunis tracked his steps.

"Pardon me," said the youth; "but you told me to come and get some information of"——

"Oh, yes. You come now when you cannot help it. Like all the selfish race of mankind; very complacent and yielding when difficulty appears."

"I ask pardon again," said Teunis; "I am now ready to follow your directions. If you know anything about them, relieve my suspense, and tell me what I should do; and your will is my law in this matter."

"Others as well as yourself, young man, are interested in knowing these things. Remember that selfishness is the bane of life. A well becomes foul when only one draws from it."

"And yet the spring at your cabin door is always clear," was the prompt reply of the young inquirer.

"That is more than can be said of the spring in every heart, young man; and if I may judge, yours is not entirely pure in the matter nearest to it. Did you see those shadows in the mist?"

"Yes, and your face more strikingly than the others. Tell me why that Englishman trembled before it?"

"Ask things you have a right to inquire after, but pry not into my secrets," was the fierce answer of the man. "Know this, that conscience is a great revealer of truth; and that villain thinks, though he affects to believe in nothing, that he saw a real spectre. You will see. But your business is of another nature than mine."

"I am anxious," said Teunis humbly, "to know where I may find Elsie Schuyler and her present companion."

"You do well young man in putting them together; and the object of your affections first. I do not find fault and I will help you in this; seek out the place which the Dutch people call their Binenkamerin."

Having said this, he turned and moved away at a rapid pace, cutting off all further colloquy. Teunis was here brought to a complete stand, for well as he knew all the apartments of Hoogenhuisen, he was entirely ignorant of the secret places about it: nor would he venture to guess, nor even now to search after, lest he might reveal, what he knew should only be known to the tried friends of the family. As the surest and most effectual method, he resolved to find out the hiding-place from Martin himself; and we have seen the first reception he met with from that worthy.

Teunis, however, had gone too far to be beaten back; so he persevered in his inquiries, after relating an account of the interview he had just had down in the glen below. Martin listened throughout with deep interest, becoming deeper every moment; when at the conclusion of the narrative he said:

"It is true that that man has had a wonderful influence over Elsie's mind, for some time past. She has spent whole days in his cabin, and if any one knows of our hiding-place, besides the Dominie, out of the family, it is likely he does. I will trust you, since the case is desperate."

"I will swear," said Teunis rising from his seat with great fervor.

"Swear not at all young man," said Martin. "I will trust you without an oath. You will stand at the back door of Hoogenhuisen—but awee! awee! there is no door there now," and the old man's eyes swam in tears, as he seized the hand of Teunis. "You will stand where we met this morning and look straight southward, and you see a three-cornered stone, half standing against the face of the hill; there seek, lift the loose stones at your feet, and you will see the rest. Go off now, while all these men are so eager upon their sport, and come back when you have good news to tell; I will know when I see you here that all is well."

After a sufficient time to prevent suspicion, Teunis left, going by the way of the cliff, where the main body were still standing looking down upon the ship and the burning house, just to show himself. He spoke to those he knew best, passing by Clifford near enough, to let him look in his face, which seemed hollower than when he saw it last. He tried to get a glimpse of Kiskataam, and his shadow Shandaagan, but not seeing them, he felt the necessity of being on the lookout for them all the way to Hoogenhuisen, to which he bent his steps hastily, reaching it before dark. From the directions he had received, he found no difficulty in entering the hiding-place. He made his way into the back chamber; where he found traces of recent habitation; blankets and quilts lay around, in places which had served as beds; and there stood three stones, which had been used as seats. He had hopes now of finding the fugitives, so crawling through a subterranean passage, calling now upon Anshela, then upon Elsie, in a loud whisper all the way, as he went, without obtaining an anwer, he concluded that they had made their escape to some other place of refuge: and as he could not discover any signs of a struggle he had hopes of their entire safety. In a corner where some straggling rays of light came through a chink in the rock, he discovered a Bible that he had given to Elsie on her birth-day; opening it he found a mark pointing to a passage which he interpreted as a message to himself. It ran thus: "Return, return, O Shulamite, that we may look upon thee. What will you see in the Shulamite? As it were a company of two armies." The tear filled the eyes of the reader, as he saw how anxiously he had been waited for, and how lately they had been there looking for him. As he sat musing, and chiding himself without reason, wondering in what way he could serve these distressed females, he became sensible that some living thing was moving around on the outside. Rising up quietly and cautiously, he made his way to the nearest opening, listening anxiously till all was quiet, when he sprang to his feet, standing on the rear of the place, and then took a rapid glance all round him in search of some one. In a few minutes, to his horror, who should appear but his hated enemy Kiskataam. They faced each other with a meaning look, as if each said to the other: "I know your business here." Teunis, as the most excited, and the most honest, was the first to speak.

"Why does the chieftain of the mountain hunt after a muskrat so keenly. Has Brandt sent spies after his allies?

"Brandt's allies," said the red man sarcastically, "have not two faces; one for the day and another for the night."

"Then Kiskataam is not one of them, for he has game of his own?"

Teunis put this in the interrogative key, striking the ear of the wily chief so that it rung again, throwing him off his guard. He intended to insinuate treachery on the part of Teunis; and the insinuation was given back with interest. Rallying himself he muttered:

"The true dog may hunt after the false fox."

"Then Kiskataam is Brandt's dog. The chief of the mountains has fallen when he has come on the Mohawk's errand. The fox can double a mean dog."

This dialogue could not have been long continued without producing results of a serious nature; and as the young Boerman was well armed, and withal a powerful man, it would not have been safe in the Indian to have struck a blow then. Nor would it have served his purpose. A quarrel at that moment would have put the man out of the way who was evidently seeking after the same object with himself. A little patience and watchfulness, and Teunis would discover the retreat of the women. The mortified chief walked off crestfallen, having been caught in his own trap at eavesdropping. Not far off, Teunis perceived that he was joined by Shandaagan, and though going with their backs toward him, they were doubtless in mind determined to turn and dog his steps. His own resolution was to keep watch on this spot during the night at least, in case, any of the fugitives should return. In the morning he would be guided by the course of events.

CHAPTER XVI.

QUEEN OF THE MOUNTAIN.

"Be thine own home, and in thyself dwell;
Palace anywhere;
And seeing the snail which everywhere doth roam,
Carrying his own house still, still is at home,
Follow (for he is easy paced) this snail,
Be thine own palace, or the world's thy jail.'
DONNE.

ELSIE and her fellow-prisoners had, in some measure, recovered from the shock caused by the late attack on Hoogenhuisen. It would be folly to deny that the brave girl felt more than gratitude toward Teunis, for the defence he had made, and her mind was wandering in that direction, when in order to compose herself she sat down with the Bible before her eyes, while in heart she was desiring human as well as divine help. Read what part she pleased, some how or other the song of Solomon would turn up. And there she found and marked that verse which Teunis afterward found and read. On looking up from the page a moment, she perceived Miss Clinton all drawn up, as if something was pressing upon her breast like a nightmare, which she was struggling to resist. She ran immediately to the lady's side, and saw the cause, which had almost an equal influence upon herself. Shandaagan was prowling around among the smoking ruins, with his face turned toward the very spot where they were hidden. Her first thought was to lift the long gun that lay loaded at her side, and finish his career; but prudence as much as humanity restrained her. She, however, took a look around the apartment, determined to resist his entrance should he come to discover it. Nearer and nearer he came, as if he was examining every inch of ground, and the extraordinary instinct of the Indian appeared now to have the power of leading him in the very direction where they were sitting. He seemed more like a dog smelling the ground than a man scrutinizing it by reasoning faculties. He was within twenty yards of the place where she sat, and was still approaching. A thought struck her; she began to hiss like a serpent, in a low, slow manner, till she saw the attention of the Indian arrested, when she changed her place, and continued hissing till it became near a whistle. Rover, who was half sleeping, rose suddenly at this, and was about to reply in his own style, when his mistress seized him by the paws, preventing what must have discovered the whole nest. But the hissing and the under growl were sufficient to awaken new thoughts in the mind of her pursuer, for after laying his ear to the ground, he rose, going quite over the spot where they were looking through at him; so close indeed that the toes of his moccasins were fixed in the holes of their cell, as he climbed to the top. A new danger now appeared. He might discover the door in the rear. Giving the dog in charge of her mother, and setting Miss Clinton to watch the road, putting a large pistol in her hand, which made Margaret look for the moment like a soldier's daughter, Elsie started for the back part of their citadel, to look out. Her courage was now rising equal to the occasion. Taking her long gun with her, she crawled through between the rocks, all the time feeling quite certain that some one was walking above. She paused that she might listen, scarcely breathing, lest she herself should be heard, when, to still her greater alarm, Rover, who had made his escape from the easier grip of Anshela, was whining low at her side, while the old woman, fully aware of the crisis, had followed after him to resume her hold. She had entered the narrow passage after her daughter, but being neither so supple nor so slim, she stuck in that place like a Dutch scow in a canal lock, and could not go forward nor back. Never was poor girl in a more puzzling plight. Her mother and Rover, herself and Miss Clinton, alike the objects of her solicitude, while the foe was now within earshot; she could, in her desperation, have gone out and faced a score of savages; but, luckily for all, the mother gave herself a good pull and got back into the main apartment, where Margaret met Elsie with the information that the Indian had returned to the front and was calling out for Rover. The two animals had, no doubt, recognized each other in their own way; but the brave girl, taking some rope, put a muzzle on the dog, and fastened him to a chest till the danger would pass.

Their tormenter left their sight after a brief space, and the three prisoners had now time to breathe and congratulate themselves on their narrow escape. Miss Clinton wept in perfect joy, and would have been content to remain there for a month. Not so Elsie, who saw that the danger was not past. "He will return," she said, "and solve this mystery.

He will bring Kiskataam with him, and they will burn us out if they cannot bring us to yield up."

"I will die first in this spot, and sell my life dear too," said Margaret. "I will prove to them how a soldier's daughter can defend herself when it comes to a battle. I fear death less than being in the hands of either Clifford or his deceitful servant. Go, Elsie, and leave me here to do as I am determined."

Elsie, who under the power of excitement was equal to any crisis, was above feeling the burden of her responsibility and musing upon what might be the best plan, suffered broken sentences to escape from her, such as, "Why does he not come? Oh, for one word of that dark man in the hollow. Let us watch."

"And pray," said the pious Angelica, who was rocking herself backward and forward as if that motion was essential to her thought and consciousness. What she had always trusted to was still with her, but in this new condition her mind had not yet obtained its balance. "Vy does niet de Dominic come? hem ay kaam in distress. Myne vader ende myne moeder hebben my verlaten; maar de Heere zal my aannemeer."

"What does your good mother say, Elsie? tell me that I may share in her comfort and support."

"She says that though my father and my mother forsake me yet the Lord will take me up."

"All true, as I can feel this moment. We have all three but one Father now. But look, Elsie, here. What is that I see moving there on the other side of the glen? It looks like some animal, but it has stood so still that I think it must be but a stone."

The mountain lass fixed her eye on the place, and after a few moment's examination she withdrew her eyes, with a shudder, merely saying: "More trouble. The master devil is there himself, as I supposed."

"Kiskataam it is," said Miss Clinton, hiding her eyes in her hand, as she cried: "Oh, God help me; help us all in this hour of sorrow. Thou beholdest all things below. Look down, we beseech thee, and hear us calling out of the depth of misery, and out of the jaws of this death which is now ready to swallow us up. Save us, O Lord, or else we perish."

Elsie stood amazed at the utterance of this prayer, and seemed to regard her friend as one inspired, while the old mother whispered to herself, "She prays goodens to Dominie." All the three became more composed and determined. Their enemy stood looking steadfastly toward them, as if he could see through the rocks; or it might be that he was surveying the fortress, before making a grand attack. To the left was the other fiend, who had, by appointment no doubt, met his master, with whom he was in consultation. The prisoners could guess his report, and judged too, probably, what would be their next move.

"They have sunk to the ground," said Margaret, "as if shot by an arrow; so noiselessly they fall."

"Yes," was the response of her companion, "some one has appeared. Now God grant it may not be Teunis at this moment, or he is a lost man, and we lost with him. If they do the deed, revenge is my word;" and she grasped the gun firmly in her hand, as if the work was begun.

Sure enough, Teunis did arrive on the ground, and was watched eagerly from behind the tree, by those snaky eyes, that moved unknown to him.

"They will shoot him from behind," said Angelica. "Let me cry to him."

"No, mammy. No, they are only wanting to see where he goes. We must try and divert their eyes from him to something else. We must leave. Oh, for half an hour. He will come straight in here, and they will follow hard on his heels. Let us leave, and we can watch them from another point to more advantage. Once get us here, pent up, and they will soon have their whole pack upon us. Mammy, go out first. It is life or death. I will wait here and watch till you get through. Push these quilts and skins before you. Who knows where our next bed may be.

Now, Martin had so fixed the back entrance after a fashion of his own. He was his own blacksmith, as he was his own mason and carpenter. He had run two bolts, with lead, into a large flat stone, which lodged into eyes that were bored into the rock. There it hung, so that it might be lifted up to the roof, and when let down it appeared in its natural place. It was a portcullis of a rude kind, but fully answering the purpose of shutting out all, except those who knew the secret. Elsie remained behind as long as she could, in hopes of getting one word from Teunis, and revealing to him her purpose of retreating; but she plainly saw that the spies were within hearing, and might succeed in preventing the escape of all the four, by some cunning manœuvre, since

Teunis was entirely ignorant of their presence. The two things she wished for most, and feared most, came at one moment. To flee was her only alternative, while there was yet hope. She let down the strong barricade, and lay behind it, to see and hear. She dreaded blood being spilt; and by the way of comforting herself, she shook a little dry powder into the lock of the duck gun, putting the muzzle through a hole prepared for such a purpose. Here she lay, and saw all we have already described, until it grew quite dark, when thinking on the possibility of being surrounded before the morning, she left, without accomplishing her desire of speaking one word to Teunis.

With great effort Angelica found her way into the open air, where she soon revived sufficiently to lift a burden of bedding. Miss Clinton took her part, and Elsie more than would cover herself, and taking now the lead of the march in deep darkness, toward what was then called the Dog Pool, since named "THE FAWN'S LEAP," they reached it without any interruption, except the obstacles which a rocky path always presents to tender feet.

The morning found the outcasts in a dejected state of mind, and with weary bodies. Had an enemy come upon them, he would have met with but a feeble resistance. Elsie soon perceived that this state of things would of itself soon destroy her hopes and the lives of her companions, so she set herself to work cheering them, and turning their minds away from themselves and their troubles. Knowing the place she had chosen, and now somewhat acquainted with her ward, she began a plan of interesting her mind, by exciting her natural enthusiasm for mountain scenery. She had formerly been sheltered there during a dreadful storm of hail; and afterward, during a hot day in July, had sat under the rock that hung over the little fall. It lies in a narrow ravine, below the rocks where the Kauterskill comes down, and falls over the shelf into a basin a hundred feet still lower down. The whole is surrounded with trees and shrubs common to the region, and forms an amphitheatre of wildness and beauty seldom surpassed. It is not so capacious as the falls lying immediately back of Pine Orchard, but it has points of interest which surpass even that famous spot. Here, in the soft sand, which is as dry as sand can be out of the sun and never sprinkled with spray or rain, was the bed of Miss Clinton, and in which she slept that night more soundly than she had frequently done in Shrewsbury Castle.

Elsie had made her own bed near that of Miss Clinton, but owing to the load of her responsibility, her sleep did not come till far in the morning. When she awoke and looked around, the first object that caught her eye was her mother, sitting at a newly kindled fire, with her cutty pipe in her mouth, seemingly taking as much comfort as she had seen her enjoying between the jambs of Hoogenhuisen, looking on the china pictures of Joseph and his brethren. The young English girl lay upon a large black bearskin, covered with a thick comforter, still asleep. "Let her lie still and sleep on; who knows when she may have another chance?" And with that she began to make her own simple toilet, with a rock for her table and a small pool for a mirror. Margaret soon opened her eyes, in evident alarm at the scene, when rising on her elbow, her eyes fixed on her protectress, she soon regained her composure. After this, she cast one despairing look upward, uttering the name of God and mother.

"Elsie, dear Elsie," said the fond girl, "it was long before I could fall asleep, and yet I am more afraid now in the daylight than I was when I looked up on the stars, which seemed to me like the eyes of angels looking down on me. Have you ever imagined those stars to be holy beings hovering over us?"

"Yes, my dear lady, I have often heard that good angels attend upon the good always; but our Dominie says a good conscience is the best guardian angel, and the surest sleeping-drops in the apothecary's store; and that a star in the breast gives more true light than all the millions in the sky. You know that I myself love to watch the stars, and last night I looked up so long, that I fell asleep dreaming that I heard their feet marching over the pure pavement above my head."

"Your Dominie must be a poet, or else he has read a book called 'The Mask of Comus,' which I feel suits my case too well. A lady lost her way, as I have mine, but she felt as I should feel, and as your minister tells you is best.

"'These thoughts may startle well, but not astound
The virtuous mind, that ever walks attended
By a strong-sided champion, conscience.'

"Did you hear the stream, how it murmured around our camp, and then roared off in the distance? It put me in mind of a crowded theatre, just before the curtain rises, when the shout of applause succeeds the appearance of the favorite actor. I lay listening till it seemed to soften down into the low crooning sound of my old Scottish nurse, when she used to sing me to sleep on her bosom. That put me in mind of home, and I cried myself to sleep."

"Rise, my lady," said the kind listener, perceiving the necessity of action, "and let me dress you. The cold air must be kept away, and here is my mother's oak-leaved quilt, which I will put around you as the Indian squaws do their blankets." And with that Elise threw the coverlet over the shoulders of the delicate damsel, on whom the air of heaven had scarcely ever blown rudely before in all her life-time. Her tall and graceful form was not hidden in the particolored shawl, and when her present lady's maid took the handkerchief which a Dutch skipper had brought from India as a present to her grandmother, tying it round the waist of Margaret, she appeared in full dress, smiling and wondering what her "London friends would say were she to walk in among them in this mask, fresh from the mountains. Lady Grantham would hold up her hands and declare that nothing could be more *distingué* and picturesque."

"Do you see how that stream leaps down among the rocks?" was the quiet question of her kind companion, all the time anxious to divert the thoughts of the stranger from herself and from her home. "Did you ever see a lighter foot than that is, trusting to the air so confidently?"

"No, never; and yet I have seen airy creatures who seemed more the creations of fancy than of reality. But how beautifully the whole stream loses itself in the haze, which covers it like a veil thinner than the purest gossamer."

"And there, again, Miss Clinton, see how it trips away down yonder below, coming out of its misty curtains fresh and fair, like a child running to its mother's arms."

This was unfortunate, though kindly intended and finely said, for the poor exile, taking up the thought, ran off in a rhapsody of affection.

"Ah, my dear Elsie, why have you touched on that string, to remind me of my joyful days, sending me back here to my sorrow? My mother is down there, just where that little stream is going to embrace the river. Why might I not follow its course and find her? Tell me, could I not go, keeping by its side? Would not I come to the river with it, and find my way to the vessel? I can imagine it waiting for me at this moment."

"You would find the rocks too hard for your tender feet, my dear lady," were the kind words of the good Angelica, "and the windings and falls are more than you dream of."

"Oh, there seems to be nothing direct in this world. How crooked has been my way these few days past! Why might I not take a winding course with that stream, and come out in the end all well?"

"Straight roads are not always the best. Our Dominie scolds the path-masters every summer, because they will go over a hill when going round it would be easier for their cattle. Ask my mother, and she will give you Scripture for it."

"Yaw," said the experienced old lady. "See de kinderen of Ishrael ta'en by vays after de cloudy pillar afore dey got to Kaunaan."

"This stream we are now watching," interfered Elsie, "is dealt kindly by, for it is let down step by step, and in a far, roundabout way. You saw the two ponds that we lay beside yesterday—no, the day before, I forget myself. They form the fountain-head. About two miles below, the waters take a far higher leap than they do here. The further down it goes, the fall is less and less, till it becomes as smooth as your cheek, and as quiet as your old nurse's voice when she found you fairly asleep in your cradle."

"Min vat de Dominie says about dat, Elsie?"

"Oh, he says that his young folk go off like the Kauterskill up here, and end like the quiet Kaatskill, in their old age joining the great river rolling into the sea."

"And is this the only stream in these hills?" was the inquiry of Miss Clinton, who now began to forget herself and her troubles. "If it be a solitary thing, it is far from showing the signs of sadness."

"This is not the only stream of the mountains hereabout," was the answer of Elsie, "for there is another spring head not far off from this, but the stream runs in the opposite direction. My father followed that when he was young. He says it follows the backbone of the mountain, going down into old Schoharie, then through the Mohawk country, joining that river till it meets the Hudson, and mingles with these very waters we are now looking at, after all that wandering life."

"What a history you are telling me!" said Margaret, pleased with the fancy which rose in her mind. "How like to some histories I could tell myself."

"I remember what you told me when we hid ourselves beside the little lakes, and I am almost sorry I spoke just now; but the truth will come out, Miss Clinton."

"That is true, and was no fault of your honest heart. Bertram and I were born near to each other. He went off to the sea when he was a boy, and we met again after the separation, on the Hudson, where these two streams you speak of are mingling in one great river."

"Come and heve somet'ing to eat," was the call of the careful mother; "leiv aff t'ese sorrowful tales, lookin' into te vater, shedding saut tears."

Upon a flat stone standing on the shelving rock that hung over the fall, were placed bread, boiled eggs, and dried venison. A cow, which came from the herd, gave them milk; the whole made an excellent breakfast, of which they partook heartily and gratefully. The mountain air gave them a keen appetite, and at the close of the meal, Elsie took her two hands and lifted up a cup of water, of which she drank herself; then offering as much to her companion, they were ready for whatever might betide.

"Come now," said the mountain lass, "and I will lead you to my favorite walk." And with their arms around each other, they went up the side of the glen toward the north. Turning around to her mother, Elsie said: "Mammy, the wildcats mew if anything happens."

"Yaw! yaw!" said the careful dame; "wildcats plenty all over. But I will mind."

"Are there enemies near us that you leave the signal with the sentinel? I had almost believed the danger to be all below, in that hollow, mysterious place we were in yesterday."

"You are too well acquainted with the customs of war, Miss Clinton, not to know that safety lies in constantly watching. But let us not talk of danger till we see it face to face. Let us walk; and please not to turn around till I tell you, for I want to point to what I think is worth seeing." When they had advanced about half a mile above the fall, Elsie called, "Now turn and look."

The sight was so overwhelming that Margaret was for a few minutes in speechless rapture. High Peak, that majestic pyramid, stood out in bold relief against the southern sky, surrounded by numerous hills, great and small, among which he rose like a king attended by his suite, who looked up to his crown with awe and delight. The October sun had spread a mysterious haze over the whole scene, which expanded rather than hid its greatness.

"What do you see there?" said the truly proud mountain damsel; proud of her own region.

"My head is dizzy. Let me alone till I get over my bewilderment, and be able to comprehend what is before me. Oh! what a stage is there for superior beings to descend upon, and see the actions of puny mortals! Elsie, have you ever known any one to ascend that height?"

"Oh, yes; I have been up there myself more than once. But it helps to humble one. I never feel myself so small as when I stand on that eminence, and think what a mote am I. And yet," was the pious thought of the rural maid, "I have felt my soul expanding above it all, when I knew that I was an immortal creature, redeemed by the Son of God."

"That is like mounting from the foot of Jacob's ladder to the top of it at a bound. I am down at the bottom yet. When I was in the city of Rome, they took me into the great church there called St. Peters; and, Elsie, do you know that when some one beside me said that he felt himself so small that he could sink, I said, presumptuous thing that I was, 'My heart swells so that I fill all this house.' You must have felt up there as I did in Rome."

"Four times a year, Miss Clinton, do I come up to this place, and look up; in June, when everything is in the greenest lustre; in August, when all is so rich and full; in October, when those various colors are painted by the hand of nature, and again in winter."

"Now I find out the cause of my confusion, Elsie: that wondrous variety of colors. This is what is called the fall and Indian summer, when the foliage changes. It is a new thing to my English eyes."

"And have you no fall in England—no Indian summer there?" said the amazed girl, who had less idea of the difference of climate than her travelled companion. "Then I do not think so much of your great island after all. No fall! no Indian summer! What have you?"

"England is always green like your June, Elsie; but what would they give there for one glimpse of that mountain, clad in trees to the very crown, and every one of these trees in different colors, from the richest purple to the brightest yellow, and the whole robe intermingled with pale and deep green. But tell me, what is that shrub covering all the ground so dark in the red."

"We call that the laurel, which is spread all over the mountains, as you see beneath our feet. But look, here is my favorite flower at this time of the year, the *sumach*. Let me put it into your hair, for a feather; and tell me if ever the queen of England had one so rich?"

"Bring me other two, and I will show you the Prince of Wales' feather. There now, a soldier of the forty-second regiment would fight with more ardor for his native hills, than he does even now, with the blood cockade in his bonnet. Oh, what a deep and pure scarlet! Never, never would they believe me, were I to tell of it just as I see it in your hands." *

It was in this manner that Elsie led the enthusiastic girl to forget her troubles. Romantic in disposition, and full of life, the picturesque in nature and in costume captivated her ardent heart, so that she forgot everything for the pleasure of the present moment, light as the bird that leaped from branch to branch. It required only the tact of producing new objects of attraction, and she would have remained for days among these hills, and been happy, and have made others happy also in return. Dressed as Elsie had adorned her in the colors of nature, with her clear, intellectual countenance, she moved with the air of a princess; and had a stranger come suddenly upon them, she would have been chosen as the genius of the region, attended by rustic wisdom in her homely garb.

"I have been thinking," said the elated captive girl, "of how happy you must be, when there is no trouble below, on a day like this, and our friend Teunis with you. For I am all the more happy in the company of those I love best; and you are of the same mind too, I am sure."

"Yes, there are days which we remember always, when we were too full of happiness. The heart, like a cup full of joy, surges over the brim, and we share it with others. I have had my share at all seasons. This time of the year is always the finest to me, though not the grandest."

"When do you call the mountain in its grandest array? I cannot imagine anything beyond what I am looking at just now. I have seen Mount Blanc, but there was nothing on it save the awful whiteness, which blinds and awes the spirit."

"Miss Clinton, to my mind the sublimest scene of these

* So the English considered Coles' Mountain scenery.

hills is to be seen in the white winter. The loneliness pleases me so, that I feel a reverence for High Peak, which I never feel at another season. All is then so still, that I can hear my heart beating. It is only at rare times that its real grandeur appears. One day, a few years ago, in January I was here. There had been a thaw and a heavy rain for a whole day, which beat upon the snow without melting it, making it so hard that it could be trodden upon by the foot without sinking. Toward midnight the wind came around suddenly to the northwest, and blew one of the coldest blasts I ever knew. The rain continued, but it froze as it fell, so that not a tree, nor a twig nor a leaf but hung in icicles, clear as the crystal I have seen on my uncle's table at Albany. As soon as my father rose, he said, 'now is the time for chasing that mischievous *painter* that has troubled the sheep so long. He will sink in the crust. Let us after him with our snow-shoes.' A company was gathered, Teunis among them. Sleds filled with skins, guns and victuals, and warm hearts. We landed here when the sun was at the highest. I had come up so far, just to take my favorite look and return; but of all the sights that mortal eye ever beheld, it seems to me still that that must have surpassed them. The mountain was one lump of glass, not a dark spot on the whole. The trees all hung in crystals. The hard snow, frozen and glittering to the very top. It was one diamond, perfectly reflecting the different colors of the rainbow. I looked, but my eyes filled so with tears, that I turned away, for I was ashamed to be seen weeping at what no one else seemed to care to look at but myself."

"Did no one enjoy the vision but you? It seems to me that I see it now as you describe it."

"Not one," said Elsie, "cared about it after a moment was passed; one girl of my own age declared that she would rather get a look at the big kitchen fire. And a good-hearted girl she was for all that. We must not judge other people by their taste in these things."

"No, Elsie," said Miss Clinton, "for we find that true love does not always unite itself with refined taste. I have known some of the most sentimental men and women in the world, who would not sacrifice a single gratification for the good of others. But I know others who can enjoy all the beautiful in nature and art, and they would this day lay down their life for me. Here I am cut off from all, and not a friend but one."

Elsie, with great art, turned her thoughts away from this melancholy theme, by saying:

"Miss Clinton, stand out there, and let me tell you what I have been planning. The Hermit that you have heard me speak of, told me about the Queen of May in England. I have been thinking that the Queen of October would be the most suitable for our country, and I would like to have you as our model."

"Well, dress me up as you please; it will put off care for the day, and give me something to tell when I return to London—that is, if I ever return. I feel for a moment now that I might act Lady Hope in the pageant."

"My dear lady, you must be my queen, since I have elected you. Let me gather the leaves and the branches while you will use your skill in putting them together, agreeable to your own fancy. Here is a piece of stick which will serve as the stalk for your sceptre. You must twine it around with the things I shall bring to you, and there is a needle and thread. Now, you are better off than Mother Eve, the Queen of Eden."

"You seem, my friend and maid of honor, as I shall call you, to use great familiarity here, in putting a queen to work. But since it must be so, let me try. Tell me who is this strange man who has informed you of old country customs so well. Is he a real hermit, or only some mock anchorite that affects these strange ways, for some good end, or in some whim of his own? I should like to see a real recluse."

"I cannot tell you much about him; at least, I dare not. He has been in this region for more than a year; he came here, no one can tell where from; and as he knows so much about the world, we think he must have been a great traveller. The common people say he is a spook; and the place he has chosen for his retreat favors the notion, for from the earliest time it has always been thought that some ghost of an old countryman frequented that spot. Some say that Hendrick Hudson comes back every year to play at bowls, up in these hills, in honor of his finding out our famous river; others, that Captain Kidd, the great pirate, hid some chests of gold there, and killed a big negro on the spot. One old money-hunter, called Fred Martin, told a terrible tale of his going at midnight, and digging under a tree. The secret of his success lay in his not uttering a single word, whatever he should see, and the whole efforts of the ghosts lay in forcing him to speak. He dug on till the hour of twelve, when round him rose the crowd of imps, led on by the big, black negro. On Fred worked till out of breath, he lay down on his back to rest; one more shovelful, and he would be at the chest; but over him whirled a large round rock, like a millstone, that rose and fell at a great rate, wheeling all the time. Speak he would not, and speak they were determined he should. Down the stone again came, till he thought it touched the hair of his head, when forgetting himself, he cried, 'Off, you black duivel.' The words no sooner left his mouth than all was pitch dark, and he was left there lying till the morning. He declares till this day, if he could only have held his peace, he would have been rich enough by this time. So superstitious are the people, that many of them think that the hermit is either Hendrick Hudson, or the 'spook' that guards the money-chest of Captain Kidd."

"But whom does Elsie think he is? He must be some one worth speaking of, when you are so interested in him."

"I dare not say all I think of him, my lady. He takes up the most of his time in reading and writing; he knows all that is going on, which makes me think he must be in communication with strange things and persons. He wanders every day to the top of the mountain, and sometimes comes this way, looking always as if he expected some one from the west. At such times he is fearful to look upon."

"You are not afraid of him yourself since you have heard his account of the May Queen?"

"No, Miss Clinton; he is always calm and quiet when I am near to him. He tells me of things he has seen and of some things he has done. He has been in battles, by land and sea. But hush! I am speaking too loud; I sometimes think he knows my very thoughts. Hark! there is Rover's bark. Hush! there is the wildcat's mew, as sure as I live. Quick! let us to the bed of the stream. My mother is afraid, and is calling us."

Here the mewing became more distinct, to which Elsie answered by putting her hand to her mouth, giving out a sound which imitated a young kitten, eager to reach its mother. Lowering her own head, she signed to her companion to follow her example as they ran toward the fall, where Angelica was waiting for them in the intensest anxiety. Rover stood trembling by her side; then running up to Elsie, he cowered down as if he had been chastised; every now and then giving forth a short, quick bark, more through terror than eagerness to be sent out on a hunt.

"Some wild animal," was the ready explanation of the experienced girl, who having been so often out with her father, had seen the dog tremble before when through instinct he perceived an enemy near. To this the mother assented, when she listened and heard a howl so fierce and deep, that it almost made her blood to freeze in her veins. All the four stood gazing down the ravine, every sense quickened to the utmost; while as howl after howl came up, nearer every time, they felt the chills of death coming over them. After a time, it seemed as if the yells were changed in their depth, and that some power stronger than the animal, whatever it was, held it in check. This was confirmed by the increasing boldness of the dog, which was seen in his running as far as the verge of the shelf, and even putting his paws forward on a tree that grew near the edge, then coming back, as if he wished to encourage his friends. The cause of this alarm must be explained in the next book.

BOOK II.

THE

BURNING OF SOPUS

AND

THE IMMEDIATE CONSEQUENCES THEREOF.

BOOK II.

Our History, to be understood, must be suspended until we gather up the other events which had already taken place within two days past, and to which some allusion has been made; therefore, our attention is directed to the town of Sopus.

This town now stands third in rank among the towns of the Province of New York. If the historian has aught of a prophet's eye, he would say, from all that he sees around Sopus—her rich and enterprising population, her fine situation—that he believes the time will arrive, when many a fair daughter rising up around her will do her honor, for the service she has done as a mother town of the olden time. Here dwell the various races, which when mixed, produce men of energy and spirit. The blood of the lively Huguenot mingles in the sluggish stream of the phlegmatic Hollander, making her people prompt and untiring, and her magistracy grave and dignified as those of old Amsterdam. She has grown, it is true, somewhat proud of her size, more especially since the stores for the northern army were placed with her for safe keeping. At the time of our history two of the most important conventions of the land were in session—no less than the Provincial Congress, and the first Synod of the

Protestant Reformed Dutch church of North America. No marvel that Sopus in matronly pride had swelled her skirts to a city size, demanding homage of her neighbors.

Alas! how true it is that a high look goeth before a fall. How frequently do those very marks of honor attract the eye of the enemy. The star upon the soldier's breast glitters, so that the marksman obtains the more certain aim.

CHAPTER I.

THE ANTEDILUVIAN DEBATE CONTINUED.

> "By ceaseless action all that is subsists;
> Winds from all quarters agitate the air
> And fit the liquid element for use,
> Else noxious; oceans, rivers, lakes and streams,
> All feel the freshening impulse, and are cleansed
> By restless undulation; even the oak
> Thrives by the rude concussion of the storm.
>
> A NEW ENGLISH POET.

THE stranger calling himself Captain Whittesley was attracting notice, and yet no one knew why, since he had shown his papers to be regular and his bearing to be dignified. Elder Swart, however, had as yet no suspicion. Too simple-minded, he believed all men to be as they seemed, yet he could not help being surprised at the effect of Whittesley's eye on some of the Dominies, and while on the way from the church to the court-house hall he said:

"So you know something about our Dominies? I supposed you to be ignorant of all our regions, and of all our private concerns on the west side of the North River. Have you been in Ulster before?"

Just at this moment Jan Freer stepped up to the captain; standing in the path before him, with the evident intention of speaking to him; but the effect of Whittesley's eye on the spirit of the rough Dutchman, was like that of a man on an inhabitant of the forest; he all but fell, and allowed the captain to pass; while recovering himself, he stared after Whittesley with mouth open and twisted legs, that showed the uncertainty of their owner's intentions. He was wakened out of his confusion by a full chorus of laughter that came from the loungers standing on the tavern stoop opposite, where, through the force of habit, he turned to go.

"What's the matter with you Jan? that you gape so after the Yankee stranger? You seem as if a witch had scalded you."

"The devil it is, or else the spy is come back again." And

so he went on to tell the same story of getting the "fifteen shillings and sixpence," and of its being the dearest money he ever earned. He only wished he could hear him say that and count it out to him as before, and he could tell more than any of them knew.

Thus the suspicion grew, and while no man would have dared to put his thoughts into words, there were few who did not feel strangely as this man passed by them even on the other side. By this time it was known that he had broken up the Classis in some way, and all felt curious to know if he was about to do the same to the Congress. Still Elder Swart, who had taken Captain Whittesley under his care, had no such suspicion in his mind.

Congress was met, and had already proceeded to business. They were a set of grave and able men, composed of the best and the wisest of our State, and of whom any State might well be proud. Philip Van Cortlandt sat as President, while round a plain deal table, covered with books and papers, sat the Roosevelts, the Dunscombes, and the Morris's of New York city; Cantine and Rhea of Ulster, with a host of men, such as Adgate and L'Hommedieu, Brasher and Van Zandt, and Wisner of Orange.

The point before the Congress was one that had been discussed warmly on the preceding day, and would have passed but for one of those artful manœuvres which public bodies see played before them, without the possibility of hindrance. The freedom of all the slaves of the State was seriously demanded, and even earnestly prayed for by many. All the members from the city were in favor it, though it cannot be said of them that their voices were raised through an extra share of humanity, but because, having none or few of their own, it would be no great loss to them; while the members in the country, being sadly pressed for military duty, required their blacks to remain and work for them at home. That kind-hearted man from Suffolk, L'Hommedieu, produced his motion, which had lain on the table for weeks, and would have been acted on before, had not that cautious man from Ulster, Adam De Witt, seen that let but one member be wanting, no quorum would be left, so he slipped out of doors, and the motion fell to the ground for that day.

The other side were now in full force, though not over strong, and their orator was in the depth of his argument, as the two men we have spoken of entered. It seemed to Elder Swart as if two or more of the leaders gave a sudden start as they caught a glimpse of his companion's countenance. The orator on his legs evidently felt something like a cold chill running down his spine, for he faltered in the midst of his sentence; and after reading a resolution against the "expediency of any measure which would liberate the slaves at the present time," sat down confused.

At the close of this act, one member rose in great fervor, arguing the humanity and the justice of a measure which would "set all free, since all were alike entitled to liberty; and what more fit and proper time than the present day, when struggling for it ourselves?"

The answer to this was plain, and regarded by the other side as complete. "Let the negroes know as well how to use their freedom as we do ours, and then shall they have their rights. But what do we hear from all the counties but the rumor of uprisings, under the impression that the day that bondage is past, the property of their masters must be divided; for how else can they be kept from starvation and misery, unless we preserve them in life as we are doing today?"

"And have not we heard," says another, "of the bounty which the king offers for the thumb of every Dutchman, brought to the sheriff by a black, if he can prove it to have been that of his master, and he a Whig?"

While these cross-firings were going on, Elder Swart observed that his new-made acquaintance was exchanging signs and motions with persons present, such as he had seen among members of the Masonic order, which excited his attention so much, that he resolved to watch more closely; for though he was but a blunt-looking man, the times had developed his perceptive powers so fully, that somnolence was no part of his real character, however it might appear. At the very moment his consciousness was awakened, Governor Clinton entered the hall, walking right into the centre, exchanging a few courtesies as he passed the different chairs. Sitting down immediately opposite our two acquaintances, he lifted his eyes in a state of abstraction, as if intending to listen, not to see; but the instant he fastened his sight on the man called Whittesley, it seemed as if a snake had fascinated him. Nor did the other shrink from the scrutiny. It was plain that the governor had the least power of eye: for, as if by impulse, he stooped forward to the ear of Swart's acquaintance, whispering: "Let us leave the hall for a moment."

"No need of that," said the man addressed, who sat in the most imperturbable coolness, while the governor shook with a visible tremor, like what an animal shows when something alarms it, though it may not move.

"How far are they from us?" was the anxious inquiry of the governor.

"At the elbow below," was all that the other said; and it seemed as if his lips did not move as he spoke.

"Who are on board, and for what do they come?" said tke state officer, quickly, "and what is the errand that brings them?"

"What he wrote to you concerning, brings himself, for he would trust no one else; and the love of adventure induced —— —— to steal on board, as she threatened in her letter to your lady."

"My God," said the distressed governor, "what shall I do? I could shoot him, after despising his bribe; but what shall I do with that romantic fool! How shall I dispose of her!"

"She is already disposed of," was the cool answer.

"God be praised," broke in the governor again. "I can turn *him* off, but *she* would wile the partridge from the hawk; and were she to come here, as she threatened last summer, it would ruin me with my enemies; and yet I would sooner die than see a hair of her head hurt. Where is she gone? You say she is disposed of."

"Stolen, and taken to the mountains," was the answer that came from the strange man; for no one, looking at him, could see that he spoke, unless they narrowly watched his mouth.

"Stolen, and taken to the mountains! Stolen, and taken to the mountains! Gracious heavens! what do you mean? How do you know? Where have you been wandering?"

"Silence, your excellency. You are observed. Carry that to the president, and sit down in your own place."

The governor did as he was told, when very soon the president rose and said:

"Gentlemen of the Congress, we have other duties before us than that which now takes up your attention. This missive informs me that the ship Vulture, under the command of Gen. Vaughan, may be expected to put a body of troops on shore, somewhere at the mouth of the Roundout for the purpose of destroying the stores in this place, and dispersing this convention of the free State of New York. What is your pleasure in the premises?"

The commotion which arose after this announcement soon gave place to a vigorous debate concerning the duty of the Congress remaining in session till driven from the hall at the point of the bayonet.

"Remain, surely let us remain in the place where our fellow-citizens have put us. It is for us, as the heads of the people, to stand firm and show ourselves to be men of nerve. Our blood may be the shower that will water the root of the tree of liberty, and the pears it will bear in the future years of the country's history will be richer, in flavor and more nourishing than the tree of England, with even Lord Chatham in the topmost branch."

This was said by Colonel Pierre Van Cortlandt, who was furious in his courage, and seemed to have in his mind more than he chose to utter. The next who succeeded him was less restrained, pointing evidently at the governor, casting glances all the time at that side of the house where Elder Swart and Captain Whittesley were sitting.

"Fight! Yes, let us fight," said Judge Cantine, who had his own reason for being envious of the position which Clinton, the son of an Irishman, occupied over him, [illegible]tive Dutchman; "there is sometimes good reasons for m[illegible]ng a man's cousin a general and another a governor. There is much in a name. Putting such power into the hands of men near of kin with the enemies of our country; more by reason that cases of Madeira can find their way before kindly offers of services are sent. Fight! yes rather lose our lives here than our heads on the scaffold."

The governor, who heard all this and understood the meaning of the insinuation, was waiting to meet these secret thrusts by something that might tell more forcibly than words; but the president, who perceived the storm that was brewing, reminded the members that they had turned aside from the question before them into undignified personalities.

"We have other work upon our hands this day," said he with great dignity, "than to fall below ourselves, by throwing out dark insinuations; which must tend to divide us, when we ought to show an undivided front to the enemy. You men of classical lore, can tell who it was among the ancients, who finding a spy in his camp sent him back to his master, after showing him all his strength, so that a good report might be rendered. How do you mean to meet the enemy, should he be rash enough to land his forces on the river bank?"

The business of the Congress was becoming so confused toward the close of the President's short speech, that his advice all but fell unheeded upon ears listening to private words. It was more of a mob debate than that of sober statesmen. Those persons against whom the insinuations were aimed, were hotly engaged with their assailants; and among them Governor Clinton was the hottest. His Milesian blood was up, and would have boiled over had not Judge Cantine met him as a man shaped out of Holland clay may be supposed to receive the knuckles of an Irishman in a fury. How far the fray might have been carried, history does not tell, but for the booming of a cannon from the river side which informed the debaters that a common enemy was at hand, which demanded both property and person. Here a calm and dignified member stood up, to whom all gave heed the moment he opened his lips:

"President and Gentlemen: We are on the eve of another struggle; and though it may sound strangely in your ears, I rejoice at the prospect of blood being shed, and of fire being kindled. You will agree with me when I read to you what has been sent hither by a trusty and careful friend in New York, written to me in cipher, with which you must be satisfied through my interpretation.

"To the Hon. Morris:

"The messenger who gives this into your hand will explain it fully. Vaughan goes in charge of an expedition to Albany, to fight as he loves to fight. Sir Henry goes to bribe his cousin: Vaughan swears he will burn the spot of blood out, if there be any cousin in this colony of rebels."

With this the hitherto silent member sat down; while a second cannon boomed through the air, which by this time was becomimg so filled with voices out of doors, that little could have been heard within, however inclined any one might be for speech making. Besides, the constant going in and coming out prevented the desire which the eager men had of rising up against the treason they imagined they saw in all from whom they differed. Another report, and they separated in hot haste, for now they knew that the danger was imminent. Since Vaughan and his soldiers were near there was no time to lose.

In the meantime all the suspecting members had their eye on Whittesley. Orders had been privately issued to watch all the roads out of Sopus, and stop every one that might be seen escaping from observation, and bring them before the commanding officer, Colonel Hausbrouck, who, being a true Dutchman, was loyal to that interest. But in the midst of the personal commotion; some say of the fright, which the approach of Vaughan occasioned in the Congress, Whittesley found his way out; nor was it observed, till Elder Swart started up from off his seat, asking where the Yankee captain had gone.

On the road to Plattekill, riding at full speed, a single horseman was seen toward the dusk of the evening, but the folks of Sopus had business of their own on hand; and the strange captain was not thought of more that day, though Jan Freer maintained till he died, that it was the same man who had hired him in the night; and gave him fifteen shillings and saxpence for a sail.

CHAPTER II.

LOVE STRONGER THAN DEATH.

" The rabbins write when any Jew
Did make to God or man a vow,
Which afterward he found untoward
Or stubborn to be kept, or too hard,
Any three other Jews of th' nation
Might free him from his obligation."

HUDIBRAS.

His majesty's ship, the Vulture—well named—was making slow progress up the Hudson River on a special expedition on behalf of the northern army. General Vaughan held a *carte blanche*, on which he might inscribe what he saw fit, provided that the general cause was advanced.

As this voyage was regarded in New York in the light of a pleasure trip for sport, more than as an expedition of a warlike character, there were numbers who sued for permission to join it, so that they might witness with their own eyes those romantic scenes spoken of and sung since the days of Raleigh. They longed to visit those grand old woods where the wild beasts lay, still undisturbed; and the red man, that western Greek of lofty sentiment and of heroic deeds, so captivating to the youthful mind. All such persons as were sick of the worn-out forms of European society desired this fresh and new world. In this way the enthusiastic and loyal sought the opportunity of a pleasure sail on board of this powerful ship.

Sir Henry Clinton either sought or demanded a small cabin for himself and family on this occasion. He held also a *carte blanche* of another character. He deemed that he himself was the sole keeper of his majesty's private seal; but a bird in the air will chirp into the ear of an envious or ambitious man, and Vaughan would play second to no one. The king had many friends who dwelt far inland. Messages must be borne thither for their encouragement. Gifts from the crown were to be scattered liberally. Every man must have his price paid to him. Before that could be counted out the man must be known. George Clinton, governor of this new State, was well known to be related to Sir Henry, and the rebel might be bought, could the colonist be seen by himself. All efforts had hitherto failed, though friendly exchanges of word and deed had passed between them, such as gentlemen, possessed of self-respect, always show even in times of war. Frequently, in a jocular vein, the knight had threatened to pay the governor a flying visit, just to see whether his good blood had all oozed out or not; while the colonist, with equal good humor, replied that Sir Henry would find that he had plenty of "blood left to show all his majesty's servants that he was still a man, though he had become a rebel."

These friendly banterings were accompanied, at times, by substantial presents and tokens of good will, in the shape of Cheshire cheeses, Burgundy and Port, landed from New York by some skiff that ran in under cover of Fort Washington, where General Clinton, the rebel, kept his majesty's forces at bay. These unloadings of good cheer were suffered to pass unmolested, the carrier being none the wiser. Sly surmises would occasionally be muttered, but with the exception of some envious Dutchman, who found fault with this sudden promotion of the Clintons, all was quiet. The Mrs. Clinton of the country, sending one time to her ladyship of the city a firkin of her own butter from the cow, with a pot of apple butter from the orchard, wrote it would help Miss Margaret's dry bread to slip down easier.

These several acts made Sir Henry come to the conclusion, in his own mind, that perhaps his cousin George might be won over to the right side. Could he but have a chance of seeing him *incog.*, who could tell what the result would be? There had lately arrived a full pardon for all past offences, and full power was held by himself to advance the colonists who might be worth advancing, to any station. This George Clinton was one of those very men, and, to tell the truth, the worthy knight was so proud of him that he declared boldly, had he been anything else than what he was, a true rebel, he would have despised him as unworthy the name he bore, and say he was no cousin of his.

These explanations are needed to account for the presence of those persons whom we find on board of the Vulture sloop of war. In the cabin were seated a deeply interested company, whose countenances denoted an agony of mind and a tenderness of feeling which were in singular contrast to the objects presented on board of a war vessel. The machinery of death is hardly the place for those of a tearful cast; and yet the lion and the lamb are never seen to lie down together in any place so generally as where the soldier makes it his home. A sense of duty will triumph over the feelings of humanity, so as to look on death and rapine without remorse.

The main person in this group was a man over fifty years of age, of deeply-lined countenance, showing determination and firmness of purpose, though at the time we refer to, his lips betrayed the yielding of the soldier to the nature of the man. The quiverings of those lips were the only signs seen of what was moving the strings of his heart. Something more than great public events was the cause of that restlessness, and the fiery glances which shot forth from beneath his bushy eyebrows showed that a crisis of some kind was near at hand. Pacing the cabin floor with uneven steps, when his back was turned he could be seen brushing away the tear, lest his weakness should be betrayed to his friends; though even with his face averted, his frame told the careful observer that deep passion was working within.

A lady, somewhat younger than he, but past the flower of beauty, sat in a richly ornamented chair, in a still more dejected state of mind than her lord. Her hair, brushed back and raised upon a frame of wire beneath, according to the fashion of our times, showed a brow of more masculine form than one loves to look at in a woman dwelling at home. Not a wrinkle showed her former griefs, if she ever had any, and all lines of care were alike absent from her whole face. She had seen only the sunshine of life; at least no cloud had rested long enough to leave its shadow. A dress of fawn-colored velvet hung loosely upon her body, clasped at the neck by a brilliant diamond, which corresponded to some smaller gems of the same water in her hair. The robe was no stinted pattern, as the amplitude of its folds showed, even when she sat; but when she rose, the long train, which she managed so gracefully, indicated that she had moved in a wider saloon than the narrow compass to which she was now confined. Not so careful to restrain her tears as her partner in grief, she was still far from showing a vulgar sorrow. Rising in one of her ecstasies, she took hold of the gentleman's arm, and in the most beseeching and touching manner embraced him before she said:

"Henry! my dear Clinton, let the young men have leave to go in search of our beloved child! Let them go but for one day. Alas, it may be too late already. Oh, my dear daughter! where are you at this moment? in the hands of that cruel monster! I entreat you as a wife, a mother, your own wife, to yield and suffer them—one of them, if not both—to make the effort. You will reproach yourself forever afterward unless you give your consent now.

Sir Henry Clinton, for it was none else than that brave man, who, for reasons of his own, was here a passenger on board the Vulture, allowed his lady to vent her grief and her desire in words before he attempted to speak; then turning around and looking calmly but decidedly into her face, he said:

"Georgiana, you must not ask what it is impossible to grant. We are but a few miles from that rebel's nest, and Vaughan has resolved to burn them out, and how can he spare two of his chief officers, when so much depends on suddenness and promptitude? Do not urge it at this critical moment. Duty is above all other considerations."

"Oh, my child! my child! and must I sacrifice thee at the shrine of duty? Oh, surely the God who gave thee to us would look down with leniency upon a neglect that would save life and restore thee. Would that I could as easily fall before my sovereign at this moment—as easily as I can before my God, and my husband, and I am sure that the parental feeling of the good king would yield at once, and save even a whole city willingly, though they be rebels, for the sake of saving that dear girl, that he put his hand upon and said, 'bless thee, child, for as thou art beautiful now, what wilt thou be in womanhood?' Could he but see her, and hear me! Oh, Clinton, yield, yield as you love me, and would save yourself from bitter days!"

"Duty, duty," was the only answer the agitated father gave, as he kindly led the fainting lady to her seat, and turned away toward the cabin door, which opened at that moment, when there entered two young men dressed in the different uniforms of the army and of the navy, to which they severally belonged. They were about the same age, and of the true English build of body; firm, stout, and yet lithe of limb; full of animal energy and of great moral force. Though evidently proud of their station, and ready to do battle in behalf of their king, they were for the moment under the same spell that held Sir Henry and his lady; one of the two bore the family contour of face, and was recognized at once as a son; while the other, of darker hue, and more athletic form even than his companion, unmistakably belonged to some branch of the Clintons, of which there are many. The one ran to his mother, who folded him in her arms, and sobbing out, said: "Spare me, O God, one child, since the other has gone. Thy ways are mysterious. The one that was truly the fawn for gentleness and grace, has fallen into the jaws of the wolf; and the other, exposed to every danger, is here. How long, thou knowest, O God! O my God!"

The son was silent on her bosom, but his eyelids swam in moisture, as he was whispering some words in the ear of the broken-hearted mother, who seemed to give little heed for some minutes, till by and by she caught his meaning, whatever that was, and became as still as a child asleep, evidently deeply absorbed in what he was communicating. He rose up kissing her cheek, which she returned with such transport, that it appeared more like a farewell embrace than a simple adieu. There were intelligent glances passing between mother and son, which a watchful observer would have understood to mean a mutual understanding as they parted.

In the meantime, the companion of young Clinton, who had just entered, was entreating his uncle to take the responsibility of allowing him to leave immediately on the search after the captive lady, whom we may guess to be none else than Miss Margaret Clinton, the present ward of our young Dutch maiden, Elsie Schuyler of Hoogenhuisen. The knight was invulnerable to all entreaty, and even angry at the urgency of the youth; though no doubt his anger was put on to save himself from an open outburst of feeling.

"Urge me no more, Bertram, as you love me and would serve your king. It would ill become even me, though I had the power, to release you from the duty just now before you, since it is mine to encourage merit and bravery, rather than to screen a coward."

"Uncle! Sir Henry, what do you mean?" said the fiery youth, at the sound of the word coward, almost forgetting the distance between himself and the party addressed.

"I mean," said the knight, "that my nephew's name must never be associated with that of coward, even by the breath of suspicion, to which it would be certainly liable if he should be allowed to have his own way."

"God knows, and Sir Henry knows, that the dangers I would encounter are tenfold more than those I would avoid, and most willingly would we encounter both were time not so precious; another day, and my d"——. He was going to say my dear Margaret, but checked himself by saying, "cousin will be on the road to the valley of Ske-nuda-wa on the Susquehanna, where that villain Kiskataam said his wigwam was still standing. Could I get within pistol-shot of him that serpent eye of his would not fascinate another bird from its twig, and that smooth, wily tongue would not tell another Indian lie in the shape of a tale."

Silence prevailed in that small circle for some minutes, and when it was broken, it was by the chief in self-reproaches at his own former laxity of duty.

"If I had but refused that bewitching child her request, of coming up this cursed fine river with us, there would have been no trouble; but her voice has always been law to me on all things where her love of nature and of the romantic are so perfect. Her raptures as she surveyed this new country and this river, that I hate to look at now, always charmed me and made herself more beautiful; and by these very means I have lost her altogether. I should have resisted her to the last, and I am justly punished for my tenderness."

"Clinton! Clinton!" said the lady, "do not blame yourself nor the dear child, for the fault lies with me. I begged on her behalf that she might see the dominions of those Indian kings that she admired; and that false-tongued serpent told her so much of those mountains which we now see in bold outline, that her imagination became fired at the prospect, so that I really thought at the time, her brain might become fevered, unless she were gratified with the sight of them. That brilliant fancy has always been to her a source of exquisite pleasure and pain. Now I fear that her death must follow. Ah, poor child! how I loved to hear thee tell us of Switzerland, and of Scotland, and wish that you could only see from the top of some high mountain on the vale of the Hudson. Thou wilt look down, but it will be as the poor fawn which is caught in the claws of the eagle for prey, and taken to the cliff overhanging the gulf, either to be devoured or dashed to pieces."

These lamentations from both the parents were more in the form of a soliloquy than as addresed to others, for they were all disinclined to hold conversation upon the subject; and yet it was necessary that some counsel should be had concerning future operations, after the attack should be passed, which had been already determined upon. Sir Henry was willing to hear propositions in prospect, but would not venture anything at the present moment. He rather wished to give the license, but after what he had said of duty, would not propose it.

"I never could bear the hateful savage," said the knight, with great bitterness; "and had my counsel been followed, he would have been dismissed from the service long since. He always quailed under my eye since I ordered him to leave head-quarters, where he was found in too close proximity for any one but a friend, or a spy. I believed him to be the man who carried the report of our planned attack upon Fort Washington."

"Yes, your Excellency," said Bertram, "it was your dislike to him that kindled his revenge, so that he has nursed it ever since his last journey to the north and west, and he found the chance too easily when he obtained the help and the countenance of another."

"Of another!" all exclaimed at the same moment. "Who else, and why should any one have any design upon such a pure being as Margaret?"

"It may not be known to you," continued Bertram, "that my cousin was urgently pressed to receive the addresses of Colonel Clifford, previous to that unhappy affair between him and his friend C——, which led first to the separation of him from his young and beautiful wife, and then to her death, when C—— vowed eternal revenge, which made you, Sir Henry, deem it best to send Clifford to the north, under the command of Burgoyne, who gave hin the charge of Fort Niagara. I go over these points for the purpose of making out what we used to call a hypothesis."

"Well, Bertram, you are very long in coming to the point; please reach your conclusion as quickly as possible."

"Kiskataam incidentally mentioned the name of Clifford, as an officer he had seen, and when I innocently asked the Indian if he knew the commander of Fort Niagara, he hesitated to answer, and then waived the reply, which I could not account for in any other way than by his being under the pay of Clifford, and he has come on here at this time, both to gratify his revenge against Sir Henry and to do the wicked work of his master."

"But Clifford," said Lady Clinton, "would not dare to return to society again. He knows that the king would never allow a man so lost to honor to see his face in the army, or his name upon the list."

"My dear aunt," said Bertram, "men under the power of a fierce passion, will rather lose their souls than go ungratified. Like a wild animal, Clifford thinks only upon the object of his desire. Honor, peace, and future reward, here or hereafter, are all thrown away for the time, so that his mind may be bent on the one thing before him. He is just such a man."

Sir Henry, who sat in astonished silence during Bertram's ricital of his suspicions, broke in here, by saying it was utterly impossible that Clifford, or any man of the army, could be so lost to honor and ingratitude as ever to act so unworthy a part, after the responsibility which was taken by myself, to remove him where the stigma would not be seen. Besides, I had a letter from him lately, in which he expresses himself in the most becoming manner. See, there it is at this moment. It refers to matters of a public nature chiefly, but a postscript is added, in which his remembrances of my kindness are made in the most delicate and appropriate manner."

"Please, sir, to say who it was that brought you that communication," said Bertram, with great readiness. "If it was the Indian my suspicions are confirmed."

"It was the villain Kiskataam," said the sorrowful father, now fairly infected with the same feeling with his nephew; "and here, in further proof, he says, that business will call him down to the frontier, where the plan is being carried out, along with the Mohawk chief, to remove some captives from the rebel's country back to the Fort Niagara. He will be happy to receive any commands from me, or from Miss Margaret, either concerning the war or the romance of this wonderful country, where nature plays on her harp equal to herself."

"Yes," said Bertram, "the dishonored man is somewhere up there, and is at this very hour watching the ship and waiting for his prey. There is no time to lose, and since we are not to be allowed to leave to-night in search of Margaret, I may as well, in the presence of my aunt and of Clarence, lay my own suit at your feet, and beg you to smile upon our plighted faith."

"Bertram," said Sir Henry, in amazement, "I have no daughter, and if all you tell us be true, there will be but pain remaining for you, and for us, increased by the consent you would obtain in a moment, did I but know how to direct you honorably."

"Oh," said Bertram, "I could run over the mountains like the deer, with the name of the loved one on my lips; and hear me she would. Your consent would give me wings."

"Hear me, then," said the grieved soldier. "Were my daughter present, I would put your hands in one, and give you my blessing. In the meantime, we must to duty, and perhaps a flag of truce to my cousin George, the Ulster rebel, may be effectual. We shall see."

The ship had turned the Elbow,* and was catching the wind sufficiently, so that she might at any moment come to anchor. A stiff breeze from the southwest was bringing her into the Roundout Creek, where, under cover of the night, they intended to land a body of men, who would march up to the village of Sopus, burn and destroy it, and return immediately. A company being detailed off, and put under the command of a superior officer, who was to have Clarence Clinton as his aid; Bertram begged, and was allowed to go along as a volunteer, he being a lieutenant in the naval service on board of this same ship.

"Now, Georgiana, I would give a thousand pounds this day, were you back in New York. This is no place for you, though you be the wife of a soldier." This was said by Sir Henry, in a spirit that showed his mortification at being caught in such a mean attack, which he would have been glad enough to have read about, but to be so near as this, would be to identify him with it. Besides, the loss of his daughter affected him almost superstitiously; and he would have countermanded Vaughan's orders, if he durst have

* A point on the river.

taken the responsibility. Lack of decision was ever his great defect.

"I could wish myself back in England, and you with me," said the Lady Georgiana, "were we honorably out of this murderous war. I believe the judgment of the Almighty is falling on us for the share we have had in robbing so many hearthstones. O God, what right have we to complain of thy justice, when we are engaged in the very act of destroying the peace of a whole village."

"Georgiana, do have mercy upon me at this hour, if you have none upon yourself. You know that this landing is entirely contrary to my mind. I feel that it must end against us; and it will ruin the plan that I have been preparing for six months past. You know what pains I have been at; indeed, I may say *we* have had, to conciliate these colonial cousins of ours, now all frustrated by this headstrong vanity of Vaughan. Never would I have given my consent to what must break up all our chances of bringing over the very head of this new State, and a general to boot. Curse Vaughan for all this." And with that he went on deck, where he found his son, who, with a restrained voice, asked his father's blessing.

While together, Bertram and Clarence had formed a desperate plan, to which the mother was to be privy—to leave immediately after the attack was completed, and have their names appear among the missing, for which no one would be responsible but themselves. They hoped to be able to justify their conduct by their success. In the meantime, it was necessary to inform Lady Georgiana, lest her heart would break at the thought of their being dead, or prisoners among the barbarous rebels. In the anxious and excited state of the mother's mind, the scheme was listened to with delight; and when parting, she exhorted her son to do his "duty like a gallant man first, and then pursue the murderous villain to the end of the earth; but bring me back my dear child—your own sister, my son, and there is my blessing." "But what shall I say to your father, when he finds you have not come in with the rest? I must weep, and yet be satisfied that you have gone on my errand."

"Sir Henry," said the youth, "will bear up well till we return, which cannot be more than a week at the most; and if you see a fire on the mountain—that second highest peak that we admired to day—at midnight, after forty-eight hours, or twenty-four hours beyond that time, know that we are safe, and have got trace of Margaret; tell my father, and he will revive."

"Go, then," said the mother, "but I tremble lest you be lost in the mountains. Now I think of it, that rebel cousin of your father's, in one of his letters, sent me this hair ring, which his daughter worked for me. You see that it has the initials of her name in the centre. Should you get into difficulty, take this, and here is a copy of the note I sent to her, with my thanks. These will prove you to be our son, and the blood relation of that same mock governor."

"We will keep out of his way, for he may play Brutus, and condemn us all the more surely that we are his kindred. I have a more certain way of escape than that," said Clarence. "I have heard that same false Kiskataam tell of his places of defence on the tops of these mountains. You saw him sitting with us a whole hour, and pointing along the ridges, marking out distinctly the cloves, and telling us of the roads which lead over the country, so that I can have but little difficulty in tracing him, with some help from the inhabitants. One spot of great interest he told us of, and which seemed to have attractions above the rest, even to him, where two little lakes lie close to each other, on the sides of these hills, fed from the surrounding heights, looking like twin sisters brimful of love, surging over their affections in a stream that quietly steals through the trees till it dashes over a high precipice a few miles below, then finds its way to this river. I can follow that as my guide, and find him safely lodged among his own thickets."

"Clarence, you are too like your sister in that romantic spirit. She told me of these lakes, and of the tradition of the Indians connected with them. She was in rapture at the very prospect of seeing them, and of telling me the story on their verge. It grieves me to the soul to recall her description as the false flatterer gave it to her. It may lead you astray, as she has been decoyed; so depend not upon anything you have heard from him, but make sure, by taking these tokens of private friendship to George Clinton. Rebel as that governor is, he must be an honorable man, possessed of a warm heart. He will not suffer you to be injured should the day go against you."

With these parting words, more the suggestions of her kind, maternal breast than the dictates of her cool judgment, the mother and son separated in doubt.

CHAPTER III.

THE SPORT OF A FOOL, CASTING FIREBRANDS, ARROWS AND DEATH.

> "The tempest falls,
> The weary winds sink breathless. But who knows
> What fiercer tempest yet may shake this night."
> THOMSON."

THE Lady Clinton saw how a false movement on her part might bring disgrace on her liege lord's fair fame. Her woman's wit perceived the ground of Vaughan's ill-advised attack upon the unoffending people of Sopus, and its consequences upon Sir Henry's mission. Vaughan would accomplish what he really intended—cutting off all hope of negotiation with the rebel governor. To counteract the certain evil effects to her family, who might be brought to plead for his help, was now her secret aim.

The two young men agreed upon their signals and on where they were to meet: two shrill whistles at brief intervals of time, an hour after midnight, unless they met earlier, should the attack be successfully made and over before that time. Bertram had possessed Clarence with the same opinion he had formed himself, that Kiskataam was on his way to Canada by the western route, and their only chance of overtaking him was to start up the mountain at the nearest point, and get beyond the rebel border, when, as king's officers, they would pass free through the country of the friendly tribes, who were the only inhabitants west of the Kaatsbergs. "We can get before them," said that ardent youth, "for they must travel slowly for Margaret's sake."

"But you said that you believed Clifford was in this scheme, and will he not be ready to receive her with sufficient force to resist our attempt at rescue?"

"Let us trust to chance for that; none but the brave deserve the fair. A traitor is always a coward; and I am persuaded that the arch hypocrite dare not show himself to Margaret, the daughter of his patron and friend, till the romance is pressed out of her mind, through her captivity and grief. He then will appear as her delivering angel, claiming her hand in gratitude."

"Your love, Bertram, has made your fancy creative; but it is as well that we be prepared for the worst. Here let us swear fealty on her behalf; living or dying, we are one."

"Agreed," said the other, as he took hold of his friend's hand; "and whoever survives to-night, shall carry out the plan to the end."

The order to march ran secretly along the line, when the sense of duty swallowed up everything of individual interest. The sacking of a village or the changing of a guard was the same to men under a rule of iron. The corps held their way, guided by some men of the country in the king's cause, through a broken piece of land for about three miles from the river. The greatest caution was used; not a word above a whisper was spoken, for the troops of king George had learned well enough that it was dangerous to go hunting, on these hunting-grounds, so far away from Windsor Castle. The reputation of the Ulster militia for bravery had been heard of ere this, and the party might be caught in their own trap—a very common thing in those times.

"Are these Dutchmen as good at handling arms as the Yankees?" whispered Clarence to a private at his side, whom he knew to be a native of the country, and who, at the present time, acted as one of the guides. "Do you suppose they will fight? or do they know sufficient of this quarrel to risk their lives against the king's troops?"

"Fight!" said the other, "yes, and on principle, too, as I am a living man. There is not one of them but knows their rights, and their wrongs too, for that matter. Their Dominie instructs them in all these affairs, and drills them into line, Sunday and week day."

"And does something of the fighting too, you think, if I may guess from your speech?" This was said with a sly sneer, which the young officer could not hide.

"The use of the sword is not despised by these Dominies; and some of them go so far as to insist that the minister should carry the ark before the army, as the priests did in the old wars; and if you, sir, had looked as often as I have into the large, black eyes of the man who teaches the folks where we are going, you would believe as I do." This was said with so much warmth of feeling, that Clarence began to suspect that he was speaking to a partisan of the country.

"So then you know and rather respect this man you call

the Dominie up here? how does it happen that we have you here in our ranks?" said the officer, with some sharpness, as he looked into the man's face to ascertain the effect it might have upon him.

"This cause, sir, like another we read of, has set father against son, and son against father." This was said with feeling. "It is enough," he continued, "that I am now under the king's flag, and sworn to be true. I can be this without losing my reverence for the Dominie, or my love of his flock. He will fight if he needs to take the field; and my advice to you is, keep out of the range of his gun, if you want to leave the field a living man."

"Ah, a good shot is he?" said the interrogator. "I love the man that can shoot straight and fair on all sides, though I should hate to be taken down by a priest. How shall I know him in the field?"

"My description," said the earnest young man, not minding the jests of his superior, "will not be required. He lets his presence be heard and felt. He has little mercy upon a Tory; and if I were to fall into his hands, he would do with me as he did to a mean Cowboy, tie me to his horse's tail, and ride me to death."

"And would you stand patiently to be tied?" said Clarence, laughing quietly at the guide's solemnity. "He must have great power over you, since he could not keep you near him."

"That is a tale by itself, sir," said the private; "but were I to see his three-cornered hat there before my face at this moment, I would stand still and deliver arms; for then would I be certain that his long Geneva bands would hang at his breast, his white locks be streaming over his shoulder; and my heart would cease to beat that instant."

"Certainly he must be a dangerous man, to be so near us at this time, and we depending on your guidance. I must watch you, and treat you as they do horses that are led out of a fire, throw a sack over your eyes; and then you will be but a blind guide. But what makes you look so fixedly? What do you hear? You cannot see anything in the dark?"

"The old church drum is beating the alarum! There will be fun in old Sopus before morning."

"Church drum!" said Clarence, in laughing surprise. "Do they call the people here to church by tuck of drum? A well drilled flock they must me. His wardens, then, must be captains and sergeants, and his clerk a bugler."

By this time the invading force had reached a rising ground, from which the village could be seen in daylight, but was now only discernible by the twinkling tapers carried unsteadily in all directions. To a lively imagination, like that of Clarence's, they were like spirits disturbed in their rest, and were now in the act of arousing their wards of the human race against the approach of their enemy, that like a huge vampire stood perched on that mound ready to descend and destroy. Silence reigned through the company. The officers consulted in whispers; all seemed to be waiting for the word to go forward; nor did they wait long, for two dark figures, that rose at a signal, stood before the rest, and were met by the chief in command, who soon returned and gave the word "forward!"

The orders were to burn the stores and the public buildings, to spare the inoffensive inhabitants, and to kill only those who offered resistance. They rushed down in double quick time, and were soon on the streets of the place, which presented a spectacle of activity, showing that some notice had been given of their approach, and that the people were moving their household stuff from their dwellings in all directions. On a road over which Bertram passed with his men, going to the north, were horses and oxen, drawing rude carriages piled with household goods, and women with their children, who were giving forth all the sounds of young humanity when suddenly raised out of their nests. With round tables, of the time of King Arthur, were seen glittering escritoirs of mahogany, brought from Holland. Clarence stumbled upon an old vrow, who bore off a set of china, while following her was a young damsel carrying a huge antique looking-glass, that had reflected the face of her grandmother when a bride in the Nederlands. A rude soldier tossed, with his musket, a bundle out of the hand of a full-bottomed matron, which turned out to be a silver teapot, and other plate of value; but his officer coming up, prevented the spoliation, so that she carried off her prize, which became from that moment the more valuable. Screams were heard from the dwellings, caused through fear more than hurt, while men were seen in the yards behind the houses running to the rendezvous, where Colonel Haasbrouk was mustering his men and preparing for the defence. Among these people were found some of the most prominent in the convention, and not a few of the reverend Dominies who had figured that day in the ecclesiastical assembly, with their lay-brethren by their side; though it is on record that the majority of both Convocations took to their heels, and never stopped till they reached the village of Hurley, where they met next day, and sent out strong resolutions against the audacious enemy who had dared to burn them out. A song called "The Race to Hurley" is sung with great gusto among the mischievous men of the place, who think it the greatest sport that ever happened.

Time pressed upon the invaders, each one being furnished with a torch dipped in tar, and his orders given to burn only public stores; but the blood of the tiger was up, and words could not restrain him, more especially when liquors in abundance were at hand. The heads of casks were driven in at a stroke, which allowed the soldier, always thirsty, to dip his mouth into the drink till he became satisfied. Fire and alcohol gained the mastery, and all the generals in King George's army, with himself at their head, could not have stayed the havoc of a general conflagration. The officers fought with their own men, swearing as only soldiers can swear at such times; but what does a drunken mercenary care for life or property when led to their destruction according to the laws of cruel war. It was not the soldiery, however, who wrought the chief damage to the private citizens, but their own neighbors in disguise, who, having grudges in their hearts of long standing, and being made aware, secretly, of what was coming, under the cloak of serving the good cause, gratified their own revenge by lighting the houses and the barns of the Whig population, and thus effecting a destruction of property which would have required an army of a thousand men in the same length of time to have prevented or stayed.

In one half hour after commencing their ravages, the bugle sounded a retreat. The deeds of fire and blood were done, and these are seeds which must yield the most noxious fruits in time to come. These blackened walls should be left, so that the yet unborn child, when it comes of age, may ask, how came these monuments of a former period to be placed there? And the answer shall be, "There came upon us a band of bloody assassins, worse than the wolves or the red men, pouring their fury upon us, and we cursed their day."

It was but the work of half an hour, and though the bugle sounded loud and shrill, it was no easy matter to gather up the stragglers, who had dispersed for booty and other objects. Such as were not insensible to danger flew to the gathering spot, while the blaring notes told the militia, who were coming in large numbers, that now was their time. The blazing dwellings showed, to their watchful eyes, many of their enemies, who were seen, some dancing like demons in drunkenness, and others, skulking behind in the dark, equally demoniac, while the sudden report of a gun, and the sharp shriek which followed, declared the death of some other victim of this night's work. The English commander saw the necessity of a rapid movement, as the danger of being surrounded was becoming every moment more imminent, and it was therefore with wise precaution that he had left a party behind to keep open his retreat; for already, on the road to the river, Captain Henry Schoonmacker had assembled a number of the true-hearted militia to intercept; and perhaps he might have succeeded had not the Dominie come up at that time and warned him, in true hunter's style, against putting the catamount in a corner.

"Give a bridge of gold to a flying enemy," said the good man, "else he will fight through and kill hip and thigh. Let us to the fences, and smite them as the wise men of the east did at Lexington—lie in ambush, as the kindereen of Israel did before Ai."

The Dominie was obeyed as if he had been captain. The men all lay down flat on their faces, but the reverend man himself and Schoonmacker who stood behind a tree, reconnoitering the approach of the enemy. The Dominie saw them the the moment they rose on the high ground east of the village; his fingers got uneasy, and his gun came to his eye; when crack went the piece, which brought the word "Halt" from the English leader, who marked the point whence the flash appeared. Captain Schoonmaker, mad at the Dominie, cried out "Vat dat for? You've fired afore the time cam once."

"I could not help it," said the enraged Dominie. "I heard that Skitilink Yaacob Tenbroek laughing among them, and I thought I might hit him; but now that they know we are here, let us all give it to them. And with that the brave, good man roared out "fire," when a scattering volley made the woods ring. No damage was done to the invaders; but as it would be risking too much to pass by the defenders, a party was detailed to dislodge them, a matter not perceived by the eager watchers, who were prepared to take the soldiers in flank; when, to their own great surprise, they were attacked with a fury in the rear, which made them tumble off helter-skelter in all directions, leaving the main road clear, down which the king's party passed at rapid pace, for well they knew that time was worth more to them than gold. The Whigs, though spread over the field for a short space, soon came together, and pursuing along the skirts of the woods and behind the walls gave out fresh volleys, which did no harm, as all was yet quite dark. These were returned at short intervals, more for the purpose of frightening their pursuers, and keeping them at bay, than in expectation of doing execution. It was during one of these halts that Clarence perceived that Gabriel Smidt, the guide with whom he had held the private confabulation on the way up, gave a start, and then fell flat to the ground, which surprised his officer very much, as he had shown more than common bravery all the night throughout, which made him ask:

"What do you see there that makes you fall back as if you were shot?"

"Do you see that black spot on the fence there, no bigger than a crow?" said Smidt. "Look how it rises higher and higher."

"Well, what of it?" said the other. "What if it be a crow, a drop of lead will bring it down, even though it were a witch. I could hardly believe that a man of your temper, from what I have seen of you, would be frightened by a scarecrow!"

"Laugh as you please, that cocked hat, as I told you, has made me more afraid than a dozen of rebels, at another time. I feel at this moment as I used to do when I could not say my Heidelburg."

"Pugh!" said an Englishman at his side, "is that all? let me put a pill through it, and I will say my catechism all the better after it is over."

"You shall not do it," said the Dutchman, "else you and I are enemies forever. The image of my old mother is now before me, saying 'Gaby, Gaby, min' de Dominie.'"

But the Englishman had no such scruples, and before his comrade had time to interfere, the firelock had spoken, and to the astonishment of all, and the horror of Gabriel, the hat stood up as brave as ever.

"Does not that prove," said Gabriel, "what my good old mother always said, that these ministers were black owls to shoot at? I never saw the man yet that prospered after he lifted his hand to smite one of them."

"Give me a good fat steak and I will venture the shot," was the unbelieving cockney's sneering reply.

"See," said Clarence, suddenly startled himself, "all the fence is lined with heads, and that as far as we can see. We must dislodge that pertinacious crew once more. True enough, they sit like so many crows—rather ravens ready to pick our bones. Not quite yet, boys." The men were ordered to lie flat on the ground till measures could be taken to dig the rebels out, or find a way to the left, and give them a wide berth. This would have been the plan, only there were voices heard in that very direction, so that appearances showed that they were surrounded, and must fight their way to the river, in the face of thousands. While waiting in council, Gabriel Smidt crawled up to the fence, and climbing over, he laid hold of that same cocked hat, which soon lost its terrors when he perceived that the whole was but a *ruse* to gain time. The hats were all put on poles, and placed on the top of the fence, so that from their regularity and number, they seemed a company of men waiting with muskets ready to discharge their fire. Gabriel took the old hat, putting it on his own head in real waggery, which nearly cost him his life; for no sooner did they see it move, than twenty muskets were fired at once, none of them taking effect, for there followed the loud laugh of the discoverer, and as loud a curse at the "old deceiver" for the trick he had put upon them, which they regarded almost in the light of a defeat.

Notwithstanding all this levity, the leaders were far from being at ease in their minds. It was plain that time was gained by the country party by these tricks, and that was loss to themselves; and it would have been fatal to the king's troops, indeed, had there been proper discipline observed on the other side. Instead of silence, they let their voices be heard, so that the ship's company were made aware of the danger, and sending up a few rockets, which were understood as telegraphic signs of warning by their friends ashore, who paused till they heard the firing of the ship's guns, that reached the field where the militia were in ambuscade, allowing a reinforcement to land and follow up the advantage. Beset in front and rear, the Dominie's party had to make way and allow the regular soldiers to pursue their course. The reverend man was seen walking in front of the men, exhorting them to keep steady and not to fire too soon.

"Yaw," said Captain Schoonmaker; "do as de Dominie bids, not as he does. But dere now; hear dat;" and there came a round ball whizzing through the air close by the rank. Then a second, and then a shower of grape that fell like hail among the trees. The men, uneasy and seeing no enemy, scattered, as the Dominie said to them when he got on the other side of a knoll: "Cowardly creatures that you are! fleeing like so many sheep."

"Yaw! yaw!" said a staid-looking farmer, whom they sometimes called Elder. "De shepherd vleeth in de front of te flock vaster dan te rest."

"And where would you have a shepherd be but in the front of his flock, as David always was? Read the tenth chapter of Johannes and hear: 'Zoo gaat hij voor hen heen; en de schapen volgen hem overmits zij zijne stem kenen.'"

"What is that he says? Can't he speak so as we can all understand him, instead of that jabber of chapters?" This was asked by a Yankee who had become mixed up with the crowd. "What does that parson of yours mean? the inconsistent body that he is. He would face a cannon, and yet he runs faster than the rest of us now."

"He says, 'When he putteth forth his own sheep, he goeth before them and the sheep follow him: for they know his voice.' He can give you Scripture for what he does."

"Yes, and if he were to run behind, he could give us the same Scripture. I do not like those men that blow hot and cold with the same breath."

"You better keep a quiet sugh, my man, for you are now among the Ulster Militia, and that is our Dominie. Touch him and you touch us. We are that man's sheep."

"And I suppose you call him the bell-wether, or the big ram, rather, judging from his two horns. But now I remember, he left his hat with its horns on the stake beside the fence, keeping his head safe."

"Vat's dat you say, you duivel snip? If you blaspheme de Dominie you must pay de fine;" and the Yankee found himself seized by the collar. Two of his comrades took offence at his freedom of speech, which brought the reverend man himself to the spot, who soon settled the quarrel by a sharp reprimand, which had its effect on all, diverting their minds from the rather sheepish flight they were now taking homeward to the burning village, after chasing their foes to the ship.

CHAPTER IV.

MORE DANGERS THAN A BATTLE.

"A double victory thou must gain,
In this emprise the merit of success.
One battle lost, makes all thine efforts vain,
Makes glory shame, and luxury nakedness."
TASSO.

THE young Clintons were cousins—the one was brother and the other lover to the lost Margaret, who had been abducted from on board the Vulture, on her voyage up the river, by Kiskataam. Both the young men were sworn to find out the young lady or perish in the attempt.

Clarence, son of Sir Henry, being in the land service, and feeling greater responsibility than his cousin, was more oppressed in spirit on leaving his command. He would be reported among the missing, but his sense of honor was so that a feather would have changed the balance between his duty and his affection. The feelings of his father and the risk he ran of being dishonored, were far more, in his esteem, than the dangers he feared of being in a hostile region. As he mused, he recalled the promise he had made to Bertram, and he became decided. When he reached the trysting place, it was surrounded by country people, who had crowded behind the knoll to shelter themselves from the ship's artillery; and nothing remained, therefore, for the young soldier but to take to the fields, and trust to luck. The flames of the burning village rose high, and by that inexplicable influence by which a fire at night attracts all animals, man with the rest, he turned his face thither, hoping that chance would do something for him. Perhaps he had something like an undefinable notion that he might fall in with his father's cousin George, the governor, and obtain, through his mother's name, and sign, a pass through the hostile ground, though his feelings and determination were to pursue his own way, so as to get to the mountains before the morning fully dawned. This was all he knew of the distance between the river and the high lands.

In walking along by himself he had time, and was in the mood, for reflection. He felt like a man who had been roused into passion, but who now becoming cool, inquires of himself why he was so mad. "Is it," he asked, "like Christians to become incendiaries? Can the king give the right to trample upon life and domestic peace? Were not these quiet people defending their homes and their altars? No wonder though the Almighty is angry with our family. Why should I and the rest of the army not suffer? I never expect to see my sister in this world. A curse on this war."

This soliloquy, expressed audibly, nearly cost him his life; for the sound of the human voice goes far in the fields at night. Superstition is quick-eared. The one who listened at this witching hour was no coward, though equally as uneasy in mind as Clarence. Gabriel Smidt, the guide of the attacking party, had also taken through the fields after convoying the king's troops to the ship, for a reason of his own. He recognized the voice and the gait of the young Englishman. Without more ado, he made himself known, and while the recognition was awkward on both sides, men like them, accustomed to sudden surprises, and in the habit of watching against them, soon get over their feelings. Their effort was to hide their real intentions.

"I have left something behind me in yon village that I would not lose for a thousand pounds," said Clarence.

"There has been many a fine thing lost there this night," said the private, "and among others, some things lie there which will never be gathered up." On saying this, he cast his eye sidewise, as if trying to scan the face of his companion, who, though he did not relish the jest, was in no place to resent it; so turning the conversation on other matters of a more general kind, he said:

"From appearances, we must be a long mile yet from the village."

"That depends," said the imperturbable Gabriel, "upon a man's feelings. It is a longer way for me now, when my heart is heavy, than it was when I worked on these fields, and went home with heavy heels, and a hungry belly; but to you, who have just gained a victory, it ought to be a short mile."

"If I remember," retorted the young officer, with some surprise at the turn the conversation was taking, and with a degree of alarm which made him finger his belt, "you had some share in that victory; I saw you fighting and firing with the best of us. And now let me ask you, in the king's name, why you are here?"

"Ha, ha," said Gabriel, "we are both equal here, where the king's word is no longer law; but lest you should be tempted to do as my superior might do, and which I might retaliate on you, though your inferior, I will open my mind to you at once, and say what I know of your affairs, and that I am under promise to help you in this enterprise."

"Who could have told you of our intentions? There is but one person besides in the world who knows about me here. No matter, then, give me the countersign and we will trust each other as far as we know what is in ourselves now, till we become better acquainted."

"Agreed," said Gabriel; "and now let me take you around, so that we may avoid all scouts outside; for you must know that I could go through these lanes blindfolded. But I have a message for you from the lieutenant, who expects to meet us near this stone barn." The young sailor, in the ardor of his feelings, had pushed forward after he found an opportunity at the river's edge of sending a token of his safety on board the ship, informing Lady Clinton of their escape from the dangers of the attack, and of their determination to pursue their premeditated plan. His eagerness carried him forward to the rendezvous before Clarence and his companion had reached it, so that he had time to sit down and reflect on the prospect before them. He was not long of hailing his friends, who came up to him, and they immediately entered upon a council of war. The two Englishmen gave themselves up into the hands of Gabriel, as their only help for the present; though it must be confessed that confidence was not lying very close to their hearts.

"My advice," said the prudent guide, who soon discovered their fears, "is to obtain the assistance of some one of the secret service-men, of whom there are many in these parts who know that snake of the mountains Kiskataam, and who for a trifle will scotch him with great pleasure. His haunts are well known to these Tory blades, who keep their tongues well in, and their knife in a sheath of hypocrisy till they get the chance of smiting under the fifth rib."

"Well, can you undertake to find the man you describe, and make a bargain that will keep him honest?"

"Bless your soul, gentlemen," said the guide, "my life is not worth a cabbage head were it known that I am now within a hundred paces of my mother's door-yard. Do you see that light twinkling there between those two trees? But you cannot see the trees—trees of a patriarchal size are before the door; and my good old mother, kind soul, is in the old house behind them: and"——

Here his voice grew thick and nature felt the desire to overflow in tenderness. Tears came to the eyes of all the three in sympathy, and yet an hour ago, they saw houses of the same kind in flames, and the inmates shrieking and fleeing from them in terror of their life.

"How comes it," said Clarence, "that you are here with your head in the lion's mouth? Some love affair, no doubt, like other men of like passions."

"Affection, gentlemen, blazes the same in rich and poor; and when it is pure and powerful, it will carry a man through deeper floods than you have ever seen on sea, and hotter flames than we have ever seen on land. I must leave you now, so that I may meet the old woman in that house; and then I shall die in peace, if she lay her hand once more on my head, and ask over me a Dutch blessing 'vaart wel;' I will send you a guide who is a Tory in his heart and a Whig in his speech, follow his direction strictly. I will keep a secret watch over you, till you get into the Indian country: of one thing be sure, that you do not trust the rascal with more of your secret than you can help." With that the unhappy man disappeared.

The two adventurers stood waiting and listening to the sounds which came up from the burning buildings, that cracked and fell, blazing up as if stirred by demons, who shouted and screamed with devilish glee. All the evil spirits had not left with the invaders, for the wicked grew wickeder so fast that they scarcely knew themselves, so sudden and terrible was the transformation wrought upon them in their struggle. Dogs howled for their masters; and for the hearth where they had been accustomed to lie; women were sobbing or shrieking throughout the whole place, while huddled in corners were groups of old men and curious boys, prophesying and listening to one another concerning the evils that would yet follow this night's work. Vengeance was deep and dark upon the faces of the old; and scudded swiftly over those of the young, as a cloud sweeps over a sunny field.

Clarence, who grew impatient, crept forward alone to the window of a low, dark stone house, that stood close by the road, where he saw what made him shrink back as if some one had struck him. It was used for the time as the hospital of the place, where lay the wounded and the dying, in their blood and groaning with pain. The Dominie had returned from the chase himself, leaving the men to watch the movements of the ship, which left the village almost without inhabitants, except the aged and the decrepit. This was so far favorable to our adventurers, keeping them from being discovered. The good man was now about his own peculiar calling, ministering consolation to the dying and the bereaved. His exhortations were made up chiefly of Scripture from the low Dutch, mixed with the vernacular of the region which would have defied the most learned body in all Germany to have translated literally.

"Goden den is villing dat you zal die, Hanse, ande you must be villing to go; you have done your duty, Hanse, as a free man dis nicht, ande if you zeek himme through Christus, you are safe."

He then offered up one of the most fervent prayers that ever the listeners heard. Accustomed as they had been to the calm, cold manner of the English church; and occasionally hearing some strolling Methodist, they were unprepared for fervor united with spirit-stirring language, which bore meaning to the understanding as fully as it gave solemnity to the manner. "He is a man of power," Gabriel would have said, "whether he be in the sick-room, or on the battle field." He could face Satan's hosts with as hearty good will as he does the red-coats. He held as part of his creed, that both belonged to the same army; and if any one had asked him that night, what was the color of Apollyon's coat, he would have said promptly, "scarlet."

As he proceeded in his devotions he grew calmer, speaking softer; and it was evident that his words had a most soothing influence upon the listeners. His language was now altogether in the Dutch tongue, as if he had forgotten all but that, which he knew was the early speech of the man who was dying, and who would recur to that in his last moments. "Hoe dierbaer is uwe goeder tierenheit O Godt, dies de menschen kinderen onder de schaduwe uwer vleugelen toevlugt nemen."

"That is true," said some one who came imperceptibly to the side of Clarence, who seemed touched with visible emotion, repeating in the English tongue what was pleasant to his heart in the Dutch. "How excellent is thy loving kindness, O, Lord! therefore do the sons of men put their trust under the shadow of thy wings." When the young officer turned round to see the new comer, he found his friend Gabriel again by his side, sobbing as a child weeps when his heart is nigh broken. It was real grief, and no one was disposed there to turn it into ridicule. There was, however, in this more than the mere sight of suffering humanity. The sight of that good man, anointing a dying sinner through the divine influence; and by this act of piety, together with former remembrances, good and bad, the services went farther into his soul at that moment than the same ceremonies, gone through at any other time, could possibly have done.

"Come away," said another person who had remained hidden till now. "If you stay here any longer, your friends will fall into the hands of the Philistines. Hear how they shout, as they come on to join their friends."

"This is the guide I spoke of," said Gabriel. "The sun will soon be up and I must hide my face in some hole; but how gladly would I change places with Hank Snyder in there, to deserve that good man's blessing."

"Quick! out of this," said the new comer, "else you will get his curse, and a horse-pistol shot to fasten it; see, he is moving to the door."

The four had gathered under the shadow of a large maple-tree, and were in close consultation concerning the future. Clarence and Bertram were confounded at the minute knowledge which Gabriel had of them, and of their purpose, and became quite passive in his hands. He entered at once into their scheme, and gave directions in such a way as betokened authority over the man addressed.

"You will take these men," said he, "by the quickest and the shortest road to the mountain, through Kiskaatam's country. There is an attack to be made upon the Boermen of the Vlatts about this time, and Brandt is to lead it. Try and get to his rendezvous, and put these gentlemen under his care. They will tell their own story to him, and obtain his assistance."

"What if we cannot get through in time to catch that red-skin? The attack on the Whigs has been made already; Dominie Schuneman had a dispatch yesterday saying that the great Mohawk was on the South Mountain, and we have had other word, that we can understand." Here he gave three snifters, which was a sign understood by Gabriel.

"Petrus Van Vliet," said Gabriel, with some haste, "you are to do the best, and no fun. These gentlemen are king's officers and on the king's business, and that, the Dominie says, requires haste; and let me tell you that it also requires honest men. Remember that Geordie's whelps have arms longer than Petrus Van Vliet's." Here the speaker held up his finger in a threatening manner.

The other gave a grin, saying under his breath, and with some emphasis: "George's bayonet is wearing shorter every hour, and that fire has melted an inch of the point. But it is time to put on these duds, so put off your buttons, boys."

This was something which neither of the two had thought of. To be disguised and taken would lead to a dog's death. To be taken in their own clothes would only cause imprisonment, and, at the worst, their being shot and honored as soldiers on duty. They hesitated.

But the new guide was inexorable, and Gabriel was silent; so making a virtue of necessity, they laid aside their buff and blue for the sheep's grey, the livery of the country. In fact, though Petrus had kept the secret to himself, he had stripped two of the men who were lying dead on the field, that he might furnish these travelling dresses; and taking those cast off from the two young men, he hid them so that he might use them, as he knew he could, profitably, on some other occasion, in deceiving the opposite party at the game of "give and take."

As short a time as possible was consumed in these preparations, under the superintendence of Gabriel; and Petrus, being one of those men who work for the highest pay, was assured of reward according as his work was well done. His eagerness at getting all that he could appropriate to himself was the key to his character.

"You may know your man," said Gabriel, when the other stepped aside to lift a button that shone among the litter at his feet, blowing the dust out of its eye and putting it in his pocket, all unconscious of doing any uncommon thing. "You will see that he has his price, so use him, by the grace of high promises, till you see he is becoming greedy of gifts, as well as of graces; and when it comes to the last and the worst, see, there is a pair of 'covenant keepers,' which you will need sometime, perhaps; but always remember, as the Dutch wives say, 'Better fazle a fool as by vecht dem.'"

With this advice, he put a pair of pistols in each of their hands, which, in addition to what arms they had already, made them well defended. With that he bade them adieu. They were now in the hands of the slippery Petrus, who took them by a foot-path, which ran along a stream, till he came near to what evidently appeared, even in the grey of the morning, to be a graveyard. The dark stone monuments were visible, while the silence which prevailed, in contrast to what had in the early part of the night been experienced, was heavy and oppressive to the hearts of those young men, who were now set out upon an enterprise far more hazardous than a pitched battle. There was not a whisper uttered by either, and even Petrus was prudently silent; but coming to the corner of a field, he abruptly seized Clarence by the arm, and standing between the two, he whispered, as he pointed with his finger to an object that moved slowly a few paces from them, "See! see!" They looked to the place, and saw the figure of a man. "See! see!" and the covetous hypocrite's teeth chattered as he tried to laugh off his fear. "'Tis only the Dominie talking to the dead. He says himself that he stands between the living and the dead. He does not know that we are here. But we must go faster than at this pace."

This was said to keep his own courage up, for the truth was, his knees had an ague fit, and had his two companions not been firm and courageous men, they would not have kept company long with him; but they seized him by the collar and dragged him a mile, till he got over his fright, when his tongue began to loosen, and to boast of what they knew was false, that he was a very bold and determined "dare devil."

A little occurrence took place a short distance further on, which showed that all three were but flesh and blood in regard to true courage, and that in reality none of them had more of that virtue than they needed. A large black dog came running toward them with a mixture of gladness and fierceness which made his gestures strange to the three men, and not understood till Petrus at last came out with the secret, and with as much unconcern as if he had done a meritorious deed. When the animal came near to them, he began to smell the clothes which the two strangers had on, and then to look up in their faces with a strange, mysterious fear, which made the blood run chill in their veins. After acting thus he left them, barking fiercely, till he got to a gate on the road, which he leaped over, when he set up a howling most terrific.

"That is Tobias Snyder's dog Pompey," said Petrus; "he knows his master's clothes. What wise creeturs these dogs are, to know about dead men."

The wearers of the dead men's garments began to realize, for the first time, the predicament they were in. All that they had heard in their lifetime of the sagacity of the dog came to their minds, together with the likelihood of being found out and suspected of being the murderers of those who had so recently worn them. "Murder will out," they said, smiling bitterly the one to the other. Perhaps, after all, there was a grain of superstition at the core, pointing to the ghost of the murdered man following the garb in which he was last dressed. This incident impelled all the three forward with increased speed, in the hope of making their way a few miles further before the day dawned. The two strangers, in their eagerness, outstripped their guide, and at one time they began to suspect that he had given them the slip. Fear, however, was impelling him as rapidly as his friends, for by this time he learned he had to do with men of determined purpose; besides, he was also aware of the power which Gabriel wielded over him behind the scenes. Tired all were, though not caring for sleep; yet it was necessary for safety that they should lie still for some time, and in some place near at hand. To this place Petrus was taking them. Arriving at a low stone house, built as if intended to last till the mountain near it should waste away, he gave three knocks, and a fourth small touch with his knuckle, when a large fat wench, of the genuine Guinea breed, admitted them, without questioning the new comers. Not so an old woman who put her head out of a recess inclosed by doors, where she lay on her bed, and cried out, with a sharpness that rose from impatience and fear, joined with old age:

"Vat's de matter noo, dats tou here at dis time oo de morning, ven oos vanted at Sopus? Te dog has been here howling like te wolf, and te old man down wid his gun vatching te Tories once. Budten vay is here?" and with that the old woman looked at the strangers with a scrutiny that made them wish within themselves that they were either on the mountain or on the sea.

"Never mind, Dame Wynkoop," said the wily Petrus; "twae Weegies on a message to the general at Albany from the governor, keeping out of the way of the konink's sogers."

This was said in the ear of the good lady, who received it as it was intended, lying down mumbling something to herself in Dutch. "Oog omoog en tand om tand."

"Yaw, yaw, granny," said the double-tongued listener; "we shall take more than an eye for an eye, or a tooth for a tooth—we shall make them stone blind, and knock all their teeth down their throat."

While this dialogue was going on, the unwieldy African wench was bustling about preparing breakfast for the family, and casting side glances all the while at the coat Bertram wore, till fairly overcome by her curiosity, she seized hold of the lappel with the evident intention of giving it a more narrow scrutiny. Petrus saw the difficulty, and coming up slily, he slipped a bright silver dollar in her hand, saying in her ear:

"Give us the high outside chamber, and keep the old vrow quiet when the old man comes."

With a sly wink he left, going up a hidden stairway, signalling his companions to follow. When he got there, and had sat down to bread, milk, and meat, which he found for them, he said:

"Now you must rest as you can till the night comes on, or sooner, as I see my way clear. In the mean time, you are to pass for what I have represented you to be, good Whigs going on business to Albany as soon as you are rested."

"Surely," said Clarence, "we may go at any time of the day through these wild regions without meeting any crowd of people or any very cunning men."

"Wild regions! Do you call these cultivated farms wild regions?" said the indignant Petrus. "The finest wheat in the world grows here, and the apples of the garden of Eden are springing out of the clefts of the rocks. And if you suppose that there are no people near, let me tell you that the road is lined with houses like this all the way to Catsbaan, and there, in the grand stone church, a garrison is lodged just to nab the king's men in disguise, and strangers would run some risk, I can assure you. They place about the same value on them that they do on foxes and the like—twenty shillings a head at the clerk's office."

"Then you would not make much by delivering us up," said Bertram, looking slily into the face of the half jocular Petrus, who was enjoying his own joke till he saw that both the gentlemen were looking to the state of their pistols.

"Judging from that barking thing in your hand," said the guide, "I might fill one grave more than you have filled already, and lie down without my fee. But let us all to bed. The old wench has engaged to walk sentry, and I always sleep with one eye shut and one ear open."

Sleep they did, as soldiers and sailors sleep, with their senses so quick that the smallest noise would have wakened them. They dreamed over the events of the past day. The dreams of each partook of the special state of mind in which he lay down. Clarence saw a procession of men—sometimes it was Indians, then it was red-coated soldiers, then mixed with others—moving around a graveyard, where were tall figures with torches, standing in a circle; in the midst of it was his sister, who clung to the man with the three-cornered hat, who stood with a naked sword defending her from Kiskataam.

Bertram's mind ran, in his dream, after a dog, who was always tearing at his coat, and baying in his ear like a wolf. Somehow he found himself fleeing from him, and sitting on a cliff that overhung the sea, with the ship Vulture below, where stood the Lady Clinton, waving her handkerchief to her daughter Margaret, who was clapping her hands with joy at the whole scene. All of a sudden he fell down, down, till he cried out in a fit of nightmare that awoke his companion, who sprang to his feet thinking of danger.

There was cause for these confused images rising in the minds of the sleepers, which they found out when they arose. Within doors, and just below where they were lodged, and all around the house, the greatest confusion prevailed, arising from the return of the people from Sopus, bringing with them one of the family who had been killed in the melee. It was a fearful sound to any listener, but to those who had so much cause to dread the vengeance of the country as the followers of the king, it was horrifying. Curses both loud and deep were uttered upon the Tories and on the soldiers, mingled with the sobs of the women weeping for their dead. The old man's grief was affecting to both the young men, who began to think on the effect which the news of their being "missing" would have upon their fathers.

"I tought myself done wid te worlt, ende dat my kinderken would have a care ov me all mine liven, budt I maien go to te ploegt, ende de harrow, ende te gun myself; nor lay te gun down till te cruel Tory be druv out of de land. Oh, mene kindren! mene kinderken woulden to Goden Ik deed for tee."

The old woman of the morning here put in her word, "oog om oog tand om tand."

"Ah, the old beldame," said Bertram. "You hear that. She has that favorite word of vengeance in her heart. You remember Petrus said that it meant 'an eye for an eye, and a tooth for a tooth.' Where is that rascal gone? surely he has not left us here in the hands of our enemies. See the crowd round the house; keep back from the windows. We are surrounded, by St. George!"

"Hush!" said the other; "hark to that voice; I know it, for I must have heard it in my sleep," and both put down their ears to the floor, listening, when they discovered that of the Dominie, who was comforting the mourners in this hour. "They have died in a noble cause; the cause of Goden and the country. They were good men that fell, and your zoon was a good lad, and you will soon follow. The cup that my father hath given. You know the rest, Fred, and must be patient."

"Do you suppose his majesty could ever conquer a people of such stern principles as these Calvinists? For my part, I have always told my father that these New Englanders resembled the Scotch that I lived among at Edinburgh, more than they did the English. And the chaplain was sure to chime in with his heretical Calvinists—Fatalists. 'No,' my father would say, 'they have a will that conquers in spite of faith.'"

"I think it will be the same here. When the Hudson runs up the stream the king will conquer human nature that has religion to help it."

At this part of the play, Petrus came slipping in at the door, when they beckoned him near, saying: "you have brought us into the panther's den very soon, but here is the cure for two at least," as a pistol's muzzle turned toward that worthy's body in a threatening manner. But he, without changing color, merely said:

"Yes, and it will depend upon how you behave yourselves if you ever get out of it. You are suspicious of this place as a trap, and so think of blood-letting, as if I had brought this on you. But who killed the old man's son? Did I hurt any one last night?"

"What have you to do with that? was it a part of the bargain between us that you should deliver us into the hands of the men who will take vengeance on us as murderers? You must account for this, and that here on the spot."

"Hear me, and then kill me if you must; but I would die with a clear conscience toward you at least, if I can. There is only one way of escape for you, and that is by giving yourselves up into the hands of these men; for they know already that two of the king's troops are here."

"Give ourselves up!" both almost shouted out. "No, by

King George, we will fight till we die first. Here we are, up in this citadel, well armed, and partially provisioned;" for as Bertram said this, Petrus was swallowing the last morsel of bread brought in the morning.

"All very fine, gentlemen," said the cool Dutchman, "all fine with a hundred men in the house, and the door all bored for balls; and look down to your feet, the board you stand upon is the only thing between you and perdition; ha! ha! thinner than the bottom of a ship."

The two confounded men looked in each other's faces, and seriously began to think of taking revenge on the fellow that had so entrapped them, as they still thought; but after a close scrutiny of his conduct, other light came into their minds. He could not possibly have known all the circumstances, and his plan of giving them up had a clue to it which must be left to the unfolding of the history as we proceed. In the meantime the young Englishmen were in a great rage, so that the guide began to think it was time for him to escape.

"Let us sell our lives as dearly as we can," said the one to the other, "and send a ball through that fool's head."

"Knave's heart, you mean," said Clarence; "for fool or knave, he deserves it alike."

Before he had time to say another word, Petrus was gliding through a side door, behind where he had stood eating their last morsel, as if he intended to strip the garrison before he starved it out. He left his two companions looking in each other's faces, in the utmost consternation, and for the first time they both obtained a glance at themselves in daylight. They would have laughed outright had they not remembered that one of them had on the clothes of the dead man whose corpse lay below. With feelings too bitter for mirth, and in a condition too critical for hasty action, they sat down to deliberate: first, barricading their temporary fortress. There being but one board between them and the room below, they heard what was said easily; and as their own fate was on the tapis, it was proper and honorable enough in them to listen, when, as the proverb runs, "they did not hear a good word of themselves."

"Petrus Smith, stand up and tell whae the men be, up in de geliedden. Put a guard on te window."

This was said at the very moment the thought had entered into the minds of the prisoners—for they were now prisoners—concerning a means of escape to the hills, when, to their exceeding vexation, the order was given to watch them; and six men marched out in front of the window where they stood, with weapons that would speak truth and death at the same moment. It would have been folly to have attempted a sortie in the face of such a force, so they yielded to their fate.

"Petrus," continued the same person who gave the command to watch, and in whom the prisoners above recognized the voice of the Dominie, "give an account of thyself, and of the company thee keeps. Who are these men thou hast brought with thee into this house, and where are they going?"

The sly hypocrite saw that he was here in a tight place himself, and that his character was suspected; so he found that the best plan for him was to go back and take up what he could substantiate. So going through a long-winded story, he came at last to say, that being like others at Sopus, through the past dismal night, he was returning home just at cock-crowing, when standing at the northwest corner of the grave-yard, he found these two men inquiring the way to Albany, as they had business with General Schuyler; and as they offered him a price to show them the way, "what, was I to refuse the men who were going to see such a good man, and a friend to his country?" He came with them so far, but beginning to suspect that all was not right, he had brought them in here, and now he left them to the care of the Dominie, and of the Consistory.

This story sounded very like something got up for the occasion, and was far from making an impression on the assembly, especially when one of Petrus' neighbors stated, that he had called at the door of the other at the time of the alarm, and the answer was that he could not leave, and he doubted whether he was out of his bed at cock-crowing.

At this point, the Dominie said that "a broder could not be condemned but by the mouth of two or three witnesses: Petrus, thee was, thou sayest, at the nordwest corner of the graveyard, at cock-crowing. What cock nearest? What did thou see at the time the cock crew, in heaven and on earth? Answer all three questions at once."

"It was te Dominie's red cock that crew; the red morn rose just over the top of the red flame, and the Dominie himself was standing beside the tombstone of old Yaakob Elmendorf."

"Enough, enough!" said the honest Dominie. "I saw

the three men turn round the corner, and go north, but did not know that Petrus was there; I thought it must be some omzwevende, de affscrapsel, but did not think that Petrus was among them."

"Dominie, I am not vagabond nor offscouring, but an honest man, and a vreedzaman in these wicked times."

"Well, we can but suspect you, not prove you guilty; and as to your being a peacemaker, let me tell you they are the best peacemakers that are pure in heart; for you must remember, my kinderns alle, that the wisdom from above is eerste zuiver daara vreedzaam—first pure, then peaceable. I thought, when I saw the three men, that it was some eenige booze mannen ait de markboeven."

"Who calls me a lewd fellow or one of the baser sort?" said Petrus, with mock passion.

"Nay, nay," said another voice here, "budt tell us once, Petrus, vy te give Dyaan tis silver milledoleor?"

This was a poser; but the ready sinner asked immediately if he had not told Dyaan to waken him whenever Tobias came home.

"Sartain sure," said the honest creature; "and no'd tell de ole man that Petrus was up stair." Here she sniggered out a true African giggle of triumph, as she drew the bright piece out of her capacious bosom, and threw it down on the table before the Dominie, with a clear jingle that harmonized with her words. "Dere, Domilie, tak it, my fingers burn," and she spit upon them before she wiped them on her greasy side.

The careful pastor saw that trouble was brewing, and that at a time when other thoughts than revenge should rise in their hearts; so taking down the large Bible, he opened it at the fifteenth Psalm, and commanding silence, he read and commented. "Heere wie zal verkeeren in uwe tente? wie zal woonen op den berg uwer Heiligheit. Die oprechet wandelt ende gerechtigheit werkt; ende die met zyn. Herte de waarkiet spreekt."

"Here is an English Bible," said Clarence to his companion; "let us see what the text is. 'Lord, who shall abide in thy tabernacle? who shall abide in thy holy place? He that walketh uprightly and worketh righteousness, and speaketh truth in his heart. Hearken to the exhortation.'"

"The parson suspects that the villain is telling a falsehood," said Bertram. "There is hope yet. Don't you remember what the fellow Gabriel said, 'Trust the Dominic before any one else with your secret. Light breaks upon us."

By this time the good man was in earnest prayer, and as there is always power where there is earnest pathos, even where the language is foreign to our native tongue, the hearts of these young men in their condition turned upward as they listened to the singing tones of the stranger, amidst the deep silence below, except as it was broken by a sigh and a sob which came from the afflicted father's and mother's heart. By the time the devotion was over, all were melted into another spirit.

"Whoever dreams in London," said Clarence, "of such scenes being acted here among these Dutch boors, in this wild country? There is more refinement and real power in that service than in the Bishop of Exeter's. It is like a chant on an old organ."

"And in an older cathedral too, you would say, looking out on these fine old trees; on that noble mountain, where, to tell you the truth, my mind was running in search of liberty all the time the prayer went forward, which, for aught I know, might be for vengeance on our heads. I had always heard that the Yankees were a canting set, and put the curses of the Psalmist on their tongues when they spoke of the king, and of his navy and army."

The door opened at this juncture at the call of Petrus, who came to it, telling them that he was alone, and had brought a message to them from the Consistory.

"Consistory!" exclaimed the two prisoners in a breath; "we have heard of the consistory of the Romish Church, but we took this to be a Protestant country; and what right have they to demand our presence? Is it a civil or a spiritual court?" To all of this, the wily Petrus was silent, afraid lest he should be heard by the people below-stairs, and not sure but that he might have a ball sent through his pate by the outraged men he stood before. He merely winked and whispered "patience," as he put his fingers to his lips, turning to lead the way as a cat turns and steps when an enemy is about to dart upon her.

"No help for it," said Bertram. "We will know the worst all the sooner."

They entered on this new stage with anything but feelings of confidence. Already disgraced, at least degraded, they were from their real position in society. Young officers accustomed to walk in Britannia's livery, were in American homespun, worn yesterday by the youth whose corpse was now laid out in Holland sheets. This was the first object which met their eyes, and went further to their hearts than a hundred balls would on the battle-field. The room was crowded with men, who looked daggers at the prisoners; but all were under restraint, for in the centre of the room stood a round table, at which sat nine men, who had the authority, and who, from their gravity and honest faces, seemed worthy of it. This was after the manner of the kerke of Holland. The Dominie sat as president, and could not be mistaken from the rest, who were all dressed in the common garb of the country, while he wore a large black coat that came to his heels, and over his capacious chest hung the true Geneva bands. He was a dignified man, and would have commanded respect anywhere. The young men were prepared, after what they had both heard from Gabriel, to yield him reverence, though not obedience. The men near him were his counsellors, though he seldom asked counsel. His word was law with all, except with one Geordie Cockburn, a shrewd Scotchman, who had found his way hither, first as a teacher, and then as a surveyor; and so, by degrees, like all of his countrymen, he climbed to the top of the heap. Possessed naturally of the controversial spirit, he stood up for his right to speak his mind, in spite of the Dominie.

"The criminals have entered," said some one, addressing the president.

"No one can be criminal," said that worthy, "till he is found guilty. Doth our law condemn any man before it hears him and knows what he doeth? Or, as our good Holland Dutch says: 'Ordelt ook onze wet den mensch, ten zij ze eerst van hem gehoord heeft, en verstat wat heij doet?'"

This was said with great tartness, and to gain time, for the president saw at a glance that the young men were of a superior class, though in disguise, so he asked in a dignified manner:

"Has any one here charges to table against any person or persons, for burning Sopus, and killing Ik. ende his brother Benjac Snyder? It is a case of Fama Clamosa."

"Wouldna it be as weel," said the Elder Cockburn, who took speech in hand here, "that we speered the names o' the twa youngsters, before we gang any furder in this business? In my kintra they aye put down the name with three or four aliases to the tail o't."

"Take down the names of the prisoners," said the president at this suggestion, as he turned sharply on Cockburn, saying, "thee always art careful to instruct the Dominie in his duty."

"In many counsellors there is safety, you ken," said the Elder, "as Solomon the wise man said langsyne. What is your name, callants?"

"May we inquire," said Bertram, being the elder of the two, "by whose authority we are here placed as prisoners?"

"At the instance of Dominie Doll, Praeses of the Consistory of the Protestant Reformed Dutch Church of Sopus," said the chief man, with some dignity; "and if you be not ready to tell, we will try you under the names of John Doe, and Richard Roe, of London. Be you ready for trial?"

"We decline pleading before this court, if court it be," said Bertram, "and claim our privilege as subjects of the king of Great Britain."

"I told you so," said the president to the others who sat near him. "British subjects in disguise, and within the lines. Make out the charge against spies and murderers, art and part."

"You will surely grant us time," said Bertram, who saw that he had made a grievous mistake, and who wanted leisure to consider their future course. "We may be able after a day to bring exculpatory proof in our defence."

"Proof!" said a little short, dumpy man, who rose as he spoke. "What need of more proof than this here patch on the knee of these tubbs, that I put on with my own fingers on Benjac Snyder, the day before he left with his gun on his shoulder. That's as true as I learned the tailor trade with Gideon Noble, of New Milford, Connecticut. That's my say, as Elihu, one of Job's friends, said, when he spoke lest his belly should burst like a new wine-bottle."

"Sit down, Eph Sly; you are one good witness, and here is another," said a rollicking, red-faced man, with a sinister twinkle in his eye. "These are witnesses enough," and he opened a bundle which contained the two coats of the young officers, which Petrus had hidden away. It was impossible to see this and remain unmoved. The prisoners felt all the shame of their present disguise, and the company broke out in a perfect storm of indignation, which was stopped only by the Dominie, who rose and pointed to the body of the dead man, saying solemnly, "We are in the presence of Death, a greater king than George III. Do the prisoners want any more proof?" he added, looking toward them in some pity for their condition.

It is impossible to say what would have been the effect of following up the disposition of the company, had not Cockburn, whose clear mind saw the difficulty, and who determined upon unravelling it by cutting the knots asunder, and by making a set speech of some length, which he was rather fond of doing. The sum of it was, that we shall be in danger of violating the place of the Safety Committee, by taking this business in hand. "I doubt," said he, "if the matter comes under our jurisdiction, for if thae men be spies, what have we to do with them?"

"Ende vat vill we do wid the men dressed in Benjae's and Ik's coat?" was asked on all sides.

"Do what you like with them," said Cockburn, "only don't bother the Kerke Session wi' them, nor wi' ony political strife. We can only tak notice of slips of the foot; moral offences that deserve the cutty stool, or sic like."

While this speech was making, there was a little-by-play going on that interested some of the parties exceedingly. The man who had brought in the coats of the prisoners went off into a corner, and began rifling the pockets, which was not unobserved by the Dominie. When he had got all out, he called to the searcher just to hand all these things here, for safe keeping. As they lay upon the table before the company, the eyes of the two officers were scanning their property which they had inadvertently left behind. There was the locket which contained a miniature of Clarence's dear mother; but what was mortifying to the very soul of Bertram, he remembered that on changing the coat, he had slipped the ribbon which held the portrait of Margaret, and now it lay before his eyes, and he could not obtain a glance at it. Clarence was fixing his eyes upon the note which his mother had thrust into his hand, just at parting, along with a small parcel which lay there with the rest, and marvelling much in his mind what effect it would have on this reverend man. It was addressed to "Governor George Clinton, of what was now called by many, the State of New York." He remembered looking over his mother's shoulder, and laughingly asking if she supposed he was going to present that as a letter of introduction to the rebel governor; but she continued to write on, saying: "Dear cousin, this is my son Clarence, and here is the amulet you sent to Margaret, as an evidence." At that instant his father came to the cabin, and hastily signing her name, she thrust the whole into the hand of Clarence, who, with equal haste put them into his breast pocket, where they were now found. A tear trickled down the cheek of the affectionate youth, as he saw the Dominie read the note, and examine behind his hand the amulet. A change came over his face, of a mysterious kind, so that by the time Cockburn was done with his speech, the president was prepared to accede to his motion; for here was something which demanded time and reflection. So saying something to himself, he called out: "The Consistory is adjourned till to-morrow, in the Consistory room, at ten o'clock. Take the prisoners where they came from, and prepare for the funeral."

Some one, it was the Yankee tailor, who suggested that it would do the prisoners great good to sit still and hear the Dominie preach the funeral discourse; but the parson had no wish to show off before them, and paid no attention to Ephraim's words; so the two astonished men were left alone, with a guard walking before the window, one of whom they thought they must have seen before to-day.

The large barn floor had been cleared out for the company. Pipes and tobacco lay round on trays which were soon reeking, so that the doors sent out "smoke like a kiln loggie," Cockburn said. Then came in bottles of cider brandy, baskets of bread and cheese, followed by slices of ham and pieces of sausage; sour krout and choice rum, with corresponding edibles, of which all partook with a hearty good will. Prayer and exhortations were the accompaniment; not the main part of the occasion. It was a regular feast, and almost a fight in one corner, and a frolic in another. Liquor will bring out human nature whether at a marriage or at a burial. "When drink's in wit's out;" youngsters will laugh at what is ludicrous, and the more solemn the circumstances the more difficult to restrain their mirth. "It's all bearin' a dry sorrow," was Cockburn's sage remark; and he went off in the determined spirit of one that hunts after an argument; no matter whether the game be large, or small deer, a mouse or a bear would have had equal attractions for him at the time. Sometimes he might be seen hanging on the loop of the Dominie's waistcoat doing his best to reason down his rising indignation at what he saw. "I'll tell you, minister, it's ill bearin' a hungry grief. They speak of stuffin' a cold and starvin' a fever. I'm agreed this is a cold time out in this big barn."

"Yaw, yaw," said Zach Myers; "but vat do you zay to dat vetchten dere?"

And sure enough there were two of the mountain birds pecking one another like hawks at the dividing of a chicken. The Dominic got his eye upon them and without saying a word, he walked up to the place, giving both a lunge with the heavy end of his cane, which set them off in opposite directions. Forming themselves in a row, men, women and children, the pastor in front of the coffin, the father and mother of the young man immediately after it, all went to the grave where a prayer was offered, and then the people scattered.

CHAPTER V.

DARKNESS, DEATH AND DELIVERANCE.

"Take care of thine own heart, for there is not a more faithful monitor."—Lord Kames.

"He that trusteth to his own heart is a fool."—King Solomon.

The two young Englishmen during the time of the burial feast, had a portion sent unto them of which they stood in need. Though not dressed after the fashion of a French cook, hunger made it savory and good to the taste. Old Dyaan had taken a great fancy to the prisoners, especially to Clarence. Her heart melted for him when she saw the tear trickling down his cheek at the sight of his mother's picture. "It vas," she said, "so buvitul, and de ribbons ov de vool on her head so yallo."

Petrus came in telling them to prepare for walking. It seemed that the Dominie had taken Cockburn's words to heart, for he had left orders to have the prisoners removed to the care of Captain Languendyck, whose company was garrisoned at Catsbaan church; and to that point the two disconsolate young men were moving by sundown. It was not the fact of their being prisoners, nor yet the fear of what might result from their separation, but the hindrance, which this delay threw in the way to prevent them from overtaking the cruel Kiskataam, who was doubtless hastening on with the one whom they were now seeking after, with all their heart and soul. They must give her up as lost, for as things appeared, they were lost themselves; and that without the power of resistance or defence.

"I will fulfill my part of the bargain, for all that has happened," said Petrus in the ear of Bertram, as they came down stairs; "keep a quiet tongue in your head and don't be blabbing of your loyalty everywhere, lest you get a lead pill through your belly, before you have time to return the compliment."

Bertram scowled a dark frown, that said plainly enough, "I will fulfill my part of the bargain with you at least, you hypocrite, the first chance that comes up." As they passed through the door-yard, they saw little knots of men and heard the jabbering of Dutch, loud and confused enough to make them believe in the confusion of tongues, had they ever doubted the fact before. As they could perceive, their own case was the subject of discussion, and, however anxious they might be to find out public opinion, there was no way of ascertaining it, except through the medium of their guard, and with him in their present mood of mind, they were not inclined to hold any communication. Their road lay along the base of the mountain, on one of those steppes which run almost nearly due north, and which are called Vlatts, extending from half a mile to two miles in breadth, rich and deep in soil; having beautiful trout streams running from different points toward the main river. The mountain seemed close at hand, and the two prisoners, when rested and in the open air, felt all the fire of youth as they saw how near they were to the region of their hope. But they were guarded too closely for them to think of escaping in that manner. After marching about four miles, they came to a stone building, which they were told was a church, now turned into a fort and garrisoned by the Ulster Militia. Here they were to be kept till further orders arrived from the governor. As they were gentlemen, Captain Laugnendyck said he would take their word of honor, and let them range at liberty. Both Bertram and Clarence were averse to so pledging themselves and set down like men determined to make the most of their conditions, by taking a survey of this singular outpost of defence. Surrounding the building were tents, and wagons with oxen and a few horses. Smoke was rising among the trees at different places where cooking and chatting were going on. Two old cannon were fastened to logs by ox chains, while about fifty muskets were stacked before the door. An endless collection of pots and pans, casks and benches, with other trumpery, were scattered in indescribable confusion everywhere, and yet the eye of the soldier could perceive that with at most ten minutes' notice, the men would be on the lookout, north or south according as the alarm might be given. The inside of the venerable building was the scene of similar confusion. All round the sides of the walls were settles for beds, on which were spread the heavy blankets and coverlets that the good wives and mothers of the men had furnished them in abundance from their heaped piles at home. In the walls were driven hooks on which hung armor and harness; with clothes and skins from different animals, tanned and used for riding, or covering out of doors. The gallery overhead held the ammunition and the more precious stuff, watched by a sentinel separate from the rest; and the very desk in which the good man had stood on the Sabbath, during many years, dispensing the bread of life, was now changed into a pantry where the choice bits sent from home were kept from the rats and mice that had followed in their wake.

The two prisoners had the belfry allotted to them. The orders were, that no communication should be held with them. Everything seemed to bear the aspect of great caution and watchfulness on the part of their guard. Night closed in upon them in the most disconsolate degree. Nor did the solemn faces of the men, who made up the militia, help them in conjecturing what might be their fate. There were none of the noises which usually keep the sleepers in a camp from enjoying rest. A loud laugh would have been grateful to their ears, had it only betokened carelessness on the part of their guard; but there was just enough of motion heard, to keep them aware that all were on the *qui vive*, and would do their duty to the death.

As night went on, and the silence grew more heavy, the scene which they had passed through during the last twenty-four hours became more confused to their vision, while the sounds of the insects that sang to each other grew fainter and fainter, till at last sleep sank upon their eyelids like a precious balm distilled from a mother's hand; and the two anxious men were, a moment afterward, as calm and peaceful as infants in their cradles, and would have likely remained so till the morning, had not a voice, which they had come to know well by this time, said, "Young men, get up; you have other business than sleep before you;" and a hand shook them both by the shoulder, while a small lamp showed them the face of the Dominie, that they had met so often of late, and knew now so well that they had become to regard him both as their good and their evil genius.

Surprise was pictured on both their faces; but they were too well trained to lose possession of themselves by a sudden wakening; so starting to their feet, they waited further development; for already they perceived that something new was on the tapis. There was not a sleeping nerve in their body, by the time they stood upright.

"Sit down there," said the good man, "and give me an honest account of your condition; and let me have nothing but the truth."

Bertram saw that kindness and severity were struggling in the face of their inquisitor, and taking advantage of the position he allowed himself to be in, he began by telling what was true; but what to a more experienced courtier than the Dominie was, would have sounded like flattery.

"We were told," said Bertram, "to put ourselves on your mercy, should we get into trouble; and to tell you all, and if you will listen to me, I am willing to trust a man whom I am now certain will not take advantage of our condition by turning the information we give him against us."

"Young man," said the Dominie, "those who advised you to trust yourself to me, did me no more than justice, for God forbid that I should hurt one innocent hair of your head: nevertheless, had I seen you about this time last night, near to Sopus, a ball would have gone through your pate, as sure as there is one in that thing there at this moment;" and with that he fingered a horse pistol in a very carnal manner, which showed that his cloth was no protection to himself at certain times; nor would he make it an excuse for silence, when either his fiery tongue, or his tongue of fire should speak.

"There is an armistice between us now, young men; so speak;" and the clerical soldier put his piece up, and Bertram proceeded to give a full and detailed account of the cause and the consequence of their apparently mad adventure.

"I find that you have spoken truth, and I am now," said the Dominie, "about to take upon me, what must subject me to much misapprehension when it is discovered, and perhaps to the getting of my own skull cracked, but I must run the risk, so follow me."

The astonished prisoners were about to say a great

deal about honor, and gratitude, and reward, but all were stopped by a motion to silence and quiet, as he led them down a way he could thread himself in the dark; for, after blowing out the light, he took hold of Bertram's hand behind him, telling Clarence to do the same by his companion, he led them out to the north of the church, where stood a man holding a horse, who seemed to be expecting their coming.

"Here is your guide," said the Dominie, "and he will tell you the rest. Be sure that you keep silent forever about this night, and whom you have seen, and God Almighty bless you, and make you successful in your race after that rapscallion Kiskataam." With these words he had vanished, and they found themselves standing face to face with their old friend Gabriel.

They almost forgot themselves in their surprise at the meeting, but he being prepared for their astonishment, immediately whispered, "let us be off, out of earshot, lest we have a ball sent after us." Gabriel mounted the horse and told them to keep one on each side by the stirrup-irons, as he knew the way. On they went in silence, increasing in their speed as they were advancing out of the risk of the sentinels' hearing; their hearts beating with joy both at their escape, and at the prospect which they felt must now be opening for them in attaining the end of their journey. It was now an hour before midnight; and in the morning they hoped to be on the side of the mountain, out of danger from the rebel Whigs.

It was under the charge of their former guide that they now were moving along through the darkness. The relation in which he now stood to them was more of guardian than of guide. The two young Englishmen, in that easy way by which those accustomed to command become subject to superior law, or to circumstances beyond control, gave themselves up at once into the hands of their servant. They perceived he had some authority, and a deep interest in them; but they were anxious to know all before they yielded up all. On their way he intimated his desire to reveal to them the exact state of things in which he stood toward them. He was in the employ of Lady Clinton. He held from her a secret message to the provincial governor, who had retired with the Congress after the sack of Sopus to Hurley, which was said to be defended by the Dominie and the old vrows of the place. Thither Gabriel hastened; sent in the sign which he knew would call the governor out; and his own words will but tell the rest.

"When he saw me he lowered his voice to a whisper, looking as Moses did, before he killed the Egyptian: this way and that way; and when he saw there was no man, he aid, 'Are you the man who sent me in this ring?' And I said, 'Yes, your excellency, a noble lady committed it to my care.'

"'And for what purpose,' said the governor, 'have you brought it to me?'

"'A case of distress, sir, in which your help is demanded,' I said promptly, looking up in his face, which by this time showed all kinds of feelings.

"'What distress can there possibly be with them at this moment, when they have it all in their own way? I am sure they burned and harried the town, and got off with clean heels to their ship without one life being lost or a prisoner left behind. The distress is all on our side.'

"'Not so sure of that, your excellency. Two prisoners are in the hands of the people of Vlatt Bush, and their lives are in danger at this moment.'

"'They must be some persons of note when Lady Clinton interests herself so much as to send this token, which was only to be sent on the last extremity.'

"'They are none else, your excellency, than young men of the family.'

"'Good God! and what can I do in their case? How could they be so foolish as to allow themselves to be taken by our people, when they had the ball all in their own hands?'

"I then gave a full and fair account of the whole matter, beginning at the robbing of the young lady, with your pursuit after the robber, and ended at the place where you were lying yesterday. Never did I see a man thrown into such distress of mind. 'Come this way,' said he; and he walked in the greatest agitation round the house, till he got me into a patch of wood, where he gave vent to his feelings in bursts of exclamation that would have sounded well in Ireland.

"'Enthusiastic little fool! She wrote me that I might look out for her some fine fall morning; and how the —— can I help these young madcaps after what has taken place? Blood is thicker than water. I wonder if the knight of the garter would help plain George, were he now in the hands of his majesty's bulldogs. I rather think I might not be known as belonging to any other family than Adam's. Ha! things change in this world. Let them take their course. That basket of deer-meat and turkeys was well enough; and the basket filled with those bottles of cognac back again were all well; but this is a new matter. It would be as much as my head is worth were Washington to hear of my interfering. No, young man, take the ring back where you got it.'

"Here he held it out to me, looking at it all the time. Then, asking me, 'who knows of these young men?' With that I told the whole story, and mentioned the name of Dominic Doll. The countenance of the governor brightened up at this: a lucky thought was evidently finding its way through his mind. Taking a leaf from his note-book, he proceeded to write, all the time swearing at the insolence of these British Tories, who threw out their requests upon us colonists, as if we were bound to listen and satisfy them, because we belonged once to the same national family.

"'Wait till I put my seal to this,' said he; for he evidently was not inclined to trust me. 'Now, take that, and see that these young fellows keep out of my road, for I will shoot them as truly as my name is Clinton.'

"I took the letter to the Dominie, and you are here. What next, gentlemen?"

CHAPTER VI.

THE PLEASURES OF SUSPENSE.

"Two ifs scarce make one possibility.
DRYDEN."

OUR adventurers, left out in the darkness of midnight, were in a more satisfied state than they had been during the last twenty-four hours; yet it was such a condition as they would not have chosen a week before, had they been offered it, with a few thousand pounds to boot, so strangely does the happiness of this life increase or diminish through comparison with other things.

The question now, what should be done? was one not easily solved, where there were different means of reaching the end sought after. Brandt, the faithful ally of the king, was in their immediate neighborhood, and by his help the Indian Kiskataam might be overtaken and punished; but, as there was unquestionably an abler mind in the plot of abducting Margaret, it would be dangerous to let matters be known in that camp immediately. Caution was necessary to obtain the ear of the great Mohawk, who certainly would listen more favorably to an officer, bearing the commission of his majesty, than to men who had the appearance of stragglers. By the time his mind might be assured, the dense forest would hide the abducted lady. Doubts gathered so thick upon the minds of both Bertram and Clarence, that they voluntarily gave themselves into the hands of Gabriel as captain.

"If you promote me to that place, then," said that worthy, "I command you, Mr. Clarence, to be off to Kaatskill, taking this letter with you, to secure the assistance of the Dominie of that place. If the mountains must be scoured, help is necessary, so that the retreat to the west side may be cut off. You see that fire burning on the face of the hill; there lies Brandt and his men. Let Kiskataam be prevented from escaping, and we can boldly go to the Mohawk and demand his aid in behalf of the king. We must trust to the current of events, and as good Dominie Doll said, 'leave the rest to Providence.'"

"True," said Bertram, "for I am more adrift here than I would be in an open boat at sea. My sailorship is all useless on these mountain waves. Some wisdom higher than my own is needed, and a power above king George must control this rash adventure. Breakers are all ahead, and we on an enemy's coast."

"A stout heart will climb the steepest hill," said Clarence. "Give the most difficult part to me; I am ready for it. I go with a better conscience than I did to that dastardly burning, where we did not deserve to succeed. The people are better than their betters. What are our captain's orders?"

"Mount you this nag," was the word given. "He will carry you at least seven miles an hour. He belongs to old Cornelius Wynkoop, as stiff a Whig as ever smoked a pipe. He loves his horses next to his wife; she says he thinks more of them than he does of her or the kinderen. If he supposed at this hour that a king's man was putting his leg across his back, he would rise out of his bed, dearly as he loves it; and I believe out of his grave, if he were in it, with a thick stone slab over it; I am not sure but he may, through some spook, be able to tell this now, as well as he can tell where to find water with a forked stick. So look out, sir. You will ride along full twelve miles, till you come to another stone church, not unlike the one you have just been in against your will. Ask for the Dominic's house, and give him that missive. Whatever he asks, tell him freely, and follow his advice."

By the end of these counsels, the young soldier was on Charlie's back, a stout, bottle-bellied animal, with a small head and a long tail, that he whisked around through habit, night and day, as a warning to the flies.

Gabriel, holding the impatient horse by the bit, gave Clarence his last advice, by saying, "You must not linger on the road till sunrise. This is the king's road to Albany that you are now travelling; keep on it till you come to the kerke; stand at the door looking east; you will see among fruit-trees, on a knoll, a stone house, covered with Holland tiles; turn to that, and you will be sure to find the man you seek—a strong-built man with a keen eye. Bid him a good morning; then, as he answers, turn to the mountain, and ask if the old vrow's nightcap be on yet. He will bid you mind your own business till the old vrow has had her morning meal, and said her morning prayers. Follow him in-doors; put the letter in his hand on the way; sit down to the table, as if you were one of the family; wait patiently till his family have worshipped with him. He will let his own pleasure be known sooner than if you press him."

"Well, that is plain speaking; I think I can remember that. Let me see—the king's road—right on—sunrise! Oh, yes, I know it all," said the rider.

"One word more, as the Dominie says, and to conclude. Meet us at noon the day after to-morrow at Kauterskill Falls—mind the name, Kauterskill Falls—and there is a whistle that will answer this one that we have."

Here both put their bone whistles to their mouths, and made the midnight air send out on all sides such a shrill sound, that the dogs all around gave out loud barks; and wild growlings were heard, not far off, above their heads.

"We must be softer than we are now," said Gabriel. "Go."

And away the horseman went at a good round gallop; a secret of Charlie's haste being, that he thought he was going home to his crib, and became all the more eager the further he went. "At this rate," said Clarence, "I will be at the end of my journey long before sunrise. But in times like these, who can foretell the adventures of a single night, within a short journey of twelve miles, even on the king's road?"

But our story, to be clear, must just now follow the course of the two who were left behind. They having a shorter distance to travel, and a more difficult path to tread, moved slowly along.

"It is but a short hour past midnight," said Gabriel, "and our part in this business is to search all tracks. For that, we require daylight. What say you to a couple of hours' sleep, and then we shall have time enough?"

"You may require it indeed, my friend, was Bertram's answer in words, though his impatient heart said go on. "We have had plenty of time to sleep, or eat, or chew the bitter root of disappointment, in yon garret all day."

"Well, if you are agreed," was the reply of the guide, "we shall turn into Cornelius Wynkoop's barn. To tell the plain truth, I am cowardly as well as sleepy. There is an enemy in these parts not easily guarded against. Hunter as I am, the painter and the wildcat, in the dark, are dangerous critters, as the Yankees say."

"Is there much of that kind of game up in these regions?" asked the young Englishman, who had seen some hunting in his day, in his own country, and also in the East Indies. "It would be good sport, to have a chase after these western tigers. The panther of this continent I have been told is a powerful animal. What of these wildcats?"

"Oh, there are swarms of them all through these hills. These mountains have their name from them; so many and so large are they, that a single man finds himself in danger of his life in attacking one of them."

"Hä! a man killed by a cat would make a great story for a picture-book in Christmas time. Since you are so skilled in names, why do they call that church we were at the Catsbaan."

"That means the cats' race-ground," said Gabriel, laughing at his own conceit. "These people are half French, and have many of their words. In the holidays the big boys and girls for ten miles round here meet, and have a regular hunt. After scaring out fifty or a hundred of the screamers, they set the dogs after them on this flat. And let me tell you it is a scratching time when one of these creatures happens to fasten on a dumpy fat Dutch girl, and the boys come round for her rescue."

"That must be fun in a small way; but these painters as you call them, must be the very thing to rouse the blood in a man's heart."

"You may meet him soon enough, sir," was Gabriel's answer, "for unless my ears deceive me there must be some wild creature up there now, in South Peak; I hope it is far off, but in the dark one cannot tell, and my counsel is that we go at once into this fortress until the enemy be off, or we be in a fitter condition to meet him."

For some time past they had been turning more to the westward, and nearer to the mountain, as the dark shadow against the sky showed. A large building which looked still larger in the night time, rose plainly before the eye of Bertram, who was at this time seized by the hand, and led through the door, which yielded to the touch of his companion, as if he were the owner himself. Gabriel led his fellow-traveller to a ladder, whispering in his ear, "follow me to the yards;" a hint which the young sailor took at once, and mounting, he found a softer hammock than any in the British navy. Gabriel was asleep in a few minutes, but the feelings of his companion were too excited to enter easily into the land of dreams; so he lay and mused, watching the sounds which came from nature, even in these lonely wild regions.

At length the old rooster of that true Holland breed, heavy behind and double combed before, gave out his first trumpet sound, becoming louder as Gabriel snored responsively, and deeper at every crow. Bertram became all the time more impatient to be away, where the dangerous Whigs would not venture near them. So giving the sleeper a dig with his elbow, he succeeded in making him conscious of where he was, and of what was required of him. A few whispers earnestly blown into his ear, were enough to a man accustomed to lie down in the midst of dangers. So keeping quiet a few moments, just to recover his full balance, he started up, saying, "Remain here till I make a visit to Dame Wynkoop's cellar, where I am sure of getting something good to eat." And before his companion had time to remonstrate with him, he was off, and already down the ladder on his way. Bertram followed so as to watch against surprise. There was no ground for fear. Old Cornelius was in his soundest sleep yet; and even had he been awakened he would not have suspected an evil intruder, but would have supposed it to be one of his dozen blacks moving along the floor.

Besides, Gabriel was as familiar with all as if he were going over his mother's kitchen. All Dutch cellars are the same in size and the same in arrangement. Butter pots and firkins on the floor. A cider barrel in the corner, and a vinegar jug on a shelf. He moved about among them more easily than the mistress of the house could: she being like a skipper navigating a scow in the Amsterdam canal without a pilot. The pies, the cold meat, and the bread all stood in a pantry on the left hand; it was but the work of a moment for the pirate to clear the whole away. He knew that the old wench who ruled the lower regions would lay it all to that cussed Ebo who came home hungry after one of his night rackets. However, the cautious Gabriel walked as if on eggs, reaching the barn with his forage, and well pleased with his success.

"There is some of the staff of life," he said to his friend. "You will need it before we get to the top of these hills, where there are no loaves growing on hemblock branches, nor roasting pigs on bare rocks. I only wish that we had some of old Kaarney's Holland gin now. He used to keep a snug grey beard in the corner of that cupboard. Confound me that I should have forgotten the value of drinking, as I thought on the duty of eating. It makes the staff limber as well as stronger on the hills."

"You are a daring fellow to venture where a hungry wolf would not." This was said by Bertram under his breath, and between the good bites he was giving to the stolen provender which he saw but partially in the star-light. All cats are grey in the dark, so all bread is white to a hungry man. Our two travellers, hearty in the stomach always, could have done justice *then* to the haunch of a bear.

"What is that I hear gurgling down your throat?" said Bertram, laughing inwardly; "have you hold of the old farmer's grey-beard after all?"

"Try it yourself," was the answer, and a square bottle about a gallon's size was held to the mouth of the thirsty inquirer, who tasted, and then swallowed with right good will. He found it strong cider brandy mixed with juniper berries; a most agreeable, but a heady drink.

"Hush!" said Gabriel, and he put his head over the loft, for they had both mounted again to their former place of rest. "Some one is coming in at the big gate. I hear the old wooden hinges squeak." The two gourmands rose to their feet to be ready for any emergency; when the stable door was opened with great caution; and some one, leading one horse, entered, and a second horse followed. The negro, for his voice betrayed his origin, began to talk to them just as he would to his fellows in the field:

"Ole Black, you'd stop de snuffin; te be 'bout Ebo's business; see dat no stories be told but de big trut."

Then coming into the other stall he commenced in the same way.

"Brown, poor Brown, been on de king's business, s'pose; vere's de fellow dat own dis saddle? vee will see in de mornin' sun-light. He be gentleman dat spok dere to us at Phœbe. Me know an English offisher by his neck, might hab left a yallow Joegey ven he vent off to de Squire Burhause himself."

At these sounds Gabriel pricked up his ears. "Something has befallen him, I fear," he whispered in his companion's ear. "The horse he rode has returned with his mate."

"Who do you mean?" said Bertram, suspecting himself that trouble had come to his friend.

"Why, the lieutenant, to be sure, Mr. Clarence—some difficulty. Hear him speak of the Squire Burhause. I have a mind to make the splay-footed vagabond tell. We may be able to remedy the evil."

Bertram saw the folly of this, and put his hand on the other's mouth as a warning, while Gabriel, feeling the influence of the cider-brandy, and knowing the superstition of the negro race, out of pure mischief, gave a squeak through the fingers held on his mouth, which made the hostler call out, "Oh, Lorra, have marcy on poor nigger," and without stopping a moment, he ran out slamming the doors after him, and rousing up all the dogs in the house.

"We are long enough here," said the mischievous fellow as soon as he got over his fit of laughter; "let us move before we get a few drops of old Kaarney's gun. There he is lighting a candle now with a coal at his mouth;" and gathering up the fragments of their breakfast for future use, they left their hiding-place with good heart and on nimble feet.

Before the heavy half-door of Cornelius Wynkoop was opened to let him and his dog Gates out into the yard, the two adventurers were well away on the road that leads to the Clove. Having no cause to fear immediate danger, they moved on at a moderate rate, discussing, as they went, the events of the last twenty-four hours.

Gabriel had an uncommon flow of spirits for him. He had been taciturn, and dark in his speech and in his looks. He had got a good draught of the inspiriting liquor; but that was not the cause. He had paid a visit to his mother, and now he was beyond the reach of bodily danger, which he had been in ever since he came up with the marauding party. To wile away the time, as well as to gratify his curiosity, Bertram led his guide to the discussion of his own affairs.

"I have no objections to the telling of it all," said the countryman, "though it is a longer story than a stranger would care to listen to, except for amusement. You see, I left old Sopus and my mother's house in a fit of ill-nature. I cared no more for King George than I did for old Mat Van Guisen; but I had taken a heart's hatred to some that called themselves Whigs, and particularly to one purse-proud old Jew, who had a lovely daughter, who loved me, but durst not move in the shadow of my shape. To get me out of the way he made up his mind that I should go off with Arnold to Canada. I took the opposite road, and have been in all the places south of this, where fighting was to be done; for I found there was more quiet for me in war than in peace. I jumped at the chance of coming on this expedition. My love of adventure, my love of revenge, my love of Nelly Labagh, and I may say it truly, the love of my mother, all urged me on board the Vulture. Standing as sentinel on deck, I soon discovered the aim of Kiskataam. I had long known the fellow to be a villain, and determined first to watch, and then unfold his designs. We had met before the war broke out, in Stony Clove, where he attempted to steal my good gun Meg, when I chased him and struck him down. So you see there was ill blood between us; our glances of defiance said—another time. When he slid overboard, carrying Miss Clinton with him, I was not there; but of all on the ship I was the man to have headed a party of pursuit; but you know it is not for us to offer advice to our betters. But I did what I could afterward in an interview with Lady Clinton. I offered my services and they were accepted on condition that I should wait on your pleasure after the Sopus business was through. There lies the secret of my knowledge of your intention, and of my present interest in you. I own that I hate an Indian, and that I will travel any time a thousand miles for the mere pleasure of shooting one. Dirty abominable wretches! how any young lady can sit and hear their soft cunning tongues close to her ear, I cannot understand. And blood-thirsty devils! how gentlemen, like you, can fight with them, or employ them to fight for you, is amazing. I am ashamed of having ever drawn a trigger under King George when I think that Kiskataam, and his like, have fingered the same bounty."

"Have you seen your mother?" said Bertram, anxious to turn the mind of the excited colonist away from a theme which burned on his own tongue. The effect of the question was all that was expected, and more, for the Englishman was almost sorry he had encroached into that sanctum of Gabriel's bosom.

"Seen my mother! Yes, but I all but wish I had not ventured over that holy threshold. Blessed woman, how she gazed on me, drinking in my soul through her old dim eyes, that lighted up with the same love she had always felt for me; prodigal as I have been. I had resolved to stand it through, but how soon all broke down, when she said, 'My own Gaby!' Well, I feel better that I went. Before, I could have killed an army, now I would not hurt a fly."

"Always excepting an Indian," said Bertram, slily. "Where did you meet her? Was it at home, in her own house?"

"You must remember, after I left you at the stile we were standing at, that I walked softly on to the cottage window, where I stood listening for a few minutes, when I heard the well-known voice, low and soothing, as if she was comforting some one. She spoke as if it were to a child. But that is her way to all sick people; so I did not expect to see a child; and yet I was startled when I saw a man's head rise up from the pillow and scream. I could stand at the door no longer; so rushing in, I flung myself into her arms. She kissed me quietly; but pointing to the bed, said, in a whisper, "Petrus is sick." That was my brother, and as I feared, he had been out in the attack, and was hurt in defending the hearthstone. A cruel fellow of ours had struck him on the head with the butt end of his gun, and now he was delirious. He recognized me, and gave a wild shriek that froze the marrow within me. Springing on the floor, he seized me by the stock on my neck, twisting it till I became like a child in his hand. I could not have resisted him, had he tried to kill me. My mother's voice, however, served to make him release his grasp, as she came between him and me.

"'Is it here,' the maniac cried, or rather yelled, 'that the cursed Tory would dare to show his face; and in the colors of the king? Ha! ha! ha! Come to burn the house, and his own mother in it? Look, see here where your bayonet is sticking yet;' and he tore away the bandages from his head, bloody as they were, and flung them at me, they falling on my face, so that the marks of blood were left all over me.

"Then exclaiming, as he looked at me, 'You bloody-faced traitor, you come home in your true colors. Take the bayonet out of the hole he put it in. Take it out, I tell you, till I put it into him.'

"At length, through loss of blood and fatigue, he became weak and quieted down, so that he fainted. This gave me some relief, when the good Dominie came in, to my great shame and mortification. He has always had a power over me more than any other man: not even the General himself could command me as that man of peace can at this hour, when I come near him. His surprise gave way, at seeing me, to great indignation, and even reproaches at first, which cut me to the heart. Then he would mellow down to a kindness, which was worse to bear; so that I stood really between two fires, and durst not resent either side.

"'O ye vile boy! Ye Absalom, rebelling against parent and country. O Gaby! Gaby! I am sure you did not find any ground for your sinful conduct in the good Heidelburg that I taught you. Sit down there, like a good lad, and see if you can say it—What is thy only comfort in life and death?'

"Just as I was beginning to reply, my brother gave a shriek that made us all start to our feet. 'Send him to the gallows, I'll be hangman.'"

"'Hear you that, Gaby?' said the Dominie, when the raving man had quieted down again. 'That's a voice calling upon God for judgment on your head; your brother has spoken his last words, and you hear them yet ringing in your ears.'

"It was true; Petrus had sunk into the arms of death, and I stood there, as I thought, his murderer. I felt it that it must be so, while the Dominie continued to pour out maledictions upon my poor head, till I sank on the floor.

"'O Dominie! Dominie! have pity—have mercy on my poor misguided boy,' was the cry of my mother. 'My kind-hearted Petrus, my first-born, the image of his father gone, and none left to me now, but this my poor wanderer;' and here she fell into my arms, and cried only as a mother can.

"'Gaby,' said the Dominie, after a few moment's pause,

'you are too long here, unless you be seeking the gallows. As sure as there is a rope in Mark Snyder's barn, if he catches you within the town of Sopus, you will have to swing for it. Up, and be off with you.'

"After that I met him, and told him all about you, and succeeded in interesting him in your affairs. So that you are here, and your friend away yonder."

"Well," said Bertram, "he must have drank deep into the spirit of his religion, when he can so help the outcast, and forgive such injuries as we put on his people. God grant that the time may yet arrive, when I may do something that will show I am still a man and a gentleman."

In this way the two went on slowly, till they reached to the head of a narrow valley, up which the road ran, when they came suddenly upon Hoogenhuisen, still smoking and in ruins.

"What!" exclaimed they, both at once, "more misery from war."

"O, God!" said Bertram, "this solitary case makes us feel more than if we walked through a sacked city. Domestic happiness in a single family we can understand, and feel a sympathy with. How many happy hours have been spent around that hearthstone!"

"Yes," said Gabriel, who was transported in grief. "Happy hours indeed have been spent around the fireside of Martin Schuyler. I would not have believed, had I not seen it, that any one could be so cruel as to level this home to the ground. Black ruins! There is the kettle that old Anshela kept as bright as a button, half melted. The cellar always so well filled, now a chaos with charred barrels and broken pottery, and"——

Gabriel's heart filled full at the sight; and mounting up on the rock opposite, he sat down on a shelf to indulge his grief, mingled as that was with burning tears of remorse—let us hope of repentance, in some degree. So long did he seem inclined to sit, that Bertram found it necessary to remind him that the day was advancing, and he knew best how far they had to go, and what must be done.

Gabriel said, "It is time we were gone; but these ruins tell us that Brandt and his crew, and I am ashamed to say our friends, are not far off, and are likely lurking about here. Both parties may now be within cry. Let us then," said the guide, "prepare ourselves for friend or foe."

With that they both proceeded up the Clove road, Gabriel intending to cross at a point opposite to the falls of the

Kauterskill, and there to lie in ambush till the appointed time for action came. Somehow, both the young men had a kind of presentiment, that the centre of attraction was there. No doubt it arose from two ideas floating in their minds, Margaret's well-known romantic spirit, and next the disposition of the Indian to seek some prominent scene in nature, as a mark for himself. To that celebrated place they now eagerly bent their steps. Here an occurrence took place which interrupted their progress, and but for their courage and experience would have put a stop to their expedition forever.

CHAPTER VII.

A PANTHER OR A CATAMOUNT.

"The brave,
None but the brave deserve the fair."
DRYDEN.

GABRIEL, sunk in reverie over the ruins of Hoogenhuisen, left the responsibility of the sentry-box to his companion, whose senses were growing keener every moment to the sounds, and new objects rising around him. He was sure that some wild animal must be in the neighborhood; but not caring to disturb his guide, he merely felt more awake, and continued more watchful. The sounds were becoming louder and louder, till at last one fearful roar roused up Gabriel, who exclaimed as he started to his feet: "A catamount! run for that rock." And they both sprang to one that was near, and balanced on the hill side so nicely, that two men in earnest, with a stout oaken lever could have turned it over, and sent it rolling down the gorge into the stream. Here they both ran, and on the lower side intrenched themselves, waiting for their enemy, who being above them on the side hill, came down upon them with tremendous fury. Their case seemed desperate, since all the advantage of superior position was on the side of the animal. Retreat was now impossible, and their fortress was insufficient should he choose to besiege them by merely keeping watch. But they were not men to yield without a struggle. Bertram had seen the real tiger slain, when there was a host against him.

Gabriel was a hunter from his youth, but this was the first time he had met the catamount, along with a single companion.

On the creature came, leaping from height to height, and evidently bent upon taking his next spring to the top of their defence, which bent over them slightly, and was only about five feet high on the upper side.

"We must fire together," said Bertram, naturally taking the command, "if we would make sure, and then spring up on the rock just as he leaps from it."

Gabriel, who had now forgotten all his grief, and thrown aside all his Dutch sluggishness, replied: "Then, captain, give him your shot in his burning eyes, while I aim for his heart."

"Have your knife ready," was the quick answer of Bertram.

"Tighten your belt, captain," said Gabe, as he drew up his own buckle one hole more, pulling his rough cap tight over his ears, and looking where he might take hold of the stones, in case he must spring to the top of the rock. The sailor was not behind in his preparations, and stood ready.

In the meantime the animal watched his foes, lashing his tail from side to side. When, crouching, he gave his threatened spring, landing fairly on the rock, where he received the contents of two pistols, which only made him more furious with pain. He gave a roar that was heard as high as the Dog's Pool, where Angelica sat smoking her pipe, till she rose in her terror and mewed the wildcat's mew that alarmed Elsie.

The two skillful men had retreated to each end of the rock, so that their enemy's attention was divided and puzzled. Falling down gracefully on his haunches, he seemed to plan carefully his next attack, and Bertram must be the object of it, for the faces of man and beast were within four feet of each other. The man's eyes penetrating so deeply into the animal's that they blinked under the power of intellect.

"Keep close to the rock, and more to your right," was the cry of the other man; "he will leap soon; let it be as far down as possible." And the warning was scarcely given and taken, when, with another roar, the spring sent the catamount down so far that by the time he recovered himself, the two men were on the upper side of the defence, waiting for their foe. The advantage was now all on their side, and the discomfited creature, as if ashamed, turned his head away a moment, half inclined to retreat. It was then that the bark of Rover from above attracted his notice, and roused him to his feet, evidently with the determination of renewing the attack, but with more caution, for taking a circuit, he moved up the side of the ravine, as if to regain his former vantage-ground. The two men were debating whether it would be best to allow him to come on to their rear; and like all divided commands, the council might have proved fatal.

"You may stand here if you please," said Gabriel; "but I am for that tree. I hate to have an enemy above me;" and with that he sprung up and sat on a branch which overhung the very rock on which his companion was ensconced. The animal, from this very motion made by his enemy, had put himself into a rapid pace, and was ready again to take a new spring as before. Down he came cautiously, when both fired, and their shots told; but, raging with pain, he sprang upon the rock, over which Bertram slid, but only to encounter his foe, which was in close quarters with him at once. Out came Bertram's sharp knife, which played havock with the beast; still the result might have been doubtful, had not Gabriel come down and finished the battle, by a ball which he planted in the ear, so well given that the catamount turned himself on his side, and gave his last gasp.

The two adventurers, wiping the sweat from their faces, mingled as it was with blood, sat down on the rock, surveying their fallen enemy with pride and gratitude.

"A panther," said Bertram, at length, "and nearly as large as the Bengal tiger we shot at Bombay, in the East, when there were fifty of us in at the death. What powerful limbs he has; and these horrible claws; see where he has torn the flesh from my arm here."

"Not a panther, sir, as you may see by these black rings on his tail. A catamount, if you please; but so far as the fierceness and the power of the creature goes, there is but little difference. The painter is sometimes seen in these mountains; but of the difference, old Frederika Sax could discourse with you a whole day, and not be tired then."

"My poor carcass, Gabriel, my boy, would be quite as sore after the description as it is now. See how these holes bleed; come, tear off a piece of my shirt here, and act the surgeon on me, lest I bleed to death."

This being done after the most approved hunter's art, the busy Gabriel commenced immediately skinning the dead animal. To the question put, "Of what use is it? for you cannot use the skin here, and you would not burden yourself by carrying it away."

Gabriel replied coolly: "You see, sir, it will serve two purposes, and more besides. It will prove good luck when we show these claws, and obtain bounty when we fetch those ears home. They are good money anywhere while fresh; and the man who has killed a catamount, as that tail will show, is not to be despised on these mountains. He will respect himself, and others will respect him."

All these reasons were given while the process of denuding the animal of his hide was going on. After it was done, the operator took the skin on his arm, and climbed up a high tree, where he stretched it out on the trunk, so that it might dry without wrinkles.

These events took place within a few miles of the Dog Pool, where the three women, in whom we are interested, had their hiding-place; but in these wild regions, a thousand men moving singly through the thickets, would be like ships in a dense mist at sea, within hail of each other, but in ignorance of being near any one. A mile more to the westward would have led the two men to the very spot on which their minds were bent.

Weary and worn with the fatigue of their late contest, they sat down on the verge of the ravine, and commenced eating the fragments of their supplies, which Gabriel had carefully gathered up at the close of their morning meal in the barn, draining at the same time the last drop of Hollands from the square bottle.

"Squeeze the sides of it," said the humorous guide, as he saw his companion holding up the vessel, so that the drops fell into his mouth. "There is more where that came from, though we are not likely to taste it till we earn it; and if my ears don't betray me, we shall have more work of the same kind before an hour passes. Hark!"

The attention of Bertram was called to what his guide was saying, when a roar went up through the Clove in the mountain, which chilled his blood, and made him start to his feet as if he had been shot.

"The mate of our dead enemy," was the answer to his fears. "She has found him out, and the skin is not so warm as it was last winter. Well, it sounds mournful, and there is a sort of humanity in that scream."

"I declare," said the other, "I wish that she could have

found the living body rather than the dead carcass; sorrow, even in an animal, overcomes one. It is nature."

"Up," said the eager Gabriel, "for there she comes at full speed; let us to the top of the hill here, and have at least the advantage of high ground. Load as you run, and see that the priming be good. We will need all our wits."

Doing as he bade, he put Bertram up first; and walking almost backward himself, he watched the shaking among the bushes, looking out at the same time for some point which might, in case of need, be a place of defence. The old rock was now in his mind, but for lack of that, he was resolving to climb the first tree which afforded a favorable harbor; and had communicated his plan to Bertram, when another roar told them that the creature was upon their wake. She had scented their track and was hastening toward them.

"Spring to that pine-tree," was the cry of Gabriel, and at the same time, he took to the one close by himself. When nearly half way up, they looked back with more security to the path up which they had come. Listening with great eagerness, their late experience told them that something was irritating the animal below them. She was giving forth low, dull growls, like those heard by themselves just before their late foe prepared to spring on them. In a moment more the report of a well-loaded gun came up to them in full volume, accompanied by a yell which told that the ball had entered some vital part, though life was far from being extinct. Before Bertram had time to speak a word, he saw that Gabriel had slipped down from his perch, and was already on his way to the scene of action; and in duty bound he must of course follow his captain. Like all men accustomed to danger, the mere prospect of seeing fair play was enough to entice them to the place.

When Gabriel arrived, he saw at a glance how matters stood: a single man was in close combat with an enraged animal; and the beast had decidedly the best of it, for the man lay on his back, and was grasping the throat of the catamount, her tongue pressed from her mouth, discharging foam mixed with blood on the prostrate man's face, blinding him completely. So closely and stiffly were the combatants clasped that neither could the man rise nor the beast extricate itself. The two forelegs of the one were held down by the arms of the other so near, that when the claws of the beast would have been raised, the strength of the man was put forth with such vigor in pulling the neck down, that all efforts were as yet vain with the fore feet; and by lifting his knees to the belly of the beast, the hind paws were fixed in the ground below, so that they did no injury.

Such a state of things could not have continued long, and considering that the animal was severely wounded, it is probable that it would have yielded had his grim captor strength left like what he still showed, to hold out; but the smallest change might have proved fatal where nothing remained but the bare human nails, against such claws and sinews.

"Hold on," was the cry of Gabriel, the moment he came near; "hold on, and I will put my pistol to her ear."

"To her heart, to her heart," shouted the man, "she will choke me with blood."

Quick as thought Bertram took the opposite side of Gabriel, and putting his pistol to her heart, while Gabriel applied his at nearly the same time, the great creature, with a scream almost human, fell over on her side, leaving the imprisoned man alone at full length.

"Are you hurt?" was the first question put to the rescued victim. Rising up, he shook himself, as if he were not sure that he was the same man who had been lying under a catamount a minute before.

"I do not feel any way injured," was the answer of the man, in the full mock dress of an Indian; "but I think I must be, after such a struggle. I forgot to thank you gentlemen, for your timely help. My throat would now have been in her vicious jaws but for you; for I could not have held out three minutes more."

All this time the stranger was panting for breath, and trying to stand on his feet. His face was covered with mud, and streaked with slaver, so that it would have defied his mother to have known him. Bertram had run and filled the bottle with water, putting it into the hand of the stranger; Gabriel was at the same time wiping his face with his handkerchief, used as a sponge. Both were doing all they could to restore the rescued man to calmness, and his strength. After these necessary things were done, they sat down to survey their fallen foe, and hear the account of the beginning of this combat.

"It appears to me," said Gabriel, "that notwithstanding your evident disguise, your voice and eyes are in my memory, like some old tune that I have heard snatches of in my young days. I am averse to ask you for a name in these times, but our late battle has put us all three on one side."

"And you might command me just now, since you are two to one."

"Any man," said Bertram, "who can fight a catamount is not to be despised even when laid on his back."

"I have recognized you from the first moment you came in my sight," said the stranger. "You are Gabriel Smith, and my name is Teunis Roe."

"Ha!" said Gabriel, "who could have thought it; and yet I might have known that the son of his father would be on the side of the king; for I see that you are wearing one of his liveries."

This did not sound very agreeable to the other, but he merely replied, "I have heard that Gabriel Smith had on the king's livery for a year past; how comes it that he has doffed it in these hills which are all under his majesty's power?"

"Reasons for all things, and you are the very man that can help in this matter, Teunis Roe; and as I knew you before to be honest, and now to be brave, I could wish to lay you under a bond of honor. We would ask of you a favor."

"What you may command as a right, since I am indebted to you for my life."

This led at once to a careful history of the reasons of Gabriel being there with Bertram, a stranger, on these mountains, and it is easy to imagine the mutual surprise of all the three, when the whole story which both parties told was communicated. Bertram of course was the most astonished, the most enraptured, and the most affected with fear lest all their labor should be lost.

"So near and yet we cannot find them! Oh, if we had but a few days to ourselves, we could hunt them. One thing we should be thankful for: she has escaped that villain Kiskataam."

"He is now hunting for them, and perhaps before you are aware of it, he will be at your back, aiming his gun at your ear. It is time that we got under cover. I have seen that snake this morning already, and I have not been able to leave the camp once, but he has been at my heels. Let us go up nearer to the Kauterskill Falls."

"Have you made up your mind as to which side you will take when the Indians are carrying off the prisoners," said Gabriel to the mock Indian: "for you know we can claim

being on the same side with Brandt and carry off our prize in the teeth of Kiskataam?"

"That is if the man called Colonel Clifford do not succeed in putting in a stronger claim and have a stronger hand in it than two men like you, in the dress of the common colonists, are likely to have with the Mohawk."

"Colonel Clifford!" both called out at once. "He here! then our cause is hopeless, unless we can obtain her by force or stratagem; which do you suppose to be the most feasible?".

"When I was met by that fearful animal," said Teunis, "I was on my way to consult a man of more wisdom than I have myself; though till this morning, I was better able to judge of hunting through these mountains than a stranger possibly could be; but I now am at my wits' end, and am willing to be led by any one in this matter. Perhaps I ought to have gone to him beforehand; still it may not be too late."

"Who is this person, Teunis, that you are now about to counsel with, if I may ask, for if we are going to take the same work in hand, it will be proper that we act together, intelligently."

"Let me here," said Teunis, "tell you candidly that my life and happiness are alike bound up in the deliverance of Elsie Schuyler, and if the young lady be the same as I have seen, your interests are mine; and so far you must trust my word. I have a plan which was in my mind before we met. It can be carried out all the better by three. Hear this, and tell me your mind. The party on the rock I believe are waiting for more prisoners, whom they expect. Some say it is the Dominie of Kaatskill. My own notion is, that it is nobody else but your Lady Margaret; and to-morrow there is to be a regular surrounding of the hills as far west as possible; now if I can get up a party of surprise it will either send Brandt off, when Elsie will come out of her hiding-place, or it may become a rescuing party, should they succeed in discovering the spot where I am quite sure she keeps her charge."

"And what did you wish from the friend below?" said the over-cautious Gabriel.

"I wanted encouragement: for my judgment has become scattered. Between this false dress, my father's wishes and my own likings and dislikings, I am like a dog that has lost its scent, ready to be whistled off by any straggler on the road that will call him master."

"Unless you have confidence in the man, do not go near him. Your plan is excellent, and for your encouragement let me tell you," said Gabriel, "that one of our party is down at the Dominie's at present, soliciting his advice and aid."

"You mean a king's man like yourself, in disguise?"

"Yes, the brother of the young lady, and he carries documents with him of such a kind as will insure his reception."

"And a warm reception it will be, as I am a living man. Your friend's neck is not worth a bushel of beans in Dominie Schuneman's hands, unless it be on the authority of General Washington himself. It would not surprise me if he be hanging like a scarecrow to the first tree he finds outside of the church."

"He would not dare to do such a thing in the king's dominions, and in the face of the authority he carries."

"My dear sir, you are an Englishman, and very loyal, no doubt; but our Dominie has more power in his parish than all the kings in christendom; but come, we have not a moment's time to lose."

CHAPTER VIII.

FUN, FROLIC AND FOLLY, FINISHED SOBERLY.

"Socrates, the great moralist, was so famous for wit and humor, that the Athenians gave him the name of The Droll."—MODERN PLUTARCH.

CLARENCE CLINTON, after parting from Bertram and Gabriel, made quick progress on his faithful nag. There was good cause for the animal's haste—his mate was on the same road that night before him. Old Cornelius Wynkoop's negro Ebo, was a dissolute fellow of his race, spending three nights in the week, besides Sunday, in some dissipation. He never went far without a good horse, and though it might be to a distance, he was sure to return before his master had shaken the ashes out of his first pipe; Kaarney's negroes were free livers, but were not the only set that lived a free life. Their masters and their sons do all the marketing, and the providing, and the visiting, during the winter, upstairs, while the blacks do the eating and the drinking down in the cellar kitchen. The frolicking is done by both classes, at their several haunts, near the villages, where might have been seen a swinging sign-board with the words "Cakes and Beer sold here," painted in the rudest shaped letters, as if patterned after an African's jaws and heels. Some crone of the real ebony color keeps the house for a white man not far off. Generally she is his own slave, of more than usual shrewdness, who presides in full freedom for the night, while he in the morning comes round from the big house for the avails of the carousal. There the negro dances, and the rough weddings are held; and under the rose the sons of the white men take great interest in these kiltocoys.

Ebo, Wynkoop's right-hand man, loved a horse, as all his race do, and mounted on black or brown, he forgot everything for the time. He treated the span impartially, taking them always out time about. The horses were brothers, and never parted from each other but they were glad to meet again. This instinct led them always to run to the same point when they could get free, and the wild Ebo had been found out before now in this very way, and traced to the very place he was most averse at being found in.

As Clarence rode along in the middle of the night, to his great surprise and sudden alarm, his horse set up a loud neighing and whinnying, which made all the fields around vocal. At short intervals, these calls were responded to, by others of the same kind, which increased in number and loudness in proportion as he advanced. All at once he was brought up standing at the door of a low cabin, where voices and screams went up, as if a hundred witches were dinning the air and performing their eldritch rites. "Black spirits and white, red spirits and grey," all seemed mingling together.

After gratifying his curiosity a moment by looking through the low window, he prepared to go forward; but to his mortification his horse would not move a foot, but sent forth one of his loudest neighs, that provoked the rider to vengeance, which caused the animal to make all the more noise, till it at last arrested the attention of the company within for an instant. One of the dancers came to the window, and seeing nothing, called to the fiddler, "Cæase, play up;" and the old fellow within gave his bow a double stroke, that skirled on the strings till the screams of the company came again in full force. Clarence descended and looked in more closely, intending to lead his horse past; and such a sight he never beheld before. There were at least forty of the genuine

Guinea negroes, of purest jet, enjoying themselves in the most outlandish sports. The dance was a cross between the wild African jig and the low Dutch hornpipe.

The astonished Clarence looked on, not knowing what to make of the scene. He had witnessed many wild outbreaks in his lifetime, but never anything like this: not even in theatrical displays.

When they had fairly run themselves down, they fell on the floor, rolling and screaming over each other, till they appeared actually like so many large black hogs, with a few white ones among them, roused in their pen, when something has disturbed them. Gradually they slackened down to a lowered key, but not less din. That was kept up in the way we may suppose the cellars of Babel were found in some night soon after the confusion of tongues took place; for not a word could be distinctly distinguished till some one cried out *sangaree*, and all rose, male and female, holding their tongues still, and their mouths open, as if they had discovered for the first time that they were choking, and could not speak another word but sangaree, till they took a swallow. It was during this pause in the state of affairs, that Black and Brown gave each other an impatient neigh, that went to the quick ear of all the delinquent negroes, who had horses there. Some one who had been out of doors ran in with the astonishing intelligence, crying, "Ebo! Robbin, your massa, come; ole Kaarney at the door."

Quick as a flash, the black rogue ran to the door, and seeing the horse that Clarence held—he knew his shape and his neigh in an instant—he prepared his back for the whip; but, in the meantime, he would try some scheme, what, he could not tell; but running up in the dark, to where Clarence stood, he screamed out, "Massa, massa, forgive ma 'passes, as Dominie says, in our Fader. Me come down to Phœbe Cauterwalikin, but didn't mean to come; forgive me ma dets."

Clarence saw that he was under some mistake, and quietly said so; asking Ebo if he would help him to take this skittish animal past the door, for he was in a great haste to get on.

By this time Ebo had opened his eyes, and had seen his error in regard to the man, but was still sure about the beast; and suddenly changing his tone, he called out:

"Ha! Cowboy stolen massa hoss. Goot; the tief found out dis time. Fox fal ente de trap himselv. He! he! he!".

And his mirth returned with something additional to pay for the fear he had incurred. All the company had felt the alarm—for the negro is of the gregarious tribes, the moment that one suffers, all the crowd suffer with him; and so let one dance, and all join through complete sympathy. Quietness had reigned till Ebo called out, "Cowboy," when a shout came out of the house, as the whole party, male and female, surrounded the man and horse. Old Aunt Phœbe, side by side with her grey fiddler, were there ready to seize the bridle of Brown, and chase the thief away with the broomstick.

Clarence, in the midst of this black nation, found himself in a complete hornet's nest and dilemma. To tell them who he was would be folly, and to go back would be to frustrate his whole plan. His first thought was to leave the horse in the hands of those who claimed it, and go forward afoot. As he proposed this, he soon found that Ebo was in as great a quandary as himself; Old Kaarney would demand of him how he happened to be there, to make the discovery, and he knew that the bringing back of Brown would not save his own carcass from the lash; so that between the doubt of the stranger and the doubt of the negro, there was rising an uncertain state of things. Old Phœbe, who was in reality the leader of the whole party, cut the knot in the right place, when she called out:

"Take 'em to de Squire. To de Squire Burhause!" To this proposition all responded with the heartiest good will, and as Clarence found out that the Squire was not far off, he hoped to prove to his satisfaction that he was neither Cowboy nor horse thief. In the meantime, he felt a little mean at the suspicion he necessarily lay under, and resolved to keep out of the presence of a white man if possible.

At the time when all were about to start for the Squire, a young lithe negro came up, blowing and puffing with importance, saying, as his breath would allow him, "the bulls! the black bulls!—Bob an' Peet."

Hooree! hooree! was the sound that went forth on all sides. The young fellow had been sent off to drive two bulls, that were kept at opposite sides of Judge Abiel's farm, into the same lot, where they were sure to fight, with a force and a fury which could not fail to be prodigiously interesting to the blacks. With their characteristic thoughtlessness of all but the present, nothing was worth looking at except the expected sport. Ebo, however, took hold of Brown's bridle, and led him down through the rail fence into the field, thinking, of course, that his late rider would follow, which he did with apparent good will. The two mad creatures were coming toward each other from opposite sides of the field, foaming and pawing the ground as they drew near. They bent their heads, then rushed together with all their fury, meeting in the centre, when their skulls cracked, as if two rocks had come to one place, flung by the hands of giants. Retiring tailwise, they flew forward again with still greater force and anger than before, continuing these repeated attacks, till the one and then the other grew weak with the effort. When fastening their horns, they pushed, as one of the ruling spirits said, when asked

"What would de Domeley say, Tom?"

"Dey push like the bulls of Bashan."

The great interest which Clarence took in the battle was in the human blacks, whose excitement was beyond bounds as the fun proceeded. Young and old, male and female, were in one perpetual movement. At every new onset they screamed and laughed, clapping their hands, holding by each other, and then falling down, seeming more like persons possessed with harmless noisy spirits, than even black mortals. Rising, they wrestled, falling down together with the most frantic yells, in which there was no malice nor misery, but outbursts of mere animal feeling, like what young colts and even old horses will at times give out, when the harness is slipped off in the field. Ebo, who by this time had forgotten all about Black or Brown, and was seen in all parts of the field kicking up his heels, turning the wildcat, with every other conceivable and inconceivable antic movement, came across old Phœbe, not seeming to know the difference between her great fat carcass and her daughter Jenny's, and taking her around the waist with his arm, she gave him a smart stroke on the cheek, telling him not "to 'sult the Missus of King's Road Hotel." Turning in his pain to old Cæse, he hugged him with right good will, who, nothing loth, hugged him back again; till, getting loose from the strong arms of the brute, he seized his bow in earnest, playing up what he intended to be "Hail! Columbia," but ending in "Rule Britannia;" a tune of more familiarity with him in olden times, and one that they all liked better from its associations.

In the midst of this horse fun, Clarence stepped to the rear, and leaving the horse tied to the fence, he took the road afoot, plainly perceiving that he would reach his destination sooner in this way than roundabout by the Squire's.

On the road he was overtaken, to his great mortification,

by three of the late frolickers, on horseback, and ordered to stop, or be "shot through the small ob de back."

Perceiving that his retreat had been discovered, soon after his secret movement had taken place, there was nothing left for him but to submit, in hope of escaping through the intervention of the Squire, to whom they said he must go for stealing that horse. After parleying with the riders a few minutes, their brains got puzzled by the question Clarence put to the spokesman of the party:

"Where is the horse that any one saw me steal? Produce the animal."

Here was something they had not calculated upon, for the fact in the case was, that Ebo had seized hold of the bridle, and was by this time far on the way back to the stable where he belonged: consequently no evidence of horse-stealing being on the ground, the fellows felt themselves utterly at a loss now when the prisoner was in their hands.

"What duv Domilie Tom say to dis in de law before de Squire?"

The person of whom this was asked scratched his woolly pate with great gravity, and said:

"Dis be de true law; the body must be found vere de murder be."

By this time other actors had entered on the stage. A company, consisting of at least sixty of rank and file, making an attempt at looking like soldiers, led on by a large brawny negro, who gave the word of command, "halt!" which took place after a while, but not till the leader vociferated savagely, and struck at the company till they screamed, as the colored race only can scream when a frolic is going through. Clarence all the while stood wondering what might be the end of this, when a new actor appeared upon the stage, in the person of a singularly dressed masque, that simply said, "this is my prisoner. Be gone;" and taking Clarence by the arm, led him off a short distance, saying at parting: "Keep the main road and make haste, for the day dawns soon after cock-crowing."

CHAPTER IX.

A DUTCH DOMINIE AT HOME.

"Thus to relieve the wretched was his pride,
And e'en his failings leaned to virtue's side;
But in his duty, prompt at every call,
He watched, and wept, and prayed alike for all."
GOLDSMITH.

CLARENCE, walking on in the grey light, followed the well-beaten road, thinking of what he had witnessed with surprise. What chiefly affected him was the voice of the mysterious commander. He had heard it before, but where was all out of his mind. The events of the past forty-eight hours, together with the entire novelty of the scenery around him, were enough to efface any sensible impression ever made upon his memory; still the sound of the call, uttered in the dark morning, by this stranger, haunted his imagination all the way he went; and had he lain down to sleep, he felt that the sounds would still ring on in his ears. He had heard the chaplain say, when preaching on the words, "The voice is Jacob's voice, but the hands are the hands of Esau," that deceivers can disguise themselves in all things but their voice. Who is this? Time may discover.

Day was beginning to dawn as our adventurer came in sight of the stone church that stood in the centre of a neat yard on the roadside. A small village was scattered around a mill. The murmur of a waterfall mingled with the dashing sounds of the wheel. There also stood the smithy, and the tavern, fashioned after those of the low countries in Europe. The fields showed a better cultivation than Clarence expected in a new country. He did not know that the whole region was more than a century old. A plain of considerable extent, running from the south as far north as the eye could see, was well dotted with dwellings, surrounded by orchards and barns; while the hills here and there had bare places on their sides, showing that improvement went on, promising fine results in time.

Clarence came up to the door of the church, surveying it with deep interest, as it reminded him much of what he had seen in the Low Countries of Europe. It was built of stone.

and covered with the same red tile so common in Holland. Posts were placed all along the road, with rings in them, for fastening teams; and a few sheds stood at the rear of the church for such as had more care for their carriages than the majority. The small belfry rose out from the middle of the square roof; and Clarence saw that a bell of some size hung in it, which, no doubt, had been the gift of some pious Dutchman of the past, whose monument stood in the graveyard near by. There the traveller went first, and read in the grey of the morning, the names of the forefathers of the place, showing that they mainly had been of true Holland origin, with less of the Huguenot blood than he had seen in some other places. Van Bergen, Van Kleek, Van Duesen, Van Vechten were most numerous. What surprised Clarence was the mixture of both English and Scotch, especially of the latter, in a place so far remote from the thoroughfares of the world.

"These Dutch," he muttered to himself, "I believe are found everywhere except where hunger and starvation are known; and there, too, are the highlanders from Scotland, that hungry country. You cannot starve them out."

Here were Salisbury and Grant, McPherson and Newkirk, all met in this fine amphitheatre, surrounded with high hills, that were washed yearly of their best soil to fatten these lands below, and these, in time, became fit to support an immense population, already flocking into it from so many countries. Here, too, was the temple, where all worshipped their Maker, blessing Him for the lands where their tents were pitched in this life. There are the graves, where pious friends come to shed a tear of grateful remembrance, and of holy hope.

With such reflections, the candid young Englishman spent the half hour that preceded the sunrise, when he was told to expect a meeting with the greatest man of the place. Standing as he did, at the door of the church, he looked to the east, and saw a stone house in the midst of a small orchard, and the whole surroundings showed uncommon thrift and neatness.

"That is the parson's house," said Clarence to himself, "no doubt, and there is the man of God himself; the instructor, the guide, the friend, and the true patriot; I wonder if he be at all like the one I have just left! I marvel if our clergymen in old England would fight and preach for their country and their people, as these men are doing here!"

The Dominie Schuneman, of Kaatskill, with whom we are already somewhat acquainted, was walking slowly from his house to his barn, surveying things to the right and left, that he might have all put in order. For having been absent on public business for his people, he had of course neglected his own affairs, and as he lived more from his farm than on a salary, it was necessary for him to watch on all sides. Clarence, in order to give the reverend gentleman time to mark his presence, had walked deliberately across the way from the church door; but as the parsonage stood on the highway to the city of Albany, every passer by was seen, and scanned carefully in those times of excitement. The Dominie had seen the stranger, and was watching his movements with the "tail of his eye," as he continued to throw out handfuls of Indian corn to his poultry, of which he had a numerous flock, including a herd of turkeys, that would have fed an army in a strait.

"Good morning," was the salutation of the stranger, to which the pastor courteously responded by a slight touch of the cap, that came close to his head, falling in flaps over the ears, after the manner of John Calvin, as seen in pictures of that great man. Indeed it was intended to pattern after that of the Polemical Republicans, of whom Dominie Schunneman was a profound admirer, equally of his "five points," and his political creed.

Clarence, folding his arms, turned his face toward the mountain, which was beginning to reflect the sun, and said, as if he did not care for an answer, "I wonder if the old vrow will doff her nightcap soon."

"Young stranger," was the quick reply of the poultry feeder, "it is not for such as you to dictate to her greatness before breakfast."

Clarence smiled assent, well pleased with the *open sesame* he had applied with such success, at the first trial; and, as if to ingratiate himself still further into the good graces of the worthy before him, he continued to speak on.

"Mother Mountain is like all her sex, somewhat freakish in her moods; such a firm bottom would promise more constancy of temper."

The answer to this was somewhat ambiguous, and warned the young man against presuming too far, and so soon. His intention was seen through, and was repelled in the outset; lest there might be a setting back afterward, of an unpleasant nature.

"When an old vrow, young stranger, prepares for a stormy journey, she takes off her nightcap at sunrise, and inexperience thinks all is fair weather; but wisdom knows, that in her good nature at home, she allows her petticoats to hang loose. When you see the top of the mountain clear, and the clouds lying on the sides, look out for a passionate burst before night."

Here the philosopher dropped his weather-wise cap, and calling out in a sharp, rough tone, "Tom! Tom! You vagabond, come with me into the stable." Looking behind, Clarence saw the one he called for, in rather a dubious aspect, looking askance upon the stranger, as if he was more afraid of him than of his master.

"What is the matter with you? What makes you look so drowsy? Ha, what is here! What makes Dick all over in a muck of sweat? Who has had him out of the stable in the night? Some black skin will pay for this before sundown."

The negro turned up the white of his eyes toward Clarence, who now recognized one of the frolickers of the preceding night—rather morning—and the one that seemed to rival his old Inquisitor Ebo, in the cantraps of the "King's Road Hotel." They cast significant glances toward each other. Tom evidently saying "a shut mouth catches no flies. Let us be friends." The negro went about his business in anything but a comfortable mood, seeing a witness of his folly in such familiar intercourse with his master; and at the same time he was planning in his mind how he might be able to counteract the evil effects of anything against himself, by something equally disastrous to the stranger. Working himself into the firm belief that Clarence had already revealed all, he resolved to pay him back with interest.

Dominie Schuneman, whose company we expect to keep the greater part of the time through which this history extends, was a man of large and wide influence in his time. He belonged to one of the oldest families that came from Holland at an early day, and which had risen to some wealth and a good position. Of their ancestors, he was one who would not boast. When his wife, who rather looked up to the aristocracy, would begin to trace back, he would curtly say:

"The less of that Maria, the better. My name is Schunneman; and you are Dutch enough to know that that is skinner; another word for plain butcher. A Yankeee would call it Skin-flint."

But the parents of our friend were able to send their son back to the Vaderland, where, at Leyden, he obtained a liberal education, and was ordained to the Gospel ministry, which he had exercised with great fidelity in this place, Kaatskill, since his return to his native country. His parish extended from Caatsban to near Albany, taking in all the mountain districts; so that he was as well known by the public now, as any man in the province, and knew as well what was going on in it, as if he were an officer of the State. Trained in the Calvinistic theology, which renders men firm in principle; drinking in the love of liberty for which Holland has been famous, and believing in the Presbyterian order of church government, which calls no man master, he was prepared to pray and fight against the devil and the king. His ardent temperament made him a fierce foe, and a firm friend, while his superior learning raised him above all the laymen in his region; and his office gave him a power which he was not slack to use, on his own responsibility. He was a fair representative of the majority of his class; both in their good and doubtful qualities. The whole colony of New York was in the hands of these Dominies, and it is praise enough to their memories, that that portion of the new States came out of that great struggle as honorably as Massachusetts, whose speeches ring like the bell of old South, in Boston, "Praise be to me! praise be to me!"

Clarence taking the hint given him by Gabriel at parting, followed the Dominie into the house, and when the breakfast was announced, sat down to the table as if he were one of the family. A large platter of fricasseed chickens, mixed with slices of pork, stood in the centre of the bountiful board, surrounded by other dishes, heaped with cold meats of different kinds. Venison and bear's meat, and hillocks of bread and bowls of milk abounded. The children swallowed gallons of a kind of porridge called buttermilk pap; and all the grown folks seemed greedy of something called apple butter. After grace, said in Dutch, the master of the feast said, "Set to, help yourselves, and your neighbors will like you the better," and suiting the action to the word, he planted his fork in the leg of the fattest fowl, and transferred it to his own plate of wood, of which material were all the vessels at the table. His guest understood the hint, and did justice to the viands of which he really stood in want, not having tasted anything since his imprisonment at Snyder's, except a piece of apple pie, that fat Phœbe had thrust into his fist as he went down to see the bull-fight.

There was but little said during the meal, and that in a language which Clarence could not fully understand. Still he knew more than they gave him credit for. Having resided himself for some time in the Low Countries, he had picked up enough of the language to enable him to follow out the meaning of certain questions and answers given, in the purer style, which an educated man always uses in his family. The wife here was a large, gallant-looking woman, with a chin that defied all competition, and her speech was with authority, not excepting the Dominie himself. She sat high like a queen; of finely rounded form. Her complexion was pure white and red, but her look was harder than one would expect, in a place so remote from the public eye. It might be the times which made her severe; but it struck Clarence that she was too masculine to be motherly, and was more likely to be feared than loved by the people of the parish. Her husband always addressed her under the title 'Yfvrow, which the stranger soon found was as much her official name as Dominie was his, which she never failed to give him, fulfilling to the letter the spiritual injunction and example of Sarah, who called Abraham Lord (Dominus). A swarm of children were round the table—not like olive plants, but more like Dutch cabbages, so round in their bodies; and what struck Clarence as remarkable, they all had the Latin terminations to their names, Johannes, Wilhelmus, Martinus. If his ideas of the ancient classics underwent a change, as he looked into the faces of these young colonists, his opinions of the future race, taking these young rebels as a sample, were, that they would yet make a noise in the world.

Breakfast over, the householder, with the handle of his knife, struck the cherry-table three times, when a large ebony wench entered, placing a heavy clasped Bible before him; when in marched such a drove of old and young negroes, that it seemed more a market-house than a single family. Where they found lodging and procured food, it was difficult to guess. The whites present took possession of the seats, as of right; while all the blacks squatted down on the floor, becoming as still as midnight, while the father and the priest read from the sacred book in English; for though it was the Dutch translation, he gave it in the other tongue freely, as he went along. He read the forty-sixth Psalm, and said, as he closed the book, "this was the favorite portion of Luther, in the times of his trouble. These are times of trouble in which we live. We need the same comfort and defence. Let us seek those from God. He then offered up fervent petitions in the two languages spoken around him. There was some comfort for all in what he said. Clarence observed that the common cause of the country was not overlooked. Defence against all enemies from within and from without; nor was the "guest and the stranger" passed by, when the wish was expressed that this "youth of fair countenance and of pleasant speech might be prospered on his way, if he had an honest heart and an upright purpose." After prayer, there was a general rush for the door; the young fry, white and black, alike eager to be off, and away from restraint; while the older and the confidential lingered behind for a word of recognition, or for orders concerning the duties of the day before them. The Dominie was evidently a man of large business; from the commands he issued and the questions he asked. Nor were these all about farming or parish work; some referred to public business, but spoken in a low tone, which told the guest that he had not yet obtained the confidence of the family, nor of its head.

The last who went to the door was Tom, who, knowing that all was not right, waited behind, like a good soldier defending his rear against his enemy.

"You were out at Phœbe's last night, you rascal, and had Dick with you," was the pointed accusation of the master.

"Lor, massa, who tol' you? Me covered up de big book, and me tought it could no speak in de dark."

"I can see in the dark, you rapscallion, that you are. Get your back bared. Ten stripes with the raw hide will save Dick another race to Phœbe's."

Tom cast his jacket at once, at the same time turning round on his master, saying, "Your spook see dis gentleman here too at Aunt Phœbe's?"

Clarence, who had not been an unconcerned spectator of the whole scene, became now an eager listener, since he knew the cause of this present trouble better than he cared about.

"What do you mean?" said the enraged master. "Do you think such a gentleman as this seems to be, would stop at such a bedlam as you have just come from?"

There was a sharpness in the tone and a look of the eye in

the interrogator that made Clarence start, and which sent a look of fury into the eye of the culprit, who evidently wished to involve the young man in the same trouble with himself; so rising from his seat, he held out the letter which had been given to him, and was stepping forward, when he was met by the reverend gentleman half way, who, with great dignity of manner, held out his hand, saying:

"You have some commands for me, I suppose, sir? Excuse me while I dispose of this business;" and with that, he informed the impudent Tom that he might look out for the full payment of what was owing to him, before he went to bed, unless something occurred that would make atonement for the doings of last night. "Look out." And taking the whip he held in his hand, he gave it a swing, which made the snapper spring, so that Tom made a pair of clean heels for once in his life.

"Sit down, sir," said the good master. "I see that this letter is from my worthy brother of Sopus. Dreadful times these; wicked devils, these red-coats. Unprovoked outrage. It would give them no more than they deserve, if every one engaged in that act were hung over these houses on a gridiron. Yesterday, too, setting that good man's house on fire. Poor Martin Schuyler. Savages, all of them. Gentlemen! Devils!"

All this sent forth in fierce objurgations, as he read the letter, which, for aught Clarence knew, was telling the passionate Dominie how he had been engaged during the night of the Sopus raid. From the interjectional sounds that came out, it was plain that the Dominie was in no good mood. He had more of the magistrate in his look than the minister of religion. Rising, he said with severe authority, "Your business will require consideration; and as there are a great many things to be done to-day, we will dispense with your presence till we have more time."

With this, he opened the door, when they were met in the hall by one of his parishioners, inquiring if the Dominie had made "up the salve for Aunt Nelly's foot." It was handed to him in a small box. Clarence saw inscribed on it: "To be well rubbed in; and this will cure *with God's blessing*."

"A droll mixture," said the young Englishman. "This man is a minister, master, magistrate, doctor, and if I may judge by my being sent to him, he is captain of the Kaatskill Whig militia. But I doubt very much if he serves me and my cause. Like his salve, I must be well rubbed; and the cure will come with God's blessing—all chance. My notion is, to bribe some one as a guide, and flee to the mountains, trusting myself to Brandt, claiming his aid as an officer in the king's service."

With these half-formed plans in his mind, he left the presence of the Dominie, wandering he knew not whither, but every now and then recurring to the idea of escaping to the hills. But it was not long before he perceived that that would be a difficult matter, for it did not seem to him that he was for one moment out of the sight of Tom, or of some one else that he had seen with Tom. At last the thought darted across his mind, "I am watched. They suspect me, and that vagabond is the spy."

BOOK III.

BURGOYNE'S FAILURE;

BEING

THE REVELATION OF SECRET CAUSES

UNNOTICED BY THE GREAT HISTORIANS OF THE TIME.

BOOK III.

THE real object of Vaughan's expedition to the north was, if possible, to form a junction with Burgoyne, who was now hard beset at Saratoga. All that was known of that daring commander's movements at the south, made the king's friends despair of his success. The communication between these two extreme points of operation was entirely cut off; and he who was willing to become the forlorn hope of the army, was regarded by the one side as a spy and by the other as a hero. Messenger after messenger was thus dispatched and caught, and still another went for help as their fate still remained in suspense, till it led in some instances to desperation. He was ready at length for any deceit or scheme, bearing the least semblance of feasibility. Once succeed in getting his spies below Albany, with the river on one side and the mountains on the other, and what was to hinder their communicating either with Brandt or with Vaughan in time to let Sir Henry Clinton know his position and obtain his aid. Having recently come all the way from Canada, a journey over the Kaatsbergs, keeping back by the Round Top, seemed to him an easy thing: nor were there wanting gallant men willing to undertake the risk, at the command of such a chief. How far their judgment was well informed or how well people of the country met these plans, must be left to our history.

CHAPTER I.

A PRISONER IN DISGUISE, BEFORE A TRIBUNAL IN DISGUISE.

"Boddikins, Master Page, though I be old and of the peace, if I see a sword out, my fingers itch to make one; though we are justices and doctors and churchmen, Master Page, we have some salt of our youth in us: we are the sons of women, Master Page."—JUSTICE SHALLOW.

CLARENCE CLINTON, whom we left in a state of uncertainty, politely bowed out of doors, and yet not at freedom, felt it hard thus to submit. He fretted himself wishing a thousand times that he had insisted on being taken up at once to the camp of Brandt. That being now impossible, he at length resolved to follow the current of events. So, composing his feelings as he best could, he set about diverting his mind by observing what was new to him.

It was evident from the unusually large number of people seen in so small a village, that something of importance was about taking place. Following the current, he was landed at the church door, where was a motley assemblage; such as he never supposed existed in this Province. He always knew that in a colony, there must be brought together a peculiar people, different from those of the mother country; but he had not dreamed of meeting such a foreign looking race, except in some country entirely different from old England. Looking at them merely on the outside, his impressions were partial; for he found a fairer representation of the Saxon race, than he at first saw. Here the substratum was indeed Dutch, as their speech proved, and also their dress. Some New Englanders, lank and sharp in features, were standing in the midst of little groups to whom they were holding forth upon the affairs of the country at large, and others of them discussing some particular point of policy, when direct reference was made to the late attack upon their neighbors; and what was best to be done both for their defence and for vengeance.

What surprised Clarence most of all, was the mixture of those naturally belonging to the country with both English and Scottish born subjects of King George. This, which became to his inquiring mind matter of great interest, was followed up; and he learned from different sources, that one reason of there being so many classes, arose from the fact that after the old French war the regiment of Scotch, which was disbanded at Albany, remained for the most part in the colony; and that a company of them, under Captain Salisbury, settled on these flats, retaining their habits and their dress: for in the assemblage met that day, Clarence saw the Highland philibeg, that garb of old Gaul, which is so picturesque in the neighborhood of hills, and recalling all the romantic associations of the ancient class of Caledonia, he could imagine himself near the Grampian hills.*

While this gathering was to our adventurer the subject alike of study and wonder, he noticed a face among them like one that he had seen in a dream. He puzzled his mind trying to recall some name that he might attach to it, but in vain. He viewed it in every possible light in profile and direct; and while in each fresh light glimpses satisfied him that he had known the man in some other place, he still was at a loss to give him a locality in past history. Tall, thin and wan in his appearance, it was evident that he was not in the spot to which he belonged. His dress was buckskin below and a small cloak thrown over his shoulders which nearly hid a coat of homespun grey. He stood high in his stout shoes, under a cap of bearskin; to which was added a beard that seemed to be but a part of the same animal's fur, cut from its neck. As his eye wandered around the crowd as if searching for some one, it fastened at last on Clarence, so searchingly that the young man found the blood rising to his eyes; and he was about to go forward and demand an explanation, when he was called aside with a slight tap on the shoulder by one that he knew to be an officer in his majesty's service; but who had been taken prisoner six months before in an attack upon Fort Washington. The greeting on both sides was warm but silent, for both saw at once the necessity of prudence.

"Clinton," said the officer, "why in the name of all that is good, are you here?"

"May I not ask of you the same thing?" said Clarence. "You seem to be in the bear's den, and so near the mouth, one might think escape was desirable."

"Oh," said the other, "I am here on my parole of honor

* The late Wilhelmus Schuneman, Esq., gave the author this description.

and must run my chances of exchange. There are ten of us here among these boors.*

"Pray," said Clarence, "is that one of your set there with the rough cap? Look cautiously around, for he is watching us, and his eyes seem as if they would search me through. I am sure he is an Englishman, and I am confident of having seen him somewhere in my travels."

Clarence's companion, by changing his place, fixed his eye on the unknown, but declared that though he must know that pale face well, yet he had never seen him before in this region; and he could only conjecture that he must be some one in disguise looking around him for sport, like others present. This was said to draw out the stranger he was talking to; but Clarence merely said he had business, which he was afraid gentlemen on their parole durst not undertake, saying at the same time, in a whisper, "we are watched, and must separate for the present."

"Well, we must of course; but," said the other, "I will gather our friends together, and we will keep ourselves on the alert lest anything befall you. Let MARGARET be our word;" and with that the two parted to different sides of the Assembly.

Clarence thought it best to mix with the colonists; and stepping up to one who had the look of an Englishman, though dressed in the fashion of the common people of the country, he saluted him so that it became a sufficient introduction.

"Is something of importance about to be transacted here to-day?" was the young Englishman's first inquiry.

"Yes, sir," was the courteous reply. "One of Burgoyne's messengers has been caught on the road from Albany, on her way to Sir Henry Clinton, whose vessel is now at the mouth of the creek."

"It is a lady then?" said the inquirer, with some perturbation of mind that almost betrayed him.

"It is a woman at any rate; as to her being a lady is another thing. We are not accustomed to calling spies ladies." This was said with a sneer, not to be mistaken; and for a hint from his new acquaintance.

"She is to be tried," he continued, "just now before the Consistory. She is a young woman, and very beautiful; above the common manners, and, perhaps, a lady. But here comes the Dominie, who will worm out her secret. You

* This is given on the same authority.

asked, I think, if this was a court to try such cases. No, not in law, but though the Dominie be no squire himself, he always sits on the bench; for he knows more than all the squires between Sopus and Albany, and rules them by his little finger, and a nod of his cocked hat.

Clarence had not asked for this information, for he understood it from experience, and was prepared to hear sentiments like these from one who spoke more like an Englishman than a Dutchman, though he was evidently a colonist.

"I perceive that you are an Englishman," said Clarence, "and are smiling at the power of this court to try a spy, as you say the lady is?"

"No, sir, not English born. My father, after the fighting at Lake George, in the French war, gave up his commission and received a large tract of land on which he settled, along with his company. We are most of us the sons of those men. The Scotch are clannish, and so you perceive a great many of that nation, though the greater part of them were so loyal that they could not live where the king's power did not extend, and have removed to Canada. Those here now are most of them true to their country, though they stiffly keep to their religion and their dress; eating oatmeal, and living in houses on the earthen floor, where they drink oceans of whisky, to 'keep the cauld out of their banes.'"

"Ah!" said Clarence, "those men with the kilt and the hose. A fine country for highlanders."

"Tell me here," said the colonist, "who you are, as you seem to be an entire stranger?" a new thought having entered his mind. He looked right into the eyes of Clarence for an answer.

"I have a case before the reverend Consistory," was the ready reply, "and I am waiting till they meet. Are not those the members who have entered in at present?" With that Clarence went in with the rest, and took a seat in a large square pew that was made to contain a whole family, from the full bottomed vrow, down to the round dumpling of the large dozen, common in those good old times, when children were like pumpkins round about the house. His new acquaintance, whose name he found was Salisbury, sat next to him, and was all alive to the business of the occasion. Suspicion of Clarence's business had induced him to take this seat, as if he meant to watch him. Nor was Clarence unaware of the suspicion.

The Consistory was called to order by the Dominie, who

sat as president. He offered prayer longer than might be necessary. Patriotic sentiments prevailed, the recent devastation was referred to, and the abduction of two members, worthy of their place, was mourned over, and petitions offered on their behalf. Sympathy for the distressed drew out sobs and tears from the multitude, and a fierce sighing, like a surging wind, ran through the whole house when the good man, in the style of one that chants pathetically, exclaimed, "Our country is desolate, our cities are burned with fire, our land strangers devour, and is overthrown by strangers, and the daughter of Zion is left like a cottage in a vineyard, as a lodge in a garden of cucumbers, as a besieged city."

It seemed to the intruder that every eye in the congregation was turned to the place where he sat, so that he felt a secret wish of sinking down into the ground out of sight. It was truly the case that the Dominie had an earthly motive in this prayer. He took heaven by violence so that this British soldier might carry back a good report. This, said the man of faith to himself, will do more to make our enemies quail than a discharge of artillery.

"Call te prisoner," said the officer who sat beside the reverend man that he might be benefited by his counsel. It was a semi-sacred, semi-civil court. Indeed, the squire was one of the Consistory, as the pastor always took good care that he should have his hand felt in all his parish. Nor did this mongrel court appear so much out of character to Clarence, who had seen the clergy of England sitting at quarter sessions in their canonicals, trying the poacher and the vagrant. The suspense of the stranger who had heard of a woman being arrested, who was described as beautiful, and of superior breeding, when he saw the prisoner brought in, was great, but he was soon relieved from his fears when the lady, who was unknown to him, stepped forward freely, and made her obeisance to the chief man on the bench. The Dominie wore his three-cornered hat, a flowing wig of three stories, newly powdered, and long white bands that lay upon his capacious chest, so that he was an awful spectacle in the eyes of his parishioners, and of the whole African population; but the lady was nothing daunted by the sight.

"Who be you? Vat be your name? Ende vere do you come fraem?" said Squire Van Bergen, who was a real peaceful common-sense looking man of fifty-five, or about that age.

"You ought to know who I am, and should have some

knowledge of where I am from before you venture to interrupt travellers on the king's road."

This was said by the lady with some tartness, as if she really felt herself to be the injured party. She stopped short in her speech, and watched the effect of her reply upon her inquisitor; whose brains were confounded by the hardihood of the woman whom he expected would have soon sunk under the question he put to her. But the Dominie whispered something in the ear of the legal functionary, when he again woke up, saying:

"Mataam, de country vants vatching, ende you were travellin' py yourself, and you must tell vere you pe come fraim; ende veder you pe goin', elz ve vill put you in de close up once."

There was meaning in these words; and though they were said with one leg thrown over the other, and the arms resting on the knees, yet they were firmly said, and the prisoner saw too well, that it would be vain attempting to carry these men by storm. So putting on her sweetest manner, she said in the softest tones, "You surely do not suppose that a lady could in any way endanger a country where there are so many brave men to defend it?" and with that she gave a look around her, on the faces of the spectators, who were really flattered by her allusions to their courage. The lady showed to Clarence great moral energy; and she was evidently wound up to the highest pitch of excitement; and as her eye for an instant rested on that of Clarence, he almost forgot himself, and felt ready to throw prudence to the winds, and plant himself by her side as her defender. He was recalled to sense by the squire asking:

"Mataam, vere you de pearer of public dispatches dat you must pe alone on de vay?"

"You do not mean," said the prisoner, "that the good people in this Christian land, with such good men for their pastors, are such savages that a lady cannot go alone where she pleases?"

She said this looking straight into the Dominie's face, as if he was the one to answer that question which involved his calling and responsibility. Nor was she disappointed, for that earnest man was only waiting for the chance of taking up the case himself, since he saw plainly that the woman was too much for his honest elder, the squire.

"There are savages in the land," said the Dominie, "but they do the bloody work of their own master."

"You mean," said she, artfully misconstruing his allusion, "that I have nothing to fear from the inhabitants of this place."

"Nothing if your own intentions be good. We are more afraid of serpents than we are of savages. There are both around at this time."

"I have heard, reverend sir, for so I esteem you, that the fierce Mohawk has been near, but surely you do not perceive in me any resemblance to that monster?"

"There are painted Jezebels, more cruel than Brandt, madam. But we have no time to parley. Are you the bearer of any message to our enemy now on the river? Answer if you be, that we may get through with your business at once."

This was said with a sternness which could not be set aside, and which had the effect of rousing up the feelings of the assembly to a nervous intensity, so that a pin dropped could have been heard as she answered:

"How should I be the bearer of a message in a country watched by a thousand eyes at every step? If your gallantry be equal to your appearance as a gentleman and a Christian minister, you will order my immediate release."

"Madam," said the dignified man, as he rose in his seat, "your evasion and your appeal to our chivalry will not avail with us. Do you know aught of this cup?

At this, a silver cup of rare workmanship was produced, and placed before the prisoner; when a slight shade of red which showed her chagrin more than any shame, passed over her fine but rather bold countenance; but recovering herself, she said, "Supposing that I do know, you surely do not expect me to say anything that would criminate myself."

"Dat's de law," said the squire, edging in a word; "budt once vere did you hide dis cup last nicht before de lads found tee?"

At this point in the investigation a young man stepped up to the Dominie, whispering in his ear, and at the same time putting a small parcel into his hand. This was immediately produced, and turned out to be a large silver hunting watch, with a silver face, to which a gold chain and seals of several kinds were attached. This rare timepiece excited universal attention, and diverted the minds of the spectators from the lady. Clarence took occasion to mark the movements of her lips and the corners of her mouth, which, notwithstanding her resolute will, showed her mortification. She lifted a wooden cup filled with water, that she had asked for soon after she came in, and took a sip of it, and this she did the whole time, showing that her coolness was more affected than real.

"Stan' up, Hanchy," said the squire, "ende tak' your oat' dat tee vill tell de trut', de whole trut' at de day of judgment."

"Vere did you find de vatch here once?" was the first question.

"Near the place where we found the silver cup."

"Ende de vere vas dat?"

"Where we found this woman."

"Ende vere did you find de voman?"

"I told you all about it this morning," said the great lout, who did not understand the object for which he was brought there. The Dominie, who was provoked beyond all endurance, rose in his seat, storming at the witness in such a way as would have driven all the brains out of ten dolts like him; and ordered him to tell his story as he had told it to him that morning. "And see that you stand on both your legs at once, and keep your nose there from snifting like old Egbert Bogardus' yellow mare in the spring grass."

His story was a long rigmarole, amounting to a few facts. He and another of the same squad had been out sparking, when they overtook on their way home something that they took at first sight to be a SPOOK, sitting by the road-side. It turned out to be this woman. She made inquiry after some one, whom the Dominie forbade him to name. They suspected her to be of the Tory side, from the person she inquired after. Pretending to take her where she wished to go, they took her to a genuine Whig's house, and left her. Thinking that she had fallen among her own class, she directed them where they would find a small bundle, which, instead of taking back to her, they put into the hand of the squire, who in duty bound consulted the chief man, and hence this investigation.

"This," said the Dominie, "is a valuable timepiece. I see here marked on the inside of it a name that no one in this colony, of the true blood, has any cause for loving—'BURGOYNE.'" *

At the announcement of this name, which the Dominie said was engraven on the inside of the case, a general buzz ran through the house, which went further into the heart of the prisoner than anything that had occurred hitherto, as she evidently feared that the crowd would take the law

* Such a timepiece, marked "Burgoyne," and a cup, as here described, came to light about twenty years ago.—D. M.

into their hands, and make quick work with her at the ducking tub; for the name of Burgoyne was as famous for loose morals as for the owner's enmity to the colonists; and in a place where a vile woman was a baser object than a vile man, Jezebel would be as likely to suffer some penalty as King Ahab.

Silence was shouted by the Dominie. "Have you no manners, nor regard for law, that you look like a set of barbarians, about to eat a woman up alive? A precious bite you would have in your mouths, rolling it like a sweet morsel under your tongue. Dick Overbagh, you great gomeril, take your seat."

Quiet being restored, the examination of the watch was continued. The case was opened and shut twenty times, the woman's eye following every movement. He stopped, shut it up again, weighed it on his fingers, drawing the seals through his hand, as if satisfied, and seemingly was about to hand it back to the late possessor. Clarence had marked her features during movements, and saw evidently her eagerness to be through with the whole. When the Dominie made as if he would hand it back to her, he perceived such a sudden gleam of pleasure that he was sure it meant relief; for he drew his hand back, saying, "We will give it one more trial." Clarence really thought it cruel in the man to torture her by this tantalizing movement, for the blood rushed suddenly to her heart, through this unexpected disappointment; and she sat down, holding her hands so that her chin might rest upon them, as if saying, "I will see the worst of it, and defy you."

The Leyden student had not dug for Hebrew roots in vain. To the search he went again, knowing now surely in his own mind that something was here, and of value. He went over the whole surface with his thumb nail, pressed upon every place he suspected; when at last he did touch a spring, which revealed a double case, within which there lay carefully a small bit of paper, bearing the words:

"De spe decidere."

"Read this," he said, with a smile. "What does this mean?"

"Nay, nay, Dominie; that is for you to read and explain, who are the only man of learning here." This seemed to be said by all, for no one would have said less of a student from Leyden, and a Dominie.

"'We have lost all hope.' God grant that it may be so," was the fervent saying of the reverend man, as he translated the inscription on the secret missive.

"What is meant by that, Dominie?" was called out by twenty voices at once.

"I think it means that Bur"—— Before he could return an answer, a rush of men to the door bewildered the Dominie, and all around him, so that they did not, for a few moments, know where they stood. So sudden and great was the alarm, some thought one thing, and some another, but it was evident that the greater part supposed that Brandt was surrounding the house. The pastor here showed his true courage. Raising his voice like a trumpet in the place where he was sure to be heard with effect; he cried out:

"Shut the door, and bolt it there, Jack Pearce. Stand firm. Salisbury, here, leap out of that window, and rouse our friends. Now, men, stand to your arms. Here, Captain Hallenbeck, take your place and muster your men."

The Dominie was first in war as in everything else; nor was he behind in the true argument, for sitting down, he deliberately took out a pair of large horse pistols, and examined them with the eye of one who knew how to use them. The whole Consistory were equally well armed, while the men in the seats were lifting up guns that were lying safe and innocently beneath their pews, and began shaking fresh powder into their pans out of their hunting-horns with something of the zest of those who watch a deer lick.

"Look well to your flints," was the order from the desk; "and when you see the first signal of danger, lie down till we know where our enemy is standing. Spare your fire till you mark your man. Some of you climb up to the belfry and snap off the leaders."

Here the squire, who had descended from the bench and was sitting humbly on a lower seat, remarked loud enough for the rest to hear:

"The Dominie might hev some pity on himself, ende hide his head in eene koormaat."

"Nay, nay; the bullet has not been cast that will take me down, squire; I have as much fat on my ribs as will hide a dozen pigeons' eggs. Come up beside me here, and let us remember how our two brethren of the Consistory are up in the mountain there, prisoners of that heathen Brandt. Oh, how I would like to tell him, and his Master George, that sent him, 'en met welke mate gij meet zal u wedergemeten worden.' For the benefit of these who do not know our good Dutch"—and here the speaker glanced toward the eyes of Clarence—let me give it in English: 'With what measure you mete, it shall be measured unto you again.'"

By this time the cause of the uproar was made known. A report was spreading through the crowd out of doors, of Burgoyne's defeat at Saratoga; and as a multitude are never too particular in trying the evidence of good or bad news, they shouted so loud that the report was believed.

"Open the doors," cried the Dominie. "Three cheers for General Gates! three times three for Washington! Now for thanksgiving to the Captain of Salvation."

In an instant that uproarious crowd were still as a Sabbath assembly, bending their uncovered heads, and following the voice of their spiritual guide, as he led them to the footstool of the Great Deliverer. It was an impressive sight, only to be seen on remarkable occasions, when the souls of earnest men are wound up to the highest pitch to meet a danger, and then suddenly to be thrown back within themselves, to record a deliverance. The prayer of that day seemed to Clarence more like inspiration than anything he had ever heard. All that passed had taken them so completely by storm, that even he, from the other side, could not refrain from joining in the rapture.

After they began to recover themselves from their ecstasy, one and another of them asked, "Where is the woman?" "Where is the prisoner?" "Vere is de lady?" said the old Squire; "I putten down mien head at de Dominie's prayer, and ven it over she vas avay." Such was the tale they all told.

"Jake Van Deuser, look after the prisoner," said the real president of the day; "and now the Consistory is adjourned till after dinner."

With that all left, evidently pleased with the doings of the morning, but expecting still more before the day was over. A signal from the leader of the day brought Clarence to his side, when he was told to be on hand at the hour appointed.

"As your case requires both *secrecy* and dispatch, you will see that nothing comes from you, informing any one of our meeting. An hour after noon, at the parsonage."

The emphasis put upon the word *secrecy*, told painfully on the ear of the young man; but he had no resource left but to stand it through to the end.

CHAPTER II.

A MASQUERADE.

"There is drollery under the blackest face;
Has not a sackcloth cloud a silver lining?"
THE ELDER BURTON.

OUR young adventurer went out from the presence of the Dominie, chewing the cud of bitterness. He felt ready for anything that might open for him a way of escape. He was becoming sure that the meshes of a plot were drawing around him.

"This man," said he to himself, "parson or judge, is a fit executioner for that mock governor, who has handed me over, through the other parson below; and I am fool enough to wait here till he has time to put the rope around my neck."

Here he looked up to the mountain, and saw the smoke that rose from the Indian's camp, where he was sure of being well received; but how was he to make his escape without exciting suspicion? In his quandary he began to whistle, when a man passing him, whispered: "that air is out of date in this region." It was "God Save the King," a tune that had become treason on the west side of the Atlantic. So Clarence, the brave soldier, stopped his breath as if he had been shot by the same air-pistol which was fired at George III. himself on his way to Parliament.

Strolling on, his eye was attracted to a strange-looking dwarf, who moved before him in the manner of the China images of the London tea-shops, steadily forward, yet shaking at every step, as if it must be the last before a fall. So interested did his study of the creature before him become, that his attention was completely riveted. We can guess what his astonishment was, when on his right hand, first, there rose a sharp whisper, "Follow him," then on the left hand, a still sharper call, "Follow him, he has something to tell you." Clarence could not help looking on both sides for the speakers, but there were none on either. But led on as he felt inclined, he stepped after the dwarf to a bridge; when coming up over the right hand guard, a voice distinctly said: "Captain Clinton!" Running to that side, the amazed passenger looked, seeing nothing, nor any one. Persuaded, however, that there was a connection between the invisible whisperer and this visible imp, he through curiosity followed on till he came to a small tavern, standing by a mill, surrounded by a few houses, built of red and yellow brick. The inn had a low *stoop*, which ran along its front, on which were forms for the lazy and the lame. A group of motley gossip-mongers were all around, made up of white, black, yellow, and other dingy colors. Dame Krouse kept the best of "Hollands imported," as she said on her sign-board; though her negro Tim, a great braggart, declared that he was a "better brewer than the bogs of Dutch lan' 'duced."

The different groups of men were engaged when Clarence came up to the tavern door, according to their tastes. The grave and grey men were discussing the late trial, and others were playing at quoits, and pitch the stone; while the boys were running at tag and leap-frog. It was a busy place considering the size of the small hamlet. Somehow a report had gone through the country, that an affair of moment demanded the presence of all who were able-bodied, and with the instinct of animal nature, they came where the carcass was. Sopus had been burned; Brandt was on the mountain; and Burgoyne had been captured, and something must be done at home to prove their interest in the public weal; even the young fry of the place were ranged under a captain of their own size as soldiers, following the sound of an old frying-pan, which a thick-set bare-headed negro, of the class simpleton, was beating with a club, in imitation of a bass drum.

Our adventurer stepped on to the piazza of the tavern, and mixed with the men who were engaged in discussing the affair of the church meeting. It was plain enough that a difference of opinion existed outside the Consistory, notwithstanding the apparent acquiescence in-doors, concerning the precognition of the woman's case, that morning; nor was the Dominie without his share of censure. The public mind, always severe at the time when treason is ripe, and when fear has the ascendency, was loud against the woman who carried such unmistakable evidence with her of being a spy, and of holding communication between Burgoyne's army and that of Clinton.

"Did na ye see the face o' the limmer when the minister put the question to her? she spoke up as bardy as you like.

Na, I thocht that the gude man himself was a wee bit bewitched, else he would na been sae easily bamboozled wi' the pawky quean."

This was said by a brawny Scotchman, who held in his hand a pewter cup, filled with the strongest kind of cider-brandy, which he sucked up with a zest that showed his experience.

"Such stuff as that is gude enough to wet one's wizzan in this country, where you canna get better; but, man, if I had but a coggie of Glenlivat, how it would mak' me fidge wi' fainness. But anent, that action o' the minister's, he should hae sent the jade to Albany."

"Donald Grant, you are always finding fault with the powers that be; and even the Dominie cannot escape your rasping tongue."

This was said sharply by a small man, dressed in silver grey, that fitted close to his body, and though worn bare, was carefully brushed. His look and his manners bore evidence of his New England origin, and his pedantic speech spoke him to be of the pedagogue order, a class of men that have done much to leaven the west side of the Hudson with the love of learning, and who had, notwithstanding the repugnance of the Dutch to all the Yankee brood, found their way among them as peddlers, pedagogues and singing-masters.

"Noo, maister," said Donald, "you would tell me that men in authority should be respected, and my mither, aye said that ministers were black craws, to shoot at; and there's yoursel', for instance, in your schule, have a gude right to use the taws in makin' your words be enforced, but if you wranged my callant there, I would lick your hide out here, till you were black and blue. Noo, as the Dominie himsel' says, you can mak' the application of this discourse at your leisure."

"I am not going to contend with you, Grant, when club-law is the rule; but law is law, and must be obeyed. The men that administer the law must be sustained, else where are we going to but down-stream?—and for my part I do not value a man more than a tenpenny whittler, who does not stand by the law. There now, something is going on among that black generation. I must look after these imps of Satan."

"Mind, maister, I'll not let you interfere with a wee bit fun, for I like it o'er weel mysel'. You are king in your ain dominion, but here you are nae mair than a common man."

"Dat's true, Grant," said a rough-looking native, with as many capes on his coat as there are plies on a tulip, and whose whole exterior was homespun in a figurative and literal sense; "budt de same ting cannot pe said ov de Dominie, who is a great man every place he goes."

"Oh, you need na mak the man mair than mortel, Myndert Overpaugh. Set him down on a rock, with a spoon in his han', and he will find as little to sup as the smallest o' us all." Grant was determined to find fault, and his spirit was up after he had drank a second cup of the cider-brandy.

"That's a fact, Grant, the Dominie can brag well enough on the bench yonder, when he has got all the congregation to carry out his will; but I would like to see him in the woods alone, and see if he would be so strong as he pretends."

"Now," said Grant, "I will not let any man say a word against the gude man in his absence, mair especially against his courage. He is a stoure bodie, and there, nae later than last Saturday nicht, that ne'er-do-well Bob Eltinge and his crony the smith, were determined to shoot the gude man, between this and Coxsackie. They hid themselves behind a tree in the woods, and lay wi' their guns ready primed; but the minute that they saw the white o' the Dominie's een, they fell down like shot doves, and let him pass. That proves, Bromie, whatever you may say to the contraer, that nae man should lift his han' against the Lord's anointed."

By this time the party had entered the mill, and were mounting to the loft, to which Clarence had ascended by the rear, unquestioned. Sacks of grain lay around the large apartment, and on these sat a crowd of different kinds of people, who were enjoying greatly some sport going on at the upper end of the gallery. Bags of the wheat had been thrown together, so as to form a platform above the main floor. On these were nine other sacks, which served as seats, where were sitting as many blacks, dressed in their masters' clothes, which they had borrowed without leave. The middle seat had on it one dressed in the true outer garb of the Dominie. His cocked hat, but crushed in at the sides, his coat, but rusty, and a large towel tied around the neck, fell down over his breast, in square ends, to imitate the Geneva bands. Four on the right hand, and as many on the left, represented the deacons and elders, while in the front stood a young negro, dressed in woman's clothes. A faded silk gown, with a high bonnet held up, so as to look like the high knots of hair fashionable among high-born ladies.

"The black devils that they are," said the man of books. "What a faculty they have for imitation. Making fun they are of serious things. I must teach them Connecticut manners;" and here he was about to act the part of select man, when Grant spoke out:

"You'll do nae sic thing as stop the masqueraud. Let them get their sport out. My certie, but they play it weel. Noo be quiet."

The mock Dominie called out in tones meant as imitation of the real voice:

"Dis Consist'ry come to order. Squia, perceed."

The man called the "Squia" had on spectacles like his model, and pen and ink before him, as if prepared to take notes.

"That's intended for mockery of the Consistory," said the teacher, "and shows how the public mind is exercised upon that trial of the woman. Hear the sham Squire, how he questions the *female lady*, that had the cup in her sack."

"Ha! but see how the black gipsy tosses her head there, imitating the white limmer in the kirk, that we saw. Her curls swing finely. See how thae blackamoors jump at the sicht. It's perfect pleasure to them. But, man, what a noise they mak'. I could hear it frae Cladich to Loch Awe on a Halloween nicht." Here Grant was getting disgusted with the capers, and stepping forward himself into the midst of the den, he lifted up a stout fellow by the nape of the neck and the seat of his tubbs, and gave him a few slaps with his big hand, that made music of a kind that brought order out of confusion, as he said, "If we are to hae sport, let us have it, and nae maer o' deviltry."

Here the president called out at the top of his voice, "Silends! perceed to furder bis'ness."

"Call in de oder prisoner," said the mock Squire. A young, lithe negro was here brought forward, charged with stealing a horse from Nellius Wyncoop, being a spy, and as guilty of forgery.

"What can be the meaning o' that?" said Grant. "Naithing o' sic kind has come up that the public kens about."

"That is, you have not heard about it, you mean. Everything is not told to Donald Grant that happens in the court of justices, or it would not be a secret very long after hè got it."

"What do you mean with your jibes and your hints?" said Grant. "If you don't tell me all you ken about that business, I'll serve you as I did that black dog there a minute since."

And with that the rough Scotchman was about taking the cross-grip, when the man of letters sputtered out, "Let me alone, and I'll tell you all I know; and listen yourself for the conclusion of the whole matter." Here a full account was given in loud whispers of the appearance Clarence had made that morning, and of the trial that was to come off that afternoon. "See that Tom there, the Dominie's chief man, sitting in the middle. He has access to all his master's secret drawers, and generally can tell beforehand what disposal the reverend man intends to make of his cases."

Clarence, who heard all the account given to Grant, looked to the prisoner, and saw a fac-simile of himself in size and dress, to the very patch on the knee, pointed out before. There was no more fun in the play to him. A strange confusion of ideas was curdling up in his brain, like what he had often experienced in a dream. He took hold of his own arm, to be certain of his own identity. It seemed like phantasmagoria. He was recalled to his case by the mock Dominie crying out:

"My freen and Bruder Doll nebber steal Nellius Wynkoop's horse. Me know nothink of dis letter; youd a spy, to be hanged at te cart tail."

Here the masque at the bar, cried out, me no spy, but true man, seeking my sistern.

Here was such a clapping of hands and screeching, that it seemed Bedlam let loose. All the dominoes on the sacks joined in the fun, forgetful of their mock dignity. Quiet being restored, the call was given to bring in the witnesses. When Caese, the old fiddler, stepped forward, and gave a rambling account of the frolic at Phœbe's Hotel, and of de man who came and spoiled de dance, in de middle of de fine tune, by de niggering of Nelly Wynkoop's horse.

"Wat says de prisoner to dat?" was the president's demand.

"O your reberence, me on de way to de mountains to seek ma sistern."

These words became the password to sport, all through the proceedings, and never failed to make the rafters ring with the echoes of uproarious laughter.

"Please zur," said the black squire, in mock gravity, "vats dat in de breast pocket? Constavel, help de prisoner to take out dose putty tings."

Here a stout fellow put his hand into the bosom of the accused, who screamed out, "Don't take dese tings away frob me, dey are for ma sistern!"

"Treason! treason!" was shrieked out, as a pair of large horse pistols were laid upon the table. Those who did not know were actually taken by surprise, at the sight and sound, while those who did know, believed that the case which this foreshadowed was more serious than it had hitherto seemed; and the cry of "treason! treason! to the gallows with the spy," rang longer and louder than mere sport called for in a masquerade trial. Had Clarence been seized at that instant, he would have felt less surprise than he did at the farce itself. Indeed, he half expected something to happen, and was preparing his thoughts for the worst. Here was an evident thrust at him. His object was known. He was regarded by the lowest grade here as either knave or fool. An attempt was making to excite public opinion against him. "Let me try and escape," he inwardly said to himself.

The farce was about to proceed, when who should stalk in but the great man himself, with a long whip, that he could use at ten yards' distance. Making it crack at the snapper like a pistol, there was such a scampering among white and black, as might well have employed the pencil of Hogarth, who has given us the Village School in an uproar. Loud natural squeals came from all sides, as the scourge took effect upon the hips of the retreating crew, who crowded out like a drove of hogs through a narrow gate, making the hindermost suffer for the sins of the foremost, while the Dominie sung out: "I'll learn you to make the venerable Consistorial Court of the Protestant Reformed Dutch Church of Holland, in these United States of America, now independent, the subject of fun. You blasphemous crew that you are! I never knew where Pandemonium was before now. You black imps, to mount up to the clouds playing your cantraps. Take that." And here another, and another full swing of the stout pastor's arm made the court and the audience tumble out in mixed confusion, that soon exhausted the wrath of the avenger. Coming upon the fellow that had played the part of the female spy, all dressed up in a full suit of the 'Yfvrow's own wardrobe, curls, high-heeled shoes and all, he roared out in loud laughter, that shook his big sides and stopped his whip hand.

The couple that stood beside Clarence had found their way out first, being close by the door. Grant coming up at the back of Clarence, gave him a hard clap with his open hand on the back, thinking that he was one of themselves, and saying:

"Frein', what do you think o' that kind of play actoring? I beg your paurdon, I thought it was our neighbour Charlie Forbes, the English officer. I never saw twa backs sae like. But nae offence I hope," said the garrulous Scot, putting his arm into that of Clarence, as if he had known him all the days of his life.

"Maister," continued the talking man, "I was just speerin at our frein' here, what he thought o' that fun in the loft there."

"There is something about to go on here at the parsonage, that will explain all we have seen in that darkness there," was the knowing reply of the pedagogue, who prided himself on being acquainted with everything before it took place.

"Oh, aye," said Grant. "You mean that we have been looking on the shadow, and that the substance is not far off."

"Or to speak more classically, we have been observing comedy, and now for tragedy," was the pedantic language of the man of letters.

"As to its being mair classical," said Grant, "I'm thinkin' Norman McKenzie, the schoolmaster of Aberfeldy, would say the scriptural figures were the maist classical of the two; but that's neither here nor there, at present. I am ready to argue that question wi you next Sabbath day, atween preaching; in the meantime, see if you can get me in to hear that tragedy you speak of, since I have seen the comedy up in the loft yonder."

Here the two followed the stream of persons who were making their way to the parsonage, with an evident earnestness, that showed their interest in what was about to take place.

CHAPTER III.

A WHEEL WITHIN A WHEEL.

"So spake the seraph Abdiel, faithful found
Among the faithless, faithful only he."
MILTON.

CLARENCE, in no better mood of mind after what he had witnessed, wandered away out of hearing, so that he might consider what would be best for him to do, surrounded as he was by suspicion. The chief man here had his eye upon him, the clowns squinted at him, and the common blacks were making him their jest. Were he only certain of getting away, he would run all risks of escaping to the mountains. Where were these king's officers? Their parole did not prevent them from helping others, though it bound them by their honor to remain here till exchanged: "I shall seek them out," said the almost desperate young man; "I have just come from seeing my own shadow on the gallows-tree; I would be a fool to run my neck into the noose after the plain warnings given in some mysterious way."

Continuing these reveries, his eye rested on the same strange dwarf that he had followed into the loft. This time the singular creature made more attempt at arresting the notice of the stranger youth, who now became interested in the motions made to him. They had both got on the same bridge, when the call "Captain Clinton," coming from the right, drew Clarence there to look with haste, and with some perturbation. Seeing no one, he still remained intently fixed, with his head bent over, when the voice was on the other side calling "Captain Clinton, follow."

Clarence, thinking that some mischief was intended, hastily ran forward seizing the dwarf, who merely looked up in the face of the captain with a dull smile, that meant nothing good or evil. Clarence was ashamed of himself when he saw that he had been rough to a poor deformed negro, whose face showed him to be an idiot. Dropping the arm he held, he merely said to himself, "I wish I knew who calls me," when the same voice on both sides called out:

"Follow him as a brave man may."

Seeing that something was meant, he pointed to the dwarf, who went on, Clarence in his wake. Turning suddenly round as if going down to the creek to fish, for the dwarf carried a hickory pole, which might serve him either for a fishing-rod or a staff of defence, he led the way as Clarence followed. After walking, and sometimes crawling through a low piece of ground covered with hazel bushes, they reached a hut built of mud, and thatched with straw, entirely different from anything that Clarence had ever seen on this continent. The walls stood nearly four square, and rose a foot higher than a common man's height, with here and there a stick of timber set in to prevent the clay from settling. The roof rose slanting to the ridge-pole, and after having been wattled with willows was stuffed with oat straw, over which was laid a covering of grassy turf, cut in squares from the meadow. Clarence thought upon the clachen of Cladich in the Scottish highlands, where he had been with a detachment of his regiment, keeping the old adherents of the gallant Pretender in check. There was the same "midden" before the door, the kailyard at the end of the house, with the place for the crummy cow at the back window. "This," said the English youth to himself, "looks like the Scottish Highlands indeed."

But his surprise was still greater, when, after his guide pointed to the low door, which stood open, he was met by an old man in the very "garb of the Gael." The kilt coming down to the knee, met below by the cross striped hose, tight to the leg above the *brawn*, having round tufts which covered the buckles of the garters. The shoes were of the kind called brogues—wooden soles, and vamps of untanned leather. The upper part of the man's dress had a mixture of the Scottish and the Dutch in them. The cloth of the coat was woven loose like a coarse blanket, and stained with the juice of the butternut, abundant in the region. An old soldier's stock was round the grim wearer's neck, and it only required the eye of a soldier to observe, in the upright form, the respectful bearing and the firm footing of the stranger, one who had marched through many countries, and was not to be startled, even now, by the sound of a trumpet. He stood over five feet ten; but, from his strength of limb and width of chest, he seemed to be of shorter stature; and though he evidently had put on his best attire, there was a roughness in his appearance, which would have made the tame citizen give him the path without further dispute.

On the entrance of Clarence, he put one hand by his side,

and the other to his cap, which the young officer understood at once. Returning the salutation with evident pleasure, as he looked on the face of the stout old man, smiling, as he said with surprise when he saw on the breast of him before him a silver medal bearing the name of the wearer, and of "PLASSY," and of "ABRAHAM PLAINS."

"Sergeant McDonald, 71st regt., Glasgow Highlanders. How is this that I meet one of the brave heroes who fought and conquered with Wolfe on the Plains of Abraham?" was the eager inquiry of Clarence.

"I am still a true subject of his Britannic Majesty, and will continue to wear his colors while this head stands higher than the earth; and when in my grave, I have sworn my auld son Oscar to come every Sunday morning, when he must lay this medal aboon my heart, where it hangs now. On the fourth of June, his Majesty's birth-day, they will fire a *feu de joie* near my auld ear."

"Whist! whist!" was whispered from a corner on the other side of the room, where sat an old woman who was busily engaged twisting a thread by a spindle, that hung between her finger and her thumb, though evidently ill at ease, as she listened to the outpouring of her husband's loyalty.

"Janet," continued the old soldier, "is wearing her life out, 'feared lest thae Whigs come in some day and put a string round my neck; and sorry am I to say, there are some of the ance gallant 71st that would help them. But, sit down, till we hear the word, *advance.*"

Clarence took a seat on a stool which stood on three feet, cut out of a rough block, which was the pattern of all the stools in the place. The visitor had time to examine the hut, and mark its resemblance to what he supposed had never crossed the Atlantic. The floor was the bare earth, hardened by the feet of the tenants. Round the centre was all the rude furniture, for there was the fire-place, built of rough stones, like an ancient altar for sacrifice. It stood about three feet high, and measured double that in breadth. On the sides were the vessels for cooking, while over the centre, where the fire burned, hung from a long chain the pot in which the dinner for that day was simmering, and sending out an agreeable flavor. Clarence looked for the chimney, but saw none. The smoke found its way upward, seeking the open air through those crevices which were left by chance in the simple roof.

"Come this way, he calls;" were the words of the old highlander, and Clarence was pointed to a steep ladder in the rear of the hut. The adventurer had gone too far to hesitate, so, mounting up, he found a door which opened at his touch, swinging back again, so that he was shut completely in.

"By George, I'm caught again," were his first words, when he looked round, him, seeing no one; but he had hardly uttered the exclamation before another person entered from the opening below, who sprung forward seizing the hand already stretched out, while both were speaking at once—"Clinton! Crawford!" looking into each other's faces to be sure of not being mistaken. Clarence, the most surprised, from being wholly ignorant of the other being near, stood dumb, while the other said:

"I knew you at a glance, whenever I set my eyes upon you. My fear was that you, on recognizing my face, would betray yourself and me at one and the same time."

"Where did you see me to-day? I have been but in one place all this morning, and there you could not be without my discovering your fair skin among a thousand of these yellow boors."

"By George, as you said, Clinton, it was my fair skin and sweet voice that have carried me through that ordeal. I must be a good looking lass when I could deceive that shrewd parson, with his black keen eye, and yourself."

"Is it possible, Crawford, that you acted the lady in that mongrel court, just now? Well, you have had a near escape with your head in the lion's mouth, and still on your own shoulders. We always in fun called you Lady Crawford, but"——

"No more of that, Clinton; you know well that it does not sound too pleasantly to my ears. Nothing but the desperate condition of Burgoyne and his brave fellows, could have tempted me to this, and now that it has failed in part, we must try and remedy the evil in the best way we can. We want your counsel."

"My counsel," was the desponding reply of Clarence, "may be of some good to others, as theirs may be to me; but the desperate state of my own affairs engrosses my soul so much, that you could not get two connected ideas from me, though this part of the globe were to sink and Burgoyne with it.

"You astonish me," said Crawford, who was one of those men of deep enthusiasm, whose countenance spoke more of levity than of earnestness; "I supposed that honor and glory, connected with your country, sat highest on the throne of your breast."

"These sentiments," said Clarence, in more haste than he intended, "are the supreme influences of my life; but after passing through the scenes of this week already past, they have been counteracted in a great degree by other sentiments no less powerful."

"Pray what may these be that tell so strongly on Clinton's mind?" was the rather bitter question of the other youth, who was evidently galling under some inward source of pain.

"Humanity for mankind in general, and affection for my sister Margaret in particular," said Clarence, with a firmness which cooled his companion down to something like patience.

"Your sister! Miss Clinton! What of her? It can't be possible that the report going round here is true, that she has been abducted from the ship, and that Colonel Clifford is at the bottom of the treason?"

It was now the time for the other to express his astonishment, as to the way in which this rumor had got abroad, and of what reliance was to be placed in it. After telling and rehearsing all that was current, and which Crawford had heard from different sources, it appeared that letters had been dropped around the camp, at Saratoga, pointing evidently to this very event as about taking place. They were written as from one of Clifford's intimate acquaintances; describing the plan and the probable consequences. Clifford and Burgoyne being bosom friends, and of a kindred feeling in pursuits of an evil kind, the secret letter did not excite any seriousness in the gay, lewd camp of the English general. It was different with another communication, which reached the camp of the commanding officer, no one knew how, when a plan of march was laid down so distinctly, for any bold adventurer, that it awakened in Crawford the desire of accomplishing—what was absolutely essential, in order that the northern army should be saved—a communication with the army of the South, under Sir Henry Clinton. A map which marked out two distinct routes was inclosed, giving decided preference to the route over the mountains, when the messenger would come under the protection of Brandt, who was engaged to be there at this time; "and"—what sounded strangely and suspiciously to Burgoyne—"Colonel Clifford would be on the mountain, along with the Great Mohawk, to lend his aid."

"You have seen," said Crawford, "how the most practicable of these routes has been closed against me, but I am determined now to attempt the other. Our brother officers here on parole have encouraged me, and I am just waiting for your counsel in this matter. All the information sent to the general by that unknown hand has been confirmed since I came here. To-day a stranger, who could not possibly know me, has pointed out the dangers and the advantages of the enterprise; that my mind is made up. Your account of your sister, Miss Clinton's abduction, corroborates the whole, making it, you perceive, to be your duty, from affection, to join me."

"And you would add," said Clarence, already half persuaded, "that honor and glory will go hand in hand. Before I can say yes to your proposal, I must see my way out of this confounded noose that I feel around my throat. I have learned caution as well as some others, where so many eyes are watching me."

"Why, my noble fellow," Crawford interposed warmly, "if the hangman be so near, are you such a fool as to wait till he puts the hemp on in a workmanlike manner? Sergeant McDonald below here has promised to guide me over the hills by midnight. He would take another under his care for the love of his king and country."

These arguments sank deep into the mind of the anxious brother when he reflected upon the necessity of promptitude in pursuit of his sister; and he all but said yes to the demand made upon his energy, when there was a slight tap at their door, which proved to be a call from Dame McDonald for the gentlemen to "take pot luck for their dinner."

"I dare not venture below," said Crawford; "but, Clinton, come back immediately after you have made the acquaintanceship of the gentlemen on parole. Some of them you know already. They waste out life here, and you will do them good in just showing your face among them."

Clarence descended the way he came up, and soon found himself seated at a deal table without cloth, but white, being evidently scoured for the occasion. The old woman, dressed in what was known as drugget, had a clean *toy* on her head, which bore the marks of a carefully put on cap, in which the wearer was confident she looked well. The skirt of the gown was drawn through the pocket-hole to prevent its dragging on the floor, which, from its length of train, it would have done. She did not sit down herself, but served the company.

Wooden plates, hollowed out of basswood, were ranged round the table; into these a ladleful of the broth, which stood cooling in the tripod pot, was emptied; and the invitation given, "sit down, sir, and mak yourself at hame. Janet has been busy preparing some sheep's-head kail to put me in mind o' Kenmore."

Clarence had seen, when he was standing by the fire, the nose of some animal pushing itself up among the vegetables in the pot like a black hippopotamus among the reeds of the Nile; but he did not expect to make his dinner of the mess. However, now like a good soldier, he sat down with a ready appetite for whatever was coming, asking no questions. To his agreeable surprise, the soup was white as milk, though the head—it might be of a ram from its size—was there in a large platter, on the centre, without the horns, and the wool singed all off. Garden stuffs of all kinds, known, and some only known to Janet, had been boiled for two full hours, with the head among them; so that it would have defied a French cook to tell the prevailing flavor of what McDonald called this dish of HOTCH POTCH. Barley bread, unleavened, baked upon a griddle, thin and tough as leather, was eaten to this soup; when at the close Janet put down a square bottle and a basket of oatmeal cakes alongside of a skim-milk cheese; all of which were intended as a dessert. The sergeant lifted a small dish made of narrow pieces of wood of different colors, hooped round, so that it seemed a Lilliputian milk tub. Into that he poured the contents of the bottle, drinking it off at a single draught, after he had, with great solemnity, given *the King, God bless him*, as a toast. Clarence had the same put before him: and so it went round the table. The rest who were there seemed to be men who merely listened and looked. When it came to Janet's turn to drink, there was evidently something more expected of her than a bare toast. Putting on the table a crystal goblet, which, from the manner of her unrolling it, she deemed sacred, liquor was poured into it till it stood on the lip. Taking an egg in her hand, she broke it so that the yolk spread through the contents of the glass. Through this compound she looked with a curious eye, as if expecting to see something uncommon in the distance. Tasting of the mixture freely, she leaned her head on her knees, singing a Gaelic song, rocking herself, as she sang for a few minutes, during which the company sat in the profoundest silence, waiting on the will of the actor. When she lifted her head, it was to take the goblet again in her hand, which she shook sharply, and gazing intently, she laid it down as if in fear at first; but lifting it up, one of those dark smiles came across her wrinkled features, which recalls to the traveller's mind a gleam of sunshine on a Scottish sky.

Tell us what you see, wife, and let us go," said the sergeant, evidently under the enchantment of the occasion. "We want the truth, Janet; but the journey must be taken, weal or woe. What does the Brownie say?"

Janet, in a moaning tone, sang, "Smoke, fury and blood all the first."

"We are ready and prepared for them. You mean that the end will be successful. Let us go, said McDonald, "and see the gentlemen;" and with that he led the way through the low door of the mud cabin, taking the path that led up the side of the creek.

On the way Clarence learned from McDonald that there were several families like himself, who were living among the farmers, and some had risen to be good landholders themselves. The most of them, however, were imprudent, and useless to the community, and to themselves. They were divided like the country on the question of the present war, and "you may," said the sergeant, "as weel break a woodie wi' a windle strae as change a Hielan man, when he wants to gang either up or doon stream."

The two had arrived at the door of a large stone barn that was snugly fenced round, and the yard swept and orderly, showing that the hand of a soldier had been in use here for some time. The door was opened by McDonald, who entered, leading Clarence, hat in hand. The company, as if expecting the visit, rose at once, and came forward with the dignity and the frankness of gentlemen and soldiers. The welcome was hearty and full of feeling. Already all had been made aware of the name and of the rank which belonged to the visitor. Of the object in his mind no one knew anything, nor was one of the ten gentlemen at liberty to ask him till he might reveal it himself. Of course they supposed public business alone could induce any one to venture into such a dangerous vicinity. Still as they had heard of overtures being made to leading Whigs throughout, it did not sound strange when one of them, with a knowing look, whispered, "Sir Harry is cousin to the rebel General Clinton, and his brother the governor, and the governor knows that these Dominies are great men among the Dutch boors."

And so the mission of Clarence Clinton was guessed at without being sought out. The opportunity was now sought after by all to make themselves agreeable, while the young soldier, feeling sympathy for them as a brother officer, in the same noble profession, put forth all his character in their presence, with promises of aid whenever he would return to head-quarters. Some of the number were old acquaintances, and the greeting between them was cordial. The strangers were no less pleased with a visit from one who was so sure to report of their privations undergone on behalf of his majesty. Hope of promotion revived as they looked to the future.

Clarence cast his eye round the place where they were met, and learned from them that though they chose to assemble here they were by no means confined to any location. Some were lodged in the little village, and others in the families of the farmers. For some days past they had been engaged preparing for a hunting excursion to the mountains. A pair of catamounts had been seen, and all who were inclined had the chance of putting forth their energies.

"I see," said Clarence, "you have all the means provided," as he glanced round the place and saw the guns, the lances, and the other articles of a huntsman's armory. "You are allowed great freedom when these are put into your possession, and time given. I hope you have ample range and verge enough."

"Of that, sir, we have nothing to complain. We have been away twenty-four hours at a time, and have travelled to the borders of civilization. Some of us on a journey of pleasure, others on a tour of research, and I myself have been to consult the wizard of the spook's den, as the people called it when I went first. We are waiting for a message from him to go on this hunting campaign. He promised to send us a special warning, so that we might be there in time; and if I am not mistaken, there comes the witch's imp at this moment.

Clarence looked toward the entrance to which Captain Willoughby pointed, who from his rank, as well as for his superior intelligence, was regarded as chief, when he saw the same misshappen dwarf move toward them, holding a letter in his hand, which he gave to the officer who expected it.

"That will do, Unga," said the captain. "You may sit down till I send you with my reply;" and the creature stepped high and low as he moved to a settle near the wall where he stretched himself on his back, with his cap over his face.

"Just as I said," were Willoughby's first words. "The hunt comes off to-morrow, and if we wish to see it we must join the party by sunrise at the Round Top, keeping round by—— But see here is a map of the region. Sergeant McDonald, see this and tell us if it be practicable. We must not trust ourselves in the hand of a spaeman."

The sergeant took the sketch, looking at it with the deepest interest, while all the gentlemen stood around him waiting for his verdict, which he gave briefly.

"You maun tak to the west o' that round hill, then climb the mountain as weel as you can, and when at the tap keep west by south, till you come to a waterfall that lies at the head of a deep glen, running to the east. The man that drew that is the same as he who drew another I have seen this morning."

"What do you draw from both, my worthy sergeant?" was the familiar question of the one in command.

Before an answer could be given, a voice, which seemed to sound on the outside of the building, called out, "Clarence Clinton!" That gentleman looked suddenly in the direction, all eyes turning in the same way, when the same voice, but louder, called from the other side:

"*Captain Clarence Clinton, the Consistory of the Protestant Reformed Dutch Church demand your presence at this moment.*"

This, which was said slowly, excited some amusement among the young men who ran out for the purpose of seizing the impudent fool, who would so speak. But no one being seen, a singular tremor came over men who would have stood at another time in the face of death. Clarence, who had seen enough of that court of late to despise it, in his present condition took McDonald with him aside, making an appointment to meet him and Crawford in case he found it possible to free himself of the presence of spies. To them he ascribed the voices he had heard all that morning.

Bidding his brother officers a pleasant adieu, and a successful time on the mountain, he hastily left for the parsonage, where that strange court was to be held, despising it in his soul, and yet forced to appear.

CHAPTER IV.

JUDGMENT AND MERCY KISSED.

"Sir Roger informed me that Moll White was dead, and that about a month after her death the wind was so very high that it blew down one of his barns. 'But for my part,' said the knight, 'I do not think that the old woman had anything to do with it.'"

ADDISON.

THE young Englishman entered the Dominie's house with a thousand revolving feelings in his bosom. The ridicule thrown upon his errand in the loft by those guissards had more effect upon him than all the arguments of his friend Crawford. In fact, the announcement of the meeting by that mysterious voice, made him, brave as he was, and in a cause which God must own as holy, step with less confidence than before he left the parsonage. The main entrance was full, as were all the rooms. Nothing of privacy seemed to be here. As Clarence pressed through, he was brushed against by some who said, "Remember, a straight story." He had got that advice before, and the words roused up his energies, which had been sinking. He said to himself:

"I have friends, and will hold up my head in the midst of all."

The inner door was opened by Tom, who was already at his post, looking demure or roguish as the one side or the other of the company would be best suited. He gave a roguish leer on Clarence, that was met by one of fire, which men accustomed to command are sure to have at disposal, and which no real slave is ever able to meet without being withered by it. The impudent fellow cowered under the glance of his superior at once, nor ever after looked him in the face.

"Massa Domilie in de C'nsistory. Gen'lm'n please to sit down till he be called for."

This was said to show the power of the master and to impress the attendant Englishman with awe.

"Tell your master, sirrah," said Clarence, with sternness, "that Mr. Clarence Clinton is here and desires admittance immediately."

The effect of this command upon Tom, as well as upon all those who were waiting, was quite evident. The negro came back bowing his best salaam, saying:

"Massa Clary vill walk in."

The moment the door inside was shut, and Tom on the outside, the rogue gave a wink to the spectators, which nearly upset their gravity. This little bit of acting between the false and the true was too interesting not to excite attention; and caused more than common anxiety concerning what was going on. The dominoes in the loft, conducted as these were known to be by the Dominie's private secretary, prepared the minds of the public for a real case of treason; and the manner and the name of the stranger were gradually producing that intensity of feeling which always follows secrecy and hints; so that pretty loud murmuring was beginning to show itself by those who were debarred admittance to the tribunal. The design of Tom was working out. He had vowed revenge on Clarence for what he supposed him guilty of—informing his master of his late peccadillo; and so he was accomplishing the end.

The prisoner, for now he was so in reality, found the court in session. He, by this time, was becoming acquainted with Consistorial forms of investigation, and knew already the strong and the weak places, of which he was determined to avail himself. There was the chief man in his canonicals in the centre, and the same Anthony Van Bergen in the threefold capacity of elder, squire and clerk.

"Mr. Clarence I think your name is?" said the questioner.

"Clarence Clinton, at your service," was the answer. At the same time he stepped forward, and half demanded the authority of this court to put him through an investigation. He saw plainly that it was a mongrel court, which did not differ much in his esteem from the mockery in the mill. For one moment his mind was so confused that he almost imagined himself standing before the other cocked-hat on the wheat-sack.

"You are charged here, sir, with stealing a horse from Cornelius Wynkoop."

"I deny the charge," said the prisoner, with great warmth, and almost starting forward to punish the insulter.

"Call the witnesses," was the cry of the Squire; when the door opened, and in stepped the same old negro; telling exactly the same story, though with less palaver.

"Vat says de prisoner to dat?" said the squire, glancing aside to his chief.

"I say," was the reply, "that all the old man says is true; but it does not show that I stole the animal. If the reverend gentleman will look at the letter I put in his hand this morning, from a worthy brother of his own, it will account for what is here produced as evidence."

"My dear sir," said the Dominie, "I have reason to believe that the letter you produced to me is a forgery. I am quite sure that my good friend and brother, whose name is here, never entered a barn at midnight, to take even the loan of a horse, for—for"—he hesitated to say the other word, but it come out "in short, for a spy."

At this word the accused felt as if nature was giving way. The scene in the mill was all present with him, but there was no laughter here. These were earnest men, looking cold and determined.

"You be a spy," said the Squire, "and vill be thrown off at de cart tail."

By this time the door was open. Tom had purposely left it so, and a crowd gathered up close to where the accused young man stood, whose faces did not show any sympathy with him. Remembering what he had been warned against, and feeling that if the worst came upon him at the last, he would suffer more in feeling afterward that he had told untruth, than the fear of death could bring, he resolved to give a full account of the whole, omitting only the fact of his being at the Sopus burning.

He began by saying in a hesitating tone, for he actually felt the influence of the farce still: "I came to these mountains in search of my sister." He continued giving a brief and touching account of her romantic character, of how she had been abducted, and of where he believed her to be, and concluded by saying, that if he must die in the manner threatened, he would die a true man, and no spy. For the moment, they believed him to be under some hallucination, and they were sensibly touched with his account. The grave Dominics' features were relaxed into uncertainty, while Grant was wiping his eyes, as he said to the pedagogue the "fule has made me greet." Tom, who stood behind his master's chair, and had fixed his mouth for the general guffaw at the usual watchword, hid his teeth, wondering that "white folks neber 'joyed any funny ting at all."

When all had recovered themselves sufficiently for business, the Dominie said, "Young man, your story is too unlikely to be believed anywhere; and even though we did receive it as true, there are others to whom we are accountable who would laugh at our easy faith in these times, when the name you give is so obnoxious through all this land to-day."

These allusions moved the spirit of the young British soldier, and raising himself up rather haughtily, he answered: "If you are amenable, then, to higher authority, I prefer to be tried by a regular court of the country."

This was unfortunate, since it insinuated the want of due authority in the court where the present judge was always the law, and sometimes the executor. Drawing himself out of his large hair, he rose to his feet, saying with a force and a loudness which might have suited the church where they had been, that morning:

"You must understand, Mr. Clarence Clinton, this is not the mill loft; nor is this Consistory of the Protestant Reformed Dutch Church of Holland, in these United States of North America, a set of mountebanks, but has had its existence ever since the sitting of the Synod of Dort; and be it known, that they have sufficient power to try you, or anyone else, of the king's slaves, that falls providentially into their hands. A mongrel court indeed! You are thinking of those blasphemous grimacers, who dared to mock me and my court, almost before my face; some of them will have to take forty stripes save one."

During this speech, every man, white and black, was quiet, as a mouse. The sly fellow behind the chair looked down and pretended to wipe his eyes.

Just at this point, when all seemed to be going against the accused, to make the matter still worse for him, some one suggested that the prisoner be searched for arms. Now Clarence, remembering again the scene at the mill, saw that he was lost indeed, and immediately produced his pistols, laying them on the table before them, saying:

"You may be sure, gentlemen, that no wise man on a mission like what I say I am upon, would dispense with the use of arms; and here they are, at the disposal of the legal power."

"We have the legal and the moral authority together in this house," said the president, with more than his usual severity; "and as there is great doubt concerning you, there is no help for us but to keep you in custody till these doubts be cleared up."

Clarence bowed low; when some one at-his elbow whispered, "produce your sealed packet." This recalled to his mind what he would then have forgotten, the letter he received just as he mounted the horse. Putting his hand hastily in his bosom, he took out a small package addressed, "To those in authority, given by the hand of Clarence C——."

The Dominie cast his eye over the superscription, and saying hastily, "I am—at least, *we* are the men here in authority," and breaking the seal, he read to himself, all the time changing color; looking first to the outside, then again on the inside, while his eye every now and then was turned on the face of the prisoner. At last he drew the Squire and other two into a corner for consultation.

During all this time every one was still as death. Something real was now before their eyes, and a *dénoûment* was about to take place as was evident from the whole demeanor of the chief men. Even Clarence was ignorant of the contents of the package, and was in as great a quandary as the spectators. At last the court again took their seats, when the Dominie, not being willing to trust his aid in this business, took up speech himself.

"We have come to the conclusion, sir, that this is another forgery, only it is of a more heinous nature than that already committed by you. The other was only the name of an obscure minister of the Gospel—as great a sin in the sight of God as could be committed; but this, in addition, is a sin against the highest authority in this State. The name of George Clinton, the chief magistrate, in which he is purported to say, 'allow the bearer, Clarence Clinton, to pass and repass unmolested.' Now our decision is, that you be retained here till evidence can be produced from headquarters of the genuineness of this document; or till you give such security as will satisfy this court."

Clarence replied: "After what you have declared, no affirmation of mine will avail. Of the manner in which the first letter was got I know something; but how the Governor of this State, as you call him, should have given me that letter, I am ignorant; and as there is no one here who will be security for a stranger lying under such charges as you prefer, I must be resigned to my fate."

At this point of interest, a slight movement was observed in one corner of the room; and after the Dominie had said, "Then you have no cautioner to give," there stepped up to the table by the side of Clarence, the tall bearded man he had seen in the crowd that morning, dressed in a still more fantastic manner; and throwing down a small card on the table, before which the Dominie sat, he demanded: "if that would be sufficient assurance for the accused." The person to whom this was addressed, rose in a moment, gave a glance at the paper, and as he handed it back, said, bowing in the most respectful manner, "Your own word would be enough;" and turning to Clarence, remarked, "you are at liberty, sir."

Clarence, before whom all this was acted, looked round for the man who had changed the whole, from darkness to light so suddenly; but he was gone, and turning to the chair again, he said:

"Reverend sir, did I understand you aright? Am I at liberty?"

The president repeated his words in the most respectful manner; leaving Clarence and the whole auditory in far greater wonder than he did when he entered the mill, whip in hand, to chastise those negro actors. He seemed to those who knew him, as if he were the one who underwent the scrutiny of a pair of eyes, more penetrating than his own; and that toward the late prisoner he became obsequious. A kind of amazement held all in silence, waiting for something, they knew not what, when a stir among the crowd at the door attracted the eyes of the court. The children in the yard below were screaming through fear, and even the inexperienced men grew a little pale when a tall young man entered dressed in the costume of the mock Indians of the region. It was evident that he was meeting but a doubtful reception. The men around were seen handling their hidden weapons, for all expected a tribe of Mohawks certainly to follow.

"No occasion for alarm," said the intruder. "I am a messenger of peace and one of your own friends, though for the present obliged for good reasons to wear this disguise. I am now on an errand of deliverance." The president on his feet answered:

"Teunis Roe, when we see the garb of the cruel Brandt stained with blood, you can hardly expect that the man who wears it should receive a friendly welcome."

"That is true, Dominie, but you preach yourself, 'judge not according to appearance.' Safer to meet an angel in the garment of Satan, than Satan in that of an angel of light, I am alone. Hear me and then judge," said Teunis, for it was our friend the young Boerman of the flats who spoke.

"You have given us a new rendering of that scripture, and something like a new doctrine upon it; but see that you do not wrest it to your own destruction. But what have you to say about that fire raising and midnight marauder; that heathen and scalper that has torn up the nests of our best folks, and left so many weeping and wailing below on the Vlatts, while he, like the hawk, sits up there looking down into their yards."

"Do not fear that I am not come to help the bloody crew, so be at rest."

"Teunis," said the roused Dominie, "we never knew fear. "A good conscience is always brave."

"No one," said the youth, "ever questioned the Dominie's courage; and it is for that reason I am here at the risk of my life; and if you will hear my story you will not be long sitting there on your soft chairs while your brethren of the grand Consistory are up yonder chained to the rock."

"Hearken to Teunis Roe," said the Dominie, striking his large fist down on the table with a force that made Tom jump a foot high, and put all the rest into silence.

"My tale is soon told," said Teunis. "You know that Elder Abiel, and Martin Schuyler are in the hands of the Philistines; and Brandt says he is only waiting till he gets a few more, and the Dominie himself, and then he will go off with them to see the great falls of Ni-a-a-gaara."

"And by old St. Nicholas," said the brave soldier of the cross and of the State, "I will meet the red sinner half-way, that he may see how the Lord will deliver me out of the mouth of the bear, and out of the paw of the lion. Go on, Teunie, and let us hear the rest of that fine tale. Here, Tom, you blaspheming rascal, that mocked me behind my back, bring me the tobacco pouch and pipes for us all."

In a short time every mouth was puffing out smoke till the whole room was so thick with vapor, that "a piece of it," Clarence afterward wrote, "could have been cut out and sent as a specimen of a Dutchman's breath."

The sum of Teunis' story was, that he was sent with a message from the captives to the Consistory, desiring assistance. Showing how it was not only possible, but highly probable, for a few men to surprise the Indians and the Tories on the next day, as it was their intention to divide off into companies, so that the whole woods and caves round the region might be scoured for some prisoners that had escaped. In the course of the narrative which Teunis gave, it leaked out that Elsie Schuyler was one of these fugitives, and that along with her was a young lady, who had been taken to the mountains. No one could tell how. It would, nevertheless, be a great act of humanity, to save two such young and beautiful girls from such a spoiling set of murderers, as these Indians were.

"O! yaw, yaw! Teunis, you have got a kindness for every piece of humanity; and for all woman kind in general; but for Elsie in a special degree. Well, no harm in that; I could tell a tale myself, if the ''Yfvrow' were here. Let that pass, and tell us something more about that other young girl: I see a pair of eyes in that corner there looking at you as if they would draw you into them. Here, Mr. Clarence, or whatever else they call you, here is some corroborative proof of your unlikely tale. What say you, neighbors, to a young man going off to the mountains to seek his sister?" and the Dominie laughed at the joke now, and all joined Tom with the rest, turning the court-room into a house of mirth.

In the meantime, Clarence had taken out Teunis by himself, making all the inquiries which affectionate earnestness could suggest. For already he was persuaded, that it could be none other than Margaret. The answers he received went all to confirm him in the suspicion he had formed the moment that Teunis had said there were two young women, and one of them a stranger. It was something to know she was out of the hands of the destroyer, but the dangers which still surrounded her made him all the more eager to be off; which he and Teunis were determined upon, whatever might be the conclusion of the present reverend conclave.

The discussions now were informal, and turned upon the best way of accomplishing the desired object. As in all bodies of men, there was a division of opinion. The Dominie headed one side and old Mat Van Deusen the other. The latter had objections to everything, and every plan. He appeared to have no heart in the matter. Clarence made up his mind that here was one of those secret friends of the king, who inwardly wished Brandt to get off with his captives. Could the young Englishman only have had the ear of the Dutchman a few minutes, he thought, an argument might be produced, that would prove powerful and efficient. As things appeared, nothing was likely to be done by such slow men; and of divided counsel.

Silence prevailed, and even darkness brooded over the place; scarcely a face could be distinctly seen, for the smoke that rose from every mouth. All took the cue from the chief man, and he was rapt up in his own thoughts; and might be following after some knotty text, or deep doctrine, while his counsellors were quite as silent, and their countenances more meaningless. But at this juncture the door was flung wide open with haste, and in stepped Grant the Scotchman, out of breath. His first words were:

"Minister, you and your session there, sit greatly at your ease, when the work of treason is going on round you."

"What now, Hugh Grant," said the Dominie, taking the long pipe from his mouth, holding it ready for the blast. "We have seen you on fire before," and with that he continued on with his smoking.

"Weel, weel," said Grant, "maybe you'll lock the stable, when the steed is stown; but I'll shake myself clear of the sin at ony rate. I'm tauld that a' those offishers o' the king, are awa' on a hunt to the tap o' Ben—I mean Roun' Tap, and that that wild Tory sergeant McDonald, has gane with them; taken a young lad dressed in the philabeg aboon the knee; and it is thocht by the maist of folks to be nae one else than her that was actin' the lady here before you this morning. She, or he is carrying dispatches to the sooth by that way, since the road by the river is closed."

Before Grant was through, not a pipe but was held between the finger and the thumb of its owner. The president had removed his, and was rolling up the tobacco bag with care, evidently working himself up into a state of excitement, before he would venture to express his determination. Even old Mat Van Deusen looked mad, at the course things were taking; and was the first to say, "It is time for us to act." The decision was becoming every moment more forcible, though as yet nothing was spoken, or a movement from the place where they sat. Clarence, all excitement and afraid lest something might come out concerning his knowledge of the real state of things, was planning within himself how he might leave without incurring the suspicion of those, who unquestionably knew more than was expressed.

CHAPTER V.

THE MARSHALLING AND MARCHING OF THE MIGHTY TO THE MOUNTAINS.

"The more haste the less speed
Said the tailor to the long threed."
SCOTTISH PROVERB.

DOMINIE SCHUNEMAN had a favorite maxim, which he put into practice most faithfully, as Cecil said to Queen Elizabeth, "Let us take time, that we may make the better haste." He made all sit down or stand quiet in their places, and knowing him well, they obeyed instinctively. He gave the cast to his face which it always took just before he spoke. They listened to what they knew was coming.

"Providence points us to duty. As Vader Abraham was sent to the slaughter of the kings, who came upon the plain, he brought back all the goods, and also again his brother Lot, and his goods, and the women also, and much people. 'Tom, bring me the big Bible, till I read how David, that good soldier and saint, did, when they came and told him that the Amalekites had invaded the south, and smitten Ziglag, and burned it with fire.' You will find it in the twenty-ninth chapter of the first book of Samuel." And he read it through with the coolest deliberation, greatly to the annoyance of the two impatient young men, who had no resource but to wait patiently.

But after reading this long text, he commenced his exhortation. "Brethren, can we sit still, and our friends all in the wolf's den? Good hunters all of you, fathers and sons. Were a painter to come out, or a whole army of wildcats to run down these hills, would not the whole congregation—men, women and kinderen—go off, even on a Sunday afternoon, to kill them; and there now is that wolf Kiskataam, and his cubs, fixing their teeth on the check of Elsie Schuyler—she that every young man in the parish would run off his legs to get for a wife; and there you are letting her fecht it out herself. I say the youth that relieves her out of bondage shall have her."

This was met by a cheer that made the stone house ring.

"Who will go up with me to Rammothgilead to battle?"

"We will all go," was the answer; "only lead us out, and we will follow the one that bears the ark."

"Oh, yes," said old Mat Van Deusen, slily, "put the Dominie in the front. He is a good mark. They will be sure to hit him."

"Shame upon you, Mat," said the Dominie, shaking at the deacon his big fist; "you have no more courage than your black dog Morgan. You, a Christian soldier that I have been exercising so long in the canons of the church! Ha! ha! deacon, there is for you," and he shook Mat by the shoulder till he made his teeth chatter, when he declared that it was through perfect fear.

"Now who is ready? Let us all to work," said the pastor, rising himself.

"I am ready," said Tom, lifting up the clasped Bible, when his master's back was turned, as if it were a stone to fling at the head of an enemy, when the Dominie suddenly wheeled to see the fun, which he perceived must be going on behind him; the comical fellow jumped to the door at three steps, saying to those near him, "O, lor'! forty stripes for supper, and one spoonful less."

"Mr. Clarence, this matter concerns you as much as any of us; but I do not see how you can fight against the king's servants conscientiously." This was said in a whisper.

"Oh," said Clarence, "I will serve humanity and affection first, and the king will receive his share afterward."

"Alas! alas! sir, these sentiments are sadly forgotten in these days of blood and rapine. Human nature is a miserable piece of inconsistency. It turns out the widow and the orphan into the wilderness, to die of nakedness and hunger, or worse; and one of Eve's other daughters is reft away in no worse manner, and we will fly through fire and water to deliver that single one."

Clarence was left to muse over these true sayings, while the Dominie called out after those around the house, who seemed to wait upon his orders.

"Leftenant Grant and Captain Salisbury, drum up your volunteers, and meet, all well armed, an hour hence, in the church, with provisions in your knapsacks for three days at least; and see that your men be like Gideon's choice troops, not greedy of drink."

A general dispersion of all here took place preparatory to a march to the mountains that night. No one was more active than old Mat Van Deusen, who gave his horse to a young stripling at the gate, telling him to "ride along the whole road to Coxsackie, and be back in time, after warning every man, though old Bet should fall in the ditch at the close of the race, and you beside her." In this way the different roads were resounding with horses' hoofs; and there was not that day a heavy-bottomed Dutchman along the Kaatskill flats. Once under way, they swept the air like a well ballasted sloop, in a fair wind, through the water.

Teunis and Clarence took to each other through common troubles, so that before an hour had passed, they were sworn friends, and bound to do their utmost for the deliverance of those who were dearer to them than life. Their fears were, that the little army now mustering would be too late; and every moment's delay rendered them more impatient to be off and up the mountain's side.

In a shorter time than Clarence could have thought it possible for any but regular troops to have assembled, he saw that the yard and road around the church were crowded with men and horses, when out from the midst of them came the Dominic's man, bowing and sniggering, as he said, "Massa Domilie 'sire de compaly of de gentlemen in de C'nsistry room."

Having gone through with his message, and walking back, he sidled up to Teunis, saying:

"Massa Teunie hab on de Ingin cloades; come frob Brandt's fireplace, eh?"

"I have been up there," was the dry reply of Teunis, "and I am going back again. Has the nigger any message to Cuff?" This was intended to sound the fellow, whom he suspected and intended to circumvent.

"Tom vud like good deal to see Cuffee, ma goot frien'; de great African king in his own lan'. He now valk beside de great Ingin Mohawk king, and, no more 'fraid ob ole' Beal and tick vip. Ha! ha! Cuffee dat licked de ole boy in de dark."

"Now Tom, what would your master say if he heard that you wanted to see Cuff? He would suspect that you wanted to do the same thing to him; cudgel him and then sell him to the Indians."

Tom looked from under his cap to see if the land was all clear, and thinking that he spoke only to the real kingsman, he said under his breath:

"O lor'! vont he roar ven de Mohawk skins him."

Tom walked off, leaving the two young men remarking to each other, "Slavery, whatever may be said of it, has two sides. There are very few of these men in black skins, who would rejoice at the captivity of their masters, but there are some who would deliver them up. "The Cuff he speaks of, has just betrayed one of the best of men."

They entered among the secret friends, who were sitting in council. The Dominie, as usual, took up the speech, and addressed them saying: "We have sent for you both, that we may have the benefit of your information, and of your experience. Teunis, we shall hear you on the first; and you, sir, Clarence, on the second; and as you are both interested in this matter personally, we have a pledge that you will be sincere."

The young colonist told them all he knew of the numbers, the intentions, and the plans of the party above. How many real Indians there were, and how many disguised Tories. "So far as I can guess, they have private instructions to remain on the flat rock, till they do all that can be done to secure one prisoner of great importance, a young lady of high note, who has made her escape, and is hidden away in the clefts of the rocks. An officer of the British army is there, and exercises a great influence over the Mohawk; so that he seems to do just as he directs. How long this may remain, no one can conjecture; but to-morrow is to be the great and general hunt; what is called by the Indian a ring. One is to start from the camp now fixed, and spread three miles wide, each man to be within hearing of two; one before and another behind. Then turning till all meet at the Kauterskill Falls. If unsuccessful they are to spread again, as wide, coming round to the *dog-pool;* then rest for the day, and perhaps give up the chase. That is all I know. My advice is to track their circle and deliver their prisoners, raising the alarm so effectually, that they will retreat suddenly, and they will leave all they have got behind."

Clarence, when asked, declined to answer, through delicacy, but really through inexperience in such modes of warfare. But he stated his willingness sincerely to follow any leader who might be appointed in an expedition that would deliver those two prisoners out of the hands of those cruel foes.

"Captain Van Vechten, we will hear your opinion concerning the best way of delivering the birds out of the snare of the fowler." The president here addressed a stout, slow-looking man, who had not said a word that any one heard that day. He opened his eyes like some one that is just wakening out of a slumber; and instead of speaking he rolled out his tongue in something of the same way that a turtle puts out its head, when boys place a hot coal upon its back, moving its point from side to side. All knew his weakness, or perhaps his strength; for though he was slow he was sure to act, and sure to speak to the point.

"We are going to the mountains you say, to fight the Indians. Let one half of our men be dressed in the disguise that Teunis wears, so that our party will mix with Brandt's, in the circle, and let the other half be a reserve to attack their main camp, when we will find no difficulty in carrying off the booty. That is all."

"Now, Grant, let us hear you," was the chief's word to that curious worthy; "see if you can keep that Scotch blood of yours cool. I declare I have more trouble with these hasty highlanders, than with all the rest of my parish."

This was said in a jocular vein, but the real intention leaked through, and Grant understood these hints sufficiently well to bridle his tongue in part.

"'Deed, minister, I own that I am a wee thought hasty, when troubled wi' such a hot spur as Sandy McLeod, or Billy Salisbury here; but mind you, that it's no the rattlin' filly that gangs o'er the brae first, and that smooth water runs deep, and the deil at the bottom o't sometimes. But minister though you be, I'll tell you this at ance, that neither I, nor any one of my company will ever put on false faces, like a set of silly hug-ma-na guissards; Jesuits, naething else; wha would pretend to be friends in the morning, then turn round before night and stick a gully-knife in a man's wame. I'm for being up and at it at ance, having a fair fecht and din we't. A true Indian is a real gentleman, we' a brown face o' his ain; but a man putting a feather in his cap, and marking his cheeks wi' a bit o' burnt cork, and calling himself a Mohawk chief, I despise him with a perfect scunner."

"What say ye, Willy Salisbury, man?"

The person addressed had a mischievous pleasure of tormenting the Scotchman, and though they were great friends, and on all important occasions usually agreed, could not resist the temptation of saying in reply:

"Grant has a great distaste to the Indian dress, but the Highlanders are only of the same breed of the wild men. Burgoyne called the BLACK WATCH, the English savages."

"Haud your tongue," said Grant, in his good-natured fury, "you Sassenach, if yo do not want me to put this whittle up to the heft in your buttock. The kilt, let me tell you, as the minister said to me, is the garb of old Gaul, and that was the pride of old Rome. When your forefathers came doon to Scotland trying to enslave us, as they are trying to put the collar on the neck o' this kintra, they had just to look at the kilt, and aff they skilped as if a dirk was in their doup."

"O, yes!" said the tormentor, "that was at the race of Colloden; my father was there, and he declared that it was the finest thing he ever saw."

"Except," said Grant, in something of hearty bitterness, "the race o' Prestonpans, where the English horsemen were the first to bring the news to Embro that they were beaten by these kilted men, armed wi' hooks an' scythes."

"I think you are even now," said the Dominie, who knew Grant too well not to see that his blood was rising. "We must come to business. Let Captain Van Vechten have the charge of his plan, as every one can carry out their own schemes best. Captain Salisbury, you will take charge of the main body, and let Grant have the reserve. We will start all together an hour after sundown; going by the north side of Round Top; and be sure that not a whisper of this be dropped outside, for that wily snake has got his ears laid low to the ground already, and might take us in a lone place before we knew what was the matter. Let our Indian captain send his single scouts in all directions, to prevent surprises. Our rendezvous at an hour before sunrise, a mile above Hermit's Hollow, on the side of the North Mountain."

"Losh keep us," said Grant, "he is nae doubt going doun to see that Warlock body in the glen. He is a fearless creature that Dominie, minister of ours. That's the way o' the minister's in the highlans; they are acquaint with a' the witches in the kintra side."

By this time the volunteers were all come in, mostly very young men, and those past middle life, as the able-bodied of the population were away in the army. A large draught had been made but recently for the army of the north, to follow up the victory of Saratoga, now crowned with complete success in the subjugation of Burgoyne. Had it been a hunting excursion, they on the ground that day could not have entered into the frolic with more zest and spirit. All present had been out night after night many times before this, chasing the bear and the panther. Scarcely a youth present but had killed some of the kinds common in the region, and was familiar with danger. Even the blacks, who are a stout, athletic race, many of them the genuine "Guinea nigger," and all of them but one or two removes from the original African, were eager for the frolic; and some of them, for secret reasons, were jumping with joy.

"Boys," the Dominie cried, at the full pitch of his voice, "before we march let us seek the counsel of the Lord." To this no objection was expressed, either in word or by look. The good man's heart was brimful of devotion, so that he poured out his soul with all the fervency of a saint—now in English and then in Dutch, and sometimes mixing the two languages in the same sentence; all hearts were melted into one stream. He alluded to the cloud that hung over the tabernacle in the wilderness, and to the safe guidance which the army of Israel had when the ark was in the van. "And now be not angry with us, O Lord, while we venture up into the mount. Let it not prove to us as the mountains of Gilboa did to Saul and Jonathan; for if thou goest not with us we cannot go up in peace." Breaking out into a transport, he forgot his English, or, perhaps, he meant to rouse up the hearts of his sluggish people through the tongue they loved best to hear; he prayed, "De lieflykheit des Heeren onzes Godts zy, ons eñ bevestigt gy het werk onzen handen over ons; ja het werk onzer handen bevestigt dat." Amen.

"Translate that last sentence to me," said Clarence, who was entranced by the earnestness of the petitioner; "it must be good, it was uttered with such spirit, and the effect of it is seen all around. I am not without some of the influence myself, though I am almost ignorant of the meaning."

"It is good," said Teunis; "but the Dominie has a handsome way of saying these things, which adds to their effect. The words at the close were, "Let the beauty of the Lord our God be upon us, and establish thou the work of our hands upon us; yea, the work of our hands establish thou it."

"There comes the 'Yfvrow! there comes the 'Yfvrow!" was sounded all through the company. "We will hear something now."

"You seem to be in a hurry," was the salutation of Mat Van Deusen to the lady of the parsonage. "You put me in mind of the big East Indiaman that my father says he saw, heavy loaded, coming down the Scheldt, on her outward bound voyage."

"Hurry, indeed, as you say, Mat Van Deusen, when a woman's life is to be left exposed to savages, and worse men. Dominie Schuneman, where are you going?" said the jolly 'Yfvrow, "leaving me here in charge of a whole parish, white and black, and"——

"These young darlings at your heels," was the filling up which the husband gave to the sentence begun by the careful wife. He knew that she would oppose his going, and had hidden it from her to the last moment; and now that he was all ready he had no objections to her bidding him good-bye, while all the family followed for the same purpose.

"Where are you going, Dominie?" she renewed her question, with a softer look. Her fine, full face glowed like a morning sun, and her tall, rather heavy form, in the excitement of the moment, had life throughout the whole, which gave it elasticity and motion, quick and graceful. The Dominie stood entranced, but not in the least hesitating, as she said energetically, "You will get your neck broken on some of these night expeditions; you will not escape the lead always that the wicked man has run for you. Can you not leave such work to them that should do it, and mind the business that properly belongs to you."

"'Yfvrow, 'Yfvrow! my work is to do good for God and to my country, as did the high priest of old, who buckled the sword of Goliah on the patriotic David, and blessed him, sending him forth to battle."

"Yaw, yaw! but he did not go himself, but stayed at home, attending upon his work in the tabernacle."

"You have forgotten, 'Yfvrow, that he went before, carrying the ark in the sight of the people."

"Dominie Schuneman," said the softened but proud wife, "we have not all been at Leyden, so I cannot argue with you in that style; but affection pleads in me more powerfully than learning."

As the tear glistened in the eye of the wife and the mother, and there was not a man there who would have ventured to call the Dominie a coward had he remained at home—but the man of God was made of sterner stuff than to yield up at such a juncture—he said:

"All that you say is true, Maria; but there are other parents in the world besides us. There is Martinus and Anshela Schuyler crying after their dochter Elsie, the niece of our good friend the general; and she is away into captivity somewhere in the mountains: and what would we say if our little dawty there was in the same place, and no one willing to risk a gun-shot for her life."

The good 'Yvfrow smiled, and looking through her tears, asked if he intended "to let all these men go off hungry to the hills?"

In a few minutes all the servants of the house were seen out on the road, loaded with all sorts of eatables and drinkables. These were spread out on the horse blocks, on the pews inside the church, and even on the flat gravestones outside. The parting meal was made up of ham and eggs, sausages and roliches. Breads of all kinds of flour, and cakes without number; ole cake, Johny cake, crawley cake, fritter cake, and buckwheat cake; with more of Dutch names than would be safe for any man to speak of. Grant said "these Dutch words always stretched his jaw so that he would as soon read the tenth chapter of Nehemiah, when he was hungry, as try to learn to speak them; unless," he added, "this wife o' the minister should be my schule master; for verily she is a perfect Abigail, wi' her loaves and her wine, and her hundred kinds o' cakes; but there is a kind she has na got yet, and that was ait cake: and as for the Dominie himsclf, he aye believed that there must be some Scotch bluid in his veins, he was sic a sensible body."

The good dame having got over her fears, went from place to place, urging upon them all to eat; flinging down at the same time a slice of rye bread on this place, and a piece of pork on that; and not passing one by, unless she showed her kindness practically. A good word she had for all. When she came to Teunis, she urged him to eat, and be sure and tell Elsie that she would expect her to come down and spend a week with her at the parsonage, till the Hoogenhuisen was built again. Turning to Clarence, she put on the dignity of a duchess, hoping he would soon find his sister; and as this was an easy route to return by, it would be good to spend a night by the way after her fright. At the time she was saying this to him, she was pouring out a glass of her best Hollands for his particular use.

"You will find us, sir," she said, "plain, true hearted folk, who know both how to treat a friend and a foe."

Clarence drank her health standing, with his hat in hand; wishing that "never worse than the present might be seen by him or his friends on any side of the sea."

All were now ready to march agreeably to the order laid down. The Dominie and about ten of the ancients of the town were in the saddle. Tom, that slippery dog, had charge of what might be called a sumpter horse, since on its back was a large bag of all kinds of necessaries; and his master's cloak, which the careful 'Yfvrow had ordered to be strapped behind, so that he might have it ready for immediate use. Coming up close to his stirrup iron, she said:

"Now, Dominie, see that you take good care of yourself, and tie this round your mouth to keep out the night air and the cauld dews; and mind me and the kinderen; as she looked up in his face more softly than she would have done an hour before.

"Get away with you, now, Maria," as he held down his head to her cheek; "you know that I am never cold; my feet are always out of bed at night. My head, you tell me, often is too hot; but you know, Maria, dearest, my heart is never cold; and for you and the kinderen it is always glowing warm."

Here the equally warm-hearted wife lifted her head a little nearer to the saddle girths, as the good man said, in his usual half jesting way, when he wished to be familiar and fond:

"Indeed, wife, I think were I laid in the clay there, my heart would throb back to you, were you to put your hand on the turf."

A tear sparkled in the 'Yfvrow's eye; and as the men had moved off a little way, she embraced her lord most heartily; as he rode away from her sight, saying, "the Lord be with thee."

BOOK IV.

THE FAILURE OF BRANDT;

SHOWING

THE STRENGTH OF INDIAN AMBITION AND REVENGE,

AND

HOW THEY WERE FRUSTRATED.

BOOK IV.

THE Mohawk chief ostensibly sought to obtain a diversion in favor of Burgoyne, but that was not his main design. He was proud of being the hereditary king of the Six Nations, cherishing the name and the fame of Hendrick, who fought for that title with a forecast and a vigor worthy of any ancient hero. The honor bestowed upon Hendrick by Queen Anne, along with other Indian chiefs, had made him mad after more honors; and as he had but one rival worthy of the rank, he resolved to contend openly with E-tau-o-quam in his place on the Hudson, at the mouth of the Kaatskill, which he had done twenty years before, coming off victoriously.

The tradition of that great event was cherished with veneration by the Mohawk nation, and induced them willingly, to make the attack upon the same point now, in full confidence of gaining honor from their Great Father, over the big waters, as heretofore. The vast West was at the command of some one, daring enough to seize the power, and who so able and willing as Brandt? The impossibility of uniting the king's armies of the North and the South, presented a most favorable chance for cutting the rebels in two, and thus leaving them like a serpent that lies on a path intercepting a march; to wriggle out life. To obtain joint possession of

Wantonia—the island at the mouth of the Kaatskill—was the purpose of the Mohawk. Divided, the American patriots must yield, or be greatly weakened by the forces brought against them at all points. To execute this scheme, Butler, the notorious Englishman, and his brother, had made themselves favorites with the Indian tribes, from their sheer desire for blood and rapine, resembling more the appetite of a panther than the generous enmity of a civilized foe. Willing to carry out their hatred at all sacrifices, they gave up the honor of commanding, into the hands of the Mohawk, who, in return for these honors, which gratified his ambition and his pride, lent them his influence and his braves, who proved themselves but too willing to follow wherever Butler led. Hence we have the massacre Wyoming to record, which was to have been followed, in due time, by similar attacks all along the lines, till it would be impossible to raise men who would be willing to follow Washington or Gates, leaving their districts open to the attack of these cruel assassins of women and children.

This savage force, which was becoming every day more formidable, had a wide territory on which to exercise their designs undisturbed. No wise general in the present state of the frontiers, would dare to venture an army into a dense wilderness where no support could be obtained, and all retreat cut off from their base of operations. It seems to be a maxim with military men, that the possessor of the heights has the command of the country. A salutary fear prevented all the officers in command from an attempt to dislodge an enemy seemingly intrenched behind the strongest wall nature herself could raise.

It was, therefore, all the more remarkable, that the attempt of the Dominic to drive Brandt and his allies back from the verge of the precipice, should be undertaken by one ignorant of such an old and unrepealed rule of war. Perhaps the very ignorance of a non-official man, possessed of good common sense, may have been the very cause of his seeming temerity. Had any of the superior men at arms come along and shaken their heads in doubt of success, it is likely that the good Dominic Schuneman would have hesitated; but having been many times after wolves among these heights, he always found that if he could succeed in mounting up still higher, there was small cause of fear, when the hunter was brave and well armed. The time may come when this daring common sense shall take the place of that theoretical caution which lets an enemy remain undisturbed, provided he is in possession of a hill-side. The historian, in faithfully narrating this first blow at the barbarians on the mountains, may show to the high authorities of the land, how the key to the vast and unknown West can be applied again successfully, in opening that rocky barrier which shuts the whole world out, and yet leaves the savage a means of escape.

CHAPTER I.

HUNTING THE LION AND HIS TAWNY WHELPS.

> "As when some huntsman with a flying spear
> From the blind thickets wounds a stately deer,
> Down his cleft side, while fresh the blood distills,
> He bounds aloft and scuds from hills to hills,
> Till life's warm vapor issuing from the wound,
> Wild mountain wolves the fainting beast surround."
>
> POPE.

ALL being ready, the rude soldiers moved away under the command of their several leaders, a motley and irregular band, at sight of which the well trained and practised smiled. They were like a fleet of Newcastle colliers putting to sea, roaring, tugging, screaming at the full pitch of their lungs, each one in the others' way. The man-of-war's man, fresh from Portsmouth, would turn the quid in his mouth, drawing up the wide trowsers, as he swore an oath at these landlubbers pretending to be jack tars. But after waiting a short time, he sees them all out to sea and on their vogage.

Every one of this straggling crew, had an individual mind, and every one watched the movements of the Dominie, who at length rode up with fury that he might take the lead in the cavalcade.

"There he goes noo at last," said the impatient Grant, "like another Abrauhaum, going after the slaughter of the kings; and literally true is it as the Scriptur says, wi' his armed servants, three hundred and aughteen, pursuing them even unto Dan."

"Do you think," said Salisbury, "that he will bring back his brother Lot and his goods and the women also."

"Nae saying, nae saying," was Grant's sincere answer, "he is a bauld creature that Dominie, and a stout body till the bargain."

Teunis and Clarence were considered as independent volunteers, and went together with more thoughtfulness than pervaded the company in general, who had not so much at stake. Even the reverend leader joked; Tom whistled what he durst not speak out, and until they got within the line of the enemy, expressed their feelings as they deemed best. After they reached the foot of the mountain, they were ordered to speak less and in a quieter tone. By and by the Dominie told them their march must be in silence.

"Down in de belly, spose," Tom said he knew "'hem nigger did dat; could make himself tink two nigger in him at once; one down cellar noder up stair."

"Hold your peace, you scoundrel; now, when I think of it, the forty stripes must come off soon, else we shall have the mountain echoes resounding with your pig squealing."

"Lor' massa, me can't help telling Brandt w'ere massa am if him gib forty save vone dis night; best 'spense wid de forty and gib de one."

"And a good one let it be then," said the Dominie, as he unexpectedly struck over the shoulders of the unsuspecting Tom; who roared out so lustily that there was some fear of wakening up the wild human and bestial.

Clarence and Teunis had made up their minds to go forward and reconnoitre the state of affairs; and there seemed to be no immediate objections to that course. But Grant, to whom they broke their mind, did not exactly relish the movement on the part of two untried men, still wearing the livery of the king. He did not exactly suspect them of treachery, but he deemed it best to be cautious. He said, as if incidentally:

"You will run great risk, callants, only twa o' you among so many Tory Indians. If they catch you they will roast you like a red herring."

"We have planned all that, you see," said Teunis. "I have got on their dress already, and I can easily get a disguise for my friend here. We intend joining them, so that we may be near the girls, should their place of refuge be discovered."

"'Wull to cooper, gang to cooper,' as they say in Fife; but I wouldna disguise my face for all the lasses that ever lilted a strathspey. An Indian garb is a mean looking thing at the best, and I cannot help suspecting the man that puts it on. You maun just excuse me for sayin' what I do say."

Teunis, who did get flushed in the face at the insinuation, put in here a word concerning his fidelity, and he was conning a speech in accordance with his fiery look, which would certainly have produced trouble, as the hasty Scot only wanted the chance of giving expression to his doubts, when

Clarence with great address, turned the mind of Grant into his favorite theme by asking:

"How that valley down below there would compare with the scenery of Scotland. You have been up here, of course, in the day time, and can judge."

"Oh, aye, sir, I have been up here hunting wi' the lads that are prisoners down in the toon; and to be honest, I think the size of the country tak's away from the feeling of pleasure I used to hae, when I looked down frae a Scottish mountain."

"But does not that make the sublimity all the more, if there be a sufficient variety of hill and dale, wood and water, interspersed. And then, surely the forest rising up as this does to the very top, must be more beautiful at all times of the year than the bare furze on the Scottish mountains."

"Heather sir, heather is the word. There is music in the very soond o' the word, and as to the sight, I have seen naething here that can stand a comparison with the bloom o' the heather. Oh no, sir; they have nae sangs about the woods up here, nor the streams. I never heard a lassie in this whole land singing the sma'est lilt about the hills and burnies in all this lan'. Man, if you gang up Ben Cruachan, or down the dale o' Aberfeldy, you would think all nature vocal."

"True, true; but then the Scotch are a singing race of people, and they have had such a noble history, it makes the natives glad."

"That's a' true, and finely said," was the answer of the flattered Scot, "frae you that's an Englishman; for nae doubt, you hae been in Scotland, hunting in the Highlands. If you have stood on the tap o' Ben Ledi, you have seen another sight than what you will see the morn at sunrise here; and you will see eneuch here to make your een glance, I'll allow."

"Keeping out of view the associations of the Scottish scenery, where to your mind lies the difference between them?" asked his new acquaintance, who was anxious to keep the good opinion of Grant, who would be a formidable enemy if enraged, or even were he to remain prejudiced, as he was evidently against him and Teunis.

"I think, sir, that the chief difference between what we see here, and that of a Scottish mountain and glen, with all the rest that surround them, lies in the fact that you can take in all Ben Lomond and the loch below, with the islands out, down to Dumbarton, and on to Tintock tap, at ae glance; and it's all grand. But, here man, everything is on sic a great scale, that I canna comprehend it. My head gets so dizzy that I feel as if a' my thoughts had turned into bumble bees. Just this minute, as I'm looking down in the dark, my brain is maer like a bike before it hives aff than anything else. Do you no feel something like it yourself, sir?"

"I confess, Grant, that my head is turned after all I have seen and heard this day," said the young man, anxious to keep the lieutenant from the subject of Teunis' departure, as he perceived his new friend negotiating the matter with the chiefs; "but if I may guess from what you say, there must be a fine uncultivated field for the future poet in that very greatness and mistiness, which meet in the far off horizon, where the other mountain tops just peer through the clouds. And that noble river, running through the centre where the forests are ever living and moving."

"You are very eloquent on what you have never seen yet; but even your description does not come up half to it; and as you say yoursel', it will require some poet like Allan Ramsay to sing about it. At any rate, it will be a lang while before this can compare wi' the hills o' Caledonia. Daunie McGregor there will tell you, that the hill o' Kenmore, where the Yerl of Breadalbane has his house, is as like the Garden o' Eden as this mountain is like that where Noah's ark rested after the flood. Indeed, I doutna but the auld carle when he looked frae his craw's nest out o'er the plains of Shinar, as the folks here do, when they look out on that valley where the sun shines noo, said that will be a bonny country when it is a' peopled, and growing o'er wi' corn, and the river Hudson there speckled wi' sails. But man, whan that takes place, we will a' be lying beneath the yird; and what the better am I?"

Grant would, with a willing listener, as his present auditor proved to be, have gone on till the morning in the same strain; but Clarence, perceiving that Teunis had succeeded in convincing the Dominie of the excellence of his plan, allowed him to give his own report, and all the leaders were called together, that there might be a proper understanding in the morning.

"We must fix upon a signal" said the Dominie, "for we have a wily serpent to deal with, and we cannot guard ourselves too well. What shall the word be?"

"The sword of the Lord and of Schuneman," shouted out

the enthusiastic Grant, as if he had made a discovery of perpetual motion and was afraid it might slip back down his throat before he could give it out. "The sword of the Lord and of Schuneman," he repeated, to be sure that he heard it himself. They were about to give a cheer, but restraining themselves said "Amen: so let it be."

And so the two young men left, careful to bid Grant the most cordial good bye.

"Noo," said that worthy, after they were gone, "it's my opinion that we have not shown muckle sense in that. What would you say if the whole o' that telling of theirs was just a scheme to get up here, where we canna help us? Ane of them is a king's man, we are sure, and the other to my mind is a great deal worse. Baith o' them are in disguise: and a man who will put on a false face for ane thing will do it for anither. It would not surprise me to fin' ourselves corbie's meat before the mornin'."

Some of the young men were so impressed with this speech of Grant, that they offered to ride forward and bring the two scouts back. But this was overruled by the general opinion of their honesty. Indeed, Grant himself did not believe all he said, for he added:

"I took quite a liking to that chiel Clarence frae the first; he tauld such a straught story, and for ane, I am ready to fecht for him, and for his sister when it comes to blows."

Teunis, having Clarence in charge, felt all the responsibility of a man, on whom the success of a great enterprise depends; but so far from sinking under the burden, that he grew stronger, able to endure anything, or to accomplish the most difficult undertaking. He was casting about in his mind the different ways which it might be best for him to pursue, when quick as a flash he fixed on the most perilous—being none else than that through which Elsie had led Miss Clinton two nights before this.

The two young men climbed a tree, so as to get a full view. The sky was lurid, and the din that rose from the camp of Brandt and his allies was ominous of coming war. This, however, was a proof of unconsciousness concerning an enemy approaching. Clarence looked down, with the eye of a romantic youth, as well as of a soldier; and as he saw the fires ranged in a half circle, cut by a deep, dark gulf at the distance, he imagined a thousand things of which he had read and dreamed of the red man.

Round each fire, men were seen moving like the black

spirits of pandemonium. The few days they had been there had quieted the rude, and made the intelligent more reflective; still there were songs and coarse jests going on, which made the woods ring with their noise.

"Is that high ground we see there on the south?" said Clarence, after a pause.

"Yes, sir," said Teunis, in a whisper, for he knew that sentinels were near. "Your soldierly eye is laying out the battle for to-morrow, but the Mohawk has not left himself without a way of retreat."

"Well for him," said the other, now also under his breath, "for, I declare, it makes my nerves tingle to see how easily the whole might be surprised, and put to flight. But how I should like to see all these dusky warriors start up at the sound of the trumpet."

"The war-whoop you mean, sir; but it makes the Dutch blood in my veins curdle when I see these fiends, not soldiers, hiding themselves till the time comes for them to shoot out their fiery tongues."

"You are right, friend Teunis; as I look down, my memory helps me to words that suit the scene before us well: 'It was a place for the habitations of carnal sinners. The winds, full of stiffened voices, buffeted their souls, forever whirling them away to and fro, dashing them, the one against the other.' There is a crowd driven in a body like *dark stars* by a sulphureous blast."

Teunis, who never had heard of Dante, and was in no mood for imaginary description, said in low tones, as if afraid the Mohawk might hear him, "You may distinguish Brandt's tent by its standing in front of all the rest; can you see figures moving?"

"I do," said the young scholarly soldier, replying in the words of the same poet; "''Tis hell, thick smoke carved into images black, yet lustrous; shapes of dignity, they dwell apart.'"

The two young men, descending from the tree, prepared for the morrow. Already Clarence had determined on joining the army of the Mohawk, as the surest way of keeping the dishonorable Clifford in view. But before he could do that effectually, he must change the dress he had on, and obtain, if possible, one of those disguises which Teunis and others had assumed. He communicated his purpose to his companion, who, though he feared the result, saw in it a boldness, which would, if anything, insure it success. At the worst he could reveal himself, and thus claim the protection of the Mohawk.

"You may obtain this," said Teunis, when Clarence inquired for the disguise, "for the king's clink. There are plenty of such garments to be had down there."

"Well, go, and I will remain here for a time; my blood boils and I need sleep to cool my brain; I shall lie down here for an hour or two."

"Not there," said Teunis; "but come with me and you shall have the bed that your sister and Elsie had on the night I have told you of."

"None better than that where I can dream of her and of home."

With that, Teunis led his companion to the place of repose already described, which he spread with branches and a fur robe he had at hand, and advised Clarence not to stir till the word of the party was given before sunrise.

They parted with this understanding.

CHAPTER II.

THE HEAD IN THE LION'S MOUTH.

"Honesty is current coin; uprightness is fine silver; probity, gold without alloy; but integrity is gold, tried and purified."

OLD DIVINE.

OUR young Dutchman, left once more alone to his own thoughts, was feeling every moment more heavily upon him the pressure of his responsibility. Everything appeared to depend upon his prudence and his boldness. The young soldier he had just parted with trusted him; the two he had seen in the morning at the falls, were waiting his return at sunrise; to-morrow the Dominie had pledged himself on Teunis's behalf; the mysterious being in the hollow was expecting a visit from him at midnight; Martin, father of Elsie, had begun to trust him; and above all these reasons, was the consideration that Elsie herself had made his fidelity to this good cause the price of her heart to him. Never did he feel till this moment that so much depended upon his faithfulness and wisdom. Under all of these obligations he did not stagger. His foot pressed the ground more firmly at every step, while he moved cautiously, where he knew the sentinels were posted; courageously going forward, he resolved at once to present himself at the camp, and thus ascertain for himself the exact state of things, and of the plan for to-morrow. Veering a little to the right, he heard voices, which made him turn from the path into the bushes, where he lay down. Putting his ear to the ground, he quietly waited for the return of the party that he knew were near. There were two of them, who came back slowly, like men who had sauntered aside for free conversation.

"I will cover you from all blame, as your superior. Acting under me, you only fulfill his majesty's orders. Have I not shown you the letter of the general, to burn and take all the prisoners, and to do nothing by halves?"

"Mohawk is his own chief," was the proud answer of the other; "Indians cannot see the mark of the goose's wing. They love the scalping-knife better. Braves cannot be tickled with a feather."

"Captain Brandt," was the hasty reply of the first speaker, "does not doubt my honor." There seemed as if there was some handling of a sword-hilt here at this time. "Have not I left my command at Fort Niagara, at the word of one of your red race? I have met you here to aid in conducting these prisoners back through the wilderness. Surely that is evidence of my sincerity, and of my interest in the success of this enterprise. And now, just when it is about to be crowned with complete success, you threaten to leave."

By this time the two men had become so much in earnest in their conversation that they stood facing each other quite opposite to the spot where Teunis lay quiet: for well he knew that his life depended on his keeping in his breath. Yet he trembled lest the beating of his pulse at the wrist would disturb the dry leaves on which he lay.

"Clifford was a great soldier when he fought the Whigs on the sand-fields of the Dutchmen. Clifford has all the fort of Ni-a-a-ga-ra in his great hand; but the king's great soldiers have soft hearts when pale squaws come between their fiery eyes and the moon."

There was a sly irony in all this; all the more provoking that it could not be met by an honorable blow.

"Cheeks that smile like the young morning, bring tears into great eyes," was the still aggravating tone of the same speaker. At last the other man broke out into fury unrestrained.

"I tell you what, brave Mohawk, that pale squaw must be mine, and if I can buy your help in bringing her into the camp before you leave, there is nothing that the Great King has put into my hand which Brandt may not command."

"The Mohawk cannot be bought with fair words; and if he could, his braves are turning their faces to the north star, where their squaws are husking corn, and their papooses singing in their swings."

"Well, I must be content and let you all go," was the infuriated answer. "But I remain till I gain my reward. Good God," said the speaker called Clifford, "am I to be baffled by a sentimental miss, and that Dutch dumpling which Kiskataam says has her in charge. No, I'll scour these woods till my toes are worn to stumps, or blistered as they have been under a Bengal sun, before I yield to this piece of painted flesh."

All this time the speaker was stamping with violent rage on the ground as if he could bring up relief from the nether regions. His comrade for the time was quietly standing till the storm would vent itself; which, like all such gusts, was soon over; and the man who was calling up spirits from the vasty deep, gave it up by saying:

"I can at least control Kiskataam and his foil by the glittering metal."

"Ugh!" was the short interjection of the Indian, "Kiskataam's good hunter for himself. A fawn will leap and play well in his wigwam on the silver water of Ka-na-we-hol-a."

The white man, at this home thrust, which he evidently felt in the tenderest part, could not express himself, but gave out that choking utterance which a man gives when his breath fails him. "I know," said he at last, "that the serpent has tried to crawl into my nest, and all my fear is that he knows too well of the hiding-place where Miss Clinton is kept; and that he only waits to weary us out. But I will die first."

"Miss Clinton! Miss Clinton," was echoed by the Mohawk. "Who is this fawn that the great soldier calls Miss Clinton? The great Englishman called her Fawn."

"Who should she be but the papoose of that rank Whig Clinton, one of the rebel generals? That is prize enough to wait a week for;" and here he bent his mouth to the ear of the Indian—the last word heard was "ransom."

"The Mohawks do not make war on pale-faced squaws. We leave when the next sun rises."

With that the two went on toward the camp; and as Teunis followed he heard Clifford chiding his companion for his tender heartedness. "Mohawk is a woman. I have a stronger heart than any of you. Delicate women whose veils were never lifted to man, have begged from me and I have turned away. The valley of the Ganges, wider than the one below, groaning with misery, and putrid with death, did not move me. Under my windows I saw the river Hoogly rolling with corpses; the streets of Calcutta blocked with the dying. The living not strong enough to scare away the jackals and the vultures from the scarcely dead bodies."

All of this was said to impress the Mohawk with the folly of being tender hearted; to which he merely replied with his significant "ugh !" and

"Clifford is a great soldier; the Mohawk shall go after the next day is past."

"Go and be ——" as he turned right round, leaving the Mohawk to enter the camp alone, while he plunged into the bushes aside, as if he wished to hide himself from the stars. Teunis only heard "curse him! curse her," repeated till he lost the sound and the sight alike.

The listener justified himself in hearkening to what ought to be counteracted if possible, more especially as he had obtained valuable information for the risk he had run. So making his way as quietly as he could, without appearing to steal in, he found out his brother Anthony's tent, who was there having a command. When they parted in the morning they had an understanding between them that Teunis should make a call at home as he passed, just to see how things "*kaam* on, and help for an hour or so." Anthony was not in the tent when his brother entered, so addressing one who was always known by the shortest part of his name:

"You here yet Phill? I feared that by this time you would be all away to Niaagaara."

"Nay, nay," said the other pettishly, "dat big soger, has de ooren ov de Indian o'er near his mouth. Budt end vere hast tou been, Teunie? bad talk here."

"What now, Phill?" said the new comer, with well-feigned astonishment. "Where is Broder Anthony?"

That kind hearted youth who loved Teunis better than his own life, and who felt all the anxiety of an earnest soul for him, had been out watching for the wanderer, so that he might put him on his guard. Coming merely into the tent door, he gave a signal which brought Teunis out into the dark, where they stood out of sight and hearing.

"Teunic," said Anthony, in a low husky voice, "thee had best gae home and watch te old folks."

"What now?" said the no less anxious brother. "What have I done that I cannot be with you at the great hunt?"

"We have not time," was the answer, "to speak of all. Whispers have been going through the camp all day. Awee! awee! for fayther, if the half of this be true, he will shoot you though he die of grief afterward."

Teunis would have entered into his own defence warmly, but the other stopped him, putting his arm into that of Teunis, leading him round, so as to reach the higher point at the south of the camp, where they had the opportunity of seeing all that was going on below. Anthony told his brother to watch the movements of two or three men whom he pointed out. The three figures Teunis soon discerned to be Kiskataam, Shandaagan and Dan, De-la-mater, a well-known desperate fellow, who aspired to the hand of Elsie Schuyler, and was thus the decided enemy of Teunis.

"Can you guess what all that means?" was the question put to the transfixed Teunis. "They are searching the tent; if you had been there till this time, your arms would have been tied behind your back. Or a ball through somebody before that could have been done. Anthony, I killed a catamount this morning, and I am not likely to let any villain, as all these are, put a cord round my wrists without a struggle."

"I have heard of two catamounts being killed, and am proud that my brother had the power and the skill to kill one of these monsters; but mind you, Teunis, that there are worse creatures than catamounts."

"True, as I see down there. But, Anthony, were as many of these wild beasts to be collected, as there are men below, they would sleep quieter and devour less; and I have been thinking that an animal with a red coat is more savage than one with a dun-colored one. The feet of the human beast are swifter to seek blood."

"Let that alone just now; you better leave before they surround the camp, and rouse up these Mohawk duivels, and you will find them to be a drove of catamounts. We are going out to-morrow to hunt up two Whig women, and you can guess who one of them is."

For that reason I must remain and protect her against harm."

"You cannot aid her in the smallest mite. After what I saw at the burning of Hoogenhuisen, I am sure that you will be less able to stand the onset, when the flower of that place is laid on the ground, and trampled upon by ruffians."

"I would send a ball through the man that dares to put a foul finger on that flower of my heart."

"Neither Dan Del-de-la-mater nor Shandaagan will keep away the less that you look gloom at them. Two men and an Indian for one woman, and she a Whig's dochter, must be in these times too many for you."

The tear was rising in the eye of the anxious lover, so that it glistened in the light of the bright fire, and trickled down upon the hand of the kind-hearted Anthony so as to startle him into earnestness.

"In the name of God, Teunis Roe, go; they will get a glimpse of that face in the light of the fire, and a ball will come from some one of these pieces, that never errs. Your eyes are glancing like a deer's at the river side, when pine knots are blazing in the boat. You have shot them in the eene yourself; go, I beseech you."

Almost overcome, Teunis began, "And you will be"——

"Oh, Teunis, I know what you would say; and I swear to you, that Whig as Elsie is, and the real dochter of a true Whig, that I will protect her with my life, for your sake. Go, Teunie go, and mother's God be with you."

"Swear again, and I will go; swear that you will not let them tie her, nor let Dan put one hand on her, and whisper in her ear that you do all for the sake of your wandering brother Teunie."

With that the down-hearted youth stepped over the face of the cliff by a natural ladder that he had frequently used before, and was no more in danger of missing his foot than by that of his father's barn, so that he was soon out of the reach of those sluith hounds who were already on his track. A vain pursuit amidst those rugged rocks and fallen trees.

Directing his steps northward to where the Dominie's party was lodged, he fell now into their hands from necessity. While the sympathies of his better nature were always with the Whigs, it is doubtful if he would have declared so soon for them, but from affection first, and now through necessity. Treading his way, as a hunter only knows how, among loose rocks and underbrush, thick as an East Indian jungle, with not a few of the dangers found in Bengal, from American tigers, Teunis moved with his knife in one hand, and his horse-pistol in the other, looking on all sides for enemies. But he had no choice but of escaping thus, nor had he any fear of being waylaid, except as some cunning hunter from above might have descended from the opposite side of the rock, and was lying in wait for his passing by. He disturbed not a few of the wildcats of the place, as he knew from their hissing and spitting sound, which would have been mistaken for serpents by a less acute sense. His aim was now the spook's den, but ere he could reach that he must come across the camp of the Dominie, where he could not rest in security till the appointed time for meeting the spook arrived. So keeping the north star in his eye, he moved on like the sailor, tacking as he found a favorable breeze. Turning round a jutting rock, avoiding some chasm, or leaping a fallen trunk, he never once lost sight of the point of his attraction.

CHAPTER III.

THE AFRICAN COURT-MARTIAL.

"Commend me to Nature, spiced over by the hand of Art; the one provides hunger, and the other sauce; so that between Nature and Art, you sit smacking your lips.'

OLD COOKERY BOOK.

OUR night walker, uncertain concerning the character of the sounds he heard, dropped himself quietly and suddenly to the ground, where he put his ear, hoping to be able to distinguish the voices which gave them forth.

"Some frolickers," said Teunis, "who have found the camp above too quiet. Maybe some Indians on an independent excursion. Both must be avoided by me to-night. I can neither join the one, nor be seen by the other. Ha!" said the listener, "these are niggers; what can they be at here, and at this time of night? But why need I wonder, they are just like all vermin; they follow the white man, and mock his ways. Why not? They have as good a right to their fun and fight as we have to ours."

Climbing up on the point of a jutting rock, he saw a fire

kindled in a hollow place, which he knew must be near to the cloven rock, where he had himself often rested, and which was a standing mark to all. Many a cup of good Holland had been drunk there by the hunting parties, who were sure to gather round it after their surroundings, and at night to make it their pillow before a rousing fire. The Dominie, after one of those frolics, which had gone to excess, came down on the sinners in a thundering discourse, in which he called this the *steen des aanstoots*—the stone of stumbling; and by that it was known among his folks, till one day the good man himself came across a party handing the cuppe round, and seeing him coming they obtained one of pure water running through the rock, and gave it to him. He tasted it, drinking it off with a loud smack of his lips, at the last saying, "Deszen Mozusst eenrots!" and it is called Moses Rock unto this day.

Cautiously Teunis crept forward till he was near enough to distinguish the shrill tenor of the negro, with the deeper bass of some white men; then a loud chorus of laughter, which went from the giggle to the guffaw. Determined to find out who these roysterers were, he sought as close a standing place as he could find, without being seen himself. Keeping well up to the westward, he came down, almost crawling, as if swimming on his back, feet foremost, to the side of the rock, which he had between him and the assemblage below. Rising up, he looked over and saw such a scene as gipsy life can only present. A large fire burning brightly in the centre, sent out a heat which made the party turn round as brown hams hung on a spit would turn were they possessed of feeling, and waiting for a regular roasting all over, and through to the bone. Here were all colors, from the jet black, glistening with sweat, to the bronze, that changed as the fancy was tickled, on to the whity-brown of those called white people.

Teunis knew them all as the slaves belonging to the farmers of the district; chiefly the same ones he had seen in the den two nights ago, attending their superstitious orgies. Cuffee, the African king, as he maintained himself to be; Cæse, with his fiddle; Jerry of Kaatsban; and Tom, the Dominie's man. These were usually the leaders in all mischief around, and though very stringent laws existed in the colonies concerning slaves meeting after nightfall, they were easily eluded by such cunning fellows, who, like thieves, knew more of the laws than the average of justices. Strong in mind naturally, and not degraded yet by long bondage, experience had made them acute in matters where their enjoyments were in danger, or their gratifications curtailed.

To Teunis they now seemed to be engaged holding a court, whether in mockery or in earnest, he had some difficulty in determining. Cuffee was the presiding spirit, as he usually was in all affairs of the kind. His sincere belief, or his assumption, gave him airs which he was not slow to put on, and being of a robust person, and possessed of great shrewdness, he generally enforced the law by physical force.

Tom was the only one who disputed his authority, and this he did, *first*, because the king was a heathen; and *second*, he himself being a Christian, should "*hab authorities*;" and *third*, the Dominic's man affected a little of the Dominie himself. From his place and puffed up pride, he had begun to assume it, and latterly he really believed he had had a call to preach.

At the time Teunis discovered these blacks, Cuffee was acting as judge, trying a young negro, whom the secret spectator at once knew; and he soon saw that this was not mere sport, but that Cuffee and his followers, presuming upon their relation to the big Indian, were acting for King George, in due legal form, which, to one who was a mere spectator, might have afforded amusement; but to Teunis, who had now wakened up to the danger of his own playmate, was no joking matter. He determined to watch and prevent mischief.

Tom acted as public prosecutor, and Jerry, the slave of Cornelius Wynkoop, was to defend the accused.

"Constable, cry de court," said the judge, with great gravity, when old Cæsar stepped forward in front of the raised bench, and mumbled over, "oh yeez, oh yeez," and left the rest in an unknown tongue.

A ludicrous imitation of a white man's trial here followed, which would defy the pen or pencil of genius to portray in its true colors. What was of more importance to our hero, the scenes were indicative to him of how the public mind was beginning to regard his own present position. Leendert, who was the son of Dora, and of the same age with himself, had, like all negroes brought up side by side with a master's son, walked in the steps of Teunis, till it had become his own nature to do whatever his young master did. He was showing signs of disloyalty now, and those of his grade had detected his tendencies. In the trial he was passing through, Teunis saw his own self foreshadowed.

A charge was formally made of leaving the service of King George, and taking part with the "revels." A jury was chosen, and exact specifications laid down to be proven. In all of which Teunis heard but his own case repeated. The pleadings on both sides were ludicrous indeed, but it seemed that the actors were in earnest.

"Bring in de prisoner guilty of treason," said the mock judge, "and den shoot him."

Teunis was here about to take part, and prevent what appeared to be the actual intention of the cool rascal, whose words seemed as positively spoken as if he were sitting in an Albany court, among his white peers; when suddenly, out of the darkness behind, old Dora emerged, to the great terror of all, including the chief actor himself. Rising, he made a low bow, saying:

"King Cuffee glad to see Queen Dora wid the Gree Gree."

Dora paid no attention to the salaam made to her presence, but turning her eye into a clear crystal cup she held in her hand, she muttered some words of incantation; then lifting her face to the judge, said in her most solemn style:

"King Gongalloo hang on de gallows dree."

Cuffee had already ordered the prisoner's arms to be unloosed; and then he called out:

"Court 'journed till abter suppa."

"'Men, so let it be," said Tom, who was man of all work at home and abroad.

A long pole, laid from two branches, sustained two pots of the biggest size in use, which were simmering over a fire of hot coals, filled to the brim. The acting cook, a full-bodied wench, was looking in now and then, stirring the contents, and scenting the savory steam that entered even Teunis' nostrils, making his mouth to water; for he had not eaten a warm supper since the night of Tobias Myers' husking-bee. Besides being really hungry, he knew well enough that the purveyors of this feast had found the best in the land. He forgot the robbing of hen-roosts, and nearly in his eagerness for food, yielded up his prudence. It was evidently in the mind of Cuffee, that young Massa Teunis had been guilty of double-dealing, and would be punished when caught. With all these willing hands about him, a larger prize than Leendert would be acceptable. There were, besides, some persons present, whose backs were toward him, and as yet he had not heard their voices above a common tone.

The festival table was the ground, raised as if a ditch had been dug round a knoll, into which the feet might be stowed away, and the edge of the bank used as seats. Many of them chose the flat places, squatting down on whatever was below them. There were at least fifty or sixty persons of the black population, with at least a dozen young whites—sons of the farmers, whose low tastes led them to seek such frolics, where the animal propensities could be gratified unrestrained. One individual kept himself hidden, notwithstanding that he lay on the ground, just below where Teunis was perched on the branch above. The spy in the tree had his fears that it might be known to the groundling that some one was in the loft.

The supper dishes were large sugar troughs, usually left in the woods for the spring opening, now washed clean in the water near by, and convenient for the revellers. Into these the contents of the boilers were poured—meat and potatoes in heaps. In the centre stood a monstrous dish of fricasseed chickens, mixed with sausages. The fowls "'greed vell wid von anoder," Dido said, "dat had been fechten cocks in de mornin'."

"An de duck swim in de gravy vell as in de pond wid de oder unda dem vings," was the intended wit of old Cæsar, who gave some extra scrapes upon his fiddle, as he saw his favorite dish.

But the attraction of the take were two full trenchers of what is known as souse; a well-grown pig's flesh, fat, and corn-fed, cut up into small pieces and stewed, all together, till it became soft and rich. Dido was in her glory when she saw that come up, slightly browned in the skin and tender to the touch.

"Dere a mess for de king, and de Dominie besides might say grace as long as turkey's neck dat runs to him's tail behind."

And to hungry men, seldom has a finer repast been spread. All sat round as they chose. Forks there were in plenty. A twig cut from the bush beside them, with a stump for handle, and the bark peeled, was equal to the best silver in the governor's-basket of plate. That stuck in at random, never failed to bring up the game that gratified the eater.

Bread came out from corners as white as Dame Dyce could produce to her New York company, in her fine stone mansion, by the Kaatskill creek; and to crown all, there was cold slaugh, and hot slaugh, which was forked into their mouths as if they were stowing away heaps of manure into a deep cellar way.

"Ho! ho! ho!" roared out Cuffee, as he fished out a huge piece which he saw would be his last bit from that platter, "me got de gobla crop; dat goes for to hollo orda!"

"He! he! he!" responded one of the young wenches; "King Cuffee got de goose's throat. Goose make good squia."

Here the faithful Phœbe produced her liquor jug, well filled with strong waters of some kind, that had the usual effect upon human brains. All kinds of frolicking commenced, and some of a nature that could not be described without defiling my page. Savage nature came out in its most loathsome forms, such as we read of in histories of paganism at its feasts. Looking down upon them, Teunis saw the rolling and tumbling as if it had been the wriggling of black snakes, in a round pit.

During the noise, our night-walker had climbed to the outmost part of the branch. He was eager upon finding out who was lying beneath him on the ground, and had just succeeded to his horror, when Cuffee cried out:

"Now for de trile of de Ingen Shandaagan, for falling in'd love wid Martin's Elshie—Clerk will read de law."

Here Tom, who had heard it many times, gravely repeated the colonial statute: "De durd Sessions of de fif Assembly Queen Anne. Be it 'nacted by de Gobernor, Council, and Assembly, in case any slave or Ingen, kiss, or marry, or court free man's daughter"——

Here the Indian, who took all this more in earnest than was intended, and who had worked himself up, under the influence of love, liquor, and mortification, rose just under the nose of Teunis, and gave the war-whoop of his tribe, so lustily, and so long, with his face turned toward the mountain, that the echoes of his voice returned as if a thousand demons had responded to him. Every man, white and black, started to his feet and fled as if the Mohawks had come into their midst with gleaming tomahawks. Nor was the commotion abated by Teunis, who, eager to see the whole from his perch, had gone so far forward on the branch that it swung, so that he lost his balance and dropped right among them, fronting the infuriated Indian, who became cool in a moment, when he saw the very man he cared less to see than any other, before him, as if demanding satisfaction for the injury with which he had just been charged.

"Ugh," said the red man, as a grim smile crossed his face, "the young bear can climb trees for sweet apples."

"And sometimes he gets sour apples for his pains," was the tart answer of the excited Teunis. The fact alluded to in the mock charge of this black court, was evidently understood by those eavesdroppers at home and abroad. He had suspected all along that the intention of Kiskataam was to remove the young English lady to the West, and the reward of Shandaagan was to be his own beloved. Putting all he knew in one, he was persuaded within himself, that the hiding-place of the young woman was known to these wily men. But there was no time to settle that question to-night, so turning away from his enemy, he stepped up to the souse dish, and putting a fresh fork into the mess, he proceeded to eat a hearty supper from the abundant fragments which remained. By the time he was through, the leading spirits of the late scene had disappeared, afraid of being informed upon. They knew the law well, and Tom in his mock fun had reminded them that

"It sall no' be lawful for more as tree niggers to meet together in von place, 'cept at kirke door on Sunday, upon de penalty of been whipt upon de naked back, wid forta lashes by de public whipper, Yankee Dorlan, the horse-doctor."

The fear of this was constantly before the eyes of the slaves, and even Cuffee did not care to be seen by a man of Teunis' character. Tom, however, came back, assuming to be loyal, and willing to excuse himself for being present with a crew of black rebels.

"The Dominic would look wild to see you here, Tom," said Teunis.

"And vilder to see us two," said Tom, as he winked a sly wink. "VE vatched dem;" putting weight on the plural word WE.

CHAPTER IV.

REVENGE IS SWEET.

"Come, dainty witch; see, there's my palm;
Read if you can; I dare to hear.
Witch.—Yet the hand trembles, and feels
Clammy, like the wall of a shut up tomb."
ALLAN RAMSAY.

TEUNIS and Tom made their way to the camp, where Grant kept guard. Among the first questions asked of the brawny Scotchman was, "where's the Dominie?"

"He's gane doun the glen to that warlock bodie. They are baith ow're weel acquaint with the diel. He is, nae doot, sitten atween them."

"Has he been long away?" was the next question put.

"Oh, yes; but when twa sic meet, nae sayin' when they will part: but for mysel', I would as sune hae a crack with auld Sawney as we' ane o' his bairns."

"Oh!" said a new comer, whom Teunis had not seen in the party that day, "you are mistaken, Grant; the hermit is not one of your Scotch witches, but a respectable spook as can be found in a Christian land, where it takes all kinds of people to make the right kind of a world."

"May be, sir," said the Scotchman, who turned to Teunis and asked with evident feeling, "where did you leave that fine Englisher, Clarence? has he heard ony thing o' his sister? his heart was sae in his mouth when he spoke about her that I began to suspect she might be a bit tenderer than a sister. There is nae accounting for such things. Bluid is aye thicker than water."

"I am going down the hill, Mr. Grant," said Teunis; "and I would hint to you that there are Indians about, who have ears that hear a great way off; and their noses can smell tobacco smoke a mile away; and you can see the fires of Brandt's party are not much beyond that distance."

"You are quite richt, sir, and I maun awa roun' all the outposts and see after things. I have heard my father, honest man, say, that when he was out in the forty-five, that he smelt King George's poother frae Loch Awe to Fort George. Good nicht with you; I'll see you in the mornin', and we'll hae a crack aboot these things."

"A beautiful night it is, Grant; but it may be an awful morning," said Teunis, his mind running in a mournful direction.

"Yes, man, that is a bonny sky. It is grand to stand up here and view that crown in the heavens. It sends me awa back again, where I herded sheep on the braes of Balquidder; when I used to watch these very stars, as they gaed round like clock-work, tellen me the time o' night. Man, hoo happy I been sometimes rolled in my plaid; and thinkin' whiles on the great Creator, and whiles on Susy McLaren. Poor thing, she was ta'en awa fra me, far aboon those stars; and I am here this very night, on ither kind o' hills, herden Indians; kittle kind of sheep, and no' a lamb among them, if we leave out that puir lad's sister."

"Yes," said Teunis, touched with this fit of tenderness on the side of Grant; "there is another besides her that I am interested in; and she is not my sister."

"Aye, man, I suspected as much as that; I'm an aulder man than you, but my heart is no altogether so cauld but I can feel for you, when I think on Susy McLaren. There's my han', Teunie, and depend on't, if Hughie Grant can help you or yours out o' trouble, he'll do it wi' right gude pleasure. Noo, awa wi' you to the glen."

Teunis left, nor was he long in reaching the foot of the hill, which he had travelled frequently; and he went now with more confidence because of his appointment with the mysterious being: still, putting his hand into his bosom, he pulled out the black pebble stone; touching the spring, so that he might be ready should danger come in his way. In spite of his convictions, his feelings dwelt on the superstitious at the time; and as he drew nearer to the door, the quicker his heart beat in his breast,

"I would not consult this witch of a creature were the Dominie not near me," he said to himself. "I must, however, wait till the two part from each other."

He came up to the door of the shanty and saw the flickering light between the crevices of the logs, that had been laid up of old, by some trapper or trader, who had built them for shelter while he gathered his peltries from the Indians during a winter's hunting and trading campaign. It served now another purpose, and long had had the reputation of being the Geest Housen. Teunis, knowing that a window was open at the rear, stepped cautiously round, that he might first ascertain the state of things within. Putting his ear to the opening, which was covered by the skin of some animal, he heard voices in earnest conversation. There was a small slit which allowed him to see or hear, but not at the same moment of time. His first effort at seeing was to obtain a perfect look of the cabin; so, fixing his eye on the fire, which had been newly supplied with pine knots and cones, he watched till the blaze broke through, when he saw three sides of the den. Two of these were covered with skins of different kinds of animals, inhabitants of the region; some of them undressed; but the most of them tanned after the Indian manner of preparing furs. These served as clothing for the person of the inhabitant out of doors, and for the bed of the restless solitary at night. Guns and pistols of different patterns, with other hunting apparatus, were suspended on deer's antlers, which were the hooks for all things that were hung up. Above the place where the couch was made, a naked sword gleamed as if alive when new fuel sent forth flame. The scabbard depended on another hook hard by, and was ornamented with some precious metal. Besides those necessary articles of furniture, there were things of which the observer could not see the use so easily. A large paper globe was suspended from the roof, covered with figures of beasts and birds, serpents and men. On the wall on the left side, were pictures, which, so far as Teunis could distinguish, were more of demoniacal than of human shape.

These observations were made at a glance, for the mind of the slow Dutchman was now excited to the highest pitch, and comprehended in a minute what an hour could not have unfolded to him at another time. As we may suppose, it was the living human figures which chiefly arrested his attention. There were two men, one on each side of the fire. The Dominie he knew, and only observed that he was in his most dignified posture. If possible, more so than when he sat in the President's chair in the Consistory. He had never seen him before with a face in which intelligence and goodness struggled so much for the ascendency. His usual humor lay hidden away in the deep lines that surrounded his eyes, and his mouth; and yet while he sat gravely, like a man who was conscious of his place and power, he yielded a deference to the man before him, which Teunis had never hitherto seen him do. But this was the first superior he had ever seen in the presence of the greatest man on the Kaatskills. The other man was of tall and upright carriage, with a head like one that was accustomed to command. His face closely shaven, and neck bare, he seemed more like one sitting in a city mansion, than the rough unshaven creature that interrupted him on his way two days ago. The obeisance given him by the Dominie—who called no man master—showed him to be of some distinction. Perhaps a messenger from the Provincial authorities, proffering help; or, after all, he might indeed be a real wizard able to change his appearance like Satan himself.

At that instant a change from one position to another gave Teunis a chance of seeing him more closely, when he almost called out "that is none else than Captain Whittesley that caused so much commotion in Sopus, the other day." Teunis had read in the Arabian Nights' entertainment, of persons going through such transformations, but he had ever believed it to be but a fable; and he almost trembled when he remembered how Granny Hoffman had said, with her long skinny finger lifted up, "Teunie, Teunie, never look on ole duivel wid hisn young face."

It was while Teunis was conning over this warning, that the object of his scrutiny turned his eyes in the direction of the place where he was standing so intently, that the hidden spectator's blood ran chill. Rising from his seat by the fire, he took down his pistols, and coming directly to the window where Teunis stood, he thrust his hand so quickly that the looker in had just time to squat on the ground, and let the inmate fire over his head, one pistol after another, followed by a similar discharge of guns, that it seemed as if the cloves and the gulf were sending back their reverberations which increased in loudness as the several pieces were fired off. The state of Teunis's nervous system made him believe that the artillery he heard must be something more than earthly; and had he been threatened with a muzzle at his ear, he would have sunk dead on the ground, so feeble were his knees when he attempted to rise. Recovering from his fear, he heard the voices again within, and ventured to look once more. This time the skin was left a little aside, so that he could hear and see at the same time. The stranger was reloading the pieces, bestowing great care upon the manner as well as upon the matter in hand.

"You are very precise and attentive to these Boanerges. Do you suppose that they will speak their thunder any louder, or with more effect," said the Dominie, who was evidently asking not for information, for he knew as well as others, but because he was leading a conversation.

"Reverendissimo Domino, know you not that a little more or a little less powder would either fail to carry, or scatter the shot without doing the execution; I am confident that Leyden taught you that loud thunder is not lightning."

"True sir, but I find that thunder frightens more people than the lightning; and when you have more powder in the flask than shot in the pouch, what is to be done but let fly, and you may chance to hit."

"Thrown away, Reverendissimo Domino, know this, that a little more or less would fail, as I said; so look here, this thimbleful is worth more than a hornful. Your piece may chance to kick you over in the—I beg pardon—pulpit. I give you this illustration from Leyden."

"You would say," said the reverend expounder, "that short sermons, short prayers, spoken cool and quiet, to saint and sinner are best. But tell me if you ever in the heat of battle thought on the thimbleful. Nature is then above all rules."

"Reverendissimo Domino, nature in war, work or worship, is but wisdom, requiring the true expression, whether it is to be given by Captain or Doctor Theologi. Be in earnest. The heart, your reverence; the heart in the right place, and then fire away wisely."

"Old Cromwell's advice, 'trust in Providence, and keep your powder dry.' Just as I said, honorable captain, nature is above all rules; and a few grains of powder more or less is not thought of. Thimblefuls in the heat of battle, sounds like folly."

"Ah! but Reverendissimo Domino, we measure the powder before the battle begins," was the deliberate words of the man loading the piece; who as deliberately took out a few grains from the thimbleful.

"As we soldiers of King Immanuel should do," was the quiet reply of the reverend man, "I accept the good advice. I have seen many a good sermon lost, by scattering the points: just as I did myself in a flock of pigeons when my piece was overloaded. To drop figure, I see that you are in earnest there, preparing for battle. If so, please to inform me, captain."

"Remember," was the quick reply of the other, "that you are not at liberty to use that title here nor elsewhere above your breath. After to-morrow I hope to throw aside all disguise, but I must first have revenge. The face of a dying mortal follows me everywhere, crying revenge! For that have I yielded up king, country and rank. Thanks to the Almighty, he has heard my prayer, and brought my enemy close to me. Now hear me, O God, again, and let him not elude my hand—the hand of justice—a second time, as he did once before."

These last words were uttered with exceeding bitterness and while the loading went on. There was a deep determination expressed as the wadding was rammed in, that seemed to say: "now let it belch forth fire and blood." There was a pause in the conversation here as if the operator was afraid to trust his feelings in words, and the Dominie was too prudent to attempt making way for the torrent that he saw lay behind. When he spoke, it was cautiously; but venturing, he said:

"Revenge, my dear sir, is a fiery demon; and I have marvelled if that be not the reason why he deals so much in powder and ball."

"Reverendissimo Domino, there you are wrong again. A pistol is a gentleman, and a musket is a hero. If they fall into malicious hands the fault is with the demon that uses them. It is the stiletto and the poison bowl that act the coward. That pistol in my hands is the executioner of justice; and all I want is to have such a good judge as yourself to see that justice is done without malice. It shall be dealt out as the Almighty apportions it to the sinner, when he sends down his thunderbolts: God's firearms have no malice in their execution."

"Noble sir, hear what that God says 'vengeance is mine.' It is too sweet a morsel, the heathen said, for a mortal man. The sinner should be dealt with according to his sin; but we must wait God's time."

"Reverendissimo ministro verbi Dei. 'He that sheddeth man's blood by man shall his blood be shed.' Wait God's time! O Heaven! have I not waited thy time, and thanks to thy great name, it has now come. You will say this yourself, Reverendissimo Domino, when I have rehearsed my history of wrongs in your ear, and my vows."

"Most honorable sir, you have hinted these things to me before, and I am anxious to be able to vindicate your honor, when you are gone, for you say that you must go."

"When my duty is performed, and that will be when my

vow is fulfilled. But mark, Reverendisimo Domino, how that Providence, in which you believe, and which I am now forced to believe in, has brought the sinner to the place of his end."

"But have I not heard something of a decoy being used to bring on here him that you call your enemy? If so, then more than Providence has had a hand in the matter."

"Ha! and that has been revealed too; some minds, and those of the greatest number, are sieves, letting all through them. The red race have as open mouths as their neighbors. But tell me, reverend sir, if Providence does not use all sorts of instrumentalities?"

"Yes, and he also controls them, when he sees that they would go too far; I have seen a fool set a mill going, and he could not stop it; and I once saw one open the sluice out of sport, when the water broke through with a force that swept him away. It is a dangerous thing, this helping Providence."

"It is having a good course yet; to-morrow will decide the whole well, and you will say Amen."

"God grant that it may; but unless the man who holds the strings of the puppet-show, understand the machine well, he may bring up the wrong figure, at the wrong time, and spoil the whole game. A wiser one than he must direct."

"Reverendissimo Domino, be patient and you will see this special Providence here, as you would say, now: did you know all that your God has put into my hand, you would yourself urge me on to make my mark in the right time and place. I must execute justice! Woe be to me if I fulfill not this mission. I see the sword at this moment; I have seen it every night for the last year, as I lay on that skin, suspended over his head: and hear me, by the God of justice, I will have revenge."

"Perhaps you will succeed," the Dominie here interposed "but does it accord with our notions of right, and propriety that the injured should become both judge and executioner."

This argument, which went farther than the roused reasoner wished, goaded him, so that he almost screamed out in madness: "No man may come between me and my victim. I am appointed of heaven. I have prayed, planned, dreamed of this hour, and tracked him like a sleuth hound; how I have lain on that bed thinking of nothing else, till I fell asleep, and the morning found me dreaming that I had him by the throat. I have bought the service of menials and flattered the vanity of fools; made myself appear to the vulgar a simpleton, a wizard, everything, that I might see this day, and now to let him go into the hands of those who will deal daintily with him, calling it justice, lawful justice. Ha! ha! ha!"

Here the speaker rose from his seat like a maniac, smiting his hands on his forehead, and laughing again, till the echoes out of doors mocked the hoarse sounds within.

During a pause in this transport, the Dominie put in a few words, saying: "Then you have not a high opinion of Sir Henry's sense of justice."

"Why should I have a high notion of his honor? This man was my bosom friend; I took him into the sanctuary of my heart, and of my home. He betrayed me; defiled her soul, which was as pure as the driven snow which I have seen coming into my hut here. Yet she died in my arms, praying to me for my forgiveness. Freely did I pardon her; but I swore on my knees, with her still warm hand in mine, and her eyelids unclosed, that the villain who had caused this should have the full punishment. That oath is recorded in heaven, and was carried thither by her whom the villain had ruined. But where is the law on man's statute book to punish the guilty seducer? Can any tribunal restore to me my pure Augusta, or give me back my peace of mind; my home; my joyous heart! Where is the equivalent on earth! Men taunted me by pointing me to the code of honor. Honor with Satan! honor with the man who had already violated all honor! But still I offered him the justice of a soldier, and of a gentleman. He sneered at me. When I appealed to that same Sir Henry, he affected to feel for me, but he had his favorite removed, where I could not find him. He promoted him instead of disgracing him, and then I swore that they all should know and feel my justice."

"And yet you know that mercy is the darling attribute of God," was the quiet insinuation of the good man present, anxious to allay the passion of the agitated solitary, who was hiding his face a minute, till waking up he said:

"I know all that, and it is well for the Almighty, who can allow himself to wait, since time is nothing with him; he has eternity to operate in, but we mortals must be quick when the time comes.

"And yet," said the reverend visitor, "you have been very patient in your purpose, and have taken a long time."

"Yes," and this was said with a deep sigh, as if it involved a confession of guilt. I left my own colors, burning with revenge, threw myself into the ranks of you rebels, whose cause was nothing to me, as compared with my own; the authority of Washington, which you saw to-day, I purchased by pertinacity of purpose. I left the world, came here, when I found that this hut lay near to the road which leads to the west. I bought the service of Kiskataam, who has decoyed the villain hither. I bought the same Kiskataam that he might carry off another, that shall be nameless. The black, the white, you are all now helping to develop my plot."

"And is this the secret," said the astonished pastor, "of the Hermit's residence in this wild region? his walks by night, and of his journeyings and disguises by day? For this he has made up with the Jew and Christian, the deist, and the pagan. His mixing with witches and saints; his influence over the old men, and the young maidens; all, that he may be revenged on one that has injured him! Verily I shall be humbled after this, when I think of the zeal of revenge—revenge on one man."

"On two men, holy parson: the one that did the injury, and the one who sheltered the sinner. Both shall see what you Calvinists call a special Providence. God has aided me in my pursuit. What say you?"

"I could believe all you say," said the calm auditor, smiling, "were it an unbiased interpreter that preached it; but our wishes make us partial commentators, and hence law has been established as the moderator between the offender and the offended."

"As the colonies should wait for the king's law, and not have recourse to arms," was the quick retort of the recluse.

"Most honorable captain, the people waited till the law was lost sight of in despotic tyranny; and we fell back upon our natural rights."

"You help me, reverend sir; I waited till I saw there was no law for me, and I have now fallen back on my rights as a man, and it is not possible for you to overlook the advantage that is thus thrown into my hand.

"I own," said the Dominie, "you make out a good case for yourself, and on that very account, I am the more suspicious of the end in view. We are apt to be well pleased with our own creations, and call them the work of God when it suits us.

"But Reverendissimo Domino, hear. There are on the flat rock above us a band of marauders, and they have in their hands some of your own friends. They are waiting for others. That noble-hearted girl, Elsie, is one of them, and the daughter of Clinton is the other. You heard the story to-day; now tell me did I bring that young lady here? Have I detained Brandt so long that the brother has had time to come and help in the rescue? If this will teach Clinton that he ought to have done justice to me, that the hand of God has followed him, and found him in his own family, so that the very man who injured my honor, is the destroyer of his own peace, shall not the punishment of the double-dyed villain lead to the deliverance of your friends, to the restoration of the innocent girls, and to the fulfillment of my vow, and be a warning to the guilty ever afterward?"

"Amen," was the hearty response of the vanquished Dominie, whose feelings were all the time on the side of the speaker. Pipes and tobacco were now produced, where amidst the thick fumes of smoke, the theologian was eager to resume the argument on special Providence in the abstract. His antagonist fought shy, not from any inability, as was evident, but he was now too much in earnest to attend to a mere display of intellectual gladiatorship.

"I am pleased, sir, to see that our discussions held before, have had some effect upon your belief, and that those vile Arminian doctrines are abandoned."

"Venerable sir," was the half jocular reply of the other, "I am too young a convert to be congratulated on my conversion. You have just now warned me against allowing my wishes to control my faith."

"Yes, honorable captain, but you have too much philosophy, and logical acumen, not to perceive the force of that canon of the national Synod of the Reformed Church, held at Dordrecht, not"——

"Oh, yes, reverend sir, that was a great convention; I have it now before my mind. You lent me the book, and I have profited by it; but you will not refuse a cup of this good liquor, for dry argument ought to have the throat well moistened, else we are apt to stick too long at the hard points."

During these passes of intellectual debate, the stranger had put his hand into his capacious coat pocket, and produced a square bottle, which he shook kindly, before he poured out part of its contents into a wooden cup; holding it out to the Dominie, as he made those remarks, in a quiet, pleasant manner. The minister, without stopping his discourse, took the offered beverage, and with his pipe reeking in his left hand, he lifted the cup half way to his mouth, looking in the face of his entertainer, continuing to say:

"That canon is as I have said to you before"——

"Yes, sir, drink;" interrupted the other. "I know it all by heart, I have been, as you shall hear, a most diligent catechumen. 'As God himself is most wise, unchangeable, omniscient, and omnipotent, so the election made by him can neither be interrupted nor changed, recalled nor annulled; neither can the elect be cast away, nor their number diminished.' That is the article. What think you of the liquor?"

"Honorable sir, that came out of Elder Abiel's cellar. I was there on the night he returned from Jamaica. He took home a barrel of the same kind; which, somehow, has run dry very quick. I have always blamed that scoundrel Tom. But, concerning that canon—correctly repeated, verbatim; and what is better, you have expressed your belief in it."

"Reverendissimo Domino, your good health, and success to our enterprise. Your amen lingers in my ear yet, like rich music. But do you not think that the authority of that Synod of Dort, was greatly impaired in its force by the strong minority in favor of Arminius?"

"There was a majority on the right side," said the Dominie, warmly, as he emptied the second cup, "and there was Calvin, a host in himself."

"So, reverend sir, you test truth by numbers; and the quality of the man that heads them. Where would it lie now with you on one side, and your humble servant on the other?"

Solomon declares that in a multitude of counsellors, there is safety."

"Then, Reverendissimo Domino, the heathen and the papists are safe."

"Honorable sir, you know that the staff of an army is the smallest part, yet they fight the battle."

"Just as King George wanted to rule by his staff, and the many would not allow it."

The Dominie was getting warm inside and out; when his teaser said to him, "here is a subject that concerns us more just now than the Heidelburg catechism."

A large skin was spread on the wall, the fur inside. The unknown captain began to chalk out a plan upon the surface, explaining as he went along the combinations necessary for future operations. These were too intricate for Teunis to comprehend. What he could gather was enough to convince him that the Dominie and the hermit did not agree.

"Your plan, noble captain, is all made with one overwhelming thought in your mind—the punishment of your personal enemy; we cannot sacrifice the good of the whole for that single point, however intensely you may feel concerning your end. Your scheme has too much of theatrical trick and plot about it to prove in all points successful You are desirous that your enemy be made to bite the dust in the eyes of an audience, whose very presence shall humble him. We have public good in view, even though your intended victim should escape the fate he justly deserves at your hands."

The Dominie's auditor was calmed by a thrust which had so much reason in it, but persisted in saying that the arrangement of the several parties was complete, that it could not possibly fail of both humbling the guilty and effecting the public good.

"You may be disappointed in what you expect. Let me say what I think. You have woven your net with such exceeding great skill that I am now afraid that the boldness of the Mohawk and the desperate villainy of the English colonel will break it; when you may find that the wise have been caught in their own craftiness. You have heard our plan of attack, noble captain, and if you can take part in either division we can make room for you."

At this point in the discussion, the captain, as he was called, stepped forward and wrote with his chalk some figures Teunis could not at his distance decipher, but which made the Dominie start, and then give a glance round. This brought the conversation gradually to a close, as if intended to deceive some one within earshot.

"When do you expect the hermit home?" was the casual question of the Dominie. "He keeps late hours in these regions."

"All hours, reverend sir, are alike to him; and as he would not relish more company than suits him, we had better march up hill to the camp."

This Teunis only regarded as a ruse, for he saw the glance and the look which was cast at the window, and that he might not be caught eavesdropping, he slipped back into the darkness for a few minutes, intending to call at the door as soon as prudence would permit.

CHAPTER V.

THE RESTLESS SPIRIT.

"Is not this it in which my lord drinketh? Wherein indeed he divineth. And the cup was found in Benjamin's sack."

GENESIS.

TEUNIS wandered down the hollow for at least forty rods. He sought to cool his brain, which was burning with what he had witnessed, and he wished to collect his thoughts before he ventured into the presence of the man of whom the whole country were in wonder concerning. As he turned his face back toward the cabin door, he was suddenly seized from behind by two men, who proved to be the Indians Kiskataam and his follower, who had been seeking for this chance since he was in his brother Anthony's tent. One of them closed upon his arms, while the other put a hopple round his ankle, thus preventing him from resisting or running. A cloth bound over his mouth prevented his call for help. By signs not to be mistaken he was directed to pass the hermit's door; when Teunis perceived that fear of the inmate held his captors in check. All at once the words of the recluse came into his mind, "In trouble sound this whistle." Suddenly drawing his hand out of the bandage, he seized the pebble, and gave a shrill call, that made the wilds resound. The Indians, surprised, found the terrible man before their face ere they were aware of it, with old Dora and the dwarf in the rear. Torches of pitch pine showed the state of affairs to the relief of the captive. The captors, finding themselves so unexpectedly caught, fled, leaving their prisoner in the hands of his deliverers. Great was the joy of old Dora over her favorite white boy, and the virtue of the black pebble, and as they entered within the abode of mystery, many a strange motion was made by the black enchantress before the wizard.

Teunis, when he recovered himself, was in the presence of the man whom he had seen before. The man with the long beard, the high cap, the robe of figured blue, the bent body, with a staff in his hand of at least seven feet in length. The captain, with whom the Dominie had been debating, was not there. A superstitious feeling swelled through the young man's breast like the tide at full moon. His first impulse was to run after the Dominie and the captain, but that was impossible with Dora there at the door, and the dwarf at her side, while the hermit sat before the ruddy fire, stroking his beard and pointing Teunis to a seat.

"Dora may go on her errand," said the grim man, "and let her be sure that she leaves one of these sets of garments at the bear's cave, and the other at the south side of the big falls."

The old creature came forward at that, and laid down the crystal cup which Teunis had seen in her hand before, on the tripod in the centre of the room; she was careful to have it stand immediately beneath a lamp which hung from the roof, and Teunis just observed for the first time that the lamp was the same in size, in pattern, as well as material, with the mysterious cup.

"Teunis Roe," said the Solitary soon after the door was shut, "you are in trouble; you are seeking those you cannot find. Your mind is divided, and how can any one obtain what his thoughts are not fixed upon! What seek you here at this hour of the night, when the very ravens, the wild-cats, and the panthers are all in beds, and no one prowling round but the tigers of humanity?"

"If I may venture to speak," said the young man, trembling from head to foot at first, but gradually recovering himself, "the man who asks of me what I am seeking, knows more of my affairs than I do myself; and so I ask at once where is Elsie Schuyler? Is she in bondage?"

"These are questions which every one has not the right to put; nor have all the right to intrude upon the privacy of that noble hearted damsel. I may not answer in words. Look into that cup. Lift it in your hand; it is the cup of the famous Begu of Moorshedabad that he called Alinagore, the gate of God; and his spirit is ever present when the like minded gaze within its sacred walls."

Teunis, sincerely afraid that he was dealing with the devil, and yet anxious to have an answer to his question, felt a wavering in his mind at first, but his reverence for the necromancer had diminished somewhat since he saw that Dora and he had some participation in the same things. Had he known less of Dora, he would have had more fear of the recluse, but having been behind the scenes with her in part, he had but a partial hold on his imagination. Still, to make himself safe against all the power of the evil one, he said the Creed secretly to himself, with the grace before meat in mistake for another prayer he was inwardly gathering up. The sides and bottom of the cup were bright and shining, and seemed, or really did, send forth the pictures of living beings, who were seen moving around in the midst of scenes wild and beautiful. The gazer looked till his head swam in confusion, eagerly looking, yet not distinctly comprehending the objects before him. He was about to return the goblet when a side glance at one of the figures discovered to him the well-known outline of Elsie; and then of Angelica's profile, and even Rover came before him at last; with another form, he could not distinguish sufficiently plain. The natural scene in which they were grouped was familiar to his eye; but the more doors unlocked in the halls of his memory, the more confused he became. This was all the more tormenting, for it seemed that Elsie looked right into his face, and was holding up her hand in an imploring attitude.

"For the love of God," said Teunis in a transport of passion, "tell me where that place is, that I may run and help her for whom I would give my life at any moment. I see that she is in danger, and every instant is worth a world to me."

"Shake the gate of God, and it will open if your spirit be in harmony with truth and justice; we know already that love is in the ascendant; but it is the symmetrical soul alone which angels admire, and for whom they will unfold the doors of paradise."

During this brief homily the cup-bearer had shaken it, and was gazing intently down into the bottom where he saw figures of men in crowds, as if fiercely contending. Figures which he could have taken to be those of persons whom he knew and feared; but all was so dark and interesting to him that he durst not define too closely, though he could not help catching glimmering hints. He was satisfied that the mysterious man before him knew more than he did himself; and that the shadows he was showing him were intended to excite in him feelings of curiosity, which maddened him rather than gratified his desire.

"You mock me, whatever you be, wizard, witch or spook," said Teunis, flinging down the goblet with a ring that startled himself more than it did the necromancer. "You show me that Elsie Schuyler is in danger and leave me in the dark. No good man could be so cruel."

"Shake the cup not in wrath, for anger never gained heart, hand or heaven," said the gloomy recluse, half smiling at the violence of the youth.

Teunis looked again, and after patience he saw a gay group surrounding a pair equally gay. All was sunshine. In the distance was a church, where offerings of praise went up from the assembly, and to the right was a ship in full sail with streamers flying in the wind; the grandeur of nature, spread out before the eye seemed to be hallowed with the incense of heaven. The scene on the opposite side was one of death and of blood. But scarcely had the curious gazer looked understandingly on the pictures than the hunting watch of the hermit struck ONE, and then, as if by real magic, the divining cup was dark and meaningless.

Teunis started at the sight of vacancy, and shook the goblet furiously in the hope of restoring the vision.

"Only three times, young man, and never after the short hour. The spirit has returned to his place."

"Good sir," said Teunis, now anxious to see more, "let me but finish the vision. I have come for counsel, and must know the place I am standing upon, before I can act."

"You must act, young man, without knowing all things. We have but glimpses of realities in this world. Faith must guide us through darkness. You have seen enough to warn you of duty. Heaven leaves us no choice of duties. There is danger near the one you love. Be on the alert, and the time to act is at hand. There is blood on the road to life. To-morrow at noon, by the Dog Pool, and let your new friends be with you, for we shall have a sacrifice there, sending up a fragrance and a smoke that shall be seen from the bay of Manhattan to the shores of Erie."

With these words, the strange man held out a cup of the good Santa Cruz, which Teunis might have shrunk from receiving from the hand of a wizard, had he not lately heard its praises given, and its pith proved by the man whose word he had never once questioned; so without a scruple he drank the whole. He left the cabin in much the same kind of feeling which a somnambulist has when he rises out of bed into dense darkness, and yet knows the way he means to take. He mounted up the hill, thinking of what he had seen and heard, and scarcely knew where he was till he stumbled upon the sentinel, who demanded fiercely, "Who goes there?" He was too young a soldier not to be surprised; so his tongue hung fire, for he had forgotten the countersign, when another voice roared out, "Fire, you careless idiot, at once." This roused the intruder's intellect, who stammered, more dead than alive, "The Sword of Gideon and of Schuneman."

"Ha! ho! that's enough, my dainty callant;" for it was Grant the Scotchman that spoke. "You have na learned your carritch o'er weel. But we'll forgive you this time. It would na been gude for you had a ball been put through your wame, this cauld night, just because Schunaman's name was na found in the Book o' Judges. But where the deil hae you been a' this time? You've had a lang claver with that warlock in the house. It brings me in min' of Saul consulting with the witch of Endor, before the battle on the mountains of Gilboa. I hope maer luck may come of it. It's no canny, laddie, and I'm sorry that the minister should show you sic an example. But gang awa, and lie down on your bed, you are quite dazed, I see. There is my plaid, take it and row it round you. It is a wee wet, you feel; but that's the way we do in the Highlands—dip it in a spring, wring it out, and it will keep the cauld keen wind frae penetrating your banes. Mair especially as I fin' from your breath that you have got a gude dram. A kind witch or ghaist he maun be; I wish he would come up this way. Now there you may lie like King Charlie himself, when he was chased like a partrick on the mountains."

Teunis was too tired to resist the attention of the kind Gael, and he slept almost before his head fell on his moss pillow, so that before his nurse left him he was heard snoring soundly. Turning away, Grant said to himself, "Ou aye puir chiel', his head doon, his house is theekit."

Silence reigned over all the hills. Every voice was stilled. Man and beast were alike gone to rest. Already, the early frosts had silenced the insect tribes, and the two carcases slain that morning, had attracted the prowling races to the southward of the two camps. A distant growl or yell might be heard as if quarrelling for a dainty bit, or a summons from a new arrival to prepare for a surrender. Man had lain down to recruit his weary body, and regain more energy of passion, now exhausted by the toil, the suspense, the anxiety, or the frolic of the previous day.

One only acted the part of sentinel-general, and seemed to move like a ghost in unrest, as he went from cliff to cliff; through hollows and brakes, as if these were as familiar to him as his native home. It was the strange and gloomy recluse who had in his time paced the banks of the Thames, and the banks of the Seine. He had fought under Clive in Bengal, and had traversed the jungle where the Hoogley rolled on its yellow sands. And now he had become familiar with scenes of a more rugged and impressive character, in harmony with his desperate nature, made more intense from the passion of revenge, which he had nursed in secret discipline, for two whole years. He found relief in these lonely wilds during the midnight hours, till every tree and spring had become an acquaintance, whose company he had courted with ardent affection. One great overwhelming passion glowed within his spirit; and but for the prospect of gaining gratification, his brain must have burned out all his reason, and his heart become crisped like the foliage of the trees, when the heavens are brass, and the hills iron.

On this night it was impossible for him to sleep, and could any eye but a spirit's have followed him, he might be seen walking in his close fur helmet, a leather doublet tight to his body, with breeches and boots of the same material, while in a broad belt round his waist were hiding those weapons which he ever had with him, though the only visible arm of defence was the long hickory pole, shod with sharp steel at the point, but containing in the head a strong dagger, which started from its place by the touch of a spring at the middle, rendering what seemed but a peaceful hermit's staff, on a sudden a lance, fit for the hand of a knight-errant. From his cell to the north of the Dominie's camp, he traversed slowly, till he came in the rear of Brandt's forces, taking a narrow and perfect view of the whole from the South Mountain. Passing down the streams and trails, where only the wild beast runs, he came to the main falls, and gave a passing glance at the pool, where were hidden the objects of that search, on which were so many minds at that instant intent and dreaming. Before daylight he returned, saying in brief soliloquy, "how easy it would be for me to deliver those captives by the road I have taken myself, and the words of that honest man still echo in my ear. 'It is dangerous to help Providence.' He would say nothing should take the place of positive duty. Relieve now, and trust the rest. But the punishment must be measured out in the presence of all. The report must be carried back, where it will tell. Sir Henry Clinton must be made to see that he has but narrowly escaped the vengeance he has proudly invoked. Yes, said the excited exile, striking his staff on the rock, it shall be heard of in the army, that the villain has been made to bite the dust. And in London too, shall it be said that the heir of Brantwood had power left to punish his enemies though they hide themselves in the lair of the panther."

Returning to his cabin, he threw himself on the skins which lay on the settle, that served for seat and for bed. His voice died away in prayer that God might give his hand strength for justice, and bitterly weeping, he cried, "thou pure Spirit, whose bosom was soiled by the slimy serpent, thou who heard my vow of vengeance, come and behold justice meted out for thy dishonor."

CHAPTER VI.

THE LAST INDIAN BATTLE ON THE RIVER HUDSON, 1760.*

"And Cush begat Nimrod: he was a mighty hunter before the Lord."
BIBLE.

THE fretfulness of Brandt with his braves was becoming every hour more apparent. The hope of succeeding in diverting the colonists from watching the passage between the north and south was almost fled. But the pride of the Mohawk was mortified when he thought of retreating back into the wilds, where he knew that he must be buried in obscurity. Could he only get a foothold on the Great Rver, making the mountain his base, he might be of some importance in the eye of the great king of England.

Upon this weakness of the Indian, Clifford was directing all his skill, holding out the hope before him of being able, after a few days, to descend and make a lodgment on those very islands which they could distinguish from their camp at the mouth of the Kaatskill Creek. Not that he deemed such an attempt wise, or likely to be successful, but anything which might detain the Mohawk here for a few days longer was deemed by him to be lawful.

The little army of red and painted men were preparing for the grand hunt that was to come off that day; and while the braves were so engaged the leaders stood out upon the verge of the cliff, watching the mist as it rolled away at the sight of the sun.

"I have heard," said Clifford, as if incidentally, "of a great battle being fought for the kingship of the Six Nations, on those two islands below these, between your ancestor Hend-

* Colonel Stone refers to this battle, and quotes from a manuscript history by one Smith of Schoharie.

rick and Etau-o-quam, the Mohican; does the great Mohawk hear me?"

"Thayendanegea was there," replied the chief proudly, "with King Hendrick, when no bigger than an eagle's height. There this wound was made: the first time blood came at the point of a spear."

At this, the chief made his shoulder bare, that the wound might appear. Clifford was gaining his end without an effort, and as if casually, said.

"Some of you old Dutchmen must remember that battle; it is not over twenty years since."

Several spoke here at once, saying that they were present as spectators; but all allowed the Elder Abiel had the most to do with it, being acquainted well with the Mohican chiefs.

"Well," said Clifford, "we have an hour to spare, let us hear the account; I am sure it must please the Mohawk chief—the present king of the Six Nations to listen to a white man telling of the bravery of Hendrick, who fought for the crown, which Brandt now wears so nobly. It would be a pity to leave those beautiful islands down there in the hands of the rebels, when another battle would secure them to the rightful owner."

The Elder Abiel, thus pressed into the service, could not escape from the task of narrating what he had seen. The subject was familiar to him; and as his audience were evidently all interested, he began as follows:

THE ELDER ABIEL'S STORY.

"The ground of that war between the Mohawks and the Mohicans, was the crown of the Six Nations. Hendrick had been in England and felt that the title went a great way there. So had Etau-o-quam, but he was of a more exalted mind, in religion and was less ambitious of distinction. He was stirred up, however, by his son Newabina and by the people of New England, who wished to cripple the power of Sir William Johnson in the West. Hindering Hendrick they hindered Johnson; so they secretly set the one chief against the other. There had been much manœuvering all over, of which we heard a little.

"The chief village of the Mohicans was down there. There are remains of it still to be seen, but it was once a thriving place, the centre of a large population. Etau-o-quam had his wigwam on the Haup-pee-naus, a high bluff at the angle of the creek. He was an old man, very lofty and proud of having seen Queen Anne, who gave him and some other chiefs royal robes. Dominie Schuneman says the whole account is in a book called the Spectator. Colonel Clifford no doubt has read it?"

"Yes," said the soldier, growing sincerely interested, I remember seeing the Indian Kings at Drury Lane Theatre, just as Addison describes them. Go on."

"The first notice which we had of the coming war was through one Drake, who was on a trading excursion; as he pretended, but who really came hither from Stockbridge with a message from these wise men of the east, to the great chief Etau-o-quam.

"That chief had gone out leaning upon the arm of his son, Newabina; himself a noble specimen of the red man. Dressed in the regalia he had received in London: he felt a presentiment of his end being near and he longed to look once more upon the lofty mountains. Rising to his full height, he held out his hands, as if to embrace the towering height. Knowing every change which High Peak puts on, he perceived that a new aspect was assumed, indicative to him of a change for himself.

"'The sun sets amidst the mist,' said he. 'There is blood mingling with the streams; I hear the music of war, I must fall with my mantle around me. Let me be gathered into Asinath, the tomb of my fathers. But first must I drink of the spring that runs close by their graves. Thereof I drank in youth; to that I ran first, on returning from the house of the great queen. I shall come from the hunting-grounds of the west to drink of that clear fountain.'

"It was on returning from this sacred pilgrimage, that the man Drake met him; putting into his hand a small package, which was not opened then, and though the curious trader felt anxious to draw the chief into conversation, he got no reply, which somewhat annoyed the inquisitor. Falling in, however, with an old acquaintance, who had come hither from Ulster, the travelling merchant found good quarters with Johannes Du Bois,* where he was sitting quietly after supper, telling what he knew, that he might get knowledge back with interest; or as he said himself, he put a little water into the pump so that he might pump all he wanted out of the cistern.

* John Du Bois, a son of the one mentioned, who died at the advanced age of 93, had a distinct recollection of this battle, and described it vividly.

"'I guess, Mr. Du Bois,' said the trader, 'you can read Ingen?'

"The Dutchman, who was a man of silence and was at that time enjoying his pipe, merely nodded his head.

"'Well,' continued Drake, 'tell me the meaning of a muskrat darting at an otter?'

"Du Bois here took his pipe from his mouth and sprang to his feet with a leap that startled the peddler up to the same position, where they stood facing each other, before either found a tongue. Du Bois spoke first.

"'Where have you seen that sight?'

"'I did not say I saw it, I only asked what it meant.'. For his conscience told him he had been guilty of violating the trust put in his honor.

"'You will know what that means before long, if I be a true prophet. The great Mohawk has sent his challenge, or else our chief here has got word of the coming he has been expecting for a month past. The muskrat is the Mohawk's totem, and the other is for the river chief. You can read the rest.'

"'Or, as a Philadelphia lawyer would say, their signmanual. But do you suppose that old chief will fight?'

"'Do you think he will die,' said Du Bois, 'He will fight as sure as death; and there, I declare they are singing the war-song now. Nay, see how the fires are burning all over the country.'

"'Yaw! yaw!' said Gertrude, the wife of Du Bois, 'there, the lights are blazing on the Hau-pee-naus.' She said this as she lifted her babe in her arms, running in terror to the door, that she might hear as well as see: She called as she looked back:

"'They are singing psalms to their God. Their squaws are loudest."

"'Rather to the devil,' said Drake, whose puritanic blood rose at the thought of these red-skins and their cruelty.

"The house of Du Bois was on the banks of the stream that comes down from these little lakes, and was situated about half a mile from its mouth. It was a strongly built stone structure, after the Huguenot fashion, one large room with chambers overhead. It could be turned into a fort in time of need; but before Du Bois would determine on his course, he deemed it best to take a quiet survey of the camp. Accordingly he walked out along with Drake, who was no coward, though a peddler. They climbed up a hill, that stood between the house and the Hau-pee-nans, where they saw the beacon burning all along the base of the mountain.

Du Bois understood the warning, and made up his mind it would be best to move his family inland, and turned back with that intent.

"'Gitty,' said he, 'is a brave creature, but there is no saying what these bloody beings might do when their wrath is up.'

"'I guess,' said Drake, 'I now understand the meaning of those dark hints that Priest Wheelock threw out about wars and rumors of war, last Sunday.'

"There was but little sleep for any of us," continued the Elder Abiel, "in that region all that night. We on the Vlatts soon heard the yells of the roused warriors, and though the Mohicans were our friends, an Indian in a rage is a very unpleasant companion. I started in the middle of the night, and took my stand on that kekute from which you see the smoke rising now, where I met a number of my acquaintances, and we looked down on the red circle, where the old chief stood in the midst, dressed as I have told you. He was dancing as a young chieftain mingles in the crowd. All night there was a ceaseless stream of their squaws and papooses passing on to Castilberg, where it was supposed the weaker portion of the population would be safe. Still these were not unarmed, nor unprepared, for Etau-o-quam himself was there in command. While on the outside of their village, to the south, a strong party were secreted under the command of the chief Newabina, and a third division was on the little island at the mouth of the creek. It was in a measure to be a pitched battle, and scouts were sent out by both armies as early as the twilight, with orders to penetrate as far as possible, and divine their modes of attack and of defence. Those of the Mohican did not require to go far till they met the Mohawk fleet, on its way down, making for the larger island out in the river, where they all disembarked. However, this was for the purpose of deceiving the enemy on the main land. Hendrick had received accounts from his spies, of how the foe was posted, and determined to surprise him in all his three points. In this he showed a lack of that wisdom he had learned when afterward at Saratoga. When Sir William Johnson was bent upon dividing his forces, Hendrick, his Indian ally, took three sticks, giving one after another to the Englishman, bidding him break them; and taking three more, he handed them to him at once, and asked of him to do the same thing. The symbol was understood and the advice taken with success. Hendrick had learned something of the art of war in this little battle, where he nearly lost all by dividing his forces.

"A heavy fog lay upon the river all night, which prevented the attack from taking place as early as was the Mohawk's intention; still he sent out one party from the upper end of Ussaman Island,* who were to follow a small stream on the west side of the river that comes down through the rising ground which you see to the north of the Kaatskill Creek, about two miles distant up the river. Scouts had already, through the dark, crawled forward one before the other, at certain distances, so as to be heard by one another through signs preconcerted; so that the whole devoted camp was encircled, and the ground fully understood before morning dawned. Every ear in the beleaguered fort was awake, and scarcely a whisper was heard, for all waited for the onset. It did come upon all three forts at once. Hendrick sailing down the east side of the river early in the fog, led his main body from a few miles below, up through the woods, where they lay coiled like so many serpents on the ground, till they heard the war-cry from Castilberg, when up the great chief Hendrick started, giving the whoop to his braves, then rushed upon the camp of Newabina, which was there to meet the onset with a vigor and a spirit which made the Mohawk fall back crest-fallen for a time. But for the renown and power of their leader, all would have been lost. As it was, they had to take to the trees and the gullies, where they crouched, and watched the movements of their enemy, whose spirit being flushed with the success of their defence, were more than ready to expose themselves to the eyes of the marksmen on the other side, and consequently lost several of their best warriors through extra zeal and courage.

"The attack on Castilberg was simultaneous with that on the Hau-pee-naus village by Hendrick, whose intention was to surround the island, where he supposed the main body of the Mohicans were lodged, and thus cut off their retreat, so that they would be entirely massacred; for little Abraham, Hendrick's brother, was hovering around the island Wantona with a fleet of canoes, ready at a signal from the land, to enter upon his part of the battle. We have seen how the attack upon Newabina's force was repulsed, and that upon the castle did not come off any better. The old chief Etau-o-quam, took the command, and felt the blood of his youth rise to fury. Like the old war-horse that the good book tells us about, his neck was clothed with thunder. He smelled the

* Now Rodgers.—D. M.

battle afar off; and said Ha-ha. Rushing from the gateway of the fortress, he shouted his war-cry, so clear and strong, that his people below who heard it regarded it as the sure omen of victory. His scarlet robe still on him, but bound round his loins with a bear-skin belt, and his crown tied under his chin, he swung his famous tomahawk, till he fixed his aim, then flung it with a force and a skill into the skull of the leader of the assailants, which felled him at once to the ground. Rushing forward on the prostrate foe, he had his hair at once in his hand, and his scalping-knife at its dread work, so that he succeeded in tearing the trophy from the head of his enemy, but was struck down himself by a blow that laid him on the ground, from which he was borne off by his people, and placed within the fort, upon his bed of skins. His example had its effect upon all, friend and foe. The Mohawks were beaten back as far as the mill which stands there to the east of Castilberg, where they took refuge. The force in the castle was not strong enough to storm them, nor was it intended that this party should act except on the defensive. They returned to watch over the old king of the rivers, who had evidently struck his last blow. Body and soul were alike yielding up, and preparing himself for his departure to the hunting-grounds of his fathers, he sent a message to Newabina, commanding his presence when Hendrick was repulsed.

"That brave chief was restraining his own followers, and at the same time watching the movements of the Mohawk. He had most to fear from the pent-up ardor of his braves, who were eager to rush out and become the assailants; but he satisfied them by encouraging individual prowess, while the main body were spectators of the fierce play. If a Mohawk was seen to skip from tree to tree, coming all the time nearer, Newabina would encourage some volunteer to rush over the defence around his camp, and scalp the skulking enemy. An instance of this kind kept the two parties at bay for a time. One of Hendrick's braves was observed by the Mohican chief himself to hide behind a large oak; and from that to take aim, so truly, that his shots told upon several of the best men of the army. The patience of Newabina was exhausted, and without any previous sign he rushed with such unexpected fury upon the hiding Mohawk, that he nearly stumbled over the foe; when with one blow of his battle-axe he prostrated him to the ground. With his fingers twisted in the hair of his enemy, he was preparing to finish his work, when the keen eye of Hendrick saw the advantage, who was soon on his way to take the combat on himself; but being heavy and stiffer than he had been, he measured his distance so that his tomahawk fell short of its mark, and quivered in the oak behind where the Mohican stood with the dripping scalp in his left hand, and his knife in the other, ready to plunge it into his great enemy, when he came up. Prudence restrained both of these wily chiefs from single combat. The crisis had not yet come.

"Like all Indian battles where they were so evenly matched, this combat continued for several hours, and but few lives were lost. Defeated in their cunning at surprisal, the Mohawks fell back. So far as the battle had gone, the Mohicans were the victors. Aware of the approach of the Mohawks, they had been ranged in fine order in the form of a half moon, behind an intricate brush fence, which had been in use before this in a former contest, and had then proved its worth. They had improved it, and made it impenetrable to half naked men. Every attempt at breaking through only hurt the assailants, and just at the time when Hendrick's braves were becoming discouraged, he received word of the failure on Castilberg, which made him decide at once on a retreat; as, in proportion to his loss, would be the gain of his enemy. Trembling every moment lest he should be attacked in his flank by the forces of the hill, he retired by degrees, fighting all the way. His retreat was masterly of its kind, and new to his pursuers, so that they were puzzled; losing ground rather than gaining new laurels, Hendrick put his men that bore fire-arms into three files, running parallel to each other, when they moved backward, but as the two outside ranks discharged their pieces they ran, leaving the middle rank to defend, as long as possible, when they also fired, running immediately and passing their fellows, who by this time had loaded, and were ready for defending, firing and running, so that by the time they had reached the place where their canoes lay off in the river, the Mohicans had not come up, nor did they see what was going on of the embarkation till the last file were leaping into the water, up to their middle, and swimming out to their companions, leaving their pursuers shouting defiance, and yet feeling that it was but a partial victory.

"Little Abraham's attempt upon the island Wantona * was

* The present Catskill landing is a small island connected with the mainland by an artificial neck. The whole point was covered with sycamore trees.

not more successful than the other two attacks. Indeed, from the first it was more a feint than intended to be serious; though from the natural fury of the Indian character, it became soon too bloody to stop at the command of a leader less than Hendrick himself. Having strict orders not to leave their canoes at the risk of losing them—since upon them lay the safety of the whole expedition, in case of a defeat on the main land—this third division did not venture far into the sycamore woods, which served so well as a means of defence to the party lodged within; still, some of the more venturous rushed over that boundary, and were cut off from the main body, falling into the hands of the Mohicans, who were hidden among the bushes, lying flat upon their faces till they saw their chance. Abraham drew his braves off without attempting a rescue, which he saw was vain, and had the mortification of seeing a few of his best men killed before his eyes with horrible cruelty. Retiring immediately to the Ussaman island, he sent down the canoes to aid his brother in his retreat.

"Newabina, considering the battle over, ran immediately to Castilberg, where the old king, Etau-o-quam, was lying ready for his son, and looking forward to the hunting-grounds of his fathers. He found him content. The fierce Mohawk, his only rival, had been beaten back; and now, contrary to his expressed wish of the previous day, he commanded that his regalia, regarded by him with so much pride, should be taken off from him, and his son put into the kingship, while his eyes were yet clear to behold him. Over forty years had he worn it. From the time he had received it in London from the Great Queen over the big waters, he had worn it on all festive occasions, whether in war or in peace. He made Newabina kneel at his couch; putting his withered hand across his brow thrice, he took the feathery crown and put it on the head of the elected king, giving him at the same time the silver-mounted tomahawk: the symbols of power to rule, and of power to execute. Bidding him walk three times before him through the tent, he called him once more near, when he muttered something like an invocation; then, laying himself back, he never spoke more. On the same evening, just as the sun was bidding the world adieu, the mountains and the sky, resplendent with the radiance of his beams, they laid the old chief in his last bed at the foot of that hill. Any one will tell you, should you venture there, where the Indians' graves are made. From that Castilberg his grave is seen with this mountain stream placidly winding round it: the Hau-pee-naus lies to the south a little way; while the great river over which he reigned so long, still winds on with majestic flow. I have stood on that rising ground at sunset, looking to the mountains above, on which there lay palaces, castles, islands, and smooth blue lakes, of spiritual beauty; and have at times envied the men who imagined those near glories to be the grounds and the streams to which Etau-o-Guam had gone, the last king of the rivers.

"Newabina, dressed in the royal attire of his sire, came down among his people, who received him with shouts, for they deemed that his crown was fairly won; but the chief, the moment he stood on the Hau-pee-naus, and looked out upon the water, perceived that his new honor was not to be retained without a struggle. The crafty Mohawk had a plan from the first, which he intended to put in force, but which he kept to himself. In the meantime he was seen strengthening his camp on one of those small fields where the Mohicans had from time immemorial raised the fragrant weed.* He affected no secrecy of his intention to remain and watch his chance for another onslaught; and though he saw his enemy on the east shore and on the west side reconnoitering his camp, he made no attempt at driving them away. As night came on, the death song for the fallen braves rang out over the waters, and was echoed from the shores, sometimes in low, plaintive tones, and at intervals with wild shrieks, which made the blood curdle in the veins of those of us who were listening upon Overpaugh's kekute; that, you see, as I said already, smoking there at this moment.

"But from that we went down to the high land that overlooks the river, where a band of us stood at night. The two islands seemed in the dark like two terrible creatures glaring upon each other with their thousand eyes; as if looking into the hearts they wished to penetrate. Yells of defiance went forth amidst the songs of lamentation, while from Castilberg was heard a more mournful sound, as the women shrieked over the grave of the departed sachem. We were becoming every hour more numerous, and had formed ourselves into a band of defence in case of any murderous attack from the Mohawks, should they prove victorious. Their blood up, any scalp would become valuable. We chose Du Bois as our captain, and were drilling under his command, while we were

* Ussaman—tobacco.

marking the movements of both parties below on the two islands.

"All night the spies of both sides were busy around. Fearlessly did they venture within the rival camps; crawling like snakes along the ground, after rising on the banks as otters lift their backs, letting the water drip from their sides; when, after having obtained all they wanted, creeping back, they would dash into the stream with as loud a plunge as they could make, giving a laugh of triumph as they swam into the current; or of contempt, at the negligence of their foes. One of these daring devils was caught on the shallows, and though he fought like a panther, now holding on as with a grip of steel, and then slipping out of their hands as an eel escapes, he was finally conquered, and condemned upon the spot to a cruel death. By some mutual sign of their own, the Mohawks were made aware of the fate of their brave spy; for, standing abreast on the banks of their own island, they saw the fire kindling that was intended for his torture. It was on a little knoll upon the verge of the creek, which could be seen from all the camps: from Castilberg, Hau-pee-naus, Wantona, Ussaman, and our hill we saw the tragedy, and heard the shouts of cruel victory that rang around us from the Mohicans; while the companions of the wretched victim sang his death song aloud and clear, so that his spirit entered the halls of his fathers by the music that he had loved best all his life.

"This last occurrence inspirited the followers of Newabina so highly, that he resolved to attack the Mohawks instead of waiting for Hendrick on the next day. He kept his counsel to himself till the last moment, confiding only in his pale-faced friend Du Bois, who endeavored to dissuade him from it by every argument he could bring.

"The attack was what Hendrick anticipated. He kept his fires burning, tied his blankets to the trees, spreading them so as to surround his camp, making the whole outside to have the appearance of a secure and comfortable sleeping ground. He seemed careless; letting the spies of his enemy come as near as they pleased, so that they might bear away reports of the state of things as they appeared from the outside. Newabina made a voyage himself to the islands, so as to make all sure, and came back satisfied that the Mohawks had gone to sleep.

"We all stood upon the hill, ignorant of what was to happen next; only that we were warned by Du Bois against disbanding for the night. We were all hunters, and ready to fight for our hearthstones, with as good heart as we ever hunted a hungry wolf. Quietly we sat on the hill, saying little. The peddler in our midst talking as if he did all the work. He dilated on the causes and the consequence of this battle, with the same assurance as he would have discussed a yard of serge.

"'These Mohawks are a wicked set, and will just do whatever Colonel Johnson tells them to.. If he has bid them kill off the white folks here, be sure of their doing it.'

'Why should Colonel Jansen do dat ting?' said one old farmer of more benevolence than knowledge of the world.

"'Just that he may rule the colonies,' was the peddler's answer, 'and Parson Wheelock says that all men should make laws for themselves. That kings were made for the people, and not the people for the kings. That's no treason. Johnson is the critter of King George, and Hendrick is the critter of Johnson.'

"'Ende vay is de Mohican de creature of?' said the old Boerman.

"'Why,' said the peddler, 'everybody in Connecticut knows that the old Sachem was on the side of the people, and we expect that the young capt'n will cast his braves into the scales against the crew that want to rule the colonies. What do you say to that, Mister Du Bois?'

"The person addressed had disappeared from our company, and was in close counsel with Newabina. 'Hendrick has one eye open. He sees the otter in the rivers. The muskrat will dart upon him in the dark,' was the warning of the Dutchman.

"'The Elk is afraid of the water after the sun is down,' said the Indian to his careful counseller, with some bitterness in his speech, and as if reproachfully.

"Du Bois felt hurt, and replied, 'I have no fear of doing what I promised; but the pale-face has his eyes without blood, and can see clear. Can the brave chief see now?' and with that he threw a bandana silk handkerchief over the red man's face. Taking it off, he said, 'we will meet on the island as I said.'

"This referred to a diversion which some of the boldest of us intended to make in behalf of their neighbors, the Mohicans, at the upper end of the island, when the fight would be at the hottest, just sufficient to alarm the Mohawks, and give their enemies a better chance. 'I have seen," said our captain to us, 'that a sudden start was better than a deliberate volley.'

"Hendrick did sleep with one eye open, for he knew all that was going on. His spies were intelligent and penetrated the design of their enemy in time to warn him of their approach. Crawling out of his camp, he and his braves lay among the bushes outside, scarcely breathing, with their weapons ready. Newabina came on, quietly at every step, till within a few yards of the place, when they rushed, yelling their war whoop, striking through the screen upon the ground where they supposed the Mohawks lay. Not a sound met their ear, but a silence which stunned them more than if a thousand voices had responded, since they expected such a meeting. As with one consent they ceased themselves, looking round for an enemy, when all at once the hidden foes started up, firing and hurling their weapons so truly from the dark where they stood, upon those within the fence, whose faces were plainly seen in the light that blazed; so that every shot and stroke told fearfully, bringing down a Mohican.

"Hendrick saw that now was his time, and springing from his hiding-place, he hurled his heavy weapon of war in the direction of his foe, so that it sank into his left shoulder. A moment more and the Mohican confronted him. The tomahawk of Newabina whizzed through the air, but it was a random blow, and missed its aim. His eyes were filled with the light of the fire, and could not discern objects in the dark around them. It was the same with the whole of that devoted band. They were shot down like deer, that come to the waters in the night. When they came out they could not see where to run.

"The two chiefs stood facing each other. The Mohawk had a sound body but it was old and stiff. The Mohican had the advantage in years, but now he was disabled, so that they might be called equal. They measured each other with the look of fierce revenge. Knife in hand, they were about rushing at one another, when the party under Du Bois landed, causing great alarm to the Mohawks, who were wholly in the dark concerning the new enemies, their numbers, or their plans; only they felt certain it could be no friends of theirs. We had no other wish but to prevent further effusion of blood, and had loaded with blank cartridge; but our volley told sufficiently to produce the greatest confusion. The preserving of their boats was their first care; and these little

Abraham immediately put out into the river, where he waited for the fugitives, who, leaping in their terror into the water, swam toward the fleet, upsetting some of the canoes in their haste. By this time the Mohicans were recovering from their fright, having discovered their new strength, and were returning in great force and spirit, when there was no foe to encounter. One after another of the Mohawks had retreated through the bushes, and all being aware of the place where their fleet was moored, had run in that direction. Some of them, however, missed their way, swimming to the different shores, and either made their escape by running homeward or hid in the brakes, till they found a chance. One poor wretch was taken a few miles on his way, and brought back to suffer all the cruelty which a red man can inflict so skillfully. Though I saw it, I have no wish to describe it. An Indian is a fiend when he becomes an enemy.

"Hendrick, taken equally with surprise, hesitated to venture upon Newabina sufficiently long to allow his foe to spring forward on him, but he met his match in that large and strong warrior. They clasped one another so firmly that their weapons were harmless. Rolling over one another it was difficult to guess which would have proved victorious. One that knew them both, would have decided for the Mohican, but since his wound he had lost blood, and was becoming all the time weaker. One turn more in this state and his right arm fell helpless by his side. His time had seemingly come, for his enemy was above him. The knife was at his neck, when Du Bois sprang forward and arrested the hand. Hendrick rose to his feet as if to meet a new foe, when Drake, with a comical air, called out, "I arrest you in the name of King George for disturbing the peace of this Province." The Mohawk scowled one of his black frowns; and seeing Newabina helpless, he turned and took to the canoe that waited for him, and left the field, in which he had gained few laurels, though he had succeeded in rendering his way to the kingship certain to himself and to his successors.

"The young king of the rivers was buried in the same robe in which his father had arrayed him. They took nothing off from him. He reigned but a single day; and that was the last of that noble race who wore a crown."

The Elder Abiel having finished his narrative, turned to see the preparations for the hunting of the fugitives, and perceived that all was ready. A small party were to remain keeping sentry over the prisoners already collected, himself with the rest. He sighed as he gazed back upon the plain below.

Brandt, well pleased with the history given of his ancestor, smiled as he said:

"Big Boerman's tongue straight as a hawk's bill: goes to many sides, but picks the real bird from the branch it was pointed to at the first."

Clifford saw that the Mohawk aimed at the islands and would continue in sight of them while he had hope of gaining a footing there. He felt satisfied with his little plot of having the history of Hendrick told over by a white man. The pride of Brandt was excited, and so was that of all the Mohawks present. At any moment they would have descended at once, sparing none in their effort at maintaining the name and the fame of their nation. Their chief brought the whole band around him, making one of those nervous speeches to them, pointing down to the river, which at the close was followed by a war song and a dance that made the blood of even the tamest white man there tingle with emotion. A word of Brandt's, and death to all.

The band of men formed round into a solid circle, having the chief in the centre, then untwined itself by two threads that went off at almost opposite points, turning gradually westward.

CHAPTER VII.

A HUMAN WHIRLPOOL.

"Het beest, dat gij gezien hebt, was en is neit; en het zal opkomen uit den afground en ten verderve gaan."—Openbaring.

Translated thus from the Dutch:

"The beast that thou sawest was, and is not; and shall ascend out of the bottomless pit and go into perdition."—Revelation.

Teunis rose that morning, and without bidding any one good bye went directly in search of Clarence Clinton, whom he left to sleep in the bear's den. Surprised and alarmed at finding the cave empty, he made the best of his way to the point of meeting with the other two young men at the

Kaaterskill Falls. His knowledge of the route soon brought him to the place of rendezvous, but he saw nothing of them. When he arrived at the falls where he had left Bertram and Gabriel, he had lost all hope of finding Clarence. Bertram was clear for going at once and claiming the protection of Brandt, and to this Teunis was acceding, when Gabriel, more cool by nature, and less interested in feeling, threw in objections which caused the other two to hesitate. As captain, elected by themselves, he had the right to command, and he was worthy of the place.

"You cannot," he said, "think calmly on this subject. Were Peggy Troumpier where any of your joes is, my mind would not be in a fit state for planning, whatever it might be for fighting in the right time."

Bertram as well as Gabriel, had been putting on their Indian garments, found by them when they wakened that morning. Some friend was watching over them in the dark, and this gave them all three new courage. Beside the tree where these were laid, lay a paper containing something which Bertram soon discovered to be in Latin, but which he would have preferred much more if it had been in common English.

"This fairy, or brownie, as the Scotch would call their good friends, surely thought we must have dictionaries on trees when he left this for us. Here it is: '*Media* autem *die* clamor factus est: Ecce sponsus venit: exite in occursem ejus.' 'And at mid*day* there was a cry made, behold the bridegroom cometh: go ye forth to meet him.'"

"Is that a correct translation, you Bible-reading men?" said Gabriel.

"All but one word, I should think," said Teunis, who perceived the meaning of all this; guessing from what he saw through the night where these things came from. "You have put the word *midday* in for *midnight*."

"Let me see," said the lieutenant: "it is midday here underlined, and is intended to be so. Let us note this. Let noon be our countersign and look out for the midday.

After hearing a full report from Teunis, they made up their minds to remain at the place where they were, as the most likely to serve their purpose. If the marauders succeeded in recapturing Margaret, they would bring their victim here, as the first place of gathering; so the three took positions where they would see, and be themselves hidden. The solitude, to minds like theirs under the most painful suspense, was as much as they could bear. The ever running water below, and the constant fall from above, affecting the two senses, hearing and sight, with the same monotonous din; and the same succession of airy spirits coming constantly through the narrow passage, and then leaping over into the cloud formed by their predecessors, produced a strange loneliness in their watching. And yet as no man feels himself alone if a child be playing around him, so these men when they saw that playful stream tripping down to the brink and then stepping off with ease, felt that they had communion with the spirit of the region. Thrown back into the recesses of their own nature, they fell into that dreamy reverie which the soul of the thoughtful loves to cherish at times, and with profit.

"This is more than I bargained for," was the expression of Bertram, "when I left in the good ship Vulture. I expected to see a wild country along the shores of the river, but not to see nature in her wildest dress. I wonder if that Elsie, whom you describe as possessed of such good sense, Mr. Teunis, would have romance enough in her soul to take Miss Clinton to see this precious gem of these mountains."

"Miss Clinton," said Gabriel, "by the time she got this length, would have something else to think of. If she be a woman like the rest of them, streams of water fell over her cheeks."

"You are likely speaking the truth, so far my captain, but there are some souls which never lose their sense of the beautiful and the grand, and Margaret Clinton is one of that kind: were she on the way to eternal exile, that silvery gossamer would, at least for a moment, relieve her painful feelings."

"Maybe," said the plain matter of fact Gabriel. "First impressions are always the most effective, and I own that my lady Margaret is the very one to see wonders, where I would not see aught but common things. I have been here when I felt the influence of the scene more than at present."

"Still, captain, you cannot help admiring the grandeur of the whole amphitheatre, as your eye ranges round in search of some single object on which to rest till you fix it on that watery spirit which springs from the shelving platform into the capacious hall beneath. Indeed, when I look again, I can imagine so many winged spirits sent forth from the Father of Spirits, meeting again below, as in airy sport; first in that dark mysterious gulf, from which they recoil as from a place of punishment, to rise where the sunbeams light upon them, forming the whole into a glorious crown fit for the heads of seraphim."

"You forget the possibility of Miss Clinton being hidden in that place down there, which you would compare to the mouth of the pit."

"I have imagined that to be possible," said Bertram, "and I am sailor enough to descend into the hold, or into the sea itself, for pearls such as she."

"That language is too deep, and too high for a common Dutchman like your captain. Perhaps Teunis, who I see is in a brown study, may answer you according to that kind of folly; but I will tell you what I once saw here. It was in the winter. A fine hunting morning, the snow all crusted over, so that it could bear man or beast. A little flurry had fallen during the night; just enough for the fox to leave his mark behind him. We had a hard run, but we earthed him, near the foot of the hill over there. As the work for that day was over, and we were on the lookout for anything in which we might pass the time, we followed the advice of old Frederick Saxe, the bear-hunter, and went down to see the falls frozen. This produced much sport with the young folks, who were inclined to poke fun at the old hunter. But knowing him to be a man of original expressions, I led the way that we might see a wonder. We came up from that deep gully below there, and arrived suddenly upon the sight of an object before which we all stood for a few minutes speechless, quite at a loss to understand its nature. They had all but myself been here before, and exclaimed, 'what is that? It has grown since I was here in the summer.' It was a high tower reaching from the bottom, up to the tip of that rock you see jutting out there, pure white, intermingled with glittering crystals. The stillness of the grave was around us. Some one whispered in my ear, 'the year is dead and that is its monument, raised by the frost king.' Imagine just now that not a sound is reaching your ear—all that din stopped, and the murmuring altogether lulled, so that you could hear the beating of your own heart against your ribs."

"You don't mean to say," was Bertram's interested interruption, "that the stream was all gone? That might be in the summer, but the winter's freezing does not dry up the whole."

"No," continued the other, "the water ran as before, up there; but was neither seen, nor heard after it left the ledge."

"That's a very droll story you tell, Mr. Captain, and may be good enough for the marines; but an old salt as I am, has spun too many yarns to believe that the water would not fall in the winter as it this moment, making din enough to deafen the old, or young bear-hunter."

"Wait till you hear the whole. Suppose that from the place we are now sitting, over to the other side of that amphitheatre, as you call it, a round thick tower were built of glass, hollow in the centre, rising up and up, till it came to that shelf from which the water now runs; where would the drops go?"

"Why through the glass tower of course," was Bertram's quick expression; "but what has your comparison to do with your description?"

"Everything, Mr. Lieutenant, for there would be no murmuring sound of water as there is now; nor thundering roar as I have heard after a heavy storm, when that stream so small, and so tame, sprung like an angry beast till it cleared the whole platform, and fell into the outer basin yonder, two hundred and twenty feet."

"Yes, captain, but your enthusiasm has made you forget your glass tower, which, as you describe, must have been a large bottle, bottomless; taking in the whole stream at the neck, and letting it run down its sides, so that it passed through below."

"Just so, and better told than I could tell it. It was full eighty feet in diameter at the base, and one hundred and eighty feet high, pure as snow, till it rose to the neck, when it became clear as rock crystal with the whole stream entering, and passing through it, plainly to the observer."

"Certainly, that was a wonderful object, and equal to any of the peaks of frost that I have ever seen or heard of. Does it rise so every winter?"

"No, sir; old Fred said that he had hunted among the hills forty years, and had seen it only complete once before. A half bottle may be frequently seen, like what comes after a drunken frolic, but the perfect full-blown vessel, out of nature's glass-house, comes but once in a lifetime."

"I hope you had something warm to drink, captain, for cold water coming through a bottle of frost, may be good in a hot summer day, but in the months of February and March, it is another thing."

"We had plenty of the hot stuff, sir; and it was dearly paid for too, with broken heads and bones nearly cracked. A little more and I would not be here to tell the tale."

'Let us hear that yarn with the rest, for after what you have told, I am ready to believe anything."

"As you please," said Gabriel, with perfect *nonchalance.* "After we had freely drank of Santa Cruz rum, our brains began to swim, and some of us did not know whether we stood upon our heads or our heels. I was ready for anything, either to scale the tower from below, or slide down from above. They laughed at me till my pride was touched, and through recklessness I began to climb. The rough sides of the gigantic thing allowed me a footing, so that I did get upon one of the turrets, twenty feet from the ground, where I stood looking round me. The sight had not lost anything from my strange position. All round under these rocks were huge pillars of ice, formed by the water which had searched through between the seams."

"I have seen the like," interrupted Bertram, "in salt mines, and in deep caverns, where statlagmites, built in the course of ages, rise to the high roofs, as if chiselled by the hand of art. Go on, captain, I beg pardon."

"No, sir, thank you, I wanted just such a description to help me through. At the time I stood there, it appeared more like a crystal theatre of display, and I have since frequently wished that lights of a sufficient size and number, could have been introduced for the sake of showing the effect of illumination in such a place."

"Oh, you must read when you can," said Bertram, who could not restrain his speech to the end of the description, "the account of the Empress of Russia's ice palace. You will see that the thing you wish has been tried with full success, lately, and after you have got through with that, turn to the 'Arabian Nights,' and you will see the power of Aladdin's lamp."

"Well, sir, there I stood on the turret, admiring my own daring as much as the wonders around me, when Jim Crapsar, that imp of Satan, thoughtlessly cried out, 'Three cheers for Gabe.' The three cheers were never given; one was enough. Such a commotion has never been listened to by me, though I have been where a few cannons were let off at my ear, as you know. It seemed as if that single cheer would never stop. Crack, crack, crack, went off the pillars, all round falling in pieces as big as a cannon, and others like the trunk of a tree; as to the small lumps they were like a shower of grape-shot, mixed with forty pounders. It sounded and appeared more like the last day than any battle I have been in. A company of more terrified beings I have never looked at in actual danger, with no way of retreat. It was begun in sport, but it closed in real earnest. As for myself I was really in the safest place, being in the centre looking on the shower, and its consequences. But to this day, I feel the shaking of that mass beneath me. If the three cheers had been given, down the whole fabric would have come, and I, below the fragments, would have been crushed."

"That indeed would have been a tale worth telling at a hunter's fireside for ever after. Buried in an avalanche, and swept away by the stream, when the spring floods came. Not quite equal to the Alpine traveller who is lying now, in just such a glen as this; nor will he be found till the last great fire thaws him out. Anything more, Gabriel, about that wonderful bottle? one glass more, if you please."

"We left in double quick time, for a look at the bottle from above. It lost nothing in effect, but it was of another character. I have looked up and down since, but mostly when the sun shone bright in June. The day I refer to in winter showed the different colors of the rainbow reflected. It was in reality, a frozen rainbow."

"Ha! better than before, captain! Do you not see one now giving us the promise of a fortunate day?"

"When the sun shines out that will follow of course, and you may go there to that step, and have it round your head if you choose such an ornament. There are more wonders here amidst the Kaatsbergs, than the king knows of."

"True, Captain Gabriel, the king has not a bottle in all his cellar like that which you held in your arms; and that is one reason why his majesty wishes to keep this fine country of yours among his other treasures."

Teunis, somewhat piqued at the merriment of the young Englishman, turned to him, saying: "The half of the wonders of this spot has not been told you. Come here in the heat of summer, and after a fall of rain, you will, if you look up from below, see an entire rainbow—a complete circle; and though you laugh, I will tell it, that I have seen my face as distinctly in the centre, as I have ever seen it in the round looking-glass that Madam Dyce has in her biggest west room. What do you say to that, sir?"

"I say his majesty has not such a mirror in Windsor Castle, and it is doubtful if he has it anywhere in his dominions, but here. I do not question what you say, you have seen; but I would require Sir Isaac Newton to explain the philosophy of it; and yet, when I remember the camera obscura, I dare not doubt, though I must laugh a little at both you colonists, holding up the beauties of your country."

"Well, laugh away, but I have stood hours looking up into that wonderful glass, where sometimes I would see a single face, sometimes one other; then as the sun would shine out differently through clouds, there would be faces all around the circle, changing their position every moment like a mystic wheel revolving, till the head below grew so dizzy, that I have believed them to be faces looking down upon me from the upper world, only they were not always of the most pleasant kind.'.

"Ah, this is the spot," said Gabriel, "I have heard of when I was a lad, where they went to speak to the vapory spook, and get their fortunes told; I wish I had come before now."

"Gabriel," continued Teunis, "this is no laughing matter; I have known some who laughed after they came on the wrong side of their face."

"Hush! hush! low down," said Teunis, as he prostrated himself to the ground, "there are runners afoot, I hear their voices calling to one another in the woods, and around us."

The three young men fell to the earth with their heads toward the gorge; nor did they lie long in that position till they discovered persons on the opposite side descending into the bottom of the gulf. There were several; some of these were in the garb of Indians, others were dressed in the common woollen cloth worn in that region, dyed with the juice of the butternut, resembling brick-dust, as much as anything known out of Jersey. They increased rapidly in numbers as the circle grew smaller, according to appointment.

"Those persons in front are not real Indians," said Teunis, "I know from their looking so much before them, as if they were curiously investigating a piece of art. I warrant the real Mohawk sees more than they do, out of the side of his face, and from under his eyebrows."

"And I would take those in front to be entire strangers, they look so astonished," was the remark of Gabriel. "I did not expect to see any but the real hunters up here."

All this time Bertram was examining the different arrivals with his pocket glass, and had the range of the party in front. Something in the outline of one of them awakened a dormant feeling in his soul, which made him keep that figure close in view, till at last, he cried out, "Clarence! by George, as I am a living man!" and he was about to rise and halloo, when the man on each side of him held him down, pointing to the numbers which were coming in from the same side on which they lay watching.

"Take the glass and see," as he put the instrument into the hand of the captain.

A long, earnest gaze, and Gabriel agreed that it resembled Clarence much in manner, but the dresses were all so much alike, it was impossible to distinguish them individually.

"But turn your attention to what chiefly concerns you both; do you see any females among them? Look into every knot of persons, and watch all new comers."

"Yes," said Teunis, "for if there be none with them, it is time we were off to the next rendezvous, the pool that I told you of, and which we must reach by noon. Behold at mid-day!"

"You think that the cry is to come in that quarter then?" was the sly question of Gabriel, who, being less interested in his feelings was the more inclined to jest a little with his companions. "Let us take matters coolly for the present, and mark the motions of the our friends below. See how they pour down like so many bloodhounds to the death. Their hunt has made them eager for more prey."

The wide hollow now seemed alive with the crowd. At that distance it was impossible to distinguish the parties, they were so much alike. Some sat on the rocks, others hung on the sides by branches and roots of trees, while a few of the madcap race were chasing one another under the shelving platform, and attempting to climb up the sides of the steep rock, to the danger of their necks. A main body was grouped into a circle, who stood as if waiting for orders. Apart from these, and in deep conversation, were about twenty individuals, whom Gabriel declared must be the commanders of the expedition, engaged in counsel. He continued:

"What a difference between that little spot at this moment, and what it was when we rose this morning. Then God and nature reigned, now devils incarnate are before us."

"Yes," said Bertram, "could we only see your tower of ice there in the centre, and boiling lava round it, and these fiends lying rolling naked in the pit, tumbling from the cold tower into the hot furnace, and"——

"Please to stop, sir; that's more than my nerves can stand; it puts me in mind of our Dominie's description of the bottomless pit."

"Another, as great as your great man the Dominie, has helped me to that description. While you were telling me of those cheerings which shook icicles on you in showers, I was reminded of how an Italian poet describes hell, where 'naked spirits lay down, or huddled sat; trying to throw from them the flakes of fire which came like snow. The devils called out to other devils, thrusting the soul back into the boiling pitch; and looking up, Dante saw them walking on a mount of ice, their teeth chattering, and eyes locked up with frozen tears."

"Enough of that horrible poet's words. Down, down lower with your heads; we are observed," was Gabriel's quick whisper, which his comrades obeyed by a sudden prostration of the face to the turf. "Rather quick to be successful, friends. There is a figure on the opposite side of the gulf, standing so erect, and so still behind a tree, that I am at a loss to know whether it be friend or foe. Teunis, you look now. The objects round here are all familiar to you."

Teunis did as he was commanded, when he saw the form and face of the Hermit, plainly gazing down into the pit, with the intenseness of one that watches from a tower, on the movements of an enemy. As he did not turn his eye away for an instant, Teunis whispered.

"Lift your heads slowly, and look. The hunters are preparing for a new start."

It was as he said; orders had been given for mustering. The whole body stood in two columns. At the word of command each moved off at a right angle from the other, straight as an arrow, up the opposite sides of the ravine, and as the one remaining at the head of several ranks stood still, till the one who had just left was at least ten rods distant, it took some time before the last two were gone. When these were out of sight, the three young men looked where their fellow watcher had stood, but he was gone also.

"The coast is clear now," said Gabriel, "and Teunis, you must be our guide. My advice is to pass straight through that circle, which these hunters are making. It must be three hours before they complete their search."

"Yes, and an hour more. Let us follow the stream as the safest and the nearest, though it be the roughest road in the world; and who knows but we may find the timid Fawn and her protector in some of the caves formed by the eddying waters."

They descended carefully, looking at every step around them, lest any spy might be left behind. For well they all knew that Brandt was a wily foe, not to be circumvented but by superior wiles.

CHAPTER VIII.

THE WINGS OF A CHERUB.

"Chastity and truth? They are two of the pillars of the Temple."

"God's Temple? Why, then, are they heaved by the earthquake, rocked by the floods, driven by the winds, and made to walk in the seven fold fiery furnace?"

"True; but they have never been rent, nor drowned, nor scorched in them all."—OLD DIVINE.

THE hunted fugitives, whose place of refuge was as yet undiscovered by their enemies, were making the best of their condition under the ruling mind of Elsie. The barking of Rover, whose quick ear had heard the growl of the angry catamount a mile off, had produced alarm in the minds of all three; more especially as this was followed by the reports of fire-arms and the shouts of men engaged in a combat. Gradually as their fears subsided, they had time and opportunity of considering the peril and security of their present position. Elsie had reasons of her own for remaining where they had already slept so soundly; and the confidence with which she expressed herself had the effect of preserving the other two from painful uneasiness. Margaret, whose experience of the world was more than Angelica's, felt as if Elsie must know more of the means of escape than she expressed. Possessed of an elastic spirit, she bounded up the moment the smallest release was given.

A trifling occurrence in itself here took place, which gave variety and interest to their solitary condition. Rover, who had suddenly disappeared without leave of absence, was heard by the quick ear of Elsie to give one of his pleased and familiar barks, which he always gave to herself when he welcomed her home. This would have occasioned no alarm; but for her present circumstances, when she believed that that sly snake of an Indian, Shandaagan, was in the hills, seeking after them, and that Rover had always a hankering fondness after the keen hunter. Hushing her companions to silence, and pointing them to their bed as the securest and most retired place of safety, she crawled off in the direction from which she was most likely to perceive the cause of alarm. Her surprise was increased by hearing the tinkling of a small bell that she felt more than distinguished to be one familiar to her ear. A moment more, and what was her amazement to find her own pet lamb, which had been driven away on the day of the conflagration to the hills, and now had found his way high up in search of food. The quick ear of Rover first discerned the tinkling of his playmate's music; and at the instant their mistress discovered them, they were fondling each other in perfect animal rapture. The dog, by his superior sagacity, was manœuvering so that he might bring the lamb where he knew a welcome awaited him; and the innocent little fellow seemed to know that friends were near: for he was following Rover, butting with his head, as if impatient of his gambols. Elsie stood up and gave the usual signal for Dickey's meal, when he rushed to her side with meek confidence, bleating his wishes and his pleasure, as she stroked him with her hand, and spoke Dutch: "*Arme Lammeshie, schoone Lammeshie*"—Poor lamb, beautiful lamb.

This new arrival was hailed with delight, and especially by the kind-hearted Angelica, who wept now when she spoke of her poverty as so great that she was not able to give poor Dickey his pan of milk. From that she naturally went off in a deep lamentation over the probable fate of Red and Brindle, and the mooly cow, wandering over the hills, with no one to milk them.

This trifling occurrence served to pass the day, giving employment in part to the good Angelica, and even diverting the mind of Margaret from herself; so that before night came on she had almost recovered her buoyancy of spirit in the communion she found with nature; into which she entered rapturously, as every new and fresh object rose before her. Her education had all tended to foster these sentiments within her, so that her mind was not untutored for any time, but was prepared for all circumstances, and so trained, that the present scenes rose up before her like dreams of the past rather than like unfamiliar pictures requiring minute investigation.

"I believe, Elsie," said the lofty-minded girl, "that I must have lived here before in some time of my previous existence; for everything I see is associated in my mind with some beautiful thing of the past. Elsie, did you ever think upon the life we came from in the past?"

"No, no, my dear Miss Clinton, I have had enough to think of in the present, and any spare thoughts are given to the life to come. This is the first time I have ever heard of a past life."

"Excuse my foolish talking, Elsie. I have read about it in some old book, and I sometimes dream of things which I may have seen. Your standing just now, with your brown October garments on, and your hand holding the lamb by his string, is just as plain to me as if I had seen you a hundred times before, my shepherdess. I am not surprised at all, as I would certainly be if something of the kind had not happened."

"If that be true, then," said Elsie, smiling, "being a queen is no new thing to you, for it sits well upon you. It would not suit us girls in this land, who are putting the crowns of majesty alongside of witches' brooms, and other trinkets of the kind. Let it be as you will. You are queen, and I am your shepherdess, while this play lasts, which I hope will not be long. We must go soon to our bed. Let us gather all around, and speak of the good before we lie down in our nest."

Night came with more pleasure than it had done for a week past with Margaret. The scenes of danger were becoming common, and the presence of Elsie every moment more endearing. So rapidly and earnestly had her thoughts grasped the circumstances of her own case, and combined them with those ot her companion, that they seemed as if linked in one bond for life and for death. She had known her a long while, for all the time they had been together they had lived in every sensation of their sentient nature, and in every thought of their rational being. With pious feelings and subdued affections, she lay down on the humble couch prepared for her by the tender-hearted mother, who saw the two young maidens laid beside each other as she tucked in the warm coverlets around them, saying, in homely phrase, what Elsie had said to her:

"Arme Lammeshie, schoone Lammeshie, de genade zij met se."

"What is that your good mother wishes for us? She is always thinking of us more than of herself. My trust is so strong when she is near me, I am confident her God hears prayer."

"She is calling us poor lambs, beautiful lambs, and saying grace over us."

The leaves of autumn, dry and in abundance, formed their soft bed, and sent forth a fragrant smell. Rover nestled in cosily at their feet on one side, and Dickey lay down as softly at the other. The stream came down, murmuring melancholy music above them, and was answered in the din of the waterfall beneath. Lulled to sleep, they lay in more composure than princesses, who, after a night of dissipation, have musical instruments of all sorts played near their pillow. Our damsels, though hunted by wicked and barbarous men, were not haunted by the spectres which glide around the pillow of the evil conscience—never at ease, be it on a bed of flint or a couch of roses.

Night passed without interruption of any kind. Pleasant dreams even flitted through the brain of the hunted women. They lay down under no absorbing sinful emotions, and were therefore more calm in mind when sleep overtook them. In the morning, when Margaret awoke and found that her ever faithful Elsie was not beside her, she threw her arms around as a child does in search of its nurse. So dependent was she, that she felt more like an infant than the daughter of a soldier, who had taught his children the necessity of self-reliance upon all occasions. But these were new scenes to the English girl, and there was not time yet, nor room allowed, to give scope to the real character she possessed. Turning round, she saw there was no one at her side, so sitting up, she called:

"Elsie, dear Elsie, where are you? Come and tell me that all is well. Oh! what shall become of me, now that my only friend is gone."

Angelica was also absent at that moment, but soon returned, wringing her hands in a transport of anxiety lest something terrible had befallen her daughter.

"Wat can I do for my dochter. Martin gone, my housen burned, the cows ande sheeps, ande niggers, alle agone. Awee! awee! Elshie, Elshie, vere are you dat you never come once."

It was now that the spirit of the deserted Margaret came out in its true energy. Rousing herself up at the sound of distress, she forgot her own troubles, and wrapping around her the blanket she had worn as a mantle the previous day. She bathed her glowing temples in the fresh running stream as it passed clear over the rock. When fully equipped, she ran back to the disconsolate mother, saying:

"I am going off to look for Elsie, and I will not return till I find her. Sit down and watch till we come back."

The astonished Angelica was startled by the ardor of the delicate stranger, and looking up in her face, saw that she was sincere in her resolution; but at the same time she knew that the attempt must be vain, and certain to result in the capture or death of one so feeble and inexperienced.

"Nay, nay," said the affectionate mother, "tee cannot do any such ting as dat, we shall go down de clove road togeder and meet Elsie coming up. If she be in de hands of de vile Shandaagan, we may help her, tree of us 'gainst von; but feeble ting dat tou be, vat can tee do?"

"O mother," said the excited girl, "have you not seen how a pigeon will swell out and speak boldly in its own language when an enemy comes to its nest. Let us go."

As the two feeble creatures were about to start, they knew not whither, they chanced to look over the precipice, when far down they saw two figures in the bed of the stream; one of them could hardly be distinguished as human, only that it stood erect, and was lifting up its arms to the very point on which they themselves both stood. The other figure Margaret soon perceived was Elsie, who had already parted from her unknown companion and was on her way back, with great haste, as if she saw the uneasiness which her absence was causing. These things occurring at the moment of their departure, made them pause sufficiently long for their friend and protector to reach them in time to set their minds at rest.

"Wat's dat down dere among de bushes?" was the earnest query of the mother to her daughter just as she put her head above the ledge.

"Never mind mammy, here is a pipe and tobacco and some fresh dry punk for your tinder-box. The steel is in the red pouch at your side."

A pipe and fresh tobacco were just what Angelica needed at that instant, for collecting her scattered senses; and so her mind was diverted from the vision that rose in the mist of the glen, to the eyes of the amazed and disturbed woman. Margaret would fain have continued the inquiry, but perceiving the unwillingness of her friend to enter upon the subject, she, with the tact of good breeding, set about helping Elsie to spread out the meal that she had brought back with her upon the flat stone, which had hitherto served them as a table.

"What a fine breakfast you have brought us; beautiful white bread and milk; warm milk just from the cow. What I used to steal out and get in our dairy at home in England. Here I am drinking it on the side of these very mountains that Hendrick Hudson saw when he came up the Great River."

"Yaw mammy," said Elsie, addressing the old lady, 'it is the milk of old Blackie. I met her mooing on the side of the hill, for some one to milk her, and when she saw me, you would have cried to see how she ran to me."

The good Angelica was wiping her eyes at the account her daughter gave her; but the prudent girl went on so rapidly, that there was no room to ask questions, and it evidently appeared to the quick-eyed Margaret, that there were things behind which the caterer did not wish to tell. Her high spirits and quick motions had a sympathetic effect upon the others, so that by the time the mother's second pipe was over and the repast partaken of, there was even cheerfulness felt and shown by all. Rover had eaten up the crumbs and was watching a chance to dip his tongue into the hole where Dickey's milk was poured. Elsie was carefully gathering up the remains of the meal and putting them away in case of a dearth of food; while the reflecting Margaret was lost in reverie as she recalled the strange being she had seen that morning with her guardian; of whom it was evident she must remain in ignorance for the present. She however ventured to ask a question, as they all sat looking down through the intervening glade. "Is there no path down through the ravine there," said she, deferentially, "that we might follow and come to the river where this water is now going? My dear Elsie, it is surely better to risk some danger, than be pent up here in this high fortification and perish. I have heard soldiers say, that it was a maxim in war, that to remain and never show yourself was the sign of defeat, and sure to end in that at last."

"Ah, my lady," said Elsie, "you forget that the weak must have walls of defence, and what the wildcats up here have not in strength is given them in cunning and claws. Despair never effects any noble purpose. Let us wait another day up here in the sunshine, before we risk our lives down in the dark valley."

"All that sounds very philosophical in words, but I would be willing to venture into the dark, and get my feet bruised for the least chance of escape."

"A hundred Indians are lying across that road at this moment," said Elsie, with her hand pointed downward, "and every one of them has the scent of the Spanish blood-hound that I have heard my uncle tell about. Do you think, Miss Clinton, that you could swim to an island, when the tide is sweeping everything out into the sea? could a hunted deer break through a closing rank of men and dogs, watching for him in the thicket? I saw one, a beautiful creature, chased by a hundred hunters, and he took to the ice. The men and dogs on the banks pursuing him, but he bounded forward at such a speed, that I clapped my hands in perfect joy at the prospect of his escape, when a cunning hunter, who had lain down in the bushes, lifted his gun and gave him a fatal shot."

"You mean," said Margaret, with a sigh, "that I am a hunted deer, and that there is no hope for my escape?"

"No hope for you down through that path; by and by there may be. Go down at this moment, and you will be like a fish going into a fyke."

"And what is a fyke?" said the interested young lady, always wakened up by any new sound or scene.

"A net wide at one end like this clove, but closed at the other, and narrow, so that the fish cannot turn."

"That gives me but little hope, my friend, my protector, my adviser; but it seems after all, that you are not without some hope. May be you would prefer me to mount the hill, and seek a refuge on High Peak as you call it. I am ready to go with you to any place."

"Come, Miss Clinton," said Elsie, anxious to divert the mind of her ward from her present condition; let us go out into the sunshine and finish that queen's robe we commenced yesterday. I have some thread that we can use in binding these leaves together, as Mother Eve did in her forlorn state. We are better off than she was in the Garden of Eden."

"I am sure," said Margaret, smiling at the conceit of her friend, "she had not more brilliant colors than we have in our paradise; though on the whole, I think her outward condition was a little better than ours to the feet."

"My lady, it is not the soft or hard walks which make the difference. Let us make the most of our place, and be the noblest of beings on the mountain."

In this way the two maidens passed the early part of that day. Elsie made a crown of the laurel, and set in it three feathers of sumach, which rendered it quite imperial. The sceptre was a peeled staff, surrounded with red and yellow leaves, tufted at the top with a deep purple knot. A wreath made of the same material, several yards in length, which when tied at the ends was thrown over the right shoulder, and biased so as to come on the left side, where the sword of state hung, made of shingle wood which they found floating down the stream. The lozenged, blanket variegated with red and blue, had a hole cut in the centre, through which Margaret's head went, and having also outlets for her arms, it hung easily, not to say gracefully, upon her stately, aristocratic form; so that she really moved among these scenes more like the queen of the mountain in October, than this description would justify.

"Ha," said the enthusiastic lady, as she surveyed herself, laughing so that her face seemed like the sun struggling through the mists; "how the Duchess of Mourtelhome would envy me, were she to see me walking into the birthday masquerade. I will keep the pattern of this until I need it;" and with that she gave a few steps in the fashion of majesty, so that her companion laughed back, and with assumed obeisance bent the knee before her, while her queenship held out her hand to be kissed.

They had not got over the novelty of this amusement when they were attracted by a scream of eagles above them in the clouds, that were slowly resting on the mountain tops, where they sometimes lie for days like a fleecy turban round the head of an East Indian King.

"See," said Elsie, who was the first to speak, though not the first to perceive, "there is an eagle resting on that white cloud. He is calling to his mate for he sees where he may find her a dainty bit."

"Hush!" said Margaret, "let him rest there till I see him a little more. His voice is that of true love. Let us listen. How calmly he sits up there undisturbed; his head is above the mist; and he only seeks glimpses of the earth. The hand of the fowler cannot reach him. Like the warhorse of Job, he mocketh at fear, and is not affrighted. He smelleth the battle afar off."

"Yes, Miss Clinton, he scents his dinner, and not very far off either, if I may judge from the growling of a wolf that I hear below us, with the quarrelling of other creatures. The shots we heard yesterday left carcasses lying there, and both beasts and birds soon find out the place."

"I become terrified at your telling me these things as I

look below; but I feel strong looking up to that majestic creature. Have you seen him ever before?"

"Oh, dear lady, he has his home up there in High Peak, from spring till the winter comes near, when his mate and he, with the young ones which they have raised during the summer, go away to some warmer climate. The Dominie says they will not stop till they reach the Andes. They know the seasons better than any old man in the country; and can find a dinner where the cunningest fox in the hills has hidden it. The Dominie preached us a fine sermon not long since from the Dutch text, 'wan alwaar het doode ligchaam zal zijn, daar zullen de arenden vergaderd worden.' It is about the carcass gathering the eagles. And it was terrible to hear the good man lifting up his hand, saying, 'wherever there is a carcass, there is a bird to tear it open. Vengeance follows the guilty like instinct; cross the sea, ascend the mountain, dive into the whirlpool, there is the eagle hovering over him ready to alight upon him. No sooner is the wicked act performed than the fatal flap of the wing follows. But I see you are up in the clouds just now, and I must wait till you come down."

"Oh, yes, excuse me, Elsie, for not listening to you. How grandly he moves. Like a ship far out at sea with sails unfurled. I could trust myself on his wings, and be free. He would lay me down at my mother's side. What is that you said about the Dominie and the eagle?"

"Doth the eagle mount at thy command, and make her nest on high? From thence she seeketh her prey; and her eyes behold afar off." So Elsie quoted, adding: "the Dominie says that 'the Creator who gave power to the eagle can give freedom to the country.'"

"Ah very true, dear Elsie, but the eagle has been the sign of tyranny as frequently as of freedom; and he is a cruel, bloody bird, though he be a true king up there, and everywhere. I wish from my soul I were on his wings. See he narrows his circles, and there he seems to sit unmoved upon the air."

"Wait, my Lady Margaret, and you will see him alighting soon. His eye is fixed on some object below; and he will dart down like an arrow upon it."

Elsie was mistaken in her conjecture, for while the kingly bird did come down it was to alight on a tree that stood on the south side of the ravine, where he sat pluming himself with evident pride, stretching out his high neck over the precipice. The two spectators watched him for an hour till their eyes grew tired. Margaret's especially, melted into tears at his movements, so natural, graceful, and at the same time evincing such power. Elsie, who had not the same interest in the bird, made while she sat a wreath for herself, and was in the act of throwing it over her head when a scream from her mother, and a howl of distress from Rover, made her run to the rescue; Margaret following with equal speed. When they arrived at the spot where Angelica was, confusion spread on all sides, of what nature, neither of the two damsels could tell. There was the mother, the chief figure, in the foreground, with Rover and Dickey at her right and left, but the most confounding thing of the whole was to see the eagle in front, striking and flapping his wings with the utmost fury at all three; and but for the prompt arrival of new forces, he must have come off the conqueror.

The history of the battle, when they came to tell it in order, was this. The eagle had seen from his eyrie, the lamb playing around the platform, and made up his mind to carry him off captive; but like a cautious soldier, he determined on stratagem rather than upon attack in face of the enemy; so sitting down before the fortress, he resolved to bide his time. At one spring, and as quietly as a cat, he descended, putting his talons into Dickey's wool, and was in the act of lifting him up, when Rover, with true courage and self-sacrifice, ran to the help of his playfellow, seizing the eagle by the wing, and holding him to the ground. The brave bird, nothing daunted, let go the lamb, and turned on the dog with beak and talons, which made him yell, and try to get off in retreat, which the enemy had no mind to allow; still keeping at him, since the woolly victim had fled. By this time the eagle deemed that dog-meat was better than none, so he was in the act of lifting up poor Rover in the air when Angelica arrived on the battle-ground; and seeing her favorite struggling to be free, she rushed forward, seizing Rover by the tail. The eagle soon found that able as he was to lift either of the two four-footed creatures, it was more than he had bargained for, when a heavy Dutch vrow had taken forcible possession of the tail end of his prey. It was at this part of the contest that Elsie arrived, who, finding that the weapons of the enemy were so sharp that they drew blood at every stroke, made an effort to seize him at once by the neck, which she, by a dexterous turn, caught in her hand, choking him so that his beak became helpless. Here Margaret came on with one of Angelica's thick quilted petticoats, which she threw around him, while the old lady, with great presence of mind, took the garters from her own legs, and bound those of the dis-discomfited bird of Jove, so that he became nearly as helpless as one of her own gobblers, on his way to the Dominie's for his Christmas dinner. Conquered, though still defiant, he lay on his side, casting fiery glances at his vanquishers, who, from the fright and the battle, were in a state of great excitement.

"What shall we now do with him?" was the question which came simultaneously from the conquerors. Margaret was for setting him free at once, remembering her own imprisonment.

"I cannot," said she in her enthusiasm, "see such a bold and noble creature in chains. You may not have read of a great man like your own Washington, but I must say it, of one who delivered his country from vassalage, William Tell, who was celebrated for his markmanship, so that he could sever an apple with his arrow at a hundred paces' distance. When out on his native hills, he saw an eagle wheeling in aërial circles above his head. With the instinctive ambition of a huntsman, he put the bolt upon the string, which all knew would have brought the king of birds down to the earth, but in a moment he let the weapon fall from his hand, shouting, 'Liberty! liberty!'"

Angelica, who had none of that kind of sentiment in her composition, was for chopping off his head at once, like any common hawk's found in a barn-yard trap.

"Te wicked tief dat he is; noting betters serve him dan drink and lap lamb's bloed; wid my mind izijn hoofd willende be gebragt in een' schotel like Johannes den Dooper."

"Mammy, that is not like you. His head on a charger, like that of John the Baptist! You may live through this day, and see the prophecy fulfilled—to the 'woman was given the two wings of a great eagle, that she might fly into the wilderness, into her place where she was nourished for a time from the face of the serpent.' I could read that in Dutch to you, mammy, for you believe the old Dutch is the true language of Canaan. Let us teach the robber a lesson, and keep him a short time, and make some sport with him."

"As the Philistines did with Samson," said Margaret, rather pettishly, because her will had not been carried out. But Elsie, perceiving that he would serve to pass the time, lifted him carefully, and mounting into the fork of a tree which grew on the verge of the shelf, fastened him there. Coming down, she left him ruffling up his plumage, spreading his wings, full six feet from tip to tip, while his head stood erect three feet high; but the spring of his limbs was lost, and he sank with noble pride a prisoner, still threatening defiance on his keepers. Margaret was in raptures at the sight, and forgot for the moment her sorrow, exclaiming as she clapped her hands:

"What a tale to tell if I ever return to England, that I helped to capture the king of birds."

"It is a good omen, my lady," was Elsie's response, "that you will conquer your hard fate. The tyrant seeking to devour the innocent lamb is overcome."

"Yaw, yaw," said Angelica, "ande de vecht ande prevailed not, neder was hims found any more in den hemel."

"Many thanks to you both, my kind friends, for your words of hope. God Almighty grant it may be so."

"Yaw, yaw," said the pious mother, catching always at good things; "de Domilie says dat Satan in Gabriel's wings can be tumbled into des afgrons—dat is de bottomless pit, by a worden of prayer."

"You see, Miss Clinton, that the signs are favorable this morning, and there is no need of your doing any rash act till the hour of desperation arrives, and then it will be time enough for us to do up to our ability."

CHAPTER IX.

THE AMPHITHEATRE.

> "I've seen myself with these two eyes,
> Far grander scenes than Cæsar saw in Rome,
> Or champion joined in when the skies
> Sent back the shouts upon him with the prize;
> I saw that scene, and felt that power—at home."
>
> WESTERN TRAVELLER.

THEIR great exploit with the eagle furnished subjects of sufficient interest to engage the minds of all three for a whole day, and thus fill up the time which Elsie was so desirous of occupying, so that the mind of her charge might for the present be diverted from herself. Margaret was the eagle's favored one. Neither Elsie nor her mother durst come near to him without meeting his fiery glances, which he sent out like flame. The young enthusiast was enraptured; taking pleasure in feeding him, and even ventured to stroke down the plumage of his neck. Climbing up on the tree beside him became one of her new lessons in mountain gymnastics; so that she came at length to swing on the branches that overhung the glen with delight rather than with fear.

The sun had by this time ascended nearly to the meridian, when Elsie spread their table once more, and insisted upon their partaking with her of a dinner she had kept for them, in the basket, from the morning's repast. There was broiled chicken and roasted venison, with plenty of home-made bread. The mountain air and the hard fight had given them a keen appetite, so that the meal was relished by all three women and their three companions, dog, lamb, and eagle—each feeding her own charge. Elsie had one more surprise for them; a small bottle of the purest port wine, which cheered the hearts of all.

"One might believe, my dear Elsie, that the eagles of Elijah have been supplying your basket this morning; and if so, we have made an ungrateful return in capturing one of our friends there."

"My dear lady, we cannot always tell how our commonest blessings reach us; and it is best for us not to know all in one day,"

"Eat as de Dominie says, asking none questions for de stomach's sake, vat is set before tee." Having said this, the old mother looked round for Rover; but though she called to him in her kindest and most pursuasive tone, he did not answer. Elsie showed most excitement of the three; starting to her feet as if she waited for some apparition. If so, it was not certainly the one that came up; for on a sudden Rover came in sight, followed by that unworthy dog, Shandaagan, who took his stand upon a rocky point above the platform where they stood. The caitiff grinned a scornful smile, as he tried to look into the faces of the disconcerted women, who knew too well that he was but the shadow of another whom they both hated and dreaded still more than himself. As they feared, Kiskataam came in sight a minute afterward, uttering his usual ugh! of grim gratification at the success of his hunt.

Margaret gave a shudder of mingled fear and disgust, recalling in feeling, as in memory, the torments she had endured since she had been kidnapped from the ship. After looking aside, as if she expected yet another besides these two, she turned her back to the dizzy precipice, standing as near to it as safety would allow; her face lighted up with a courage and defiance which made the human tiger turn his eyes away, conscious of his weakness in the presence of virtue. To relieve his growing embarrassment, he ventured to address the young lady, more to keep his own courage up than in any hope of daunting her determination.

"Will the Fawn run now, or wait to be eaten up by the big teeth of the red wolf? His feet are on the trail of the weak Fawn. He will be down in the length of ten arrows. Let the Fawn run now with the Indian. He will carry her to the big canoe down there, and put her beside the great soldier and his squaw."

This artful speech, delivered in the softest tones, and with his finger pointing down the clove to where the river is almost seen, was well calculated to make an impression on a young female, imprisoned among strange scenes, and trembling still more in the prospect of being captured by one that she hated with a perfect hatred. Had any other man on earth offered her the same convoy, she would have accepted of it; but she had proved his hypocrisy already, and was not a moment in deciding against the proffered help. Elsie, who had been watching the movements of her countenance with the keenest scrutiny, was prepared to thwart the sinister purpose, had there been any wavering on the part of her ward. But the hesitation, if any, was but for a moment; for the face of the captive assumed the most ineffable scorn, which the wily serpent interpreted without requiring verbal expression, which provoked the savage more than a torrent of words. These feeble women, even the simple Angelica, had put on a calmness which confounded their enemy, and rendered him almost mad; all the more because he expected to hear the voice of Clifford in the rear every moment. Whatever, therefore, he had to do for himself, must be done quickly. Perceiving that Elsie was the prime mover of Miss Clinton's action, he tried that string, gently at first, as if conscious of the tenderness beneath. Knowing from past experience that the least scratch of an unsheathed claw would bring upon him a storm, before which he must retire, he partly addressed both the young women, as he said, in his most smiling way:

"The Boerman's young Wildcat will go with the Fawn. Shandaagan is good Indian hunter."

Elsie had not the self-restraint of Miss Clinton. Having

always full freedom at home, her speech was ever the ready utterance of her feelings, and now that her contempt for the mean red-skin was so deep, it was all she could say to bid him—

"Go off to Stony Clove, where the squaws are lying hungry beside their pappooses, whimpering for their double-tongued daddies."

A flash of savage passion crossed the face of the smooth deceiver, when he leaped down on the step beneath, along with his attendant, coming up close to the very spot where the three females were standing, with their faces toward their enemies. Elsie was all alert, and whispering to her mother to keep an eye on one savage, she took the chief to herself. In the front of Miss Clinton she kept Kiskatam at bay. On the other hand, Shandaagan was pressing forward with the evident intention of pushing the old lady aside, so that he might aid his master in securing Elsie, who was the one most to be dreaded. But Angelica had not stood so long unprepared, for with a stone in her strong hand, she struck the skull of the Indian such an unexpected blow that he reeled, and all but fell. A moment more, and his tomahawk would have done its work on her head, when Rover seized the calf of his leg from behind, giving it a bite which would have made a white man scream; this gave the old lady a chance with another stone to strike the hand that held the weapon of death, when he let it fall just at her feet. She picked it up so aptly that the coward sprang back, and wreaked his vengeance by a kick on the dog's ribs, which added to the music of the day.

In the meantime, the Indian chief was pressing hard upon Elsie, whose courage was rising equal to the emergency, as she prepared for the worst, though it was not the intention of the wily foe to do more than frighten her into compliance, since he could not wheedle them into his charge. He said fiercely:

"Does the Wildcat seek a lead nut through her brown hair," as he pointed the muzzle of his gun in the direction of the brave girl's breast, who, not in the least daunted, to the evident surprise of the enemy, drew from her bosom, where it lay concealed, a beautiful silver-mounted pistol, armed with a small dagger, that flew out at the touch of a spring.

"Does the bloody Catamount want a ball through his false heart? Let him come one step nearer and there are two ready for him."

Foiled alike in his attempt at flattering and frightening these feeble women, he was put to his wit's end, and was evidently intent upon something desperate, when, to his increased mortification, the chief actor in this wicked drama stepped suddenly upon the stage. Standing upon the bank that ran across the ravine at a higher point, Clifford looked down upon the whole party with an interest and a hesitation which a wicked man, still possessed of some honor, may be supposed to have when he sees the victim of his desire, and when his conscience tells him that he is sinking in his own esteem. He stood pausing and preparing himself, not unlike the eagle before it descended on the lamb, hating the act, yet forced by insatiable appetite to devour. To none of the parties was the arrival of Clifford more unwelcome than to to Kiskataam. His intentions had been, up to this moment, to carry off Miss Clinton. He would have taken her back into the wilderness if possible; but rather than not be revenged on the Englishman, he would have set her down safe in the ship from whence he abducted her. Sick of the bargain he had made with the unprincipled rake, he had been nursing his vengeance ever since their quarrel on the night of his arrival; but now all his selfish schemes were blown aside, and he must deliver up the prize to the one who had bought him. Grinding his teeth with rage and disappointment, he had no alternative but to smother his wrath, and seem to yield, by showing an extra zeal for the master's interest, so that even the simple Angelica said:

"De Yudas petray his maister for ane kiss."

"Miss Clinton, I have found you at last, and after an eternity of anxiety," were the first words of the cold, passionate hypocrite. "You have the cunning of the fox with the beauty of the fawn, so well do you hide, and so fleetly and gracefully do you move."

With these words, he bowed so like one paying deference to beauty and innocence, that none save the most knowing in the art of the spoiler could have guessed that aught lay beneath the surface but the purest stream of sincerity. To his bow the lady gave no further heed than to look toward him, watching his smallest motion.

"Miss Clinton," said the artful villain, coming nearer and standing quite over the place where the others were grouped, for all were waiting his motion; "you look in that dress as if you were prepared to come with me to the place where nature is exhibited on her greatest scale, and when I have you there, standing in the island that divides the tumbling waters, a poet would call you the genius of Niagara."

Margaret had been so absorbed in the events of the morning, up to this moment, that her fantastic attire was the least of her thoughts, but being now reminded of that, and casting a rapid glance over her person, a slight blush tinged her cheek as she reflected on her folly in the midst of her distress, but this was no time to be affected by trifles; important realities called for action, and for endurance; now she could neither be flattered nor frightened out of her chaste dignity, by the man who had tried before this to fascinate her, as the snake draws the helpless bird into his jaws.

"Miss Clinton," repeated the artful seducer, "you never in the days of your greatest beauty, in the brilliant assemblies we have attended together, looked half so queenly as now, standing amidst all that rugged grandeur around you, and yourself so seemly in the trappings of that holy nature you love so well. Could you but see the great lakes of the North and of the West, your spirit would expand to a breadth which you are as yet a stranger to."

"Defile not the pure air around you with such flattery. Your breath is hateful to me; I hate the pure things you put your praise upon; I have become tame, and tired of my childish romance, since it has cost me so dearly already. My liberty has been bartered for it, and before night falls, my life may be the sacrifice. But, thank God, my virtue still remains and"——

"May not," interrupted the smooth sinner, "virtue and love dwell together in a cottage, while romance would ride out in company on play-days? I remember some such sentiment sung, in a home we wot of. Our own Shenstone, you know, sings:

> "'I have found out a gift for my fair,
> I have found where the wood pigeons breed.'"

"No more!" said the impatient lady; "you have touched the wrong chord; I will sing the real truth, as Shenstone sung

> "''Tis his with mock passions to glow,
> 'Tis his with smooth tales to unfold;
> How her face is as white as the snow,
> And her bosom be sure is as cold.'"

With that he leaped down on to the same platform where

the three fugitives and the two Indians were already standing. Margaret stood in the centre, her autumnal crown on her head, the wreath round her person, in a diagonal direction, and her blanket robe bound at the waist by another wreath of willow twigs, that confined it, so that she moved without tripping on the skirts. As she saw Clifford approaching her, she exclaimed, with more force than could be expected of her:

"Stand back wretched man; God has still provided me with a retreat, that I may escape from your hands."

"God himself cannot save you now, Miss Clinton. See on either side of you my two faithful servants, the brave Indian chief Kiskataam, and the cunning Shandaagan, and behind you is the roaring fall. You see that that Providence you speak of has delivered you into my hand. Surrender at will is your true courage now, and you may make your own terms. Margaret, in yielding to your fate, you conquer your conqueror."

With these half earnest words said in a serio-light manner, the bad man took a step nearer, partly bending himself forward, taking off his cap as in deference to the presence of a queen; while the whole group presented a picture worthy of a painter's eye. It was well that a pause was taking place, since it gave time for the working of those passions within, which ever gain force as they are restrained, and the time given allowed Elsie an opportunity of reflecting on the critical position of her friend. Her bosom heaved, as the veins of her neck swelled, her whole frame expanded a size which seemed above common, and yet there was a symmetry of proportion which filled the mind more than the eye.

"Stand back, caitiff!" was the frantic exclamation of Miss Clinton, to the still approaching Clifford. "Stand back! Soldier though you be, you are a coward in attacking women, and I will not trust myself in your hand. I have at least one chance of escape."

With this she sprung up into the tree at her back, climbing to the branch on which Aurelius stood, welcoming her with his curved neck, and spreading wings as if he invited her to her chariot; she sat out on the branch swinging over the deep gulf, making the heads of all but herself dizzy.

"For God's sake, Miss Clinton, do not tempt Providence

in that way; come down and I swear by my honor, that you may go where you please rather than have your blood on my hands."

"I will not trust a man whose cheek grows pale at the sight of death, and calling himself a soldier; first mocking God, and the next moment invoking his name, then swearing by an honor that has been tarnished by ingratitude and violated friendship."

The blood came back to the face of Clifford at these reproaches. He was mad, and knew not how to wreak his vengeance, or on whom. He felt himself weak in the presence of such daring as he saw. Besides, the scene before him, wild and romantic, had a charm which captivated his cultivated, and experienced eye. Margaret was dressed in her queenly robes, and unconscious of her beauty at the moment. Her face flushed, her hair hanging loose on her shoulders, she stood balancing herself on the branch with one hand on the proud eagle's neck, and the other ready to loosen the string that bound him to the tree. Clifford, at the moment, would have given all he called his own to have had the lady at his command, whose spirit so proudly defied him.

"Clifford," she called out in transport, "you see that the God you mocked has provided for me a way of escape; I am not without a friend since I can rise on this noble creature's wings."

"For the love of God, Miss Clinton, do not think of trusting yourself thereon. I swear on my knee that you may do as you please, only come down."

"I will trust the eagle before I will an ungrateful and dishonorable man misnamed soldier and unworthy of his flag. I feel safe. I am not the first that has been thrust upon a pinnacle, and who came down safe in angels' charge."

All this time the noble Aurelius was excited to the highest degree, by the loud speaking and the gestures of the different parties. He felt the sympathy of human passion, in which he joined so fiercely that he kept the soldier in check, by his fluttering and his screaming. It would have been more than a strong man durst have done to venture without arms near to him. Without measuring the full strength, skill and rapidity of such an enemy, Clifford made a spring at the eagle, hoping to bring him down, and thus cool the ardor of his mistress, but before he could seize his feet the proud creature, quick as thought, struck the intruder's cheek with his beak below the eye, for which he aimed, and sent him back with a force and a pain which brought both blood and tears, as he stood the object of secret ridicule and contempt. His rage and bad passions were now up, and pausing a moment so as to gather force, he said:

"Miss Clinton, I have no time to parley, and since you will not yield yourself to me, your protector must pay the penalty of insulting one of his majesty's servants."

With that he levelled his pistol with the intention of putting a ball through the bird's wing. Quick as a flash, Elsie stepped forward, and struck the muzzle aside, when the shot fell harmless in the gulf below. The hot-brained soldier, now in a transport of fury, looked like a demon on the brave Dutch girl, whom he had hardly noticed before, and who now stood his glance unappalled, as he demanded, "Who dares to interfere with my game?"

"No soldier of King George shall insult the sign of my country in my presence," was the prompt answer.

"Ah," said the mortified man, "and have we got a young rebel Whig up here in the mountains, and beyond the lines too; come bold chief, let us bind these rebellious arms and carry her along with old Abiel and Schuyler to Fort Niagara. She will serve as maid of honor to the queen when there: I see she wears her livery already."

During the excitement of these few minutes, the three men had closed round the beleagured women, and seemed about to make the final charge. Angelica had another stone prepared for her foe in one hand and the glittering tomahawk in the other. Elsie had her finger at the trigger of her pistol and Margaret's courage was wound up to the highest pitch, so that she seemed to court the chance of taking her aërial voyage rather than to fear it. If she had fear, it was of that kind which would have made her blood circulate more freely, as when stepping into the parachute of a balloon, in which she had perfect confidence. With eye and hand firm, her dress carefully freed from the twigs of the tree, she was ready for the final spring the instant her enemy was within a yard of her person; when a voice startled all as if it came out of the rocks:

"Clifford! coward! stand back and face your sworn enemy."

The apparition was not calculated to allay the sudden alarm of the parties; though it was a human form that stood before them and a human voice that spoke to them. It was human, but dressed in bear-skins, with a high crowned hat of the same material; the face, rough with hair, seemed as if the same animal had provided the man with a beard from his jaws. Standing erect on the north side of the shelf, the figure confronted the three men, who stood waiting for the next movement. The Indians fell back to the upper side, while Clifford moved to the south extremity of the platform confronting his new foe. The stream of water, shallow at the time, ran between them; while the females standing with their backs to the precipice, were about equal distance from the two men, who were already eying each other as malignant enemies ever do, when suddenly brought face to face. As soon as Clifford sufficiently recovered himself, he demanded haughtily:

"Who dares to insult a king's officer on duty or to interfere with the king's business in any way? or what menial in an idiot's garb has the temerity to call Colonel Clifford a coward."

"His duty! the villain's duty! ha! ha, ha!"

The laugh froze the blood of even the stolid Indians, who looked on as if they had been turned to stone. "Your duty to employ a savage to decoy an enthusiastic, artless maiden into your toils! The child of your best friend, the man who defended your black name from eternal disgrace. Your duty! to hunt after women as tigers are circled round! Duty!" and the figure laughed again in scorn, until it seemed as if the echoes were the responding of the fiends from the pit of damnation. So voluble and full were the answers from up the clove that Clifford, though accustomed to scenes of danger, shrank from the voices that called upon his conscience to reply and defend himself against those superstitions which were unmanning him.

"Fool that I am," he burst out, "to be foiled of my purpose by a madman, spook, or wizard; I have heard of you before. This is too much, and a dose of powder and lead must silence your gibberish. See if you are witch enough to catch that in your skull cap."

And with that there was a flash and a report. The ball pierced the high hat of the strange being, bringing it to the rock; and when the smoke passed away, the soldier was waiting to see the effect of his fire, when to his utter amazement the rough robe of the figure had also dropped off, even to his beard, and there, instead of a maniac, stood an officer of his majesty's 13th regiment of foot, in his undress, fully armed and equipped for battle ; all except that his head was bare. Great beads of perspiration broke out on the brow of Clifford, while his lower jaw fell as if smitten by death, and his lips involuntarily muttered " Calderwood."

" Thank you, Clifford, for that shot," were the first words of the unveiled man. " See, here is a better mark for you. Aim at this star, won by your side on the banks of the Hoogly. Aim at it, for it lies on the heart you have already riven asunder. Two full years ago, I warned you of the coming day of vengeance. It has arrived. There is a just God in the heavens."

At this part of the action, going on in that lately solitary chamber of nature, the different parties who had been collecting from all sides, were arriving, so as to surround the little, but perfect water-fall. The ledge of the rock served as a stage on which the main actors stood, while all around, at different points, were the spectators. Down the stream, and looking upward, were the mock Indians, gaping in astonishment. The Mohawks stood on the sides of the gulf like statues of bronze, gazing on the marvellous scene. The officers on parole who were in pursuit of game, came in from above. While Cuffee and his crew were perched like crows on the high trees outside of all. They were rooks in a gallery of nature.

The now unveiled and chief actor gave a glance of grim satisfaction around him, saying, " One of us must die. Surely, the brave Clifford, whose praises have been sung by the belles of St. James, will not show the white feather! You coward! you seducer, you ingrate, can you not be provoked; can the blood of the proud Clifford not start at the epithet coward!"

The petrified and quivering sinner at this leaped as if he had been stung, and looking up, he cried with a husky voice, " It shall never be said of Clifford that he feared death at the hand of any man : I am ready."

The two combatants stood at the extremes of that stage; the Indians on one side, and the women on the other, so that the balls must pass between them. Elsie grasped her pistol tighter, for she had a terrible purpose in her mind, in the event of one falling. Margaret bent forward from her seat, so steadily, that her plumes did not quiver ; but the pious Angelica hid her face in earnest prayer, as she thought of an immortal soul passing in blood to the presence of the Great Judge. The red men dilated their eyes to the utmost, but stood in an evident transport of expectation that showed an inward pleasure, whatever might be the result.

The deadly weapons were raised: a flash and a report, and a fall. It was the conscience-stricken Clifford. Calderwood ran forward with his sword drawn, for he feared the treachery of the deceiver; but he soon found that it was needless, for the ball had struck the right arm below the shoulder, shattering the bone.

"I bargained for nothing less than life," said the enraged Calderwood. Confess to be a liar or die. The steel is at your throat."

"Never! never!" was the bitter reply of the vanquished but still unhumbled man. The foot of the victor was on his breast, and the weapon ready for the last plunge, when it was thrust aside by a powerful arm from behind. It was Brandt, attracted by the reports of the pistols, and just in time to save the life of his companion in arms.

CHAPTER X.

FAWN'S LEAP.

"For my part I would rather kiss the lips I love, than dance with all the graces of Greece, after bathing themselves in the spring of Parnassus. Flesh and blood for me, with an angel in the inside."—STERNE'S TRAVELS.

WHILE the grand tragedy recorded in the last chapter was acting, the spectators, as if spell-bound, stood waiting the issue. A common feeling of horror and surprise pervaded all. It was one of those seasons when the mind grasps the whole at a glance, the daring, the danger and the sublimity of the position which the young lady had taken, and where she sat with such grace and majesty. The other figures in the foreground were ranged according to their place. But the fear entertained by all, lest the fatal leap might be taken, overwhelmed every other emotion.

Every one was relieved and drew a deep breath when the danger was past. The villainous pursuer had fallen, and they had time to follow out the doings of the rest. The most prominent were four men dressed in the assumed Indian garb: one of them without any previous warning, seized the vile Kiskataam with a vigor and skill that nearly overcame him at once. But that traitor was no common enemy. The savage saw that the cup of death was put to his lips and he resolved to sell his life dear, and then enter the council hall of his fathers in company. So, measuring the gulf toward which he was rolling in the death grip of Bertram, he determined to draw over the young Englishman with him if he must fall himself. Seeing that the lady from her seat had now recognized her lover, he gave a fiendish smile of delight at the agony she was undergoing. It seemed impossible to elude the fate which the Indian aimed at, and which Bertram in his eagerness to punish, did not see. Like a young lion twisted around by a serpent, the sailor felt the coil about his body, but with a sailor's skill, springing suddenly upon his feet, he brought up the red man, who received as suddenly the grip and throw of a practised wrestler, bringing him to the hard rock with a crash that made him feel as if every bone in his body was broken: before he had time to recover his scattered senses he was bound hand and foot, and left lying on his back with a stoical indifference, waiting for his fate, which he saw was now sealed.

During these fierce combats the minds of both Margaret and Elsie were wrought up to the highest tension. A double beat of the heart indeed was felt by both as the four young men leaped on the stage of action, disguised in their Indian garb; for then they really deemed their time had come; but the quick eye of Elsie soon discovered that Teunis was present, and she knew instinctively that he had brought friends with him.

"Courage, my lady," was her piercing whisper, "deliverance has come at last; but let us stand still till the battle is over and render help if we can."

And there they remained fixed till Kiskataam was conquered. Clarence had rushed forward to the tree on which his now agitated sister stood, pale, as death. The blood ran to her heart, as she fell nearly fainting in her brother's arms. Teunis showed no sluggishness now, for, leaping to the side of Elsie, he grasped her round the waist as if afraid of her being taken from him, imprinting a kiss that was not unheard, amidst even that tumult, and which she returned as warmly; but it was followed by as hard a slap of the hand on the cheek of her lover which made it glow a whole hour afterward.

"A pretty kindereen you are, Teunis, to leave two helpless women folks upon the hills."

"Elshie! Elshie!" said the overwhelmed Angelica. "Ye kenen nae dat de kind lad was liken to go out of himself on de day dat he lost tee on de hill; sae hold ty peace, and be tankfull for all our mercies."

During this little byplay, which even in the times of the greatest commotion will be played out, Bertram and Clarence were bending over Margaret, who, soon recovering from the shock of this sudden deliverance, opened her eyes, fearfully looking into the face of Bertram, lest all might be a deception. The latter dropped a few warm tears such as a heroic heart will send forth when love returns fond glances as it did here. The kiss of affection was freely given to both brother and lover.

The guilty Clifford sat where he saw the whole. Writhing in his pride and remorse, wounded and defeated, he turned himself away from the sight, gnashing his teeth with rage and pain like what we may suppose Satan to have felt when he saw our first parents in the midst of their happiness.

There was a lull in the tempest, and the late busy actors were enjoying the benefit of the quiet, waiting for the command of some master; no one exactly knew whom, for as yet they had been thrown together as by chance. An underhand movement there must have been, which had succeeded it is true, but the very skillfulness of the operator had nearly undone the whole. An hour sooner or later would have changed the face of things. The dangerous experiment therefore of allowing the *dénoûment* to come out in a public display, was more worthy of a playwright than of a wise man, who never waits for a better chance, when he has an almost certain issue. The man who arranged the plot might have delivered these fugitive women a day sooner, but having ulterior views of revenge, he tempted that Providence, who, notwithstanding his rash folly, crowned his scheme with success.

Calderwood, as he was now known to all, was in earnest council with Brandt, whose mind was evidently yielding to what was presented to him. A piece of parchment, such as bears the commission of an officer in the army of Great Britain, was held out to the Mohawk, while the other hand, with earnest gesticulations, was pointing to the several parties within sight, as if he were expounding to the mind of the puzzled Indian some point of difficulty. All at once the face of the red man shot forth a fierce light. He saw that he had been imposed upon, and coming forward to the place where Margaret sat, still arrayed in her queenly robes, he smiled and looked from her to the eagle that perched above her on the tree. Gazing on the bird, he folded his arms, absorbed in thought; then cast a glance at his own form, which a reader of nature would have interpreted to mean, "We are the true children of the Great Spirit."

"Does the Fawn wish her bird to cross the big water when she goes to the green fields of the great Father George?" This was said evidently with the intention of drawing out something else than a bare answer about the eagle.

"No, Great Chief; the bird shall be set at liberty when I go from here, if my will be law; I love England, and he loves his mountain home. He is screaming for his mate; I have found," she was almost saying—mine; but stopping in the midst of the sentence, she sprang again into the tree, and bidding Elsie look, she loosened the string that bound the legs of Aurelius, stroked his noble neck down with her hand, while he returned her fondness by rising to his full height. Feeling himself at liberty, he rose on his wings, as they spread at their full length. For a moment he hung over the deep lin, then slowly rising, he soared away to his mountain home.

As he ascended, and until he was nearly out of sight, not a word was spoken by any one, when the Mohawk turned on Margaret the look of perfect approbation, saying:

"The Fawn shall be Brandt's sister, for her love to his brother, in setting him at liberty; she will wear this, and be one of the Mohawk wise squaws." With that, as she descended, he put a silver pin in her blanket robe, having a shell attached to it. He moved back to where Calderwood waited for him, and as he passed the place where Clifford sat, he gave him one of those looks of contempt which only an Indian can put on.

"The tongue of the big warrior folds in two," said he. "The Fawn is the kid of the king's Clinton."

By this time the true and the disguised Indians had come in, and were lying all around, waiting the will of their chief. The hunt was past, and had ended so entirely different from the expectations of all, that their minds were in wonder at what should next come up, when suddenly the chief Mohawk started to his feet, and all his tribe seemed to have risen at the same moment. Their quick ears had discerned their own war-whoop swelling over the hills and the glens, till it reached them. Then came the repeated reports of fire-arms, declaring that a skirmish was taking place not far off, which demanded the presence of the leader. Brandt, without further warning, shouted his war-cry, followed by the united voices of his men around him, till the rocks and the dells sent back the sounds doubled, and redoubled, as if the departed spirits of ten thousand warriors were raised from their slumbers by the call, to repeat the music they loved so well, once more amidst the scenes of former glory.

In a moment, Brandt had cut the bark that bound Kiskataam's ankles and wrists; ordering him to his feet, he put him under a guard of his own men, who drove him off before them at full speed. Then pointing Clifford to the westward, he said, or seemed to say, there is now your only chance of escape; the bad man did not hesitate, for though fainting through loss of blood, and suffering from the spiculæ of the bone in the flesh, he was forced into motion. Leaving the former companions of his proud days more like a prisoner than a colonel of his majesty's troops, and the commander of Fort Niagara. He had no alternative but to go, for the looks of scorn and contempt that met him withered his soul; yet still, with the proud step of the soldier, he walked off with the Mohawk.

After the coast was clear, and none were left except the Clintons and their attendants, they looked round on one another, as if a feeling of forsakenness had come over them, and that some one was expected to take the command.

"Where is our captain, Gabriel?" was the cry of more than one. That faithful follower had singled out, as the special object of his vengeance, the mean caitiff, Shandaagan, whose fear had early in the fray got the mastery of his desires. While the attention of the company were engaged by the conflict between the sailor and the chief, the parasite minion slunk away behind the scenes, taking the bed of the stream as his road of retreat. Gabriel, who perceived his motions, and knew him of old, pursued after him in hot haste. The Indian, who knew the path better than the pale face, and who had not endured quite so much fatigue as the other, was soon out of sight, leaving the crest-fallen Sopusonian without a laurel to carry away of this great victory.

"We are about moving," said Bertram, "and were beginning to fear that the cannibals had eaten you up. 'Better the end of a feast than the beginning of a fight.' You know the glutton's proverb."

"Yes, sir, but not the maxim that rules you, judging from the hearty good will with which you encountered that red rascal. But hark! there is the Dominie and his congregated troops, on the rear of the Mohawk. Gracious heaven, there must be hot work there, if guns speak the truth to-day."

"I am off," said Teunis, "to help the Dominie. He helped me and mine, and Martin Schuyler is one of the captives."

"I will lose an arm in his defence," said Clarence. "Brave soul that he is, with all his oddity."

"And I am with you," said Gabriel. "Let the sailor navigate the ship now. Carry your passengers to port, Elsie will be your pilot; and let us all meet, if we can settle this affair, at the Flat Rock, before sundown."

CHAPTER XI.

A BRIDGE OF GOLD FOR AN ENEMY'S RETREAT.

"A wolf peeping into a hut where a company were regaling themselves with a joint of mutton, exclaimed: 'O Lord, what a clamour these men would have raised had they caught me at such a banquet.'"—ÆSOP.

THE plan adopted by the Dominie's party had been scrupulously carried out, and at the same time so secretly, that not a rumor of their approach had reached the camp of the Mohawks. Their reverend leader had two objects in his mind: *Firstly*, as he would have said himself, to prevent any communication between the North and the South through Brandt's aid. It was reported that the lady spy was a young man in woman's apparel, who had succeeded in making his escape by the way of the Round Top. Every member of the Consistory present said "he must be prevented." "The he jade," said the roused pastor; "we must skin her this time."

"Aye, aye, minister," said Grant; "skin for skin, as the Scripture says; and fegs, sir, your name is Skinniman; but it's no easy putten saut on a mouse's tail."

"We must keep the rascal from getting on board the ship: and *secondly*, my brethren, deliverance of the captives. If we can drive the savages back, well and good after that; let us try."

There were some who insinuated concerning the officers on parole, as if they were on a pretended hunt; but the Dominie would not allow a word to be spoken against their honor; and when any one whispered suspicion of Clarence, the good man got so angry that all were glad to hold their peace except Mat Van Deusen, who wanted to know more of those "paper things that had such power."

As to Clarence, who did not appear till the close of the chase, there was before him a daring course, which he did not hesitate to pursue. He entered into the circle that morning, resolved to follow the chief robber, and either thwart him or die. The attention of Clifford was early arrested to the movements of his mysterious countryman. The experienced soldierly air of the youth, who held his head up so firmly, and the manner in which he stepped from stone to turf, put him on the alert. Perhaps the features of Clarence might recall an image discovered by his conscience of late in his dreams: a face which he was impelled to follow, though it spoke of vengeance. Once he was upon the point of demanding of Clarence who he was, and why he followed him, when some call in the chase diverted him from his present aim. When the hunters made their first stop, the two did not meet in the bed of the cascade. During the second part of the chase, Clarence was not so successful in keeping Clifford in view. That wily sinner had more persons to watch than one. The two Indians, Kiskataam and his foil, had made a sudden turn around the corner of a rock, and being suspicious of treachery during these two days past, Clifford followed them at full speed, coming up to them just in time to take the captive out of their hands, and to meet his own reward. When Clifford and Clarence did meet, it was to scowl that fierce frown, which proud men, whether victors or defeated, send out upon each other, when hate burns freely, but which passed over Clarence's face the moment he saw his sister safely out of the traitor's hands.

The division under Van Vechten fell back, so as to release the captives taken off by force from the Vlatts, while that under Salisbury drew away to the west, so as to intercept the Mohawk on his retreat. The moment he perceived the treachery of Clifford, and found out that Miss Clinton, whom they had been waiting for so long, was not the daughter of the rebel Clinton, but of the great soldier, his men were ordered to the west through Katrina Montour's country. The red men, impatient of delay, were already on the road, and their chief only remaining behind that his mind might be fully satisfied, when the war-whoop of his tribe was sounded with the nona—retreat.

Salisbury, who had posted his men on the side of a rising ground, which looked to the southwest, lay down, quietly waiting the van of the enemy. The orders were, "do not rise till the party has passed at least half through; then take him in the flank. Keep your ears open for the word."

The Dominie, who came up to this party, after surveying their position, insisted that the space before them gave the Indians too good a chance for keeping clear of the ambuscade, and that they would be discovered before the main body came forward. "I am for giving the scoundrels a bridge of gold to retreat by, but not quite so wide as that." The reverend pastor was right. Some impatient, undisciplined militia-man gave a loud call to a comrade just as the Indians were turning the angle of the hill, when a pause was ordered, and a wide sweep taken; skulking among the trees and by the knolls, Salisbury ordered one volley, but the bullets fell short of the aim. The rest was a scattering fight, with the exception of a show of battle; but when Brandt himself came up, the skirmish was a mere frolic. The moment that chief appeared, the blood of the Dominie rose so that it took all the force of the company to restrain him.

"Let me alone if you will not help. Don't you see the heathen tiger there, how he stalks before us, with as much assurance as Goliath did with his greaves of brass and his weaver's beam. Let me give him one stone at least, I tell you, from the back of that tree on the other side of the valley. I may bring him down and revenge the country for the blood he has shed at Cherry Valley and Wyoming."

"Yes, but Dominie, he will send that tomahawk of his through your skull before you load again; and you are too heavy to run fast." This was said by the captain, with a sly wink to the rest.

"Stop there, you bloody pagan, till I get one shot at you," shouted out the earnest man; and with that he let fly, but his mark had a tree between him and the muzzle before the trigger was drawn. Well was it for him, for the aroused minister was a good shot, and the ball sank into the trunk of the tree. Brandt, to show that he did not despise the black coat and cocked hat, came out suddenly and returned the fire, so that the bullet whizzed over the mark, but without injury.

"Come out from that, you skulking red-skinned murderer," the Dominie roared out at the full pitch of his voice, "and let me have as good a chance, and see if you ever reach the Mohawk flats again."

By this time the Indians had succeeded in finding their way by the bed of the stream that runs by the foot of the hill, and it would have been folly to follow, more especially as all the prisoners, with the exception of Elder Abiel and his son, had been recaptured by the reserve under the command of Grant. That eccentric mortal, on the watch for a chance to distinguish himself, came upon the enemy's rear at the time of the surprise produced by the sudden appearance of Salisbury, and carried off Martin Schuyler, with others, in triumph. The guard set over the captives were some of their disguised neighbors, who, justly dreading the wrath which would come on them, now that their cause was lost, ran in double quick time away from vengeance.

"Tak care o' thae puir captives there," Grant roared out, "a deel's dozen o' you; let the rest o' you follow me after thae fause guissards, deceitful loons that they are. Were I but within ten yards o' them, if I would na pepper their doups for them—'Dredge their drodem,' as my granny, honest woman, used to say."

All this time the big brawny fellow was running at the head of his party, uttering all kinds of speeches against the heads and hearts of the renegades before him, till he got as near to some of them as was safe for himself, he being actually alone, when there were half a dozen of the terrified false faces turned upon him in desperation. For the time he forgot that a mean fox, when earthed in his hole, will snarl and bite the largest mastiff. One figure, who turned out to be the town tailor, wheeling round in terror, plunged a knife into the fleshy part of the Scotchman's arm, and nearly succeeded in giving Grant his last lesson.

"You miserable neer-do-weel," said Grant, "is that the way you meet your neebors in the woods that have come sae far, and at sic expense, to see you?"

So taking the frightened artist by the nape of the neck and the seat of his breeches, he shook him with a force which made his teeth chatter and his eyes to start out of their sockets.

"Tak that, you limpin limb o' hungry humanity, and see

if you can learn to behave yoursel at hame instead of here, shewen your campsie grey claith." And with that he renewed the shake, till the tailor, in an ague fit of horror that made every hair stand on end, screamed out:

"Mercy, mercy, Hughie Grant; let me go, and I'll be as true a Whig as ever breathed, all my life long."

"Mercy, indeed," said the other, "after you've tried to put that whittle up to the heft in my brisket bane. You see by that bluid rinnin there what your bodkin has done, you fause loon. I'll tear the garment aff you, as Ahijah did the son o' Jeroboam, and send you hame to clip the tails aff lice."

And with that he put his great fingers up to the throat of the tailor, stripping him from head to heel of all his Indian garb, then taking whatever steel was in the dress, he left him to buckle on what was left of it, while he ran in search of other renegades.

But it was every man for himself there on that day. The place was favorable for hiding, and the few that were caught were punished on the spot, if worth punishment, or suffered to run out of the way, lest they should know them and be obliged to notice who they were. Some followed in the trail of Brandt, afraid to return.

On Grant's going back to his party, he met the Elder Abiel, together with his son, walking westward at full speed, as if retreating. The Scotchman, confounded at the sight, came up to them, saying, in his broadest style of speech:

"Whare the warl are you gaun noo, Mr. Abiel? One might think you had got eneuch o' the hill, by this time, to mak' you turn your face the ither way."

"I am running after Brandt," said the old man, sorrowfully. "I am afraid I shall not get up to him. David, here, will follow me, though he is not obliged to go. See if you can get him to return back with you. We can be both ill spared from home in these times."

"What does this mean?" the Scotchman cried out, scarcely comprehending what he heard. "Are you gaen fey? Tell me, Dauvit, for you seem to have some sense left."

Abiel's son, to whom this appeal was made, said, in a grouty way, that the whole company had had the chance of escaping that morning, had it not been for his father.

"When I awakened," said he, "the Mohawks were asleep every man of them, their arms all stacked against a tree. I whispered, now is our time, when dad just raised his head, looking round, and, as he lay down, said he would not do that for all King George's dominions. Some nice freak of what he calls honor. For all that, where he goes I go, though it should be to the gallows."

"David," said the Elder, "do not speak in that way, else I will command you to return. Here is the Dominie coming, I will leave it to him."

That earnest leader of the camp of Israel had, after his own personal combat with the big Mohawk, all but forced Salisbury and his party back from pursuing the enemy. Though his own blood was so hot that he was ready to meet Brandt, or anything else on the open field, he was too cautious a man not to see the folly and the danger of attempting to intercept or pursue an Indian army, under such a leader, far into the wilds. For with all this prudence, he had no small idea of his own knowledge of military affairs, derived from an extensive reading in ancient and modern history, which he was apt to quote a little too freely, and in the circumstances of the times—laughably.

He was laying down the laws of war to Salisbury in his loudest tones, with his usually violent gestures; the latter impatiently listening to what he thought he knew better than the reverend soldier. As they both came along side by side, they were seen by the others who were waiting for them. The Dominie, in no hurry now, riding as he was, a favorite hobby, came on striding over the narrow bridle path—for he was what jockeys call, a wide traveller—stopping every tenth step, putting his broad body in the irritated captain's way, who had been robbed of a share in the laurels won.

"You see, Billy, you were nearly caught in the woods like Absalom: you and your men would have been cats' meat to these savages. You see, Billy, when the Trojans and the Greeks fought with each other, the one had the goddess of wisdom, Minerva, on their side, and the other, Mars. Had I gone with you, then it would have had these two, and we might, with God's help, as I always write on all my prescriptions, have prevailed. But, Billy, I could not do anything without your arm; nor could you do without my counsel."

"That may all be true, Dominie," said the person lectured; "but when a man is taunted with cowardice, he is willing to throw all on the chance of proving his courage."

"Poh! is it there where the pain lies? You are no coward man, if that will please you; and that you have not had Ulysses by your side, is not your fault. You are Hector himself, only had you but chosen that narrow passage on this side of where you planted your men, you could have riddled those red skins, so that they would have fallen like the soldiers of Xerxes at the straits of Thermopylæ; and we would have hailed you like another Leonidas this day, bearing you back on our shields in triumph. That would have been something to be proud of. But what have we here? My own honest brother, Elder Abiel, once more free! God be praised, that our war has not been in vain. We shall have a day of thanksgiving for this blessing, were it for nothing else. My right arm is restored to me."

"Nae sae fast, minister," said Grant; "the Elder says that he is on his way to Neaugra. He's neither to haud nor to bind, willy illy."

"What is the meaning of this?" was the really anxious inquiry of the Dominie, who feared that the mind of his friend had suffered in his captivity. "Surely you cannot be so taken up with a heathen's company, that you should prefer it to the fellowship of the saints."

The Elder only shook his head, for his heart was full. David, his son, took it up by saying that his "father had taken it into his head, that he was bound in honor to Brandt, for some kindness he had shown to him, and he was now on the road to offer himself up."

"Let us hear," was the alarmed Dominie's words, "what is that point of honor that makes you so sensitive; for it must be very clear and strong before I will consent to such a loss as Garret Abiel. Our labor and our blood must not be thrown away in vain."

Grant, who had been impatiently waiting for a chance to put in a word, hastened here to say, "that's true, minister; I am for carrying the Elder back. We are strong enough, a' hands of us, and though we read in the second book of Samuel, the twentieth chapter, and the aughteenth verse, if I'm na mistaen, that they were wont to speak in old times, saying 'they will surely ask counsel of Abel,' and so they ended the matter; I'm thinkin' it was na this Elder Abiel, for they were not sae foolish as to put themsels into the hands of the Philistines."

The Dominie who stood perfectly confounded at the position of the Elder's affairs, looked Grant in the face all the time he spoke, seemingly thinking on something else, and not conscious of anything that was said by the Scot, at the close drew a long breath, repeating his own words, "all our labor in vain, and what a loss!"

"Yes, minister, I've just been reflecten," said Grant, "that this wee fecht o' ours is waur to us than the battle o' the Shirra muir was; whare a neebur o' my toon lost his faither and his mither, and a gude braid swourd that was worth them baith. What think you o' that?"

The good man smiled. In other circumstances he would have laughed aloud; but turning to the Elder, he desired a full account of his pledge given to the Mohawk; which when he heard, he sighed and said:

"I am sorry; and I am rejoiced. We must part for the present. Such honor is not seen but in the true-hearted; and God shall reward it. Proud am I this day. Your example will weigh heavier than the hills; and what is best of all, our good Dutch Church is represented in you this day, and the fame thereof will go far among the Gentiles even unto the ends of the earth."

The Elder here held out his hand firmly, which the Dominie grasped, taking off his hat as all did, feeling that an act of devotion was to follow; for the good pastor poured out a most fervent prayer, ending with the apostolic benediction in Dutch: *De genade onzes Heeren Jesus Christus zij met uwen geest! Amen.*"

"Now, David, see that you watch over your old father; and watch every chance for escape. Don't forget your catechism, and the canons. There is a copy for you; have it all on your tongue's end, when you come back; and you can read the marriage service now and then, and I'll join Susy Myers and you together. Keep up a good spirit."

"Oh, yes," said Grant, who was always ready, "a stoot heart to a stay brae; faint heart never gained fair lady."

The two companions parted here, the Abiels with a white handkerchief on the top of a pole as a flag of truce in case of accidents on the way to the camp of the Indians, and the Dominie to the Flat Rock, where all were gathering preparatory to their descent down the mountain side. Already the chief persons were assembled, and waiting the decision of some controlling power. Bertram and Clarence, agreeably to their intentions at the outset of their adventure, had with the assistance of Gabriel kindled three fires, south of the pine orchard, as the signal of success to the ship that lay along the shore waiting. Just at the moment when the

Dominie had reached the verge of the cliff and looked toward the moon there came forth the reverberations of cannon thrice repeated, as answers to the flame that rose from their fires. Then came up as many Roman candles burning clear, and shooting out sparks brilliant as star dust. These attracted the different classes to whom the sight of fireworks was a new thing.

By and by, when all supposed these rejoicings over for the time, lights of different colors were seen to spread from prow to stern of the ship, till she seemed to stand out upon the darkened sky, a fiery image of some terrible being, ready to mount on wings. They who were ignorant of how all that was produced stood in amazement, not unmixed with terror. The name of that vessel was one that created fear all along the river; and recent occurrences had not served to allay these fears. The Clintons, however, saw in that brilliant object, the signal of joyful enthusiasm in which the whole ship's crew united as one man.

"I can hear," said Bertram, "their hearty cheers; I am sure of it. The voices of four hundred men can be heard that short distance. There again."

"You imagine, Cousin Bertram," was Clarence's cooler word. "You may as well say that you see them; but by George I do see them crowding the deck. There, take the glass and see for yourself."

"I see no men," said the sailor, who looked with a seaman's eye; "but there, I see our initials hung out in flaming characters, B. M. C."

The other companies viewed the illuminated vessel with different feelings, and it would not serve any good purpose to record these in detail. The Dominie was impatient to be gone, as the next day was the Sabbath, and he must be at his post. As many as chose to encamp for the night, had the opportunity, as the booths erected by Brandt's army still stood, and the embers still smoldered on the fire-places, where they had been burning during the week.

"But for my part," said the stout-hearted minister, "I would rather be in my own roost beside my careful hen, than lie here under the stars high above my head, where the hawk and the eagle have their nest so near me. Let poets say what they please of such sublimities."

Grant as usual put his word in, saying: "Ane might suppose when they hear you preach, that the higher up and the nearer to that terrible crystal, the better for the health o' the spirit. That's to say when you get into your taundrums."

"All true, Grant, and proper enough to be said at the right time, but I hope," and here the good man's voice quivered a little, "I hope I may die in my nest; I have no wish just at this moment to mount to heaven from this footstool. You captains must lead the men home according to your best wisdom. I shall leave my nag here for the use of the young lady; I can get one at the bottom of the hill from Hanshee Goetchius."

With this the Dominie left. Tom had been sent away an hour before with orders to go straight to the parsonage, so that all might be in readiness there for strangers. Another messenger had been sent secretly to the ship so that nothing remained but to finish what had so far made such good progress.

"Where did you leave your master, you cowardly scoundrel," was the first salutation of the anxious Yfvrow, "that you have come skulking home like a fox that has lost its tail in a trap?"

"Leab massa!" was Tom's astonished answer. "Me neber leab massa; him leab Tom shooting de big Indian and King Cuffee. He! he! he!"

Whether it was Tom or the Dominie that shot Brandt, she could not make out to this day; but this did not prevent her ordering a couple of sheep, and fowls in proportion, to be killed, so that she might be prepared for a company, "like another Abigail," as Grant said.

CHAPTER XII.

TEARS AND SMILES.

"The joy of grief."
OSSIAN.

TOWARDS midnight, under the guidance of Teunis, the whole party found their way to the parsonage. On the road, old Martin, in the gratitude of his heart, yielded to the plea of the Tory's son; and Elsie, in the warmth of her long-cherished affection, consented to be a bride on the next day. "It would," she said, "make Miss Clinton so happy before they parted."

Agreeably to the command of the Dominie, the two maidens were put under the charge of the 'Yfvrow, who, with true maternal prudence, merely kissed them both, bidding them good-night in the sleeping chamber to which she conveyed them. Their sleep was that of youth and health, after undergoing perils on the heights, perils in depths, and perils in the wilderness. Weary and overcome with their exertion of body and of mind, they had sunk into a deep slumber, which continued till the sun was far up in the heavens. Margaret dreamed all night of the dangers and of the deliverances of the past week: the one class of images mingling so with the other, it would have been difficult to have disentwined them. A prominent figure in the foreground was an eagle that grew in her sight large as a ship; its wings spreading out till they became sails, by which the vessel moved fleetly on the waves, as she had seen a sea-gull playing in a storm. On the head of the glorious creature was a brilliant jewel that glowed like a crown of bright flame. All round the points of the wings were lamps that hung like lambent fringes, and were so soft, that though she had taken a seat between these wings, the fire did not scorch her in the least, as the eagle sailed down the broad river, with Bertram on one side and Clarence on the other; guiding their ship as they might a chariot of fire on the land, which went as she willed. It was sometimes land, and then water. All at once the vessel, winged as it was, hung over the gulf below the Falls, where they had found refuge. The spars seemed so fine, and the hull so transparent, that the appearance was more magical than real. The ropes were threads of yellow light, and the waving ensign, a sheet of red flame, as the ground, on which were intermingled the lion of England among united stars. At that instant, in her sleep, she heard a cry, and saw her cruel enemy near her on the height above. Here she leaped into the airy ship, and sailed away above the clouds, when the joyful sailors fired off their artillery, giving out cheers of gladness and continued huzzas.

At this moment the enraptured maiden awoke; nor was it all a dream. Some of the youthful crew outside, noisy in their mirth, Sabbath though it was, were celebrating the events which gave the elder portion of the population such pleasure.

They had succeeded in firing off a small canon, which of itself was a great feat, and worthy of their vocal music. The two young women, recovering their scattered senses, looked in each other's faces and smiled. Margaret calmly kissed her friend, as tears filled the eyes of both—tears of gratitude to God and of love for one another.

"We are here and safe," said Elsie; "let us thank the Great Deliverer, and be ready for whatever else may come."

"And next to him who has delivered me, I owe all to my dear Elsie, who took her life in her hand for me, a stranger, and the daughter of one who is the"——

"Say no more of that, Miss Clinton; there is a Providence which overrules all these events; and now that they are transpired, I would not have them in a different form than they are at this moment, though it may sound strange to you."

"Some good thing is about to happen then to my own Elsie."

"Yes, Miss Clinton, Teunis will be mine. An event I never expected to see; my father is reconciled to him, and I am as happy as a young maiden can be. All has come out of your captivity, so that I am as much released as you can be." Here Elsie hid her face on Margaret's bosom.

"That is your own good heart speaking that has cheered me so long: for it seems so long since we became known to each other, that it sounds strange to me to hear my brother say we must be at the ship to-morrow."

"Yes," said the thoughtful Elsie; "you return to your home, and I remain at mine; and our experience of trouble will not be lost, if we both fill our places the better that we have been at school up among the mountains. But, hark, there is the horn of warning to rise. There is more to be done this day than you have dreamed of; nor could you guess though you were to try all day."

The countenance of Elsie, while it retained its usual quiet soberness, was more cheerful than it had been for some time; showing that pleasant thoughts were passing over the zenith of her heaven; and yet there was no levity nor trifling in her demeanor. Her conversation was as lively—more lively than ever, but intermixed with sage maxims which she had heard and stored up in the past; and while the experience of the high-bred English maiden was gained in a far different school, yet the results to both at this hour were not unlike; showing that virtue is eternal and unchangeable; impressed upon the soul within, and not upon the body without.

"But," continued Elsie, "you must not suppose that my heart is any lighter, though I smile in your face this morning: like the keystone of an arch, I am firmer and stronger the heavier my responsibilities are becoming! Ha! but here is something that will interest us."

With these words the country girl drew out into the middle of the floor a strong hairy trunk, studded with brass nails, and bound with iron, such as English travellers take with them to foreign countries. Margaret soon expressed her surprise; for it was the very chest which she herself had carefully packed with what she intended to wear on this journey to Ulster. Her wonderment was how it could possibly be on that floor, when she left it last Sabbath morning in her little cabin. Had she been told by her old Scotch nurse that some kind fairy had brought it hither, she was likely to have believed her. The truth must be told here. Bertram had secretly made a journey to the ship during the night; and this among other matters was a result of his interview with his uncle and aunt. The day was to be spent in this inland village, where in gratitude to the good man who had aided them so efficiently, and in pure friendship for Elsie, Miss Clinton was to be allowed to remain. The dresses which the chest contained were sent, so that she might appear worthy of her name and place in society. Other garments lay there folded, which were intended for the daughter of Martin Schuyler, who, as the relative of the noble man at Albany, felt as dignified as a queen, and must be arrayed that day "in as handsome a manner as becomes her standing." So the proud 'Yfvrow said to her careful spouse before she went to bed that night.

The two damsels were soon into the mysteries of dressing. Elsie had worn the gown she had on, the night she left Hoogenhuisen, and Margaret had not thought after being caught in her parti-colored blanket, of changing it for another. Once afterward at a masquerade in Fortheringame Castle, England, did she appear as an Indian Queen. The blanket was kept among the choicest treasures of her gay wardrobe.

At the breakfast table both the visitors were welcomed by their host and hostess; the lady giving them the warm embrace of a mother, while the Dominie with dignity and paternal voice bade them welcome, handing them at the same time to chairs by his side.

Margaret felt the blood tingling through her veins as she sat down reflecting that she was now in the presence of the man whom she had learned to respect, by what she had heard of him. With all her experience of the world and of different companies, she was not without anxiety as to the result of this interview with one whose sentiments she knew must be of a high order. Forethought was unnecessary here, as all was done in decency and order.

"You have at least been fortunate in one thing, my lady: in your late excursion in seeing our mountain at this season, for it is the only object of interest we have to show a stranger. We think it beyond all other hills."

"I have been unfortunate, my dear sir, in not being in a fit frame to enjoy it, as I would have done had fear not prevailed over my admiration; still I shall take impressions with me so deep that they never can be worn out."

"Yes, my lady, in misfortune we receive such impressions. Had you sailed over the highest peak in one of those newly invented air boats, that the French are trying, your voyage would be sooner forgotten, than if you walked every step up to High Peak."

"So moralists say," was Margaret's reply. "Still a balloon would have been welcomed yesterday morning, and could I have made one I would have ventured in it."

"And fallen, lady, down the precipices where your crushed body would have been lying now. God's ways are not our ways, neither are his thoughts our thoughts, for as the heavens are higher than the earth, so are his ways above all those inventions that human wisdom would try."

At this point Tom put down the large clasped book on the table, while at his heels there came in the whole household of this holy patriarch, taking their seats according to their rank. The ninety-second psalm was read, followed by a brief exposition and a prayer, solemn, earnest and direct. The household, the country and the church, were all remembered. What chiefly affected Margaret was the touching reference made to herself; showing that he who spoke for them, knew all about her and felt for her as a kind father does for a wandering child. As he rose in fervor he became more pointed and his voice quivered as he supplicated, "Divine compassion on the head of her, who had been chased like a young roe, among the hills, and who had been followed after by a love strong as death. Now, O Lord! may her eyes this day see Him who is fairer than the children of men, who standeth behind our wall; who looketh at the windows, showing himself through the lattice, saying, 'rise up my love, my fair one and come away. For lo the winter is past, the rain is over and gone: the flowers appear on the earth, the time of singing of birds is come and the voice of the turtle is heard in the land. Let this daughter of the stranger, comely and delicate, be surrounded by the shepherds and their flocks in token of her future peace; even as the young lions have roared upon her yesterday; then shall she be like the young roe upon the mountain of spices."

At the close of this prayer, made eloquent by the occasion and the words of inspired devotion, every eye was suffused in tears. The good man himself went to look out at the window, and blew his nose with a blast that would have wakened a sleeping Samsom, in his cradle, but which was not observed at this time, by any one, as they were too much engaged like himself in hiding their feelings. Just at that instant a drum was beat loud and furious, and with something of an attempt at music which made Margaret start up to her feet in some alarm. The Dominie smiled as he said:

"Lady, I thought a soldier's daughter would not fear the sound that calls to battle; but that is the warning of peace, not of war. We have not got a bell yet, such as they have in London and Amsterdam, so we take what we have, and we never want. The drum does for both armies; the soldiers of the cross and the defenders of the state. But here comes the 'Yfvrow with the call for breakfast."

They sat down to a breakfast similar to that of which Clarence partook; only ladies being present now, and one of reputed high rank, the mistress of the house was ambitious to do her best. Indeed, if there was any fault to be found, it was the over-attention she bestowed on her chief guest; which led her, sometimes, sharply to remind her spouse of his duty and of even his behavior at table. There was great abundance, too much—and it lay on as white a linen cloth as ever was spread. The dishes were of the finest china, and the urn of silver; with corresponding plate of the heaviest kind. Proud enough was the dignified housewife, when she saw Margaret glancing quietly down into the saucer, at figures there drawn, and then holding up the tiny cup in her delicate hand, admiring its shape and transparency.

"Take another cup, Miss Clintòn, of the Bohea. It came directly from China, in my uncle's ship, just ten years since. My uncle was a great skipper in his day, and died very WEALTHY."

A heavy emphasis was laid on the word, and she rose in her chair a few inches, though that was hardly needed, for she would have matched the Duchess of Walkinghame in size, in dignity, and even in ease of manners, as Margaret declared afterward.

"So you do drink the taxed tea after all, 'Yfvrow," said the Dominie, with a sly look to that end of the table.

"It is none of your affairs, Dominie Schuneman," retorted his wife, good-naturedly. "We can keep our secrets as well as the best Whig in the country, though we be not officered by Dominies that scour the hills and woods shooting Indians, and standing to be shot at like tied turkeys on a Christmas day."

This little byplay was a quiet hit at the careless husband's exposing himself to the fire of the Mohawk chief, of which she had heard, though he was keeping the whole a secret. He did not feel any sting in the arrow shot, so smiling in self-complacency, he rose, saying:

"Elsie, my lameshie, you will be ready when I call you, and do not tremble at the sound of your own name."

"I may tremble, Dominie, but be short, for you know that we have had hard work to go through these few days past."

"True, Elsie, lass," continued the pastor, "but the form must be gone through religiously. The dochter of Martin Schuyler must be an example to others."

At the appointed time, Bertram and Teunis Roe came to the parsonage for the young ladies, who were dressed, and waited upon one another with sisterly affection. The occasion, and the day, had brought the minds of all into delightful harmony and sober cheerfulness.

The Dominie, who went out after breakfast, did not return for an hour, when he seemed a little flustered, which arrested the eye of his careful wife, who immediately put the question:

"What has happened now?"

"Oh, nothing, but that imp of Satanus and his belly tongue. I believe he will make all my folks seek unto familiar spirits, and unto wizards that peep and mutter."

"Do you mean Unga?" said the quick-witted woman.

"Dominie, like priest like people. What wizard was seen yesternight?"

The Dominie left her, looking at her with a warning eye. After a little while he came out, ready to enter the sacred place: his cocked hat on, with his Geneva bands hanging low on his breast; except these, not a spot of white upon him. Over all was his ample cloak, made of thick worsted stuff, imported from Holland, and sold by Abram Van Est, at Coenties Slip, Manhattan, now New York.

The 'Yfvrow, who was herself superbly dressed, made her spouse turn round till she examined him thrice over, continuing her critical investigations till he grew out of patience, and broke away from her hands in assumed fury.

"Nay, nay, Dominie, you must allow me to straighten out that wrinkle in your coat-tail, careless man that you are. Can you not lift it aside when you sit down? It is the 'Yfrow will get all the blame. Dame Brinkeroff will say,

"'Did you see the Dominie's hands? They were as yellow as a duck's foot.'

"'Yaw, yaw,' Mammy Demond will squeal out; 'and his wig was mairs like tow on my rock than good hair.'"

"Never mind the clashing jades," said the well pleased and happy Dominie. "I'll have them all before the Consistory for their slander. You're the best wife in the colony." And with that he stole a kiss, as if in perfect exuberance of pleasure.

"Fie, fie, Dominie! and before ladies, too," said the no less happy wife, "and we going to the kerke. If old Mat Van Deusen hears of this there will be some noise."

With that all marched out to the church. The Dominie, as of right, led the way, having Miss Clinton on his arm.

CHAPTER XIII.

THE IMMORTAL SOUL.

"Pure religion, and undefiled before God and the Father."
ST. JAMES.

"I'm not in sportive humor now; tell me, and dally not."
SHAKSPEARE.

It was one of those beautiful sabbath mornings, which occur at the close of the fall of the year, that resemble the face of a devout matron, just before the winter of her life commences; who, still conscious of the happy life she has passed, surrounded by her children, who revel in the fruits she has gathered for them, looks with devout gratitude to God, as sensible also of worldly delight. The sunshine of youth not only lingered round the hills, but rested richly on the valley. The people were evidently at rest in their minds, and as the clear cock-crow wakened the echoes, voices of praise were prolonged so sweetly that they reverberated from stream and knoll, till all sounded in blessed unison.

After the stirring events of the past week, a large congregation were assembling. The majority came for worship, but many to obtain the news of how the good cause was prospering. Where every one contributed his part, each carried away a full account, to be told over at home, to those who could not come to the common gathering place.

The strangers present, guests of the Dominie, sat in his large square pew, along with the 'Yfvrow and her little flock. As they looked up to the desk, and saw the pastor in his full Geneva cloak and bands, admiration filled their minds. Spreading out his hands, he said:

"The Lord bless you, and keep you; the Lord make his face to shine upon you, and be gracious to you. The Lord lift up his countenance upon you, and give you peace: Amen."

He read the commandments in a slow, solemn voice; varying his tone as he went through each, so that the ear of his auditors might receive the separate precept by itself, and ponder upon it with prayer, and in meekness.

Here he sat down, when the clerk, who was placed in a smaller pulpit below the high desk, rose and gave out a psalm, which he led in a tone between singing and chanting. Horridly grating to refined ears; but the people were pleased and paid to Zach Goetchius twenty shillings, and ten cheepens of corn for serving as Presentor. Zach also read the lessons from Scripture. The prayers were in part from a liturgy in the Dutch language, and in part extemporaneous English; which the transient worshippers supposed was in deference to them, as well as for their edification.

The same might have been said of the sermon. It was intended by the preacher, when he began, to be in English, but as he grew warm, he branched off into the vernacular tongue. This more especially when he wished to give something very terse or hitting, or which might be disagreeable to his new auditors; for he wished them to carry away a good impression. His side strokes were the spiciest. Bertram, who had been in Holland, gave these afterward to his friends. He, moreover, declared that the style of speech was as pure as the doctors of Leyden used.

The text which was pronounced in a clear deliberate voice, had the effect of quickening the ears of the assembly, who leaned forward to catch every word; and from the stillness which succeeded the announcement, as well as the curiosity on their countenances, they seemed to say, "What can the Dominie have to say from that?"

"I knew a man in Christ, above fourteen years ago—whether in the body I cannot tell; or whether out of the body I cannot tell; God knoweth—such an one caught up to the third heaven . . . . . . and heard unspeakable words, which it is not lawful for a man to utter."

He began, "I knew a man yesterday who was up on the mountain, and as near to the third heaven as any man in this region can be; and from Paul's experience, and that of this other man, we deduce the sound doctrine that the GREAT SPIRIT COMMUNICATES WITH THE SOUL OF HIS CREATURES, THROUGH NATURE AND GRACE; AND CONSEQUENTLY YOU HAVE SPIRITUAL AND IMMORTAL SOULS, AS WELL AS YOU HAVE DECAYING BODIES.

"Keep that doctrine before your view, all through; for though I will say a vast deal before I be done, it is all on this foundation."

At this point the preacher went minutely into the history and the meaning of his text; telling his hearers that it was a page taken out of the private journal of Paul's autobiography: "We could wish he had left more of the same kind; but we shall see the other parts when we get to heaven. It would seem that fourteen years before this time, and twelve years after he met the Lord by the way to Damascus, when the Apostle was in the prime of life, and after having had large experience of holy visions, he had this one, that transcended them all in matchless glory; and which even he, great as he was in the use of words, could not express."

"Others as well as Paul have had visions. There was Ezekiel, who was caught away from the banks of Chebar by a lock of his hair, and placed at the door of the temple of Jerusalem: there again was the Exile of Patmos; and with humility be it spoken, there was I myself on the mountain, when I felt like one transported out of the body, as I looked out upon the river, the woods, the fields, and the mountains far off on all sides; so that though I have come to declare my feelings before you, I find them to be unspeakable; at this moment I am sincerely sorry that I have chosen this subject. O Divine Spirit! thou who taught Paul to speak right words, indite for thy feeble servant, and make his tongue like the pen of a ready writer."

At the close of this introduction he paused, blowing his nose, looking round, at the same time, to see that all were in their places and quiet, and then in a formal, pointed, and emphatic manner, gave out his first point:

"*God communicates with the human soul above nature, and in an inconceivable way.*"

There followed this annunciation of his main point, a long rambling talk, in which it was plainly seen to the initiated in extempore speaking, that he was struggling through the mist.

"I am not," said he, "a Paul, mind you; I am not supernaturally endowed. But, after all, Paul was human, and he could have sympathized with me up there, as I am humbly sure I could have felt with him further up. He had a sense of the beautifully divine, as I have now of the divinely beautiful. Such a speechless delight is in us all. We feel more than we can comprehend; we understand more than we can tell. When I was up on the side of the mountain, I could not help looking down on the different men whom I knew dwelt here below. I said, there is one, and he never sees anything beyond his line fence. When he looks out on the stream that runs through his farm, he wishes it were a mill stream; another is always calculating on the loads of hay he will cut from that meadow; one more sees a flock of sheep, and it is of the wool and the mutton he is thinkiug. These men are but a little way removed above the brutes they feed. If I had them up here I would say, 'Were God to give me the power, brother Paulus, brother Johannus, brother Jacobus, brother Petrus, receive thy sight, and be filled with the Holy Geest.' And I am sure that I would enjoy the surprise which all of these brothers would show when the scales, made of milledoleors, of wheat, of flesh, and of blacks, would fall from their eyes: and the glorious kiverlid would be spread out, and their eyes made clear enough to see it, with all its colors and patches of wood—with its border of blue sky, and its centre of meadow-land, through which the silken stream runs so pure that it reminds one of the stream that maketh glad the city of the Lord after a storm has shaken the earth.

"Brethren," said the good man, now becoming more earnest, "your eyes must be unscaled if you would see with the spirit, and see with the understanding also. You could not penetrate the thick mist of a fall morning, but you could believe that snugly resting under it there are happy homes, and that above it there is clear sunshine. Roll away the cloud, and all is beautiful and sublime. The beauty was there all the time. So the spirit of faith can see the throne of God, and the dwellings of the blessed, unchangeably the same in their everlasting radiance.

"Some of you cannot understand these things. How can you, having never seen them? You are blinded by your milledoleors, and your grain, and your blacks. But shall my horse Dick, that was up there with me, and looked out snuffing at the fresh grass below, say that there was nothing down there but grass, when your dog Watch wags his tail at the sight of a hare? Or shall horse and dog say there is nothing more than they see, when Paulus and the rest see the fine farms in the Bught? And how dare Jacobus and his friends, who see nothing but farm-land, presume to say that the gentleman sitting there in my pew did not see beauties beneath all these visible things? And, finally, shall the gentleman in my pew deny but I had a more penetrating view of God below these fancied things, which made him leap with rapture? I am sure, after these things, you will allow that St. Paul, even in the body, might hear sounds unspeakable in the third heavens."

Here the venerable pastor paused, wiping his face with his Indian bandana, of which he was a little vain, as one might judge from the manner in which he spread it out, lifting it softly in his big hand before he pushed it down into his big pocket. By that time he was into the mysteries of thought, and was launching out into the scriptural doctrine of divine communications with the soul out of the body. He quoted liberally from Scripture, placing himself on safe ground.

"But, my brethren, do we not see, and feel, and guess at things, after seeing a great sight like what I saw, even when we cannot put the ends together? I went out in my body over a bridge that hung across the gulf, till I could not move another step; and then I looked down till my eyes dazzled, and then my spirit crossed still beyond, till even my spirit sank, having no ground to stand upon. Who shall hold me up? There must be an arch broken. Where is the power to rebuild it? My imagination is away off—my dreams show me a country I am afraid to enter when I am awake. I am, while in my study, sometimes eager to see my Maker. I cry, Oh, that I knew where I might find him. Behold, I go forward, but he is not there; and backward, but I cannot perceive him. Why is all this? I am a sinner; but there may be in me some fragments of a broken sense, which, like the pieces of the 'Yfvrow's looking-glass that Betty let fall, still showed bits of her black face. Like some great men I have read of; she tried to join the parts, but after she had done her best, it was a fractured mirror, reflecting only glimpses of light. Who shall mend this broken spiritual glass? That glass of the 'Yfvrow must be melted over and renewed. God can renew the spirit of the mind. He can build up the broken arch, over which the spirit can pass safe and sound, so that the eye, not satisfied with seeing, nor the ear with hearing, may behold the face of the Maker, and the man become fit to hold fellowship with Him. Oh, ye men, put the milledoleors from off your eyes, your houses and your lands, your orchards and your cider-presses, with all: and ye vrows must get your spiritual looking-glasses mended, and made bright as your silver, else you will never see on the other side of your milk-pans."

The faithful pastor found it necessary to make these familiar illustrations of a very abstract subject, and it was doubtful even then if he made it plain to the limited understanding of his regular hearers. But on this occasion he knew that he had some of the élite before him, and he was not unwilling to show them that he had learned something at Leyden. Still, some of the old women there could not help saying, with admiration, "What a wonderful man our Dominic is!"

He went on: "You know, brethren, there is a difference in tastes; there is Tim has a taste for good eating, and there is Egbert has a taste for a fine book, and there is Wilhelmus has a taste for praying. When they told me that the cloud at Pine Orchard showed the faces and the figures of those who looked into it, I could not help thinking how differently these three men would come from seeing it. The glutton would start like a beast away from it and feed the next hour; the man of mind would be for giving reasons from the nature of things; but the good man and the true, would look through all, and see that hand which turned the wheel behind. What of the three men—the glutton, the thinker and the praying soul? The first man is but an animal, the second is a reasonable creature, but the last is a spiritual being allied to the Great Spirit.

To me, men and brethren, those sights and sounds are foretastes of the heavenly and of the divine. They are full of meaning, eye hath not seen it, neither hath ear heard it. It is not possible to utter it. They are unlike any other blessedness here in this world. Yet they are not beyond human experience as Paul testifies, as I can testify; and as some of these old mothers there can assure you who are in doubt. The mountain top, to the man whose vision is purified, is another round in the ladder, down on which the angels descend in their visits to us, and up which we may ascend in our visits to them; hearken van nu aan zult gij den hemel zien geopend, ende engelen Gods opklimmende en nederdalende op dem zoon des menschen. Oh, dear me! what am I saying now? I forgot," said the fervent preacher, "but the English is, Verily, verily I say unto you, hereafter ye shall see heaven open and the angels of God ascending and descending upon the Son of Man."

A fashionable congregation would have felt that time enough had been spent, but these people were accustomed to sit their full two and three hours patiently, sleeping or looking through vacancy, to be roused up as their pastor got up himself. This day he was in the happiest mood, and having an appreciating audience he gave them full measure. He drew a long breath, and gave out another main point which he said was deduced from the preceding: *that since the soul could hold communication with the Maker either in the body through nature, or out of the body, through pure spirit it followed* THAT THE SOUL WAS ITSELF SPIRITUAL AND IMMORTAL.

He dwelt at least ten minutes here in giving scriptural proof of this, which could not fail having good effect on the honest believers before him. But getting his eye on the strangers again, he launched away upon the abstract, in what he meant to be forcible eloquence. Said he, "Listen to the word of Paul in one place—'Father of Spirits. We are his children still; he begot our souls. Do you not feel that you are his children? I felt it yesterday as I stood gazing down into the deep profound, where I could see nothing, save the unknown; and as I mused, I thought what if I should step out into that space; where should I fall? On the bosom of my God, my Father! We who have been at sea, looking from the stern with eyes fixed on the vessel's track till we lost ourselves, have felt it. There never was a horizon yet that we did not wish to fly beyond! What are these longings but the conflicts kept up between the earthly and the heavenly; what but the instincts of the child longing for the bosom, from which it has been rudely torn by some foul tyrant—the returning fragments of a broken dream of yore—the strains of a broken harp-string recalled to the ear of memory, where they have long lain disconnected through violence?"

Here the preacher entered with great force and unction into the power, which the Gospel has, of healing this breach between the child and the parent. "The first Adam lost his place and we in him, but the second Adam is the son of God and we are renewed in him. The spiritual flame expired, is now rekindled and burns as it is replenished from that fountain."

The discourse was drawing to a close, and the preacher, like a strong racer, was gathering himself up for his final spring. "It is," said he, "fearfully true of many here that they have had no interest in all that I have said this day. I can read it in your faces. Had all of you been up beside me, where I felt myself rising as on eagle's wings, some here that I wot of, would have said: 'I wish I were in my own barn, over a good roast turkey:' and one or two here I see, are thinking now of the pot of silver hidden in the garden. Oh, you are a carnally-minded crew, and would not be happy had you all these things at once. You need not smile ye youngsters there; as for you, my young colts may serve as examples of the uneasy restlessness of your hearts, when they leap out of the clover into the sorrel. Can you tell me the cause of all this changeableness? Your souls are spiritual, and long for communion out of the body; and cannot be fed on good dinners, nor grow on a thousand acres of the best land in the world.

"You have been expecting something else here this morning. I want to show you that there is another and a greater cause, than even our country's cause. I saw when I commenced, that your ears were cocked up to hear of battles; but there is a great battle to be fought by every one for himself; when the last enemy appears on the field, and by the way of preparing you to meet him effectually, so as to come off conqueror, I have lifted you up into the THIRD HEAVENS. You expected me to tell you of the wonderful advantage we have gained in the north, and I have been thinking, 'want wat baat het een mensch zoo hij de gehule wereld gewint, en lijdt schade zijner zeile. Of wat zal een mensch geven, tot lossing van zijne zeile.' You that understand English only will find it in Mathew xvi., 26: 'What shall it profit a man if he gain the whole world and lose his soul.' My heart is full of sorrow when I think on these things. Let us sing:

"Oh, were I like a feathered dove,
Soon would I stretch my wings,
And fly, and make a long remove,
From all these restless things.

"Let me to some wild desert go;
And find a peaceful home,
Where storms of malice never blow;
Temptations never come."

CHAPTER XIV.

"THE CONSUMMATION DEVOUTLY TO BE WISHED."

"Let us hear the conclusion of the whole matter."
SOLOMON.

THUS the usual services were concluded, the congregation preparing to make a rush for the door, and were standing up, the men with hands on their hats, and the women adjusting their trains, paying but little attention to the desk, expecting only the well-known words of benediction, when to the amazement of all, young and old, the Dominie said in a firm, clear voice:

"The congregation will be seated while the solemn and interesting ceremony of marriage is being performed. The parties will stand up and present themselves before the altar."

Here Teunis Roe and Elsie Schuyler took the specified place. Bertram at the same time taking the place assigned by custom to the groom's man, and Margaret that of the bridesmaid. Martinus Schuyler moved slowly out of the Consistory's pew, to the side where his daughter stood; the mother, attempting to do the same, was prevented through her emotion, so that she merely leaned forward in her pew, in the act of inward prayer.

All of these arrangements were completed before the assembly had wakened out of their astonishment. When they did perceive them, whispers might be heard among the elder portions: "The Whig has yielded at last to the young Tory." The young men were hiding their mortification by winks and smiles, while one louder than the others gave utterance to his feelings: "She was always a haughty heifer; Teunis will have his own task in breaking her in."

Grant, who sat in the front of the gallery enjoying the whole scene, for Teunis had become, after what had lately taken place, a great favorite with the Scot, here felt mad at the ill-concealed envy he saw around him and had the greatest difficulty in holding himself within due bounds, whispered aloud:

"Sit doon, you haverils that you are. Do you no see true love gettin' its reward?"

"A hemp neckcloth would be more like the young traitor's wizzen," some one here bitterly said.

"Whist! whist! I tell you," said Grant, still louder, "or I'll fling your yellow carcage over the laft there."

By this time the minister had opened at the place in his book where the "form for the confirmation of marriage before the church" is contained, and began in a full, firm voice to read. Being himself a great admirer of that ancient liturgy, he believed that all his people must be, so he never omitted aught of the good service. As he said in the morning so he showed at noon: "Martin Schuyler's daughter must not be slighted."

The good man's heart was so full that it surged over, so that there were no triflers there by the time he lifted his hands over the newly married pair, giving them truly his blessing.

Nevertheless that all, male and female, were affected even to tears, Elsie's bridal attire did not escape the scrutiny of those watery eyes. Had it been such as they knew her to possess, and that in which they had seen her before, there would have been but little said; but since it was well known that Hoogenhuisen was in ashes, it became at once a question with a hundred mothers and maidens, "where have all these fine silks and laces come from?"

That was a secret known but to the 'Yfvrow. The moment she became acquainted with the intentions of the young people, her wits were set to work without even consulting the bride herself, who had no other prospect than that of appearing at the altar in very common attire. Lizzie Schuyler, the daughter of the general, and the affianced spouse of the gallant Hamilton, being at the very time on a visit to her aunt, at the Manor of Livingston, close by, was the very person to supply all deficiencies. The hint was enough for the busy 'Yfvrow. A messenger brought back a choice of dresses, such as would have decked a queen. Elsie felt somewhat displeased at the officiousness of her well-meaning hostess; but her present circumstances compelled her to comply. Of course all the parish were ignorant of the good genii that had furnished these ornaments; but they were none the less objects of marvel to every one present, possessed or not possessed of the critical skill of the milliner.

"An' vere did Anshela's dochter get all tese fine tings, bjudten ?" said Peggy van Steenberg to a visitor then in the country for her health, as some said; others because New York red-coats were too enticing; "vere did tese vain tings kaam into dis lan' ?"

"You up here in the country have not seen all the fine things in the world, though you may have the highest mountains at your elbow," was the half-jesting reply of the New York damsel.

"Vy have'n ve grand tings? Is'n de 'Yfvrow a great voman once, an her uncle de Skipper? Budt dere vas de gown like sky, on de summer afternoon; beneat it, de vite petticoat, clean as de snow packed wid de rain ven de vrost comes and make de glitter."

"Oh, Peggy, let me tell you, that is all the fashion now; a celestial blue satin gown, and a white satin petticoat shows all below. Did you not see how they were trimmed with stripes of the same color up the edges?"

"Yaw, yaw; but de corsets vas vat myne eyes beheld; yallow and crossed wid de blue stripes. Budt do tell me all about dere head. Awee! awee! how Elsie did look on her."

"Oh," said the initiated lady, "the head-dress was a *pouf* of gauze, made like a globe; and you saw how the hair was curled, so that it fell in ringlets down each side of her neck."

"Awee! awee! vat a time it must tak'n for ou to tell it so: now, vat about de neck?"

"Oh, the neck! She had on her a thin gauze handkerchief, that looks like the snow on a frosty morning. You saw that it hung full, at the edges trimmed with the richest Brussels lace."

"Awee! awee!" was all that Peggy could say, in perfect admiration; but whether at the wonderful dress or at the wonderful eloquence of her companion, could not be distinctly known. However, not being tired of what she affected to deplore, she listened with increased admiration to the city lady, who went on to tell her the meaning of those mysteries which Margaret had on.

"You saw that other lady. She is English, I know, from the rose on her cheek and the blue in her eye. How beautifully she rose up and stood. Your country lass has a fine figure, no doubt; and the gown fitted her very well, only an inch too tight all over; but, then, that other one is slender and quick in her movements without seeming to know it."

"Elshie Schuyler," said Peggy, "can stan' wid de best; vat of de oder one's gown?"

"Oh, that's what they call a perriot, made of grey Indian taffeta. You saw it had dark stripes of the same color, with two collars—the one yellow and the other white; both of them trimmed with blue silk fringe."

They went on in this way, and we must let them, and return back to the church, which was not dismissed when these two came out. At the close of the service alluded to, a note was put into the hand of the Dominie, as he was about to dismiss the people, which ran thus:

"Rev. Sir:

"If there be no impediment in the way, we wish to engage your services at present, for the same purpose as our friends now made happy by you.

"Bertram Clinton.

"P. S.—We prefer being married with a ring."

The good man smiled assent, saying, with a cunning eye, as he looked around:

"Another marriage service to be gone through; all who are tired may now leave."

He knew very well that curiosity was at too high a pitch to allow any one to go out, but he sat down, more for the purpose of considering within himself than for anything else.

"Let the parties desirous of entering the holy state of matrimony come forward." Here Bertram and Margaret stood up, with Teunis and Elsie on either side, supported by Clarence. At the same instant, and while the arrangements were going forward, there stepped up through the middle aisle a man and woman, muffled in large cloaks, taking a place behind the bridegroom and bride. The house had been so crowded, no one had observed them till that moment, and all were taken so with surprise that every pulse ceased. The Dominie almost stumbled at the beginning of the service.

However, he proceeded as before, with the additional part of the ring, which being out of the line of a Dutch minister, was handled somewhat awkwardly by him; but remembering what he had seen in England, he was not entirely ignorant.

The closing prayer was this time improvised. The good man's heart was too full to follow any form, and throwing his soul into his words, he uttered himself, so that tears fell from eyes unused to weeping.

"O Lord God of our fathers, bless these parties, in their basket and in their store, in their soul and in their body. Make them a blessing to the church, to the world, and to each other. May every thread of roughening earthliness be disentwined from the connecting bond; so that between themselves it may be soft as divine love, and yet strong and inseverable as that which unites the saints to one Lord; in one faith, in one baptism, and one marriage, till all four be presented, without spot or wrinkle, in the presence of God, at the marriage supper of the Lamb in the New Jerusalem, where love and righteousness only reign. Amen."

The AMEN was responded to in a clear, full voice by the stranger, who stood up behind the parties along with a female muffled in a veil that fell low to her waist. The sound of the Amen startled the whole house, not excepting the Dominie himself; for it rung like the word of command, heard at the head of a regiment. And by the time the audience had recovered from their amazement, the new bride had turned and flung herself into the open arms of the unknown woman, merely saying MOTHER: but so piercingly that it thrilled through the soul, as if Nature herself spoke by human lips. Margaret's transport was so great that all began to fear for the effect of that joy. The cup became suddenly full and surged over, so that she became for the time unconscious of happiness or of grief.

The stranger, vigorous and resolute, in a moment lifted the fragile creature, pale as a lily, in his arms, walking through the aisle with a step that clanged on the floor, making every one hold his breath, till he reached the door, where a vehicle stood ready, into which he put the unconscious bride, mounting himself with a bound up to the seat, saying at the same time, "drive briskly." Two other wagons drove away the rest of the party, including Teunis and Elsie. The swooning and over happy Margaret soon recovered her joyous smiling face, so that by the time they came in sight of the river and the ship, she was weeping anew, in thought of parting from her dear deliverer. They took a warm embrace and then another, waving adieus till the vessel was out of sight.

The explanation of these sudden transformations is easy by him that understandeth. When Teunis told the 'Yfvrow of his good luck with Martin, and of their intentions for the morning, that careful lady said:

"Who will be your bridesman? Do you think the young lady would stand with Elsie?"

There were difficulties unforeseen by the young Dutchman, but his counsellor was equal to the occasion, so rising up she said:

"Go your ways, and engage the young gentleman for your side, I will see the other side supported."

This hint was taken by Teunis, who made Clarence his friend. The thought darted through the young heroic brother's mind, "Why not make both parties happy, so finishing what has been worked for so hard by Bertram?"

It only required his earnest voice and warm heart, to plead for his cousin, and the thing was done. He told the whole story of Elsie's self-sacrificing devotion to Margaret, so that nothing could be refused to her or to her friends.

I promised, said the knight to Bertram, on the eve of that miserable attack, that if Margaret could be recovered, their hands should be joined. I shall keep my word of honor; only Georgiana we must go up in disguise. This pass from our cousin George Clinton, will carry us safely through.

And as the Dominie said afterward, "he came, and saw, and yielded."

A short time after the events recorded in the preceding history had transpired, and before the wonder was entirely past, the Dominie was sitting in his study when Tom entered, followed by Unga, the deformed child of Dora. He stood in the middle of the room puffing out his breath, while his head rose up, and as it fell he drew in the surrounding air, so that the spectator could imagine that he saw a swirl, like a small whirlpool, around the strange creature.

"What now, you limb of Sathanus," said the student of Leyden, lifting up his eyes from a large Latin folio that he was amusing himself with. "What news from the realms of darkness?"

"Pleas youd reberence," said Tom in a very low manner, "Unga hab someting frob de high'd legions to 'municate frob de prince ob de air an' powers."

"'Prince of the power of the air.' You fool, quote the Scripture correctly and go out with you, for I see that you want to know all about Unga's message, but begone."

Unga's head rose a few inches higher, and was followed by an eldritch scream, out of doors, that made the minister's man run to see what was the cause. In the meantime the Dwarf put a package into the hand of the Dominie, sitting down himself as if he were at home. The letter ran thus:

"REVERENDISSIMO DOMINO: When we last met in my retreat, we parted scarcely agreeing in our opinions concerning that particular Providence which you Calvinists believe in. Occurrences which have lately taken place, have gone to convince me, whatever Calvin would say were he in your place, that no plan ever is carried through agreeably to that laid down by its architect. Were I going to preach to you, as you have held forth to me, it would be from the words of our immortal bard, a man, though you may not allow it, equal to Calvin:

"'There's a Divinity that shapes our ends,
Rough hew them as we may.'

"I have been marking out my timber, and hewing it like the great King Solomon in the wilderness, deeming all the time that my fabric was coming to perfection, when to my amazement I found that the tools I was using rose up against me, and have carried out a purpose not of my own invention.

"You have pronounced me to be a double-sided man; and if appearances were to be your ground of judgment, I am many sided; but in the face of all those signs, I have had one ruling passion—REVENGE."

"I tell you now freely I sought to be revenged on Sir Henry Clinton, because he favored my enemy; but my design on him was only a step toward the depth of my purpose—the deep damnation of Clifford.

"I have lived these two years past for nothing else. I found my way to the presence of Washington, obtained a commission in the secret service, took up my quarters at the foot of your mountain, on the lines between the contending armies; assumed characters that were obnoxious to me; wizard, spook, hermit; anything that would further my fell purpose—REVENGE. All kinds of persons were taken into my service; forgetful as I became, that every man and woman, as well as I, had a mind of their own, and a purpose of their own to carry out; which could not in all parts harmonize with mine. Yet I went on planning, as if they were passive instruments, molded after my wisdom and for my ends.

"I found out my mistake; that villain Kiskataam, whom I employed to decoy Clifford here, by offering to abduct the knight's daughter, had *vengeance* of his own, that he sought to visit on the head of Sir Henry Clinton; and while carrying that out, another passion for her took possession of his bosom, disappointing me of my expectations of retaining her under my guardianship, as a punishment upon her father and future surety for myself.

"Nor did I succeed better through my agent Elsie; one of another and of a nobler nature. By degrees she was winning upon my own affections, and I shall not now avow all that was in my heart concerning her. One thing I was certain of for the time, when I found that Miss Clinton had fallen into her hand, that all was at my disposal; but the high-minded mountain maid was too direct in her purpose to be led into any labyrinth of mine. What you were pleased to designate as 'theatrical' could not be understood by her in her exceeding truthfulness; and I was prevented from taking possession of the person of Miss Clinton entirely through her determination of purpose. All came within an ace of an utter failure. I have just escaped being caught in my own craftiness, and the villain Clifford has only received a part of his punishment.

"REVENGE burns still in my breast, and must till the vow recorded in heaven be fulfilled. I am off, prowling like the wolf, round Fort Niagara; and woe to my victim, should he leave that place of refuge. His blood only can cool this malignant fire that burns, *burns* for REVENGE.

"I am, Reverendissimo Domino,

"Your admirer,

"S. C."

THE END.

W. H. Tinson, Printer and Stereotyper 43 & 45 Centre St., N. Y

THE STANDARD FRENCH CLASSICS.

NEW AMERICAN EDITIONS.

**(*Uniform with* Derby & Jackson's *Standard British Classics.*)

EDITED BY O. W. WIGHT, A.M.

TRANSLATOR OF M. COUSIN'S PHILOSOPHY, AND EDITOR OF SIR WILLIAM HAMILTON'S PHILOSOPHICAL WORKS.

There having long been felt among book-buyers and scholars generally, the need of library editions—convenient in size and reasonable in price—of the greatest and best FRENCH AUTHORS, Derby & Jackson have undertaken to supply this desideratum, by the publication, in uniform style of print, paper and binding, translations of the works of those celebrated French Writers, which have become classic in the History of Literature. Fifteen volumes are now ready, as follows:

MONTAIGNE'S COMPLETE WORKS.

In 4 *vols.*, 12*mo.*, *Cloth*, $5; *Sheep, library style*, $6; *Half calf, gilt or antique*, $2.

FENELON'S ADVENTURES OF TELEMACHUS.

12*mo.*, *Cloth*, $1 25; *Sheep*, $1 50; *Half calf, gilt or antique*, $2 25.

PASCAL'S PROVINCIAL LETTERS.

12*mo.*, *Cloth*, $1 25; *Sheep*, $1 50; *Half calf, gilt or antique*, $2 25.

VOLTAIRE'S CHARLES TWELFTH.

12*mo.*, *Cloth*, $1 25; *Sheep*, $1 50; *Half calf, gilt or antique*, $2 25.

MADAME DE STAËL'S GERMANY.

In 2 *vols.*, *Cloth*, $2 50; *Sheep*, 3 00; *Half calf, gilt or antique*, $4 50.

VOLTAIRE'S LA HENRIADE AND OTHER POEMS.

12*mo.*, *Cloth*, $1 25; *Sheep*, $1 50; *Half calf gilt or antique*, $2 25.

PASCAL'S THOUGHTS.

12*mo.*, *Cloth*, $1 25; *Sheep*, $1 50; *Half calf, gilt or antique*, $2 25.

CHATEAUBRIAND'S MARTYRS.

12*mo.*, *Cloth*, $1 25; *Sheep*, $1 50; *Half calf, gilt or antique*, $2 25.

LA FONTAINE'S FABLES.

Two vols., 12*mo.*, *Cloth*, $2 50; *Sheep*, $3 00; *Half calf, gilt, or antique*, $4 50.

MADAME DE STAËL'S CORINNE.

12*mo.*, *Cloth*, $1 25; *Sheep*, $1 50; *Half calf, gilt, or antique*, $2 25.

THE STANDARD FRENCH CLASSICAL LIBRARY.

Embracing the preceding 15 volumes, in a neat case, cloth,	$18 75
Same—Sheep, library style, ...	22 50
Same—Half calf, gilt, ...	33 75
Same—half calf, antique, ...	33 75

LIBRARY OF SACRED CLASSICS.

PRINTED FROM NEW AND BEAUTIFUL LARGE (PICA) TYPE.

BUNYAN'S PILGRIM'S PROGRESS, 12mo., $1 00
THE SAME—full gilt sides and edges, ... 1 50
THE SAME—half calf antique, ... 2 00

DODDRIDGE'S RISE & PROGRESS, 12mo., 1 00
THE SAME—full gilt sides and edges, ... 1 50
THE SAME—half calf, antique, ... 2 00

BAXTER'S SAINTS' REST, 12mo., . . . 1 00
THE SAME—full gilt sides and edges, ... 1 50
THE SAME—half calf, antique, ... 2 00

TAYLOR'S HOLY LIVING, 12mo., ... 1 00
THE SAME—full gilt sides and edges, ... 1 50
THE SAME—half calf, antique, ... 2 00

Other volumes of a similar character to follow.

John Bunyan! Philip Doddridge! Richard Baxter! Jeremy Taylor! "Pilgrim's Progress," "Rise and Progress," "Saints' Rest," and "Holy Living." What Authors! What Subjects! What Books! Writers for immortality on immortal subjects, familiar to every reader from early infancy—household names and words and books for our maturer years. They will live forever, and do good to all. Old and young alike can drink at this well, "pure and undefiled," certain of refreshing draughts of pure and wholesome literature.

***** The above will be sent by mail, post-paid, on receipt of price**

W. H. Tinson, Printer and Stereotyper, 43 & 45 Centre St., N.Y.

THE WORKS OF CHARLOTTE BRONTE

(CURRER BELL.)

Comprising "Jane Eyre," "Shirley," and "Villetté." Complete in 3 Vols., 12mo.

Price in Cloth, ... $3 00
" Sheep, library style, ... 3 75
" Half calf, gilt or antique, ... 6 00

EVELINA;

OR,

The History of a Young Lady's Introduction to the World.

BY FRANCES BURNEY, (*MADAME D'ARBLAY.*)

With a Life of the Author by T. B. Macaulay. 12mo.

Price in Cloth, ... $1 00
" Sheep, library style, ... 1 25
" Half calf, gilt or antique, ... 2 00

"Frances Burney was the wonder and delight of the generation of novel readers succeeding that of Fielding and Smollett, and she has maintained her popularity better than most secondary writers of fiction. In painting the characters in a drawing-room, or catching the follies and absurdities that float on the surface of fashionable society, she has rarely been equalled."—*Cyclo. of English Literature.*

CORINNE; or, Italy.

BY MADAME DE STAEL.

TRANSLATED BY ISABEL HILL.

With Metrical Versions of the Odes by L. E. Landon. 12mo.

Price in Cloth, ... $1 00
" Sheep, library style, . . . 1 25
" Half calf, gilt or antique, . 2 00

"It (Corinne) possesses the highest merit as a work delineating character, and descriptive of scenery, and inculcates a pure morality. Its eloquent rhapsodies upon love, religion, virtue, nature, history, and poetry, have given it an enduring place in literature."—*Goodrich.*

** The above will be sent by mail, post-paid, on receipt of price.

W. H. Tinson, Printer and Stereotyper 43 & 45 Centre St., N. Y

MARION HARLAND'S WORKS.

ALONE, ...	12mo.,	$1 25
THE HIDDEN PATH, . . .	12mo.,	1 25
MOSS-SIDE, ...	12mo.,	1 25
NEMESIS, ...	12mo.,	1 25

Of the success of MARION HARLAND'S "ALONE," "HIDDEN PATH," and "MOSS-SIDE," in this country, it is hardly necessary to speak. Nearly

500,000 READERS

testify to their wonderful popularity. In the language of the *New York Observer*—"There is genius, pathos, humor, and moral in her charming pages; much knowledge of human nature, and power to delineate character;" And of the *New York Evangelist*—"Home, sincerity and truth are invested with most attractive charms. While engaging the imagination she makes all submit to its moral impression, and enlists the reader's approbation exclusively with the virtuous and true."

The *New York Evening Post*, in a review of the "HIDDEN PATH," says:

"The following notice of this work, which we find in the *Richmond Enquirer*, is from the generous pen of MRS. ANNA CORA RITCHIE, and contains a just tribute to the literary talents of the most successful female writer Virginia has yet produced:

"'Let this *noble* production (we use the adjective in its fullest sense) lie upon the table, enliven the hearth, be the household companion of every true-hearted Virginian. Foster this gifted daughter of the South with the expanding sunshine of appreciation, the refreshing dews of praise—stimulate undeveloped genius, which has never yet "penned its inspiration," to walk in her steps, emulate her achievements, and share her honors—let Virginia produce a few more such writers, and the cry that the South has no literature of its own is silenced forever! The "HIDDEN PATH" is a work that North or South, East or West, may point to with the finger of honest pride, and say "*Our daughter*" sends this message to the world—pours this balm into the wounded hearts—traces for wavering, erring feet this "HIDDEN PATH," which leads to the great goal of eternal peace.'"

As much, or more, can be said in praise of

"ALONE," "MOSS-SIDE," AND "NEMESIS."

***** The above will be sent by mail, post paid, on receipt of prices.**

DERBY & JACKSON, PUBLISHERS,

498 Broadway, New York.

"Miss Evans may well be called the Charlotte Bronte of America."—*Troy Whig.*
"We place BEULAH' beside 'John Halifax.'"—*Baltimore Advocate.*

BEULAH.

BY AUGUSTA J. EVANS.

One neat 12mo. Price $1 25.

From MARION HARLAND, *herself, the writer of the most popular series of Novels ever published in this country.*

"TO MESSRS. DERBY & JACKSON:

"I speak my honest sentiments when I pronounce 'Beulah' the best work of fiction ever published by a Southern writer. To my mind, no American authoress has ever produced a greater book. Can it be true that Miss Evans is young? There is a life-time of thought and research, of struggles of mind and heart, in 'Beulah.' I have read every word with intense interest. The character-painting is fine, the description of passing events and scenery graphic and striking; but to me the chief charm of the book lies in the vivid portraiture of the doubts, the conflicts, the yearnings and the final triumph of a great soul seeking for truth. If the public can appreciate a thoroughly good work, they will thank you for having given them 'Beulah.'"

From Rev. Wm. H. Milburn (the Blind Preacher Eloquent).

"I have no hesitation in saying that few books have ever interested me more. The plot, the delineation of character, and the action, I think, are all admirable. It would be an extraordinary work from the hand of any woman, but it is peculiarly so from one so young. The reading of it cannot but do great good."

From Frederic S. Cozzens, author of the "Sparrowgrass Papers."

"I have been greatly interested by this story of the Mobile heroine, and I am convinced that the story will produce a sympathetic impression on the public mind. There is not a word in it, nor a phrase in it, that I have not meted and measured. Over and above the method of telling the story, the story itself wins, commands, controls the sympaties of the reader. This, I take it, is the highest test of excellence."

From the Home Journal.

"Since the appearance of 'Jane Eyre,' no volume has fallen from the pen of a lady writer evincing more power and learning than the novel 'Beulah,' and we do not hesitate to say that in the production of this volume, Miss Evans has achieved the highest rank among novelists of her sex in this country."

From the New York Evening Post.

"She has, at any rate, established a rank among the best novelists of her sex whom our country can boast, and we do not remember any work of fiction which has been produced in this country for years, which is written with more power and is more full of promise than 'Beulah.' She has achieved a decided literary success, a success which will at least be as cordially recognized at the North as at the South."

From the Boston Post.

"'Beulah' is a book of great merit, and one which will bear critical and close inspection. * * * The volume is one deserving the attraction of the reading public. It is healthy in sentiment, pure in its influences, and *grand in its treatment of great moral questions.* As a literary work, 'Beulah' will rank with any issue of the day."

***** The above will be sent by mail, post-paid, on receipt of price**

W. H TINSON, Printer and Stereotyper, 43 & 45 Centre St., N. Y

www.ingramcontent.com/pod-product-compliance
Lightning Source LLC
Chambersburg PA
CBHW031815270326
41932CB00008B/429

* 9 7 8 3 3 3 7 3 0 0 9 1 3 *